Awakening Victory

AWAKENING VICTORY

How Iraqi Tribes and American Troops
Reclaimed al Anbar Province and
Defeated al Qaeda in Iraq

LT. COLONEL
MICHAEL E. SILVERMAN,
U.S. ARMY (ret.)

CASEMATE

Philadelphia & Newbury

Published in the United States of America and Great Britain in 2011 by
CASEMATE PUBLISHERS
908 Darby Road, Havertown, PA 19083
and
17 Cheap Street, Newbury RG14 5DD

ISBN 978-1-61200-062-6
Digital Edition: ISBN 978-1-61200-077-0

Cataloging-in-publication data is available from the Library of Congress
and the British Library.

10 9 8 7 6 5 4 3 2 1

Printed and bound in the United States of America.

For a complete list of Casemate titles please contact:

CASEMATE PUBLISHERS (US)
Telephone (610) 853-9131, Fax (610) 853-9146
E-mail: casemate@casematepublishing.com

CASEMATE PUBLISHERS (UK)
Telephone (01635) 231091, Fax (01635) 41619
E-mail: casemate-uk@casematepublishing.co.uk

Contents

*This book is dedicated to the memory of the Soldiers who
were killed in action under my command:*

Private Matthew T. Zeimer, U.S. Army, age 18, February 2, 2007
Specialist Kelly D. Youngblood, U.S. Army, 19, February 18, 2007
Specialist Forrest John Waterbury, U.S. Army, 25, March 14, 2007
Sergeant Adrian J. Lewis, U.S. Army, 30, March 21, 2007
Staff Sergeant Steve Butcher Jr., U.S. Army, 27, May 23, 2007
Private First Class Daniel P. Cagle, U.S. Army, 22, May 23, 2007
Specialist Stephen Allen Alexander, U.S. Army, 27, Died of Wounds,
March 14, 2011

*The Soldiers, Sailor and Marines killed in action
while supporting my command:*

Specialist Alan E. McPeek, U.S. Army, 20, February 2, 2007
Staff Sergeant Dustin M. Gould, USMC, 28, March 2, 2007
Hospitalman Lucas W.A. Emch, USN, 21, March 2, 2007
Sergeant Peter Woodall, USMC, 25, April 27, 2007
Sergeant William J. Callahan, USMC, 28, April 27, 2007
Staff Sergeant Coby G. Schwab, U.S. Army, 25, May 3, 2007
Specialist Kelly B. Grothe, U.S. Army, 21, May 3, 2007

And to the nameless, faceless Iraqis who died under my command.

*They paid the ultimate price for our victory.
I'll never cleanse the scars of their deaths from my psyche or the
sins of their deaths from my soul.*

Preface

As this book is published, the Iraq War begins to move from the realm of current events to the realm of history; and with that transition come the post-mortem analyses of the war's causes, prosecution, and outcomes. Although the jury is still out, it certainly appears that liberal democracy has taken hold in Iraq and that its example has spawned a democratic zeal throughout the region. The so-called Arab Spring is a direct result of U.S. actions in Iraq; and the evidence is crystal clear that the Freedom Agenda of the Bush administration was successful in changing the terms of the dialog in the Muslim World. By showing young Arabs that dictatorship and authoritarian regimes are not the only possible political condition for a Muslim majority nation, we allowed their dreams of political freedom and self-determination to become goals and those goals eventually became action. The final outcome is not yet determined, but clearly the trend in the Arab World is toward liberal democracy, not away from it.

I wrote *Awakening Victory* to answer the questions that I continually hear: "Why must America sacrifice our blood and treasure to free Arabs and Muslims from dictators? What is the vital national interest that drives us to fight wars in Muslim lands? And did the invasion of Iraq make us more or less safe at home?" These questions assume that the focus of our broader war should be protecting our homeland from terrorist attacks and that we can do that by simply hunting down and killing all those who would attack us. That hypothesis fails to recognize the central truth of the "War on Terror" or, more correctly, the Long War.

The truth is that the Long War is not about America. Nor is it about religion. It is a struggle over political control of the Muslim World—that area that generally stretches from North Africa, across Southwest Asia and onto the Indian Sub-continent and surrounding islands. Al Qaeda and their ilk would see the Muslim World unified under one Taliban-like state that would rule with hate, intolerance and brutality. A new, forward-think-ing class of Muslims, however, sees a world in which individuals can be empowered to control their governments. Although the Long War is not about America, we are involved through our very existence. Many "mod-ern" Muslims see America as the example of all that they want: we represent the values of the Enlightenment—freedom, democracy, and inalienable human rights—transformed from abstract principles into the most pow-erful nation in the world. For the same reasons, al Qaeda hates us but they were willing to ignore us until they realized that our very presence in the Middle East prevented the series of insurgencies that would establish their new Caliphate. So they attacked us. They thought that attacking America would force the U.S. to withdraw our influence from the Muslim world. Al Qaeda attacks against American targets were not designed to provoke a new Crusade, but rather sought to drive America away. Their attacks failed to achieve their goal because they miscalculated our response.

As we invaded Iraq, the nature of the Long War changed. Although al Qaeda didn't predict that fight, they chose to capitalize on it. Al Qaeda threw all their might into the Iraq War in an attempt to finally export their control into the Arab heartland. A careful reading of *Awakening Victory* will illustrate to readers just how close al Qaeda came to achieving the first step toward that goal. From late 2004 through late 2006 we were losing the Iraq War. Our heavy-handed military actions, wholesale abolition of the Iraqi security apparatus, and condemnation of all Ba'ath Party members led to a schism between Sunni and Shia Iraqis that eventually exploded into civil war. In the chaos we created, al Qaeda saw a grand opportunity to establish a new base from which to launch a campaign that threatened to destabilize the entire region. Forging an alliance with the strong and alienated Sunni nationalist insurgency in Iraq and fanning the flames of civil war, al Qaeda found a strategy that nearly led to its victory in Iraq.

Awakening Victory describes how America and our Iraqi partners turned the tide in the Iraq War by finally realizing what the war was about. It was a battle to win the aspirations of the Iraqi population, or as it was termed in a previous conflict, their "hearts and minds." Central to this narrative is the transition that U.S. Army counterinsurgency doctrine underwent and how it influenced the actions of leaders and units on the ground. The invasion of Iraq was conducted by a U.S. military that employed the same tactics that brought us victory during the 1991 Gulf War. Those tactics served us well from the 1980s through the turn of this century. But it rapidly became clear that they would not work this time. The Iraq War was not the Gulf War. It was something different: an insurgency. And over the course of several years it became painfully obvious that U.S. counterinsurgency doctrine—developed during and immediately after the Vietnam War—had to be rewritten. So, while engaged in some of the most brutal fighting seen by the U.S. in 60 years, the Army's new counterinsurgency doctrine was released and the very nature of the campaign changed from focusing on killing and capturing insurgents to protecting the Iraqi population and winning their hearts and minds. *Awakening Victory* describes that change as seen through my eyes.

Memorial Day Weekend, 2011
Midway, Georgia

Acknowledgments

I would like to thank some of those who made this book possible. I cannot thank my wife, Randi, enough for tolerating my chosen profession. Without her support, I couldn't have done half of what I did. Thanks to Nathan Kline for his friendship, support, enthralling discussions, and honest comments on the early drafts of my manuscript. Thanks to Mostafa Remh for his hard work as my Arab voice in Iraq, patiently furthering my education about both Islam and Arab culture, and for his corrections of my Arabic translations in the manuscript (any mistakes remaining are mine alone). Next, I need to thank my aent, Matthew Carnicelli, who immediately saw value in *Awakening Victory* and tenaciously championed the book, ultimately finding exactly the right home. Big thanks to Casemate Publishers, David Farnsworth, Steve Smith, Tara Lichterman and the whole organization for welcoming me to the team and for working so hard to bring my dream to fruition. Thanks to some of the great soldiers who taught me through their examples: Elbert Smith, John Veasy, Chuck Lange, Nathaniel Jones, Scotty Craig, Roger Alford, Mark Hertling, Bill Reese, Dan Williamson, Bob Williams, Adam Machell, Kenny Akers, Jerry Relf, Mike Swenson, Mike Altomare, Mike Milano, Bill Hadley, Farhan al Anazi, John Moody, Mike Trenchz, Bryan Roberts, Don Campbell, Gian Gentile, Dave Hogg, Myron Reineke, James Hickey, Larry Wilson, J.B. Burton, Ray Odierno, and the one who kept me grounded and sane in the toughest time in my career—Randy Sumner. To the Iraqis—sheiks, politicians, soldiers, police, and citizens who gave me their support at grave personal risk: You will always be my brothers—Fi Aman Allah. Last, but certainly not least; I must thank the Soldiers, Sailors, Airmen, Marines and the Iraqi Security Forces who served under my command in Iraq from February 2007 until April 2008. Through your blood, sweat, and tears and your trust in my leadership, we snatched victory from the jaws of defeat. This is your story.

Introduction

The professional quality video shot from multiple angles and cameras showed an insurgent crawling through mud and sewage several inches deep to a Bradley infantry fighting vehicle that sat, seemingly abandoned, on the war-torn road in Ramadi. The Arabic narration explained that the brave *mujahid*, or holy warrior, had caught the Americans sleeping while on duty. I watched as the terrorist in the video placed two large homemade bombs under the belly of the vehicle—a process that took several minutes. Then, as the narration hit its climax and the soundtrack of Quranic verses set to music hit its most dramatic point, the bombs exploded, sending pieces of the thirty-eight-ton vehicle scattering and engulfing the mighty machine, a symbol of American strength, in flames. As the cameras panned out, I got a sick feeling in my guts. It was one of my vehicles at my most vulnerable position—Combat Outpost *Sword*—and I knew that, within days, that position would be overrun if I didn't take drastic action. The Battle for Ramadi was raging, and al Qaeda was on the cusp of defeating the world's most powerful force, the U.S. military, and establishing a permanent base in al Anbar Province, Iraq, from which to pursue the group's ultimate goal of establishing a new Islamic caliphate.

I didn't sense it at the time, but the winds of change were blowing. American troops and Iraqi tribes were about to deal a death blow to al Qaeda's Islamic State of Iraq, and my battalion was to play a pivotal role . . . but it sure didn't feel like we were winning yet.

This is my story and the story of about one thousand Soldiers, Sailors, Airmen, and Marines who were assigned or attached to the 3rd Battalion, 69th Armor—unique but similar to thousands of other American servicemen and women who floated in and out of Iraq through years of tough combat without ever knowing victory. It is also the story of the brave, patriotic Iraqis who will remain mostly nameless and faceless to the world but who finally made victory possible. This is the story of *Awakening Victory*.

CHAPTER 1

Invasion

September 11, 2001, 8:30 a.m. found me sitting in my office as the operations officer for the 1st Battalion, 66th Armor at Fort Hood, Texas. I had just showered after morning physical training (PT) when one of my soldiers came by my office and told me that an airplane had flown into one of the twin towers of the World Trade Center in New York. We spoke about how odd that was and how unfortunate for a pilot to make such an egregious error. As I did other days, I called my wife that morning. Because she was asleep when I left for work at 5:30 a.m., I always called her after PT so I could speak to her before she went to work. She told me that two airplanes had hit the World Trade Center, one on each tower, and that there was strong suspicion that it was an act of terrorism. Within thirty minutes, we had a TV set up in the battalion conference room and watched as our lives changed forever.

Within one month, as we watched from the sidelines, special forces and light infantry forces invaded Afghanistan to destroy al Qaeda and remove the Taliban regime. A big portion of the U.S. Army was at war, but not the heavy mechanized and armored forces. For us, it was business as usual, but the war in Afghanistan kept us focused and added relevance to our training.

Months passed, and my first hint about the coming war came in January 2002 as President George W. Bush gave his State of the Union Address in which he named the "Axis of Evil": North Korea, Iran, and Iraq. This speech led to some speculation in my circle about how that might affect us. The consensus was that a storm was brewing. The phrases "War on Terror" and "Global War on Terror" began to be used by media and the administration and seemed to provide more fuel for speculation about future wars.

That spring I became the operations officer for the 1st Brigade Combat Team (BCT), 4th Infantry Division (4ID). A BCT is a unit composed of two to five battalions, usually about 3,500 soldiers, but when deployed it can have up to 5,500 because there are numerous odd attachments made for combat. The BCT was training for a rotation to the National Training Center (NTC) at Fort Irwin, California, scheduled for January 2003. As part of that process, we went to the NTC for leader training in the summer of 2002. While at the NTC, I heard a rumor from Fort Hood that the U.S. III Corps and 1st Cavalry Division planners were working on a new plan. This fueled much discussion and speculation about what the plan was and how it would impact us.

After arriving back at Fort Hood, I found out that the plan was to invade Iraq and remove the Saddam Hussein regime. By September, I was devoting some time once or twice a week to the plan. Sometime around mid-October, the decision was made that 4ID would take part in the invasion of Iraq, and I began to spend twelve to sixteen hours a day, six to seven days a week writing the BCT's portion of the plan. We were to invade from the north, through Turkey, and control northwestern Iraq from Fayish Kabur on the Syrian border down to Tikrit. This area would have included Mosul, Bayji, Tikrit, and possibly Tuz Khormato near Kirkuk. The plan was broken down into four phases. The first phase was deployment from Fort Hood and onward movement through Turkey. The second phase was "decisive action" against the Iraqi armed forces. The third phase was consolidation and reorganization, rebuilding, and establishing a new regime. Phase 4 was redeployment. The first two phases were written in great detail. The third and fourth phases were "to be published."

However, the plan to which I committed one thousand hours of my life didn't even happen. The government of Turkey failed to consent to U.S. forces staging there for an invasion of Iraq, and at the last minute we deployed to Kuwait and made a new plan (in three days). The plan, ironically, called for us to go to the same stopping point, Tikrit, only we came from the south instead of from the north. We executed the plan, having a few brief and largely insignificant engagements against the Iraqi armed forces, and without a single friendly death or serious injury, we owned Tikrit.

Tikrit, Iraq, is the birthplace of Saddam Hussein Abdul Majid al Tikriti, the former president of Iraq. Tikrit is also the capital of the country's Saladin Province. It ranges from Balad in the south to near Mosul in the north, west to the Thar Thar Reservoir, and east to Tuz Khormato. The province had a population in 2003 of about 2.1 million—mostly Sunni Arabs, although it did have a significant Shia population and some Kurds, Turkomen, and Christians, mainly in the southern cities of Samarra and Balad—and it comprised about one third of what would come to be known as the "Sunni Triangle."

Operation Iraqi Freedom introduced into the mainstream U.S. Army lexicon a new concept—the idea that warfare comprised two "kinds" of operations: kinetic and non-kinetic. Most of the Army was extraordinarily well versed in kinetic warfare. That is, killing the enemy and destroying his equipment and facilities. We were not nearly as familiar with the non-kinetic—influencing with information, winning popular support—and, least of all, with assisting to rebuild, providing humanitarian assistance and developing new governments. So, on April 16, 2003, I found myself serving as the operations officer for a huge area of Iraq that was the heart of the former regime's homeland. We had defeated most of the Iraqi military with not much of a fight and had outrun our own plan. We had planned in great detail for the destruction of the Iraqi military, the control of its facilities, and, indeed, the control of Iraqi territory. We had no plan for what came next.

Over the next several days, what unfolded in Tikrit (and in all of Iraq) was not what anyone had foreseen, nor had we addressed it in any of our plans. The people of Iraq cannibalized the infrastructure of their own nation. A few anecdotes will give you the general idea of how significant this was. On our second or third day in Tikrit, I was traveling from the main presidential palace in Tikrit to a smaller palace where we had established our BCT headquarters when I saw a gathering of people on the north side of the main road behind a building and went to check it out. I was traveling in a two-truck convoy (unarmored humvees with canvas tops and no doors) with myself and my driver in one truck and Command Sgt. Maj. Larry Wilson and his driver in the other. As our trucks approached, we saw that the small group was gathered around a fuel storage tank at the back of what we would later know to be the local Department of Education compound. What I saw there was shocking. Several men had removed most of the fuel from the storage tank and put it in fifty-five-gallon drums in the back of pickup trucks. There was a small amount of fuel remaining in the storage tank that they could not reach. In order to loot the remaining fuel, one man had tied a rope to his son (maybe six years old) and lowered him into the tank with a bucket on a rope. The kid was standing in four inches of diesel fuel, scooping it into the bucket and then sending the bucket to his father. The boy could barely breathe, and when we pulled him from the tank, he had severe chemical burns on his legs from the fuel.

A day or two later, I was again near the main presidential palace when I saw smoke coming from one of the exterior walls of the palace. We went to check it out and found two men digging up the main telephone trunk for the city—braided, insulated copper wire about six to ten inches in diameter. They were burning the insulation from the wiring and cutting it into three-foot sections that they loaded into a truck. The copper was valuable and easily sold in Syria or Jordan as scrap. Prior to that week, Tikrit had a usable publicly switched telephone network; it has no land-line phone network to this day.

Tikrit was home to two massive Iraqi ammunition depots. Within days of our arrival, all the fencing had been stolen from the depots, and many of the bunkers had been breached, allowing the ammunition (small arms, artillery, tank and APC ammo, rockets, etc.) to be looted—much of it initially for the harvest of the metal, some of it for more nefarious purposes. Again, using children for these thefts was widespread, since they could fit through the vents in these large bunkers and either open the bunkers from the inside or hand munitions through small holes. Doing just that, several children lost their lives in Tikrit.

An Iraqi Solution

After about a week in Tikrit, a force called the Free Iraqi Forces (FIF) came to town. I was introduced to the commander of the FIF in Tikrit and immediately became the primary interlocutor with him. The soldiers of the FIF were Iraqi nationals (mostly ex-pats) who had been recruited by the U.S. government to fight against the Saddam regime, then serve as guides and scouts for U.S. forces. Simultaneous with their arrival, I had a discussion with my brigade commander, then–Col. (now Maj. Gen.) Don Campbell, about our need to establish some sort of provisional government to begin controlling the security situation, reestablishing basic services, and generally getting Iraqis to solve Iraqi problems. Colonel Campbell gave me permission to begin working to establish a local government in Tikrit. Things were moving rapidly by the end of April 2003.

Something else had changed in late April and early May; I acquired an interpreter who appeared out of the blue at our forward headquarters. Muhammed al Jabouri would become my constant sidekick and companion during my time in Tikrit. Later, in Baquba, he worked for my boss. (Unfortunately, he didn't live to see a free Iraq; Muhammed was killed by the Mahdi Militia in Najaf in April 2004 while working for U.S. forces.) A few days after getting Colonel Campbell's blessing, I approached the commander of the FIF and asked him if he knew any prominent citizens in Tikrit. After spending ten days or so with each other, we had developed some trust, and I explained to him that I was interested in finding someone to lead a new government. He told me he knew a good man from an area just east of Tikrit who belonged to a family that had fallen out of favor with the Saddam regime. He thought we could find this man, Brig. Gen. Hussein al Jabouri, whom he had met while they were both in prison in Baghdad.

Once I got over the shock of hearing that this prominent member of the community had been imprisoned, I found out that General Hussein was arrested for possible involvement with a plot to assassinate Saddam in the 1990s. I later found that many prominent Iraqis did time in Saddam's prisons. So, with the idea that this guy might have some ideas about how to set up a new government and that he might be a good candidate for the job of mayor of Tikrit, I set off to find Gen. Hussein al Jabouri. We headed out to al Alum village east of the city: the commander of the FIF, Muhammed al Jabouri (no relation to the general), Command Sgt. Maj. Larry Wilson and his driver, an AP reporter named Dave Rising, his photographer, and my driver and me. (Dave Rising lived and worked with Command Sgt. Maj. Wilson and me for several weeks, and chronicled much of what happened in Tikrit early on.)

Once we arrived in al Alum, it was clear we were the first Americans to be there. Though we had several FIF soldiers with us, no one admitted to knowing the whereabouts of General Hussein. As we were about to give up on the search and head back to Tikrit, the FIF commander saw one of Hussein's cousins, whom he recognized from his previous association with the general in the 1990s. After a brief discussion between the two, we were invited into the courtyard of a house just yards away from where we were standing. After a couple of rounds of tea, I was informed through my interpreter that General Hussein would be there within the hour, and before long, we were enjoying a great Iraqi meal and having a discussion with Brig. Gen. Hussein Jbarra al Jabouri and his brother, Sheik Naji Jbarra al Jabouri, about the current dire conditions in Tikrit and how we might remedy them. By the end of the conversation, I was prepared to recommend to Colonel Campbell that we make General Hussein the mayor of Tikrit. I asked Hussein to come to our forward headquarters (which had now become the civil/military operations center or CMOC) in two days so that we could finish our discussion. Meanwhile, I received Colonel Campbell's permission to appoint Hussein mayor.

General Hussein al Jabouri arrived promptly two days later and gave me my first lesson in Iraqi hardball politics. I offered him the job of mayor of Tikrit, and he said he accepted and would like to make an official announcement to some prominent citizens and the press. He said that he could be ready to do so in a couple of hours. I agreed, and a couple of hours later in the conference room of the same building, with some prominent sheiks and businessmen from Tikrit and my friend David Rising of AP present, General Hussein started to make his statement. He spoke about the need to reestablish safety and security in Tikrit. He spoke about the need to move past the Saddam regime into a time of prosperity. He spoke about getting government employees back to work and getting pensioners paid their pensions. Muhammed al Jabouri translated it all simultaneously as the general spoke, like the translators you see on TV news.

Muhammed was quite a character, with a clouded and possibly nefarious past. He all but told me he was a former employee of the Iraqi
Intelligence Service. He was fluent in Arabic, Kurdish, English, and French,
and spoke very passable German and Spanish. He had spent some time in
Paris, maybe years, working for (ostensibly) the Ministry of Tourism for
the Saddam regime. So, I was a little taken aback when he paused during
Hussein's statement. I asked him what was wrong, and he looked me in
the eye and said that General Hussein had just announced to the gathered
audience (including the AP) that he was honored to accept the appoint-
ment as the governor of Saladin Province! I told Muhammed that he must
have meant the mayor of Tikrit. He said, no, he definitely said the governor
of Saladin. Just about the time that Muhammed and I finished that conversation, Governor (right, Governor) Hussein introduced me to make a
statement. Well, there I was, meeting many of the most influential Iraqis
in Tikrit for the first time and knowing that we needed their help to get
things back on track. Hussein had put me on the horns of a sticky dilemma, but my choice was easy: I could correct Hussein's statement, causing
him to lose face and sending us back to the drawing board, or I could back
his play and have a new Iraqi partner. I said something like, on behalf of
Maj. Gen. Ray Odierno and Col. Donald Campbell, I am honored to give
our support to Governor Hussein Jbarra al Jabouri, the provisional governor of Saladin Province. The first governor of a province in post-Saddam
Iraq was in office. For about three weeks, Hussein al Jabouri was the most
senior Iraqi in the Provisional Government of Iraq.

For the next ten weeks I spent most of my time with Governor Jabouri.
There were no teams from either the military or any other U.S. government
entity dedicated to rebuilding civil society in Iraq. The task fell to maneuver
brigades and divisions who "owned the battle space" to figure out what to
do next. As the operations officer, my commander assigned this task to
me; and as a political scientist, I was quite excited about it. So I spent
countless hours with Governor Jabouri appointing his cabinet and organizing both the physical capitol and the business of governing.

We made progress in fits and starts, but the one thing that we made
rapid progress on was establishing relationships between Americans and
the prominent tribes and families of Saladin. Several nights a week, I would
go to al Alum village and eat dinner with members of the Jabouri tribe and

their neighbors. These meetings were invaluable. It was in this setting that I met people from all over the province. They all had needs, but they also had great insights into the goings-on in the province. At one of these dinners, I met one of Governor Hussein's brothers, who was previously the director of Ba'ath Party operations for most of Saladin Province. He and I had a discussion about how former regime elements were beginning to organize themselves to fight "the occupation," and he told me that he knew who these men were and where some of them could be found. He said that he was not comfortable talking about it in the open and asked to come to the CMOC to discuss it. The next day, he came to the CMOC, and I showed him the "most wanted list." At the time, we were focused on capturing or killing the "deck of cards," or top fifty-two most wanted. He told me that we would not find the top fifty-two without catching their closest operatives. He told me about a man named Muhammed al Hadoushi and his brothers who formed Saddam's inner circle of security. At the time, Muhammed al Hadoushi was approximately number 170 on the "black list" and nobody was actively searching for him.

Days later, there was an attack against the CMOC in which a soldier from our BCT was killed. Governor Hussein and I went to the CMOC soon after, and he helped us to reconstruct the attack. Above all else, Governor Hussein was a military man like me. He looked at the aftermath of the attack and taught me and my officers and sergeants at the CMOC how to look at an RPG hole and tell where it was fired from. He coached us on our sandbag and barrier placement. He told me that although he believed the U.S. Army was the greatest fighting force in the world, we didn't know how to defend a position. He was right—for years we had focused on attacking. He taught us a good deal about defending that day. Most importantly, after assessing the attack, he concluded that the leader of the force who attacked our position was a skilled military man. He suspected it was Muhammed al Hadoushi, and so began the search for the chief of Saddam's personal security detachment and his closest associates that ultimately culminated in the capture of Saddam Hussein in December 2003.

So it went for the May, June, and part of July; I would spend the day from 8:00 a.m. until about 2:00 p.m. with Governor Hussein and his cabinet. Two days a week, "petitioners" from all over the province would come to present and discuss issues with the governor, his cabinet, and me. One of the initial issues we dealt with was figuring out how to access the money of the province in order to reestablish community services. (Remember, there was no team to help us with these issues.) We eventually persuaded the bank that held the province's money to release a portion of it to the governor, who was able to reopen the schools and clinics in Tikrit and reinstitute some services.

One of the most successful policies of Governor Jabouri was his idea to pay pensioners and Iraqi military men. As the rumors of discontent began to grow in May and early June 2003, and sometime very shortly after the attack on the CMOC, Governor Hussein expressed a desire during one of our daily meetings to pay military men: officers first, then non-commissioned officers, and finally soldiers. I was initially not supportive of his idea. Although I didn't tell the governor, out of a desire not to insult him, I felt that the Iraqi military, who had deserted in droves both in 1991 and in 2003, were cowards who had little honor. Governor Hussein argued that these men only knew one skill and had put food on their tables and a roof over their families' heads the same way that I had, by training for and fighting wars. He argued that the conscripts went back to their families and would be okay, but the professional soldiers found themselves with no livelihood and no way to feed their families. The former regime leadership, he continued, had a great deal of money, and they would recruit former military members to organize, train, and equip an insurgency against coalition forces. His reasoning made a good deal of sense, and after a few hours of discussion (everything takes a long time in Iraq), we agreed to explore the possibility that we pay former military personnel.

I sought and received permission from Colonel Campbell to develop a program to register, track, and pay retired and former active-duty members of the Iraqi Armed Forces. In order to administer this program, the governor and I both thought we could use a new cabinet position and organization. We decided to make a Saladin Department of Veterans' Affairs. After screening several candidates, we agreed that the best was Governor Hussein's nephew (Sheik Naji's son), Staff Brig. Gen. Abdullah Naji Jbarra al Jabouri.

General Abdullah was a regular at the dinners in al Alum village and visited the provincial capital building often. Because he spoke English very well, he and I had had many conversations, and I had come to respect him as a fellow military officer and a friend. General Abdullah was (and remains) the most honest, forthright, and civic-minded Iraqi I know. He designed and administered a program that rapidly registered the vast majority of pensioners and servicemen in the province and started distributing a stipend to them. The stipends were modest (between one hundred and two hundred dollars' worth of Iraqi dinar per month) but were enough for a man to put food on his family's table. The program also had the dual benefit of allowing coalition members to meet with and question any of the former regime military officials we chose, which was a boon for our intelligence collectors, and they soon had several intelligence sources from this pool. The program cost $375,000 the first month. The money all came from Iraqi government funds.

Unfortunately, not everyone was as excited about the program as we were. The 4ID had a finance battalion in its task organization, and it had, unbeknownst to me, been tasked to account for the money that was in all the banks in Tikrit. Technically, I guess, that money belonged to the U.S. government (much to my chagrin). So, as I was heading to the governor's office one morning, I received a radio call that I needed to go to the division headquarters and see some guy named Lieutenant Colonel Schmidt—I didn't know who that was, and I thought it was an odd request, but I complied.

I drove the two miles to division headquarters and asked around to see who this guy was, and then I was brought to the finance battalion's headquarters, where I was shown to the battalion commander's office. I walked in, saluted, and said, "Sir, Major Silverman reporting as ordered." Behind the desk sat a lieutenant colonel I had seen once or twice before but never met. His first words to me were, "Major Silverman, you're going to jail!" I didn't take that so well. I asked him, in rather colorful language, just what it was he was talking about and why I should stay and listen. He proceeded to tell me that I had stolen the equivalent of nearly one million U.S. dollars, including a single withdrawal of about $375,000 worth of Iraqi dinar. He showed me an English/Arabic document with my signature authorizing the director of veterans' affairs to withdraw money in order to pay the military. He explained that this was the first document any of the banks could produce that had an American's signature and that he was planning to prepare a charge sheet against me and forward it through the chain of command.

I explained to him that there was a government in Saladin Province and that it was their money we were talking about. I told him that as soon as there was a government in Baghdad, I'm sure they would hold the province to account for the money. I told him that I was certain his charges would not go very far but that he was welcome to proceed, and if he had nothing else, I would get back to work. Clearly, he didn't understand one of the most fundamental principles of counterinsurgency: money is better than ammunition.

Within weeks of Governor Hussein taking office, Tikrit was a relatively safe place. For certain, there were attacks, but they never reached the levels that they did in other major Sunni cities. The city never belonged to the insurgents the way that places like Fallujah, Ramadi, Baquba, and Tarmia did. Yet Tikrit was home to the central characters from the former regime; if any place should have been an insurgent hot spot, it should have been there. I believe the reason Tikrit never saw the level of insurgency seen in other Sunni strongholds was that the 1st BCT, 4ID developed relationships early on with the major tribal and community actors in the area and quickly moved to integrate them into finding solutions for problems and moving forward with an agenda of rebuilding.

I'll never forget a conversation I had with one of the battalion commanders from that brigade. He believed the solution to the growing problems in Iraq in 2003 was to kill or capture all former regime members. He lectured me one day about how I should be more focused on that task as the brigade operations officer. He said I was wasting my time with sheiks and the "phony" governor and asked me, "Don't you have something more constructive to do with your time?" I assumed that to be a rhetorical question!

Iron Fists and Velvet Gloves

The remainder of 2003 and early 2004 saw an internal debate developing in the U.S. military. The subject of the debate was how best to counter the bourgeoning insurgency in Iraq (once we admitted there was an insurgency). There existed two schools of thought. The first school, we'll call it "iron fist," was associated with the 4ID and then–Maj. Gen. Ray Odierno.

(Whether it was a fair association or not is another discussion.) That school focused on destroying the enemy, and its central purpose was to kill or capture both former regime and international terror insurgents, and to kill low-level insurgents like improvised explosive device (IED) emplacers, indirect-fire cell members, and direct-action cell members. This school of thought put a premium on the elimination of enemy personnel as if they were part of a military force. It treated enemy fighters as if they were finite and as if their attrition could cause the insurgency to fail.

When this school of thought was employed, there was little consideration for collateral damage or for wrongful capture and wrongful imprisonment. As part of the iron fist school, one might round up every military-age male in a village and hold them for twenty-four to seventy-two hours while one sorted through the good guys and the bad guys. The idea was that if you rounded everyone up, you were sure to get the bad guys. I planned and conducted these operations both in 1st and 2nd BCTs and believed that they were the best way to destroy the insurgency. These operations came to be known in the Army vernacular as ITAVs, for "it takes a village"—the ironic allusion to Hilary Clinton's book was a reflection of our collective sentiment that there was no "kinder and gentler" way to win this war.

We'll call the second school of thought the "velvet glove." The phrase actually refers to an op-ed piece in the *New York Times* written in December 2003 by then–Lt. Col. Carl E. Mundy III.[1] Mundy's article specifically addressed the heavy-handedness of the 4ID in and around Tikrit. He was specifically critical of General Odierno. He proclaimed that the Marines would extend a velvet glove to the Iraqis in al Anbar Province. This second school of thought came, after some time, to be associated with then Maj. Gen. David Petraeus and his 101st Airborne Division, which controlled Mosul. Under Petraeus, Mosul was the epitome of the velvet glove school.

I made a trip to Mosul in late April or early May 2003, where I was reprimanded by a lieutenant colonel for pointing my weapon at Iraqis as I drove through town—in Tikrit that was standard procedure. The velvet glove technique focused on the population, with the goal of creating popular support for the coalition. To gain that support, the premium was on assistance, rebuilding, and ignoring potential insurgents. I believe this school of thought was the probable cause for the former regime insurgents to choose Mosul as their command and control headquarters and why Uday and Qusay Hussein (Saddam's sons) went to and ultimately were killed in Mosul. I also believe that is why Tal Afar, just down the road from Mosul, became such an attack hot spot in 2004–2005. Furthermore, because the Iraqi Security Forces in Mosul never cleared the insurgent sympathizers from the city, and because the Sunnis of Mosul never felt the real sting of al Qaeda, Mosul became the last urban concentration of al Qaeda in Iraq.

George Wilhelm Frederick Hegel, the German idealist philosopher, famously argued that history can be defined by a series of dialectic interactions where thesis and antithesis violently clash to create a new idea—synthesis. I believe that Hegel would have seen that very interaction occurring between the iron fist and velvet glove schools of counterinsurgency. That synthesis occurred when Gen. David Petraeus and then–Lt. Gen. Raymond Odierno, two brilliant military leaders for whom I have the greatest respect, presided over the time in Iraq when we, collectively as a force, broke the code on counterinsurgency. Neither method alone could win the war; rather, elements of both schools of thought finally led to tactics that I believe turned the tide of the war.

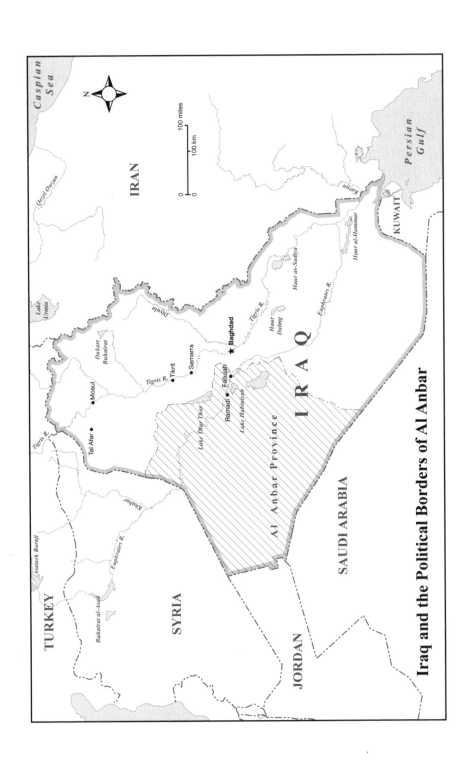

Iraq and the Political Borders of Al Anbar

CHAPTER 2

Rise of the Insurgency

Sidestepping the valid and charged debates about whether the Iraq war met "just war" requirements and the related "chicken and egg" debate concerning the presence of al Qaeda in Iraq prior to the invasion, this chapter addresses events after April 2003. Many Americans, including soldiers who have served in Iraq, don't understand the nature of the Iraqi insurgency, its history, or why it matters. The Iraqi insurgency was not monolithic, but rather there were actually three distinct insurgencies with different goals, tactics, and end states. The one thing they had in common is that they all attacked U.S. and multinational coalition forces in Iraq. Let's start at the beginning.

Most of the Iraqi Armed Forces deserted when the U.S. invaded Iraq in 2003. There were individual units from the regular Army, Republican Guard, and Special Republican Guard who fought, but generally most did not. There was one particular group that fought valiantly, if not stupidly, to the death. That was the Fedayeen Saddam. The Fedayeen Saddam (literally in Arabic, "men that would die for Saddam" or "Saddam's martyrs") was a paramilitary organization of young Ba'ath Party loyalists who reported directly to Uday Saddam Hussein until 1996, then to Qusay after that time.[2] The Fedayeen were poorly equipped and trained. They were primarily used to terrorize the population, killing and threatening individuals who opposed the regime. During the 2003 invasion, many Fedayeen Saddam members fought and died against coalition forces as the initial invasion force (3rd Infantry Division and U.S. Marine Corps forces) moved north. The tenacity with which they fought surprised many military officials. In several places, the Fedayeen fought as though they were ideologues who truly had no reservations about martyrdom.

As the fighting died down in April 2003 and the Fedayeen died or dispersed, there was a brief period of little violence, except for coalition-initiated violence against looters, ammunition thieves, and an occasional former regime figure who fought back when U.S. forces came to capture him. By mid-June, however, there began to be attacks against U.S. forces that were clearly orchestrated and planned, not spontaneous. These attacks ranged from ambushes using small arms and rocket-propelled grenades (RPGs) against U.S. convoys, to significant attacks against U.S. positions with larger forces and heavy, medium, and light weapons. The early assumption was that most of these attacks came from former regime loyalists who were attacking U.S. troops in order to force us from Iraq and allow the Saddam regime to return to power.

Saddam's Money

As coalition forces conducted operations against former regime figures, they found money in many of the houses they raided. In fact, at one farm on the outskirts of Tikrit, soldiers from the 1st Battalion, 22nd Infantry Regiment (assigned to 1BCT, 4ID) found over ten million U.S. dollars. Within days of that event, U.S. forces near Tikrit seized a car going through a coalition checkpoint with 800,000 U.S. dollars. Why these individuals kept such large amounts of cash on hand is a matter open for debate. Some supposed that it was "mad money" to help family and friends of the regime flee the country if the regime fell. Some speculated that it was money stolen from the regime by those closest to it. My personal belief is that this money was stashed by the regime in order to fund an insurgency in case U.S. forces invaded and occupied Iraq.

In the summer of 2003, we developed multi-source intelligence that told us that individuals were being paid to attack Americans. The going rate was initially fairly cheap, as low as $50 per attack; but as coalition forces began to kill those who attacked them, the cost went up. Over the period of that summer, sources told us that the price was anywhere between $50 and $2,500 to attack U.S. forces, depending on several factors. Regardless, it was clear that some individuals were attacking Americans merely for money, which meant that someone was paying for it. The most likely source for the earliest funding of the Iraqi insurgency was the former regime. All our intelligence pointed to them as the early organizers of the insurgency, and I know of no evidence to the contrary. The most likely political goal of this insurgency was to return the Saddam regime to power.

Unfortunately, while former regime elements paid money to have unemployed young men, probably mostly former soldiers, attack U.S. and coalition forces, the senior military leadership on the ground in Iraq stuck their heads in the sand and refused to "believe in" an organized Iraqi insurgency. Lieutenant General Ricardo Sanchez, the corps commander, and his division commanders chastised subordinates who referred to enemies killed, captured, or otherwise as insurgents. The term *insurgent* was forbidden in any reporting, nightly summaries, or official intelligence assessments. Clearly, if there was no insurgency, then there would be no need for counterinsurgency tactics. U.S. forces would continue to employ either iron hand or velvet glove tactics.

So the response to the growing pro-Saddam insurgency was either massive retaliation with operations that captured every military-aged male in an area or village, or completely ignoring the budding insurgency while begining the process of rebuilding. Both of these tactics led to more insurgents. The former caused strained relations between the coalition and local populations, while the latter gave money to contractors, many of whom had direct ties to the insurgency and provided great targets to the insurgents for propaganda. In many places, insurgents would wait until a project was nearly finished and then blow it up. This demonstrated that the coalition had no control over the population and could not provide safety and security.

Al Qaeda in Iraq

The pro-Saddam insurgency was well underway by the fall of 2003. Meanwhile, there were others who had a deeper and stronger hate for America and her allies—the global *takfiri* movement. *Takfir* is the act of excommunication in Islam, and declaring takfiri is generally frowned upon by mainstream Muslims because it supersedes God's judgment. However, groups like al Qaeda readily excommunicate other Muslims or declare takfiri, therefore they are called takfiris by many mainstream Muslims. I use the term *takfiri* for the same reason many Muslims do—it immediately challenges al Qaeda for sole possession of the moral high ground. Often Americans refer to these groups as *jihadists* or *mujahidin*, but both of those terms grant immediate religious legitimacy—much like the terms *paladin* or *holy warrior* in European history. These takfiri saw the opportunity to strike against the U.S. in Iraq.

Abu Musab al Zarqawi, a Jordanian citizen, was in Iraq before the invasion. Zarqawi was a terrorist with ties to al Qaeda dating back as early as the mid-1990s. For a time, he lived in Pakistan and facilitated the training of terrorists in Afghan terrorist training camps run by al Qaeda. In 2000, he ran a training camp for al Qaeda in Herat, Afghanistan, specializing in poison and explosives. In early 2002, as U.S. forces expelled al Qaeda and the Taliban from Afghanistan, Zarqawi fled to Palestine. By summer 2002 he had left Palestine, using his new Hezbollah ties to establish a training camp in northeastern Iraq with a local terrorist group.

In May 2002, Zarqawi went to Baghdad to seek medical treatment. While there, he organized over twenty extremists and terrorists in Baghdad to form the cadre for Jamaat al-Tawhid wa'al Jihad (followers of unity and struggle, aka JTJ)[3] or al Qaeda in Iraq (AQI). In August 2003, AQI perpetrated its first major attack, launching a suicide truck-bomb attack against the UN headquarters in Baghdad. Very shortly after, the group conducted a series of suicide attacks against Shia Iraqi civilians in southern Iraq, including the massive suicide truck-bomb attack in Najaf on August 29, 2003, that killed over a hundred Shia citizens, most notably Mohammed Bakr al Hakimi, the leader of the Supreme Council of Islamic Revolution in Iraq (SCIRI). Within a few months, Zarqawi was one of the top half dozen most wanted individuals (also called high-value individuals, or HVIs) in Iraq. His organization was responsible for attacks against U.S. and other coalition forces, the infant Iraqi Security Forces, and, most notably, Iraqi Shia.

There are several possible explanations for why Zarqawi's group attacked Shia. The most logical is that although SCIRI had significant support from Iran, the group was not, initially, anti-U.S. and coalition. Group leaders were pleased that the Saddam regime had been removed and were making significant noises about supporting U.S. efforts to reorganize and rebuild Iraq. Nothing could be less palatable to al Qaeda. For years, Sheik Osama bin Laden and Dr. Ayman al Zawahiri had preached against the evils of supporting Western powers in the Middle East, particularly U.S. military forces, who they referred to as "crusaders" who served "Zionist masters." So any Muslim who supported the U.S. was, in the eyes of al Qaeda, an apostate. Never mind the fact that most Sunni extremists viewed Shia as heretics or apostates already because of a misperception that they worship Ali. Of course, in Islam, idolatry, saint worship, or worshiping any being other than the one God, Allah, is a sin; moreover, it is the only unforgivable sin. Many Sunni view the Shia preoccupation with shrines as a "mortal sin." So, although it is likely that the initial attacks against Shia were merely proxy attacks against the "invaders," there is a component of long-standing hatred of Shia by extremist Sunnis. But, there is also a much more sinister possibility for these attacks. It is possible that the true reason for the AQI attacks against Shia was to precipitate a civil war and prevent a new government from being seated in Iraq. Whether that was initially the intent of the AQI attacks or not, it certainly became the intent later.

Although SCIRI and its military wing, the Badr Corps, were not patently anti-coalition, there would be a Shia group that was. Initially, the vast majority of Shia were supportive of the U.S. forces and multinational coalition. Truly, many of them viewed coalition forces as liberators, not invaders.

However, by July 2003, a new Shia voice had emerged. Muqtada al Sadr, the son of the late Grand Ayatollah Mohammed al Sadr, who was believed to have been assassinated by members of the Saddam regime in 1999, was speaking against the coalition. In July, he announced his intent to form a militia in order to fight occupying forces and the newly appointed ruling council, which he saw as a puppet government. In October 2003, Sadr announced that he had seated a new Iraqi Islamic government. Over the next several months, Sadr's militia, the Jaysh al Mahdi (JAM), conducted attacks against both Iraqi government targets and U.S. and coalition forces.

So, by early 2004, there were three insurgencies in various stages of formation in Iraq. The first was made up of the nationalists, including "the return party," "the patriotic front," and "the 1920 revolution brigade." These groups were mostly Sunni Arabs who wanted the coalition "occupation" to end and a return of some secular Iraqi government, if not the Arab Ba'ath Party. The second was the Shia insurgency formed almost exclusively by the Jaysh al Mahdi. They wanted a Shia religious state in Iraq and an end to occupation. Last were the Sunni extremists, both Iraqi and international. Although these groups had many names, such as JTJ, Jaysh al Mujahideen (the Army of Holy Warriors), Islamic Army in Iraq, and the Islamic Salafist Boy Scout Battalions (seriously), they all wanted the same things: to kill as many coalition forces and Iraqis who supported them as possible and to form a Taliban-like Islamic state in Iraq.

The one thing all the insurgent groups had in common was their hatred for U.S. forces and the multinational coalition. So, over the next three years, they all waged war against us . . . and we didn't know how to stop it.

The Intervening Years

I left Iraq in April 2004. Shortly thereafter, I left the 4th Infantry Division and Fort Hood. I was reassigned as an Army officer detailed to the Central Intelligence Agency (CIA), where I wore civilian attire every day (except for about four special occasions in two years). My duties there had me interacting with Department of Defense (DoD) officers regularly, but as a CIA officer, not a soldier. My job was to provide advice and expertise for the CIA from the perspective of an Army officer, and to spearhead interactions between the CIA and DOD on several special programs. My interactions at the Agency gave me a unique foxhole from which to observe the changes in the Iraqi insurgencies over the years 2004–2006.

The one change that would mean the most to me (and therefore to this book) was the alliance that developed between nationalist groups and Sunni extremist groups in al Anbar Province. Several factors played into that relationship. First and foremost was the situation in al Anbar between 2004 and 2006. Al Anbar Province has a population that is nearly homogeneously Sunni Arab. During the Saddam regime, the men of al Anbar provided a large number of officers to the Iraqi Armed Forces and other security organizations. Fallujah and the surrounding suburbs were a popular retirement locale for military officers and other government officials. For those reasons, and because U.S. forces were extremely heavy-handed in Fallujah and Ramadi early on, the nationalist insurgent groups were strong and popular in al Anbar Province. As AQI began to grow in Iraq, the group found refuge and safe haven there. Group leaders chose al Anbar for several reasons. First, it shared borders with Jordan, Saudi Arabia, and Syria. These borders made it possible to smuggle support into Iraq, support that took several forms but primarily consisted of money and foreign fighters who entered Iraq through al Anbar and were largely used for suicide attacks. Second, U.S. forces were having a difficult time subduing al Anbar. As troops surged into Fallujah, insurgents went to al Qaim or Hit or Ramadi, and there were just not enough forces to cover all the cities—the place is huge. Third, the province is directly adjacent to Baghdad and provided an excellent place from which to stage attacks into the capital. Finally, many people in al Anbar were receptive to the message of extremist Islam.

In spring 2004 and again in winter 2005, U.S. forces fought major battles in Fallujah. Although they had temporary success, these battles caused significant civilian casualties and brought new and wide support to both nationalist and extremist groups in the province. By early 2006, the large nationalist insurgency in al Anbar entered into an alliance with AQI. Together, they became a formidable enemy for U.S. forces and began to cause significant U.S. casualties and to control large populated areas in the province. As members of AQI moved into the population centers, they worked to recruit and establish a network of imams and muftis willing to spread their message and to enforce their version of Sharia, or Islamic law, on the population. Women were not allowed to work and were required to cover themselves with the burka. Men were not allowed to drink alcohol or smoke in public, among other rules that were brutally enforced. The population was unhappy but powerless to drive AQI from the cities. A new Islamic state was being born.

CHAPTER 3

The Train-Up

Out of Fort Stewart, Georgia, the 3rd Battalion, 69th Armor (3-69 Armor) is a combined arms battalion assigned to the 1st Brigade Combat Team (BCT), Raider Brigade, 3rd Infantry Division (3ID). Unlike armor battalions of ten years ago that had only tank companies, 3-69 Armor has two mechanized infantry companies (A and B Companies), two tank companies (C and D Companies), an engineer company (E Company), a forward support company (E Company, 3rd Brigade Support Battalion), and a Headquarters Company. It has 830 soldiers assigned or permanently attached. The battalion deployed for both the initial invasion of Iraq in 2003 and for a second tour in Operation Iraqi Freedom in 2005–2006, returning in January–February of 2006. When I took command of the battalion that June, the soldiers had already begun training for a third deployment. The Raider Brigade was the first unit to deploy to Iraq for a third tour, and was the first unit to deploy with less than a year between deployments, so there was much hoopla about that.

When I attended the pre-command course at Fort Leavenworth, Kansas, many Army staffers spoke to our group about how the Army was working to solve problems that were developing as a result of the high operational deployment rate. They would usually caveat their talk by saying something like "This is how we are going to make things better for deploying units. However, if you are going to the Raider Brigade . . . I apologize; it won't be fixed in time for you." That was my first clue that my battalion and I would have a tough summer ahead of us—and we did.

Normally, the training cycle between deployments gives a unit about ninety days to reintegrate after deployment (that is readjust to life at home), another ninety days for individual training, from six to nine months for collective training culminating with a mission-readiness exercise, then a month of leave prior to deployment; ideally, about eighteen months from one deployment to the next. The Raider Brigade would have less than a year. That meant that we had to cram about ten months' worth of training into six months. Where we would normally have a week or two between major training events, we had no time; in fact, on several occasions the training events overlapped.

Preparatory training for combat deployment of a mechanized or armored force is quite a process. A unit must accomplish several key tasks prior to deployment, plus several tasks that are desirable but not required. The events are designed such that one builds on the last. For example: first, a unit conducts individual marksmanship training on weapons like pistols and rifles, then the unit moves on to two-man firing exercises and crew-served weapons qualification (crew-served weapons include all the heavy machine guns), then finally the unit trains on tanks, Bradley infantry and cavalry fighting vehicles, and mortar live-fire. Each soldier must fire each of these weapons systems for qualification during both day and night and in degraded system modes or other unusual environments. The practice and qualification ranges go from single-day affairs all the way to week-long exercises. Units cannot begin "collective training" until these weapons are qualified at the lowest level (individual and crew). Collective training, simply put, starts to combine individual soldiers and vehicle crews into units: squads, sections, platoons, and companies. Additionally, key leaders go through various simulations so they will be familiar with their tasks prior to taking troops into the field. This leader training is intended to limit the number of opportunities wasted once all the soldiers are involved.

Doctrine, What Doctrine?

Previously, Army doctrine had identified three levels of war. Low-intensity conflict ranged from peacekeeping/peacemaking operations where U.S. forces merely separated two warring factions, to guerrilla warfare where U.S. forces either supported the state or the insurgency. Mid-intensity conflict ranged from a shooting war against an inferior ground force to an air, land, and sea conflict against a near-competitor (say China or Russia). High-intensity warfare referred to total war, meaning global, multi-theater, and nuclear.

U.S. Army forces generally had a fairly narrow focus. Prior to 2003, light infantry, airborne, and air assault units focused on low-intensity warfare; heavy mechanized and armored units focused on mid-intensity conflict; and Strategic Air Command (now U.S. STRATCOM) and the U.S. Navy focused on high-intensity conflict. Generally, the culmination of a mechanized or armored unit's training cycle would be a trip to the National Training Center (NTC) at Fort Irwin, California, to fight the vaunted opposing force, or OPFOR. The simulation at the NTC was and remains the most realistic military training in the world. The old saying was that the only thing simulated at the NTC was dying, and occasionally that was real too. Having conducted actual mid-intensity conflict twice, in Operations Desert Storm and Iraqi Freedom (the initial invasion), I can attest that the training at NTC was as close to the real thing as one can get. Each rotation drew from a menu of "standard missions." They included defending, attacking against a known enemy (good intelligence on enemy locations), attacking against an unknown enemy, and, finally, meeting a moving enemy. Each type of mission had tomes of doctrine that laid out guidelines for the conduct of that mission. Leaders and soldiers knew doctrine; they studied it, and they could recite lists and explain concepts associated with it.

But it wasn't 1986 anymore, and we weren't preparing to meet the Soviet Union on the plains of Germany, nor were we preparing to destroy Saddam's military in the open desert of Kuwait. We were preparing to return to the confusing and chaotic counterinsurgency fight we had seen previously. We all worked very hard to develop meaningful, germane training based on the model with which we had grown comfortable. We also worked hard to learn a better way to fight this war.

U.S. Army counterinsurgency doctrine was woefully inadequate. Written in the aftermath of Vietnam, the doctrine was outdated and confused. That left Army leaders with no meaningful lexicon from which to draw. Not to be left adrift, we turned to contemporary and historical academic articles and books to attempt to sort out the "how-to" of counterinsurgency. Several readings were in vogue among Army officers at that time: David Galula's *Counterinsurgency Warfare: Theory and Practice*, David Kilcullen's "Twenty-Eight Articles: Fundamentals of Company-Level Counterinsurgency", and T. E. Lawrence's classic *Seven Pillars of Wisdom*, along with many others. These three works in particular captured truths about counterinsurgency that were rather obtuse at first read. The works all required a good deal of contemplation, scholarly thought, and discussion to digest. They all provoked a good deal of healthy debate and laid bare the differences between the velvet glovers and the iron fisters. But these works would never pass for Army doctrine.

Army doctrine is generally written at about an eighth-grade reading and comprehension level. The beauty of well-written doctrine is that it can digest some of the most complex concepts in warfare into easy-to-remember concepts and lists. For example, in mid-intensity warfare, there is nothing at the tactical level more complex than breaching an enemy obstacle and attacking a prepared defense. Leaders can study and practice for years to do so. Units practice extensively to achieve even decent results at NTC. Watching it done well, either in training or in combat, is like watching a masterfully presented ballet (only with really cool explosions). Army doctrine reduced this complex operation to a five-letter mnemonic acronym, SOSRA, for **Suppress** (the enemy defending the obstacle), **Obscure** (the enemy's view of your forces), **Secure** (the breach site), **Reduce** (the obstacle), and **Assault** (to penetrate the enemy's defense). Simple, logical, easy to remember, SOSRA was a powerful word tool that guided individual and collective actions from the conception of a plan all the way through an infantryman engaging targets with his rifle. SOSRA made the nearly unfathomably complex task of breaching a prepared defense simple enough for good units to execute effectively at least half of the time. We desperately needed SOSRA for counterinsurgency.

Unfortunately, while we trained in the summer of 2006, the Army was just publishing its new counterinsurgency doctrine. We didn't have much time to read it, so we plodded on through our training. We made it reflect, as much as possible, what each of us knew from our previous experiences in Iraq, but one training event epitomizes the lack of focus that summer, since it was so incongruous and confused.

As mentioned above, 3-69 Armor was a battalion of tankers and mechanized infantry. We were relatively comfortable with gunnery tactics, techniques, and procedures for our tanks and Bradley fighting vehicles. However, we all knew that we would spend much of our time in our trucks: M1114 and M1151 up-armored humvees. Therefore, we needed to conduct training exercises focused on crew- and platoon-level gunnery in trucks. The crew-level qualification in trucks was simple and straightforward: move down a range road and engage the targets presented. No issues. It was the platoon wheeled gunnery qualification that captured the confusion of our train-up.

The scenario started with the platoon planning and preparing to occupy a series of observation posts (OPs) overwatching an IED hot spot (an area that has had many IED emplacements). The members of the platoon moved to and occupied their positions on the range and then received a report that their positions had been compromised and an insurgent force was moving to attack them. The insurgents were in Bongo trucks (the Kia Frontier Bongo is as ubiquitous in Iraq as Ford and Chevy pickups are in Georgia) and were armed with AK-47s and RPGs. Platoon members were then presented several targets. Some of the targets were standard black-plywood truck targets representing civilians, and some were white-plywood truck targets representing insurgent vehicles. (If only it were that simple in real life!) The members of the platoon were also presented with personnel targets. If the target had on a traditional Arab robe—called "man dresses" by most soldiers—he was friendly; standard black silhouettes were enemies.

So, from their first positions, the members of the platoon engaged these ridiculously simple target arrays. The platoon leader was then given an order over the radio to meet a sheik in the woods about five hundred meters to their front and left flank. The sheik, the radio report said, would provide information to the platoon leader about the insurgents who had just attacked his platoon. The platoon leader then took a small dismounted element into the woods and met with the sheik. The "sheik" was quite a piece of work—a three-dimensional target mannequin wearing both a white robe and the red-and-white-checked Arab headdress. A role-player (usually one of my staff officers) played the voice of the sheik. The sheik told the platoon leader that the insurgents had fled to a set of houses near the end of the wood line.

As soon as the sheik had divulged his info, insurgents attacked the dismounted element. The platoon was presented with a series of personnel targets that "fled" through the woods and led the group to two house facades they needed to clear. After engaging the enemy in the woods, the platoon leader ordered his trucks into a position to fire on the houses, and he and his dismounted soldiers moved to clear the houses. Once the houses were cleared, the platoon leader received a report that another observation post to his south had been engaged and that the vehicle was last seen moving in his direction. He was ordered to proceed down the range to a new OP at the end of the range road. En route, the platoon was attacked with an IED on the road, causing two simulated casualties. Platoon members had to react to the contact and call for medevac (aerial medical evacuation). Finally, the platoon occupied its new position and engaged a series of moving truck targets, ending the strange scenario. I'm not sure what that hodgepodge of events trained for, but I am damn sure it *wasn't* counterinsurgency.

The rest of the summer and fall went by much the same, with training scenarios that were neither fish nor fowl—neither mid-intensity conflict nor counterinsurgency. But, these events did exercise skills, committing many of them to the level of muscle memory, and they made leaders and soldiers think. We trudged through the training and generally had very good results in developing skills and battle drills that would serve us well.

The National Training Center at Fort Irwin remains the best training venue in the world. However, with our accelerated training and deployment schedule, our leaders decided that, in order to maximize time with our families, NTC would export a training package to Fort Stewart, Georgia. I was initially very skeptical. Having trained at the NTC nine times in my career, I was not sure that the same training environment could be built at Fort Stewart. I was wrong.

The U.S. Army pulled out all the stops to ensure that we received excellent training. First, Fort Stewart contracted to have several rudimentary villages built in the training areas consisting of multiple buildings with shops, streets, clinics, etc. Second, contractors built battalion-sized forward operating bases (FOBs) on Fort Stewart with tents, showers, latrines, motor pools, and dining facilities that accurately simulated and were on par with those of many of the actual bases in Iraq. Third, the Army sent its counterinsurgency experts from the Asymmetric Warfare Group (ASG) to interact with junior leaders and soldiers during the training. The ASG is a special mission unit that was formed in 2004 to serve as training and operating advisors to non–special forces units training for and conducting counterinsurgency. These partners spent a great deal of time with my battalion, both in training and while deployed, and helped us to develop our mind-set as well as our tactics, techniques, and procedures for conducting effective counterinsurgency.

Finally, a cadre of nearly two thousand personnel from NTC came to Fort Stewart, including trainers (also known as observer/controllers or OCs), OPFOR, support personnel, and, most importantly, role-players. These role-players were mostly Iraqi-Americans, many of whom had only recently immigrated to the United States. They were, for the most part, raised in Iraq, understood the culture, and were committed to assisting us to understand it. Many of these role-players were great patriots who truly wanted to see us learn the culture and succeed because they had a vested interest in both the United States and Iraq. The most important thing that the NTC training package afforded us, however, was a thorough understanding of the Army's new counterinsurgency doctrine. The OCs (and a very special guest trainer) introduced us to the SOSRA of counterinsurgency: the tactical defeat mechanism.

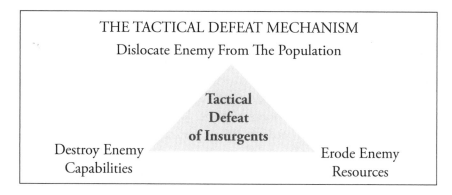

THE TACTICAL DEFEAT MECHANISM

Dislocate Enemy From The Population

Tactical Defeat of Insurgents

Destroy Enemy Capabilities

Erode Enemy Resources

The Tactical Defeat Mechanism (TDM)

Again, good Army doctrine presents complex concepts in simple fashion, and the TDM is no exception to that rule. This simple diagram actually shows the marriage of the velvet glove and the iron fist approaches. It demonstrates that all three tactical tasks—dislocating the enemy from the population, eroding the enemy's resources, and destroying or degrading his capabilities—are coequal parts of an overall campaign to defeat insurgents. Brilliant in its simplicity, the TDM gave me and several of my subordinate leaders an epiphany: it was possible to employ an iron fist and a velvet glove simultaneously. Here was our SOSRA for counterinsurgency. Unfortunately, I didn't have a whole career in which to figure it out; we would be in Iraq in four months.

I didn't have to grasp all this by myself, however, nor did my leaders. We had help from the Scorpions. Three OC teams at the NTC trained maneuver battalions and task forces, and all had nicknames appropriate to their desert home at Fort Irwin—the Cobras, the Tarantulas, and the Scorpions. We had, by the luck of the draw, been assigned the Scorpions. Each team includes a senior trainer who is a former battalion commander, a second-in-charge, a senior noncommissioned officer, trainers for each staff section (intelligence, operations/plans, administration/personnel, logistics, fire support, engineering, communications and automation, etc.), and trainers for each company and platoon. Ultimately, the team brought about fifty trainers to Fort Stewart. The senior trainer was an officer with whom I had previously served and for whom I had great respect. Then–Lt. Col. Gary Brito and I had served together in 4ID. Gary was the 2nd BCT operations officer when I was the 1st BCT operations officer. Gary had most recently served as a combined arms battalion commander in 3ID and had just completed a rotation to Iraq with his battalion. All this gave Gary huge bona fides with me. Gary and I had several discussions about how we had done things in Iraq with 4ID and how we needed to change. Many of our discussions centered on countering IEDs.

IEDs have killed more Americans in Iraq than any other form of enemy attack. If you ever doubted Charles Darwin's theory about survival of the fittest, spend a few months fighting insurgents. Insurgents come in two varieties: smart and dead. And Iraqi insurgents during the war quickly learned that direct confrontation with Americans caused insurgent death more often than not. Therefore, they sought ways to engage Americans without being in the line of fire, and the two methods that rapidly developed were indirect fire (mortars and rockets) and the use of improvised explosive devices.

Mortars and rockets were plentiful in Iraq in 2003–2004. As mentioned earlier, the ammunition holding areas in Tikrit were huge and contained tons of mortar and artillery rounds and rockets of all kinds. Those were but two of the hundreds of such facilities in Iraq. Long before they could all be secured, the Iraqi population (for whatever reason) looted hundreds of thousands of rounds of mortars, artillery, and rockets. However, it took a certain skill set to employ these rounds accurately, and while some insurgent cells were capable and became formidable, accurate, and deadly, most merely harassed American forces. But there were other things one could do with the ammunition.

The other weapon that kept insurgents out of the line of fire was the IED. Initially, insurgent IEDs in Iraq were crude devices that had to be triggered by someone relatively close to the device. (I'll not bore you with details, but it's all about the loss of voltage that occurs when electricity is conducted through wire.) The devices generally used military-grade munitions (the same artillery, rocket, and mortar rounds used for indirect fire). However, as insurgents realized these devices were effective weapons against the unarmored wheeled vehicles of U.S. forces, they began to build more and more complex and effective types. Many of these devices mirrored those used against Israeli Defense Forces in the occupied territories. (Another indication of the global assistance given by Islamic terrorist groups to Iraqi insurgent groups—but that is another discussion.) Soon, IEDs were killing and crippling Americans far too frequently. Then Iraqi insurgents developed into the worldwide experts on these weapons. They became the innovators who designed the most lethal, easy-to-use IEDs in the world.

Our strength in the U.S. Army is not in our numbers but in our training and technology. Therefore, we, as a military, immediately began to search for technological and training solutions to the problem of IEDs. In fact, it was this effort that spawned the ASG. It also spawned a flurry of activity from defense contractors. We began working on several methods to defeat the weapons. Vehicles became heavily armored, electronic coun-

termeasures where developed, and equipment and teams were built with
the sole purpose to clear IEDs off of roads. However, I watched—sometimes as a participant in my CIA job, sometimes as an observer—and
wrung my hands. The only way to really defeat IEDs is to defeat the insurgency. Don't attack the tool, but focus on the people. This brings us
back to the TDM.

Then–Lt. Gen. David Petraeus was the commander of the U.S. Army's
Combined Arms Center. Among other duties, he was responsible for developing Army doctrine and establishing the training standards for the
force. General Petraeus had also recently been named as the replacement
for Gen. George Casey, commander of the Multi-National Force Iraq. As
he prepared to move to Baghdad and take responsibility for all coalition
forces in Iraq, he took the time to come to Fort Stewart and spend two
hours with each battalion commander. For those of you who don't have
the perspective, this is like the CEO of Walmart spending two hours alone
having a discussion with a store manager.

Among the many things that General Petraeus did as the commander
of the Combined Arms Center was oversee the writing of the Army's new
counterinsurgency manual. He was responsible for the TDM. My prior
experience with General Petraeus was limited, since I had only watched
him from afar. As a 4ID veteran, I saw him as the opposition to the 4ID
way of war. As a result, I was not excited to meet him; he was the velvet
glove to General Odierno's iron fist. My meeting with him quickly dis-
pelled my previous views, however. Petraeus was genuine and extraordinarily intelligent. Although he never mentioned the tactical defeat
mechanism, that's exactly what we discussed. By the end of my two hours,
not only was I a huge Petraeus fan, but I also began to understand what it
took to win in Iraq

Focus on the Population

The scenario for our mission readiness exercise was as follows: the BCT
was taking over from a redeploying unit in an area of Iraq that was heavily
populated with insurgents. Members of the local population, however, were
beginning to dislike the insurgents and were slowly warming up to the idea
of working with the Americans. In our battalion area of operations (AO)
we had three villages: one still strongly insurgent and two neutral. The vil-

lages were occupied by about twenty role-players and fifteen or so OPFOR. During the fourteen-day training exercise, things happened much like they happen in Iraq. There were spectacular attacks against civilian targets, insurgents attempted to emplace IEDs, and patrols had chance encounters with insurgents. Meanwhile, a local government needed U.S. support, the population had hardships brought on by the combat, and the people of the villages needed help with infrastructure. We ebbed and flowed through the two-week operation very much as we would in Iraq. The leaders and soldiers learned real, meaningful lessons from the training. Several incidents during the training contained great lessons for me, personally.

During training, we received a report that insurgents had captured three soldiers near our AO. For the next several days, intelligence began to point to a village just outside the AO as the possible location where the soldiers were being held. Ultimately, this intelligence drove us toward a time-sensitive raid against a group of houses in that village. We quickly planned an operation to extract the captured soldiers and kill or capture the insurgents. About three hours elapsed between the time we received the intelligence about the houses and the time we moved to clear them.

One of the decisions I had to make was from where I would control and monitor the raid. The raid force was A Company, but it really was a larger action because the battalion used several of our systems to help the company. Additionally, we had Apache helicopters and unmanned aerial vehicles (drone airplanes or UAVs) that supported the raid. As a company commander and battalion operations officer, my tank had always been close enough to the fighting to be able to see and engage the enemy. I had always found that to be the best way to have situational awareness. So, as I always had, for this training exercise I decided I would go into the village with Alpha Company.

In Iraq, commanders can't move alone. My first time there, I always moved with just one other truck; CSM Larry Wilson and I traveled over 2,500 miles in two unarmored HMMWVs with just our drivers, but those days are gone. My personal security detachment (PSD) in 2006–2008 consisted of five to six trucks with over twenty-five soldiers. So, I took my PSD and my operations officer, and we rolled into the village right behind A Company. In fact, I cleared two of the houses with a rifle squad. As the squad went on to the third house, I moved back to my truck about two

hundred yards away. Twenty seconds later, all hell broke loose. The third
house was a safe house with about twenty insurgents in it, and they put
up a hell of a fight.

As the fight progressed, I stood near my truck and spoke to the company commander on the radio, as well as the battalion tactical command
post and the aircraft. The night was black, a deep black you only see in
coastal Georgia woods. As I talked on the radio, two OPFOR soldiers stood
up out of the woods twenty feet away and threw simulated grenades. The
grenades landed right next to my truck. Three of my PSD soldiers were
wounded, and my personal bodyguard was killed (all simulated, of course).
For the next forty-five minutes, my world became the area fifty feet around
my truck. We hunted down and killed the two insurgents, evacuated the
wounded and dead, and prepared for our exit. During that time, I contributed nothing to the larger fight. By becoming embroiled in my own
little firefight, I had left one of my companies without my leadership. Not
to mention the fact that I now had simulated deaths and injuries to the
soldiers charged with my safety. The members of the PSD were like a family, and I had let them down. I would not have to learn that lesson again.
I finally understood that there are times when, for the sake of an example,
a battalion commander must be right in the heat of the fight, and then
there are times when he must be removed enough to think, analyze, and
make critical decisions.

Another incident that had a huge impact on me occurred when an
informant approached one of the companies around midnight and told
them that insurgents would sleep in one of our villages that night. He said
they were there then and would remain until about 3:00 a.m. He gave us
descriptions of the insurgents and told us in which buildings they would
be. We had been attacked in the village earlier that day and had a sustained
firefight against insurgent forces in and around the village. We also received
a separate report about a possible insurgent gathering in the same village.
The two reports and the previous attack led us to plan an operation to
search the village. It was normally one of the neutral villages in our AO. It
had a mayor/sheik and a police chief. They both claimed they wanted to
work with the coalition forces but had done little to prevent attacks in the
area. So, at about 2:30 a.m., we went in to conduct a search of the village.

Not only were the inhabitants of this pseudo-Iraqi village surprised, but the role-players who had actually been sleeping there were surprised outside of their characters. They came out of their shacks in their sleeping clothes and started to raise hell with the OCs who were with us. I could see these folks were upset and frightened. Even though they knew this wasn't real, I could see they were truly afraid. After all, men with guns had just woken them and pulled them out of their beds. The impact was not much less than what one would see in Iraq. I walked over to the group of role-players and OCs and began to tell the role-players that we had no intention of disturbing or harming them; we were just training the same way we would fight. They explained to me that we were fighting like goddamn idiots! After a few minutes, most of the actors got back into their roles. The mayor/sheik and the police chief immediately began to harangue me about our not having coordinated the raid with local authorities. The police chief informed me that he could have had his police go in and bring all the males out to be screened and questioned. I didn't think that was a particularly viable option and told the mayor and the police chief so. I told them we had experienced several attacks immediately adjacent to the village and that the insurgents almost certainly came from there. We agreed to meet later that morning to discuss how to improve our cooperation.

None of the reported insurgents were in the village. Nor did we find any weapons. We did, however, pull several females from their sleeping areas and totally disturb the hospital staff (one of the buildings we searched was the hospital). When I arrived back in the village mid-morning, I was greeted by many really sour looks.

So, Maj. Chuck Krumwiede, my operations officer, and I met with the elders of the village to discuss why the raid had happened and how we could have done it differently. Based on my previous experience, I found the meeting very authentic. There is a rule I found must be applied to meetings with Iraqis (and I found the same with Saudis): it takes three to four times longer to conduct a meeting than it would with most Americans. Reasons for this phenomenon include the following: first, the obvious language barrier. With even a good interpreter/translator, it just takes a long time to have a conversation in two languages. Second, and more important, Arabs are the most hospitable people I have ever met. For that reason, most meetings start with polite interactions. Usually included are at least a few cups of tea (chai) and a couple of cigarettes. (Arabs will normally offer everyone at the meeting a cigarette before smoking one, and they do this every time they smoke. If you accept one, you will often be given an entire pack, and your host will insist that you take it.) The ritual greeting process can also take time. One enters the room and greets the entire gathering with the standard greeting, "asalaam aleukum" (peace be upon you) or the more advanced and formal, "asalaam aleukum a rhahman tu Allah wa barakatu" (peace be upon you and may the mighty God grant you happiness). The entire gathering stops what they are doing to reply, then all present stand and the newcomer moves around the room and shakes the hands (or kisses the cheek or shoulder if they are friends) of each person in the room. The status of the newcomer may dictate that the seating arrangement for the room change. There is a well-defined hierarchy for seating in these rooms. Also, the Arab sense of punctuality is very different from ours. If a meeting starts at 10:00, it is not unusual for key attendees to arrive at 10:45. All these factors contribute to the length of these meetings.

So, the meeting that morning lasted about three hours. During it we negotiated some fairly straightforward rules for future interactions. First, village leaders would be responsible for the environs of the village, and it was their duty to ensure we would not be attacked within it or nearby. Second, as long as they did that, we would coordinate with them for any operations we needed to conduct in the village. Furthermore, if we had information that a member of the village was an insurgent, they would go with us to arrest or detain that individual. Third, we would focus jointly on the needs of the village. And finally, the villagers would provide us with any information they had regarding insurgent activity in the AO.

With these rules in place, our relationship with the once-neutral village began to change drastically. At our meeting, we had discussed several issues they saw as critical, and two of these issues could be solved immediately. The first was that the village had no electricity. This was both a common issue in Iraq and a real issue for the role-players. You see, they actually slept in the village about half the time, and they really had no electricity. The second issue was water. Again, both notionally in the training event and in reality this was an issue. The NTC cadre had been providing water to the village but not enough for hygiene, tea-making, and cooking. After our meeting, we delivered a generator with light sets and two pallets of bottled water to the village. That day, the village market opened for the first time during the training. The police chief informed us that one of the shop owners was an insurgent for whom we had been searching, and with the police, he and I went and arrested the insurgent. Although there were several attacks against police and villagers there, we were never attacked in the vicinity of the village again. This example was a little too pat, but it drove home a valuable lesson to me. The best people to identify and fight against insurgents are those who can recognize them. Get the people on your side, and you can win.

Of course, the OPFOR from NTC were tough, as usual. Each engagement resulted in simulated wounded and killed-in-action soldiers. Every time we raided an insurgent safe house or caught insurgents planting IEDs, the fights were furious, and the casualties during the training exercise were adding up. I was concerned about this, but I attributed it to the prowess of the NTC OPFOR. The veterans in the battalion, including me, thought they were too tough to represent Iraqi insurgents. Based on our experience, they were much more tenacious than the Iraqi insurgents we had fought. Time would show us how wrong we were. The really tough insurgents *were* in al Anbar.

Simultaneous with the whole summer and fall train-up, we conducted leaders' forums and symposia in the battalion in which all leaders platoon sergeant and above discussed counterinsurgency. We talked about the importance of winning over the population and the importance of having Iraqi Security Forces (ISF) that could serve as partners in our work. We discussed the tactical defeat mechanism, and at our last gathering, we discussed what I had seen in Ramadi.

John Charlton

Part of the training for leadership in our brigade included a trip to the NTC for the Leader Training Program (LTP). Although this training was excellent, it is not terribly germane to this story, save for one crucial anecdote. During the LTP trip to the NTC, the members of the BCT fought a simulated battle on a computer model called JANUS. JANUS allowed leaders and command posts to maneuver their virtual forces against virtual OPFOR. In my past experience with JANUS, the engagements were generally fairly realistic and provided good training effects. The simulation we fought was on NTC terrain; specifically, we were attacking an enemy-prepared defense on a hill known as C130 Crash Hill, or just Crash Hill. I was very familiar with this terrain and had fought a similar scenario at least three times on the ground and several more in JANUS. My battalion was to be the assault force for the BCT (remember SOSRA?).

There were, of course, many routes we could have used to attack. My brigade commander, Col. John Charlton, directed me to march my battalion around an area called the Goldstone. The Goldstone road is a long, circuitous route that goes around the foothills of the NTC. The route of march the BCT staff had selected was about fifteen miles long and had a significant stretch that went uphill at about a 15 to 20 percent slope. When I received the order, I expressed my concerns about the route to Charlton. I told him I had taken that route a few times and that it would be very slow. In fact, I said that it would take more than five hours to reach Crash Hill. I recommended a route that was much less obvious and would provide great surprise. The route went through a little-known piece of terrain called Coyote Canyon, and we could exit the canyon through an area called OPFOR Cut. This was literally a bulldozer cut through the wall of the canyon. Very few units used it, but I had been through it twice before and found it to be an excellent approach to Crash Hill. It would cut the travel time in half, and the OPFOR would not expect us to use it. Colonel Charlton looked at me as if I were stupid (not the last time) and proceeded to explain to me that I had M1 tanks, that they were fast, and that the route was only ten to fifteen miles, so it should take no more than one hour. I attempted to explain that I had lots of vehicles that were not M1 tanks and that the slope was steep. My recovery vehicles, mortar carriers, and other stuff would not go fast up that hill. He abruptly told me that I would take his route and do it quickly, and then he dismissed me.

Two and a half hours into the simulation, I had covered about seven miles, and he started calling on the radio and ordering me to "go faster, there's no way it should take this long." Try though I did, it took five hours. Once out of the Goldstone, the battalion quickly destroyed the defending enemy, but that didn't matter. I realized that day that although I had been doing this since I was eighteen years old, I would never convince John Charlton that I was right if it meant he was wrong. Several times during the fall train-up, Colonel Charlton and I had similar disagreements. It was becoming a habit.

I have deployed to combat three times in my career. All three times I have found out when and where I would deploy not from my chain of command but from the news media. This time was no different. While I was in the field at the mission-readiness exercise (MRE), my wife told me during a telephone conversation that the media was reporting that the 1st BCT would deploy in January to Ramadi. Three days later, I got the same word through my chain of command.

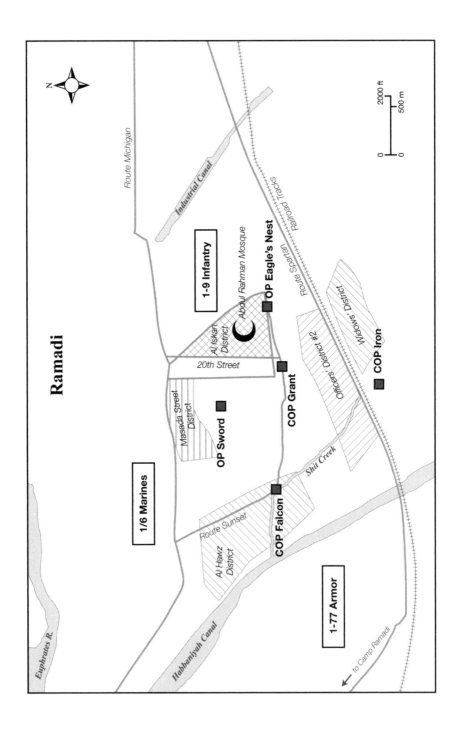

Ramadi

N

2000 ft
500 m
0
0

Route Michigan

Industrial Canal

1-9 Infantry

Abdul Rahman Mosque

OP Eagle's Nest

Route Spartan

Railroad Tracks

Al Iskan District

20th Street

Masada Street District

1/6 Marines

OP Sword

COP Grant

Officers' District #2

Widows' District

COP Iron

Shit Creek

Route Sunset

COP Falcon

Al Hawz District

1-77 Armor

Habbaniyah Canal

Euphrates R.

to Camp Ramadi

CHAPTER 4

Through the Looking Glass

As soon as we came out of the field from our MRE, BCT leadership began planning a pre-deployment site survey (PDSS) to Ramadi. *PDSS* is the modern Army term for reconnaissance of an area to which you will deploy. Normally, these recons are conducted prior to a unit's MRE, but for us, we did not know where we were going then. I had my staff find all the information they could on Ramadi, and what we found was shocking. On May 21, 2006, Michael Ware, writing for *Time* magazine, had depicted Ramadi as the most dangerous place in Iraq.[4] He goes on to describe in detail the situation in Ramadi as follows:

> There's no reason to believe that the Americans' battle against Iraqi insurgents is going to get better. ... even as commanders try to turn combat duties over to Iraqi forces and pull U.S. troops back from the front lines, parts of Iraq remain as deadly as ever. At least 18 U.S. troops died last week, raising the total killed since the invasion in March 2003 to 2,456. . . .
>
> Nowhere is the fighting more intense than in Ramadi, the

capital of Anbar province and for the moment the seething heart
of the Sunni-led insurgency.[5]

Michael Ware expressed what many people thought. Ramadi has been
lost, and as Ramadi goes, so go al Anbar Province and, possibly, the entire
Sunni Triangle. In fact, the senior Marine Corps intelligence officer in Iraq
wrote as much in a supposedly secret document leaked in September 2006,
as reported by Thomas Ricks in the *Washington Post*, saying that "the
prospects for securing that country's western Anbar province are dim and
that there is almost nothing the U.S. military can do to improve the political and social situation there."[6] A read of both Ware's and Rick's articles
also illustrates another widely held belief, the myth that "we just don't have
enough forces to secure Iraq." It was all over the media from mid-2004 to
early 2007. That false belief was based on the assumption that safe and
secure equals U.S. forces patrolling an area twenty-four hours a day; the
places where we had boots on the ground were safe. This myth rose from
the iron fist school of thought. If we only had enough forces to raid every
insurgent stronghold, guard every seat of Iraqi government, and visit every
hot spot every day, we could keep the insurgents from acting. Much like
the war on IEDs, that approach treats the symptom, not the illness. The
real answer rests with the people. To win a counterinsurgency, one has to
stop insurgent recruiting and end their cause's popularity.

What we found in official channels mirrored what Ware wrote. Ramadi
was bad, with around thirty attacks against U.S. positions or patrols daily.
Many of these attacks were sustained firefights, not just an IED or single
RPG. The insurgents in Ramadi were fighting a war. Earlier that summer,
reinforcements had been sent: the 1st BCT, 1st Armored Division (Ready
First Brigade) was ordered from Tal Afar in Ninevah Province to Ramadi.
The Ready First BCT had already been successful in securing Tal Afar, a
former insurgent stronghold, by using a technique BCT leadership called
"seize/hold/build."

Seize, Hold, and Build

The technique was fairly simple and brilliant. It consisted of three phases:
Phase one was to clear an area of active insurgent presence (easier written
than done); phase two established a U.S. or joint U.S./Iraqi outpost in the

heart of the former insurgent area; phase three was to rebuild the area both physically and socially. Members of the unit had developed techniques that allowed them to establish the physical site of a base while they were still fighting insurgents in the same area. They adapted our normal Army logistics equipment to haul concrete barriers, Hesco baskets, and pre-fabricated guard towers complete with bulletproof glass and steel walls and then brought them into a fixed site to create an "instant" combat outpost (we called them COP-in-a-box).[7] Over the summer, the Ready First BCT had created a number of these outposts. Once the outpost was manned, a U.S. force lived in the former insurgent area. The force could then conduct patrols without having to "commute" through dangerous roads and ambush positions. The idea was that the U.S. force would become part of the community, an idea that grew out of the community policing that had become popular in many American cities. The Ready First BCT fought hard to establish outposts in Ramadi, but the gains came at the cost of significant casualties. They had seized the final outpost late in the summer and were well into the hold process when we made our PDSS visit.

While my staff did their research, so did the Raider BCT staff. They provided several briefings prior to the PDSS and gave an initial plan for which battalions would trade battle space. The 3-69 Armor would take the place of the 1st Battalion, 37th Armored Regiment (Bandits). The Bandits were a "legacy" tank battalion as opposed to a combined arms battalion, and they had three tank companies and a headquarters company assigned. They had also been task organized with two of their own tank companies, a mechanized infantry company, and an extra mechanized infantry platoon. Initially, I thought that my battalion and the Bandits would compare to our advantage. I had a little more combat power to work with than they did.

As the PDSS drew nearer, we had a series of meetings to discuss plans for movement and reconnaissance. In one meeting, we discussed what we were bringing on the trip. Colonel Charlton mentioned in passing that we would only bring pistols, and I was shocked. When I went to Iraq in 2003, I remember well our urban operations training. The trainer was an old retired special operations soldier, and at one point, he looked at the battalion commander and told him, "This ain't Desert Storm, battalion commander, you better make sure your rifle is zeroed just like everyone else's."

That had a big impact on me, and even as an operations officer, I went nowhere in Iraq without a rifle. Here we were, heading to the most dangerous city in Iraq, and I was told, "no rifles." I told Charlton I was not comfortable with that, and he chuckled and said, "I don't think we'll be needing our rifles." A few of the other battalion commanders got a big kick out of that too.

Traveling to Iraq is always a painful process, and this time was no exception. Our trip started in the Savannah International Airport, where we boarded commercial transport to Atlanta and then Dulles. In Dulles we put on our uniforms and traveled via military charter to Shannon, Ireland, then proceeded to Ali al Saleem Airbase in Kuwait. The trip takes twenty-four to thirty-six hours and, like most international travel, leaves you feeling spent. We didn't stay long in Kuwait, flying in U.S. Air Force transports from Kuwait to Baghdad International Airport. There we boarded U.S. Marine Corps helicopters to make the flight to Ramadi. As the most dangerous city in the world, Ramadi was given its due respect by Marine pilots. They would only fly into the city at night, blacked-out, and once on the ground, they wanted to touch down and take off as quickly as possible, and for good reason. Many times during my tour at Camp Ramadi I watched helicopters come and go and saw streams of enemy tracers arc into the sky in their general direction. We landed safely at Camp Ramadi and were ushered, most unceremoniously, off the aircraft.

Camp Ramadi was a large and active base. It housed, at the time, about three to four thousand soldiers, sailors, airmen, Marines, and civilians. Our accommodations for the first night were transient tents, but bright and early the next morning, Chuck Krumweide (my operations officer) and I moved to live with the Bandits, who were anxious to get started on our recon. This was the third PDSS they had hosted. They had hosted a unit in Tal Afar that eventually replaced them there, and they had hosted a unit from 1st Cavalry Division, which was scheduled to replace them in Ramadi but had been diverted to Baghdad. In fact, that very week I had run into two battalion commanders from the 1st Cav with whom I had previously served and who were heading to Baghdad instead of Ramadi. The Bandits (and their entire BCT) had just received word that their tour would be extended from twelve to fifteen months, obviously word about which they were less than thrilled.

The Bandits as part of the Ready First Brigade, had earned a reputation during their time in Tal Afar for being tough and smart. Now they worked for the only Marine Corps division in Iraq, the division known as the Multi-National Force West, or MNF-W. The Bandits were one of five combat arms battalions in the fight in Ramadi. Forces included 1-37 Armor Bandits, 1-77 Armor Steel Tigers (another legacy tank battalion with some mechanized infantry and engineer troops), 1-9 Infantry Manchus (a light infantry battalion turned task force with seven maneuver companies), and 1/6 Marines (a U.S. Marine Corps infantry battalion, reinforced). North of the city, in Jazeera, was 2-37 Armor, also a legacy tank battalion minus one company.

When we arrived at the Bandit headquarters, we got started right away on orientation. They had, as all units do, a standard operations and intelligence (O&I) brief that described the enemy and friendly situation in their AO. Most units gear these briefings to communicate a certain message. The briefings are normally delivered to VIPs, and often those individuals are decision-makers and can effect changes. Therefore, units usually use these briefings to "beat the drum" for something they need. The Bandits geared their O&I brief just to be scary! It focused on how much enemy contact they had seen, how tenacious the enemy was, and how lethal the battalion was. It came complete with videos of firefights and large ordinance impacts on "insurgent houses" in the city.

The briefings took the best part of the first day. In addition to the O&I, there were briefings on "enabler support" from the BCT. *Enabler* is the latest Army-speak for combat support providers. Because the Ready First BCT was assigned to the Marine Expeditionary Force that served as the Multi-National Force West (MNF-W), the support provided to the Army BCT had a multi-service flavor. The explosive ordinance disposal (bomb disposal) unit was from the Marines, as well as the local working dog teams. There were Army engineers who performed route clearance and Navy Seabees who did construction support. There was a crime lab that could process evidence gathered from attacks or seized in raids. There were also Naval Criminal Investigative Service (NCIS) agents who investigated major crimes on and off the post. Each organization gave us a briefing on its capabilities and a description of standard operating procedures. Once the briefings were done, the rest of our time was to be spent visiting the combat outposts (COPs) the Bandits occupied, so the morning of the second day found us loading up in HMMWVs to head out to the COPs.

As we prepared to leave that morning, Lt. Col. V. J. Tedescu, the Bandit commander, asked me, "Where's your rifle?" I relayed to him the story of my conversation with Charlton, and we commiserated about brigade commanders. He was happy to provide me with an Egyptian knock-off of the Heckler and Koch MP5 submachine gun and two thirty-round magazines to supplement my feeble 9mm pistol. That taken care of, we loaded into the trucks and prepared to leave.

I had not been in an up-armored HMMWV since 2004, and they had changed quite a bit. The trucks were now equipped with intercoms and headsets, like a tank or Bradley. This allowed the entire crew to hear the radios and converse without screaming across the truck. They also had significantly more armor and had recently been outfitted with the "Frag 5" kit. Frag 5 is the highest level of armor for humvees. It consists of heavy, bulletproof glass ("pope glass") in all windows and huge, heavy armored doors. The trucks had also been fitted with fire-suppression systems, and some had electric turrets for the gunner. The gunners' stations were also fitted with additional armor so that the gunner was not exposed to ground fire but rather scanned through pope glass windows in the turret. Each truck was manned by three to five soldiers, and each had a driver, vehicle commander, and gunner. Some had soldiers in the backseats who could dismount from the truck with the vehicle commander, if needed. Each truck was armed with a crew-served weapon in the turret, usually either an M2 .50-caliber machine gun (a highly reliable weapon, in constant service since World War II) or an M240 .30-cal machine gun. Each crewmember also had at least one personal weapon, and the truck was normally equipped with vehicle-mounted screening smoke grenades, hand-thrown smoke grenades, and pen flares (signal flares launched from a pen-shaped projector). The trucks could carry thousands of rounds of ammunition, and they normally did.

I don't recall the order in which we toured the COPs, and it doesn't matter a great deal. I'll describe them from south to north and give an overview of the major checkpoints and routes in the AO. There were no routes free of IEDs in Ramadi. In fact, the only routes considered relatively clear were those that had been overwatched twenty-four hours a day since the last route clearance mission. Every other road was assumed to have IEDs, and the Bandits didn't use them. This logic necessitated a plethora of observation posts (OPs) and checkpoints. For the Bandits, OPs mainly consisted of single tanks with three-man crews that normally rotated every six hours or so. The Bandits also had one OP manned by a three-man crew in a common remotely operated weapon system (CROWS) humvee. CROWS is a system that allows the crew to acquire and engage targets with a TV camera sight and joystick from inside the truck.

The Bandit AO was in south-central Ramadi, but Camp Ramadi was in the northwest of the city. They therefore had to travel through another unit's AO each time they left Camp Ramadi, and they didn't like that one bit. The choice was to go through north-central Ramadi, owned by 1/6 Marines, or through western Ramadi, owned by Task Force 1-77.

Approaching through the west, at the southern end of the city was a rail bridge over the Habbaniyah Canal with a joint OP manned in the west by TF 1-77, and in the east, just on the western side of the canal, by a CROWS truck from the Bandits. This was OP Bridge. OP Bridge overwatched the southern east–west route and controlled the traffic flow over the railroad bridge. (The trains hadn't run since 2003, and the bridge was used by both tracked and wheeled vehicles to cross the canal into central Ramadi. The train tracks were badly damaged, and the rail bed was, as well.) Just east of the bridge was COP Iron, a three-building compound south of the railroad tracks that stood about 1,200 meters from the nearest dwellings north of the tracks and, for that reason, was attacked significantly less than the others. The COP had a motor pool outside of the wire that was overwatched by the guard towers. COP Iron was occupied by a mechanized infantry company/team—which also manned three OPs in addition to OP Bridge—and about fifty Iraqi Police (IPs).

OP Trans Am was east of the COP along the road that ran adjacent to the rail line. Route Trans Am was the only way to bypass the heart of the city east-west, so it had significant traffic. The road was mostly unimproved, however, therefore the Bandits didn't use it and were not happy about guarding it.

OP Central was due north of COP Iron at the intersection of routes Central and Spartan. Spartan was a wide route consisting of two parallel, improved roads and the open area between them, which was known as the

Bowling Alley. About four hundred meters east of OP Central was OP Bowling Alley. The Bandits did not travel Route Spartan often, but they did have many engagements in the Bowling Alley against insurgents attempting to transit the city.

Route Central was one of two major north–south routes in the Bandits' AO, and both routes were needed to move through the AO north–south or vice versa. Route Central, as a major road in the community, was lined with businesses and residences. About eight hundred meters north of Route Spartan were Route Baseline and OP Baseline.

A left turn (west) on Baseline brought us to COP Falcon. COP Falcon was home to a tank company reinforced with a mechanized platoon. The mech platoon was from another battalion, not the Bandits, and stayed with us through our time in the city. COP Falcon was home to the al Forsan IP Station—with about 350 policemen split into two seven-day shifts of 175—and a company of the Iraqi Army from the 7th Iraqi Division. COP Falcon was a multi-building position that took up a corner of two main routes: Baseline ran east–west, and Route Sunset ran north to link up with Route Michigan, a four-lane east–west route connecting al Anbar with Jordan to the west/southwest. COP Falcon had two OPs, OP Baseline and OP Sunset, both manned twenty-four hours a day by one tank each.

East along Route Baseline were two more COPs: COP Sword was two blocks east and two blocks north of COP Falcon and was occupied by a reinforced platoon and a company of the Iraqi Army from the 7th Division. COP Grant lay at the intersection of Route Baseline, Route Farouk, and 20th Street. COP Grant was occupied by a U.S. company with no Iraqi security forces. COP Sword and COP Grant lay smack in the heart of darkness. About three blocks north of COP Grant and five blocks east of COP Sword was the Abdul Rahman Mosque, widely known to be the "capitol" of the Islamic State of Iraq (ISI).

On October 15, 2006, a terror group formerly known as the Mujahideen Shura Council released a statement announcing the founding of the Islamic State of Iraq. Although group leaders claimed that the state was made up of several groups of jihadists, the group was, in actuality, a front organization for al Qaeda in Iraq. We have previously discussed (Chapter 2) the rise of the insurgency, leaving off at the unlikely alliance between Iraqi nationalist groups and the takfiris. This was the alliance that allowed the rise of the ISI. Between the nationalists and the takfiris in al Anbar Province, anti-coalition groups were able to control many of the major population centers, including Ramadi. The ISI had literally and figuratively planted its flag in the al Iskan District[8] of Ramadi and was the de facto government of the city.

During my PDSS trip to Ramadi, several things jumped out at me. First was the devastation that had been wreaked upon the city. As we rolled through the streets, there was not a single area that had been left untouched by over three years of combat. Nearly every building had pockmarks or holes caused by direct fire. Many streets were filled with sewage. It was, in fact, difficult to tell which streets were paved and which were not. (In fact, nearly all are paved, but it was many months before I would know that.) On every road traveled by Americans, there were myriad craters from IEDs and parts of destroyed U.S. vehicles. The streets used by U.S. forces were lined on either side with rolls of concertina wire to make it more difficult to emplace IEDs. Trash and debris were stuck in the wire, and occasionally a dead dog or cat that became entangled rotted adjacent to the street. The residents were too frightened to remove the carcasses because they could easily be shot as insurgents if they were seen handling the wire.

I cannot do justice to the fetid stench of Ramadi. It was a mixture of sewage, rotting garbage, burning garbage, and rotting flesh. The people of Ramadi (once a great city of four hundred thousand—in November 2006 it had maybe one hundred thousand occupants) went about their business with looks of terror and hate commingled on their faces. Those still there in 2006 fell into three categories: insurgents, those too poor to leave the city, and those too stubborn to abandon their homes to the terrorists. None were very happy. There were never children on the streets, and citizens only went out when they had to.

Amid all that fear and destruction, the city still had some basic functions. Markets and shops were open, and people could purchase basic foodstuffs. None of the markets were on roads used by Americans, but you could see them a block or two off the beaten paths. They were by no means crowded, but there were shops and shoppers. Rarely did a U.S. patrol enter these markets, nor did IPs go to them. As a student of sociology and political science, I understood that markets could only exist if there was sufficient security to prevent theft and control interactions. It was clear to me that the security was provided by the Islamic State of Iraq and, therefore, al Qaeda.

Choosing Sides

As part of the PDSS, Chuck Krumwiede and I went on several patrols with the Bandits. Most often they conducted what had come to be known as census patrols. The Bandits had developed an absolutely brilliant census database for their AO. The database was built and linked so that one could access each dwelling by building number in a database. The building numbers were one color if the building had been "censused" and a different color if it had not. If a census had been conducted, one could click on the building, and it would bring up pictures and descriptions of each male occupant. If you clicked on a name, it searched the reporting database and showed any intelligence reports that referred to that person. The system was phenomenal but very labor intensive. It required constant updating. The initial data and any updates came from patrols that went to the house, photographed all male occupants, and asked a series of questions (through an interpreter) about the household. This data was put into a patrol debrief that was then entered into the census database. In order to conduct these operations efficiently, the Bandits would enter and search a house, separate the men from the women and children, and question the men. They brought bags of sugar (an expensive and desirable commodity in war-torn Ramadi) and delivered them to the household at the end of the census work.

I clearly remember one such census patrol in which Chuck and I participated. One of the households had three young (thirty-ish) adult males, their wives, their mother, and about ten children. As the patrol queried the males, two kids kept looking out at the strange Americans clad in their armor, helmets, and dark glasses (eye protection is a must in combat), bristling with weapons. They were clearly frightened but also very curious. There were several other children who were hysterical with fear. I walked over to the children, removed my helmet and eye protection and got down on one knee to talk to them. In my best broken Arabic, I interacted with them and soon had them hugging me and laughing. All the while, the members of the patrol looked at me as if I were crazy. I could tell from their reaction that this was not how they conducted business. The women were initially terrified, but as I interacted with their children and grandchildren, I watched their terror dissipate. We entered that house as occupiers, barely human, looking like storm troopers from a sci-fi movie, but we left as human beings who hugged and kissed their children and did what we could to make them feel safe and comfortable. On the way out, the eldest woman invited us to stay for lunch. I graciously declined and explained that we did not have time, but maybe we would be back one day to stay for lunch. We left as we had come, bounding over the walls of the compound and keeping behind cover to avoid the omnipresent threat of snipers in the "most dangerous city in Iraq." Upon our return to the COP, I asked the lieutenant who led the patrol if they normally spoke to the women and children in the houses. He told me that they had no time for that; they had to get the census data and move on.

That family had most likely sat on the fence in the war that was raging outside their house. The men were relaxed and did not behave as insurgents do, but I'm sure they had never thought to help the Americans and the few IPs in the city. I'm convinced that that day they finally chose sides.

I had known for years that we could not win in Iraq without winning over the Iraqis. My time with the Bandits showed me that even though they had fought extremely hard to gain their footholds in Ramadi, they were not willing to make the Iraqis their friends and partners. My interactions with them at every level indicated that they had no trust or love for Iraqi security forces or the population in general. They had fought so long and hard against the Iraqi insurgents that all Iraqis had become the enemy. I set out to ensure that my unit would not suffer the same fate but rather would take the hard work done by the Bandits and move forward to the next phase of the fight for Ramadi.

CHAPTER 5

Bad Guys and Good Guys

There are politicians, political pundits, media personalities, and average citizens who contend, quite vovcally, that we did not fight al Qaeda (the "real" 9/11 organization) in Iraq. They contend that al Qaeda "lives" in Afghanistan and Pakistan. They are wrong. In order to fully appreciate who we fought in Iraq, one must first appreciate the nature of al Qaeda.

Let's start with the word itself. Although the term is not usually translated because it is a proper name, it has a literal translation. Often translated as "the network," the term's more accurate translations are "the base" (like the bottom of a pyramid) or "the foundation." I find the word *foundation* to be the most useful because it has the same multiple meanings in English that *al Qaeda* has in Arabic. Al Qaeda is the foundation in the sense that it is the solid structure upon which things above are built. That analogy describes exactly how its members feel about their version of Sharia (the Islamic law as handed down by the prophet Mohammed and developed since his death). Only upon Sharia can anything good be built, according to their thought; and anything added or subtracted from Sharia makes the society built on it evil. *Foundation* also means the primary idea upon which a philosophy, theory, or way of thinking is built. That meaning is fairly self-evident. Finally, a *foundation* can be an institution or charitable organization, particularly one that provides funds. Al Qaeda is to global takfiris what the United Way is to U.S. charities and the Ford Foundation is to the arts. It funds terror groups throughout the world. Al Qaeda is the "foundation" to militant takfiri extremists the world over. It provides direction and guidance, raises and distributes funds, and interprets and judges ideas, regimes, and people. What al Qaeda doesn't have is a membership committee, directory, who's who, or official website that lists each member for all to see. Contrary to the beliefs of some Americans, there is no al Qaeda headquarters with the flag planted in the front yard and Osama bin Laden's office on the seventh floor. Al Qaeda is an opportunistic organization that changes its alliances based on the current state of a particular movement or organization.

The members of al Qaeda understand and thrive both on and in the media. Like the members of most terror organizations, a large part of their effort is to inform, intimidate, and influence people whom they have never and will never meet. Abu Musab al Zarqawi obviously paid attention in class. During late 2003 and early 2004, Zarqawi and his al Qaeda in Iraq (AQI) organization went on a media blitz. Through an extensive media network, AQI publicized the vast majority of its attacks. These attacks fell into three general categories: attacks against U.S. and coalition forces (crusaders and their Zionist masters), attacks against Iraqi security forces (traitors to the faith), and attacks against Shia (apostates). AQI publicized these attacks for three reasons: First, they formed the foundation of a murder and intimidation campaign designed to keep neutral Iraqis from resisting AQI. Second, these attacks were used as recruiting tools both inside and outside Iraq to bring fresh recruits to the takfiri cause. Finally, the attacks were used to raise money, internationally and locally, in order to finance the war in Iraq.

AQI included in its organization media and propaganda cells. At the local level, these media cells were responsible for filming attacks, and often they would be filmed from multiple positions in order to present different camera angles of the same incident. The best footage was sent to regional or central AQI media cells that would edit the films and provide post-production effects like soundtracks, narration, and graphics (often including credits) to produce professional-grade video that could then be distributed in several ways. The videos were always burned to CDs that were then mass-produced and distributed through local Iraqi propaganda cells. These CDs could be found in most Iraqi markets from 2004 through 2007. Sometimes they were distributed at no cost, but often they were sold for a small contribution to the "brothers of the jihad." The CDs were also distributed internationally throughout the Middle East, typically through mosques sympathetic to al Qaeda, and were used to recruit foreign members to the group. Many of these "films" were also uploaded to takfiri websites on the Internet. Among the features on these websites is the ability to donate funds to al Qaeda front organizations. AQI made great use of these websites.

One of the unintended consequences of our invasion of Iraq was to provide to global takfiris a 9/11 or Pearl Harbor–like rallying event. Osama bin Laden and Ayman al Zawahiri had painted the U.S. as Crusaders and allies to Israel who desired to take over the Holy Land and control it from Egypt to the Persian Gulf,[9] a land they called Greater Israel.[10] In 2003, we finally took action that reinforced that belief. Abu Musab al Zarqawi capitalized on that theme in his fundraising and recruiting efforts and hit pay dirt. Zarqawi used his professionally produced videos as fundraising and recruiting vehicles, and by the beginning of 2005, he was seeing great success.

As previously stated, the first funding for the Iraqi insurgency came from Ba'athists of the former Saddam regime. However, by the end of 2004, the money was coming from al Qaeda. There was a subordinate-to-superior relationship between Abu Musab al Zarqawi and Ayman al Zawahiri. This relationship can be seen in the now famous letter from Zarqawi to Zawahiri that was reportedly intercepted by U.S. government officials in February 2004, in which Zarqawi laid out for al Qaeda senior leadership his intelligence and operations assessments for Iraq.[11] It is unclear if al Qaeda was funding AQI in February 2004, but it is likely that it was. There apparently was oversight from al Qaeda because Zarqawi wrote:

> You, gracious brothers, are the leaders, guides, and symbolic figures of jihad and battle. We do not see ourselves as fit to challenge you,

and we have never striven to achieve glory for ourselves. All that we hope is that we will be the spearhead, the enabling vanguard, and the bridge on which the [Islamic] nation crosses over to the victory that is promised and the tomorrow to which we aspire. This is our vision, and we have explained it. This is our path, and we have made it clear. If you agree with us on it, if you adopt it as a program and road, and if you are convinced of the idea of fighting the sects of apostasy, we will be your readied soldiers, working under your banner, complying with your orders, and indeed swearing fealty to you publicly and in the news media, vexing the infidels and gladdening those who preach the oneness of God.[12]

However, by the time the July 2005 letter was written from Zawahiri back to Zarqawi,[13] the senior al Qaeda leader was asking for money from AQI. Clearly, by mid-2005, AQI's fundraising campaign was working.

AQI was not getting money by merely posting ghoulish videos on the jihadist network. The group was also kidnapping Iraqis and foreign nationals for ransom, exacting taxes in areas that it "controlled," perpetrating theft and extortion, and hijacking and selling stolen goods and oil. All of these activities were leaving Zarqawi's organization flush, and all that money allowed AQI to develop quite an elaborate operation.

AQI came into the public eye in late 2006 with the declaration of the Islamic State of Iraq, although, by that time Zarqawi had been killed in a June 2006 air strike, and Abu Ayub al Masri was the new AQI leader. The Islamic State's capital was Ramadi, and the ISI was to al Anbar Province what the Taliban was to Afghanistan. In fact, one of the goals of the ISI was to establish in Iraq a replacement for the area lost in Afghanistan. What al Qaeda wanted in al Anbar was a place from which to launch a war to conquer all the Middle East. With its access to Jordan, Syria, and Saudi Arabia, Anbar was perfectly located to provide both training and toughening for takfiris from around the Middle East and, ultimately, to export those terrorists to the surrounding nations. Zarqawi wrote:

Among the greatest positive elements of this arena is that it is jihad in the Arab heartland. It is a stone's throw from the lands of the two Holy Precincts and the al-Aqsa [Mosque]. We know from

God's religion that the true, decisive battle between infidelity and Islam is in this land, i.e., in [Greater] Syria and its surroundings. Therefore, we must spare no effort and strive urgently to establish a foothold in this land.[14]

Al Anbar Province, and therefore Ramadi, also had huge symbolic significance. Al Anbar had long been viewed as the most violent and dangerous place in Iraq. Since 2004, when four American contractors had been killed and their dead bodies hung from a bridge in Fallujah, al Anbar had been seen as the seat of the Sunni insurgency. Although the Marines had come into al Anbar in early 2004 bragging that they would extend the velvet glove to those Iraqis, they soon found themselves in the most lethal fighting in all of Operation Iraqi Freedom. The brutality of the combat drew the attention of the entire insurgency and helped to convince many Iraqi fence-sitters to fight the Americans. With its newfound wealth and support from international takfiris, the ISI was ready to have a go at unifying the Sunni insurgency in Iraq.

Initially, Iraqi nationalists felt they had enough in common with AQI to form an alliance with that group. Pinpointing exactly when this alliance began is difficult, but I would say that it started to form after the first battle for Fallujah in April 2004 and was cemented after the second battle for Fallujah in November–December 2004. Nowhere has the adage "the enemy of my enemy is my friend" been more apropos than with regard to the relationship between the nationalists and takfiris in al Anbar Province. There is also an Arabic adage that describes the relationship: "My brother and I against my cousins, my cousins and I against our tribe, my tribe and I against the world."

The long-term goals of these two insurgent groups were greatly divergent, but their short-term goals were not. They both wanted to inflict maximum damage on coalition forces in the hope that they could drive them from Iraq, and they both hated the new, largely Shia government of Iraq. They also both saw the Iraqi Security Forces as traitors who had sided with an occupying force to oppress the Sunni population. With the same tactical goals, the two movements began to coordinate operations in al Anbar and export their attacks into Baghdad. In a May 2005 statement called "A Letter from a Soldier to His Emir," Zarqawi asks bin Laden to give the signal, "putting the plot into action." It's no coincidence that the level and ferocity of suicide attacks increased steadily throughout 2005. Clearly, al Qaeda was pouring the resources—money, suicide operatives, explosive precursors, and trained cadres—into al Anbar as quickly as it could. So, into 2005 and early 2006, the insurgency in al Anbar began to look monolithic.

The short-term goals of the insurgency in al Anbar were two-fold: to drive U.S. and coalition forces from the province and, ultimately, from Iraq; and to overthrow the government of Iraq. AQI had a fairly well developed plan for achieving the above goals. The group's leaders understood that the real target of any insurgency is the population. They also correctly identified that the target population was not merely that of Iraq but included all populations involved in the struggle. Specifically, they targeted the U.S. and other coalition populations through their attacks and information operations (propaganda) as well as the Sunni Arab population of the rest of the region. The leaders of AQI assessed that if they caused sufficient casualties, the American public and its allies would lose stomach for the war.

On March 11, 2004, al Qaeda launched what have been called the 3/11 attacks in Madrid, which killed and wounded nearly 2,000 people aboard trains. The goal of the assault was simple—break the will of the Spanish people and cause them to pull out of the U.S.-led coalition in Iraq. The 3/11 attacks were clearly a strategic effort by al Qaeda and consumed a good deal of capital and planning, and they were successful. The Spanish government, already a shaky ally in Iraq, capitulated and pulled its troops. Heartened by this result, al Qaeda launched similar attacks on July 7, 2004 in London, attempting to force the British from the coalition. Group leaders also assessed that through a protracted and deliberate campaign to target the mostly Shia government of Iraq and the Shia population at large with both kinetic attacks and propaganda, they could convince the Sunnis in surrounding nations that AQI fought on their behalf against an Iranian puppet regime that was attempting to re-establish a Persian empire. The tactics that they adopted to achieve these goals were equally well thought out.

Tactics

Unlike in most areas of Iraq, in Ramadi, the IED or roadside bomb was not the only (or even the most deadly) threat. The insurgency in al Anbar fought like a well-trained Army. Back in the days when the National Training Center ruled the U.S. Army and we were training to fight "big wars," one of the lists that we all memorized detailed the seven forms of enemy contact. They were visual, direct fire, indirect fire, electronic, chemical/biological/nuclear, mines, and aircraft. The idea was that one developed a standard operating procedure (SOP) for dealing with each. A good enemy would attempt to put you in as many forms of contact as it could in order to make things as complex and difficult as possible. We also strove to put the enemy in as many forms of contact as we could. There is a truly synergistic effect to be gained from complex engagements in combat. The confusion caused by them can actually slow responses to the point that soldiers (or insurgents) are paralyzed, not with fear, but with inaction born of confusion and shock. In Ramadi, the forms of enemy contact were visual, direct fire, mines and IEDs, indirect fire, counter-technology, civilian shields, infiltration, propaganda, money, and murder and intimidation (M&I).

Visual

Insurgents were everywhere in Ramadi, or so it seemed. Through informant networks, sympathizers, and even children, insurgents had eyes and ears throughout the city. It seemed as though an American patrol couldn't set foot out of a combat outpost without the insurgents knowing our whereabouts. Much of this information made it to the enemy in near-real time—they used messengers, flares and other pyrotechnics, tactical wire communications, some hand-held radios, occasional satellite telephones (there was no cell phone service in Ramadi until the summer of 2007), and physical signals (such as changing where a rug was hung or changing the position of a blind or curtain); purportedly they even used carrier pigeons and kites to communicate. They also tracked U.S. and ISF forces by using lots and lots of gunfire. The enemy spent a great deal of time observing, tracking, and recording our movements in order to plan operations.

The insurgents launched fake attacks against U.S. and ISF positions in order to watch and record our reactions. They put out dummy IEDs so they could film our methods of securing and destroying them. They were masters of reconnaissance! In fact, it was nearly impossible to hide from the enemy in order to spring an attack. Even our smallest, most stealthy elements, our sniper teams, were compromised within hours of their insertion.

One technique was so simple and ingenious that it epitomizes the emphasis the enemy placed on knowing where we were at all times. Insurgents paid children to stack pebbles in front of the gates and doors to empty buildings knowing that our small kill teams (sniper teams with an infantry squad) preferred empty buildings to occupied ones. The children would go check the pebbles just before sundown and just after sunrise to see if they had been knocked over. If the pebbles were moved, insurgents would plan an attack against the building and normally spring the attack within two to four hours.

The enemy also used visual contact to draw U.S. and ISF forces away from or to an area. Often an insurgent would cross a road with an RPG in order to be seen from an OP. If the soldiers pursued the insurgent, they might come back to their position to find it had been seeded with small IEDs, or they could be drawn into an ambush. Visual contact was a constant game of cat and mouse that could be navigated only with great skill and cunning. Double and triple tricks were the norm both for coalition and insurgent forces.

Direct Fire

Previously, it had been my experience that the use of direct fire by insurgents was akin to suicide. However, there is nothing more Darwinian than an insurgency. By that I mean that the stupid, unthinking insurgent is quickly taken from the gene pool. Remember, by 2007 some of these insurgents had been doing this for four years. In Ramadi, insurgents had figured out how to use direct fire very effectively.

First and most dangerous were snipers. My battalion would eventually lose three of the six soldiers killed in action to snipers (purportedly even the same sniper). The complex terrain of the urban environment made it the perfect venue for snipers, both ours and the enemy's. Nearly all the buildings immediately adjacent to our positions were vacant (mostly because the daily fighting made it far too dangerous to live right next to an American base). This allowed insurgents to use those empty buildings either to shoot from or to shoot through to attack U.S. positions. I know it sounds easy to keep insurgents from entering buildings right next to you, but believe me, it is actually quite hard. With patience, reconnaissance, and a covering force, a sniper could move into position, shoot, and leave without ever being seen. These snipers would often wait hours for a shot. Usually, they had a larger force designed to engage our positions immediately after the sniper fired in order to allow the sniper to escape unharmed. Snipers were the most lethal and psychologically damaging weapon used against my battalion. They were effective and hard to defeat.

Snipers were not the only insurgents effectively employing direct fire. Others employed direct fire from medium and light machine guns in attacks against our fixed sites or as part of ambushes against our patrols. Many of these machine gun attacks resulted in coalition and ISF casualties. In fact, for the less-well-armored ISF, several deaths were the result of accurate machine gun fire.

Insurgents also made great use of hand grenades in Ramadi. Rarely causing serious injury, these nuisance weapons were a great way to keep coalition forces from firing. Hand grenades thrown in close proximity to a soldier effectively suppressed his action, thereby allowing the enemy freedom of action. RPGs were also used extensively by insurgents in Ramadi. The key to insurgent direct fire was that it was almost always used as part of a complex attack, rarely alone.

IEDs

So-called roadside bombs had been favorite weapons of Iraqi insurgents since late 2003. They gave insurgents the ability to engage coalition targets from protected and concealed positions without exposing themselves to a firefight. By early 2007, IEDs had progressed to a point that they were quite powerful and ingeniously designed to protect insurgents while maximizing damage against coalition forces. The IEDs in and around Ramadi were some of the most lethal and sophisticated in all of Iraq. Two types were the most prevalent: the first, known as a "speed bump," or improvised-container IEDs, were built in factories. They were generally housed in welded-steel containers of various sizes, normally built in the shape of a rectangular base plate with sloping sides welded to it and a smaller steel plate welded to the top. The steel container was filled with high-explosive material and fitted with a blasting cap and detonation cord. The high-explosive could be either military-grade explosives or homemade explosives

(HME), which can be made fairly simply in home labs and became a huge problem in Iraq. These explosives were made from relatively simple and easy-to-acquire materials. Much like a methamphetamine lab in the United States, an HME lab is easy to spot if you get close, but if the community ignores it, it may survive for quite some time. These speed bump IEDs were easy to transport, and since the majority of the complex work was done in a factory, they were very easy to emplace. The device could be hooked to multiple initiation systems ranging from remote detonators to command wire or a "victim initiator" like a land mine. They were also very easy to booby-trap or set with an anti-handling device that could target bomb disposal personnel. A "good" insurgent team could emplace a dozen of these in less than an hour. These devices were rarely lethal but frequently caused catastrophic damage to vehicles and accounted for numerous injuries.

Large buried IEDS were also prevalent in and around Ramadi. These devices were, just as the name implies, huge explosives buried below the surface of roads or trails. They started as buried air-delivered ordinance, i.e., bombs from Saddam's air force, but they progressed to mostly HME devices buried in plastic or metal containers. The net explosive weight of these devices could be as high as five hundred pounds and frequently was in the one-hundred-pound range. Unlike speed bumps, these devices were difficult to install. In most places, insurgents had to bury them in holes as deep as four feet and usually four to five feet across. For that reason, these devices took up to two hours to emplace; however, with the right tools, a large, well-rehearsed cell could emplace a large buried IED in twenty to thirty minutes. These IEDs were fatal for crews in all but the most mine-resistant vehicles, and caused catastrophic damage to vehicles as indestructible as M1 Abrams tanks. It was because of these devices that the Bandits warned us to stay off of dirt roads, advice we would follow for our time in the city.

Indirect Fire

Mortars and rockets had long been a favorite tool of Iraqi insurgents by the time we arrived. Very difficult to counter, these systems allow insurgents to "announce their presence," not only to the targeted force, but to the locals residing or working near the target. Although these systems rarely caused significant casualties in our experience, the potential for casualties was there, and they had a strong psychological effect on the targeted force.

In order to understand why these weapons are hard to counter, first you need to understand something about them. Mortars range in size from 60mm to 160mm. The most common systems used by insurgents in and near Ramadi were 60mm, 82mm, and 120mm. A 60mm mortar warhead is about the size of a soda can, an 82mm warhead is roughly the size of a one-liter bottle, and a 120mm warhead is larger than a three-liter soda bottle. Obviously, these devices produce very different effects. Small 60mm mortars are unlikely to wound anyone more than fifteen feet from the blast seat. They typically cause superficial fragment wounds, and, although I have heard of one soldier who died in a 60mm mortar attack, I have never seen one kill a soldier. (I have experienced over fifty 60mm attacks in my career and over one hundred total mortar attacks.)

Larger 82mm rounds can cause injuries out to thirty or forty feet. The injuries, again, are primarily fragment wounds but can be significantly deeper and more serious. If someone is very close to an 82mm blast seat, he or she can suffer from substantial burns and minor blast wounds. Occasionally, broken bones occur from these blasts. Attacks with 82mm mortars can be fatal, but that is very rare. However, 120mm mortars will kill. These melon-sized warheads cause significant blast injuries and can decapitate or cause traumatic amputations. People as far as one hundred feet from these blasts can be seriously injured, and minor injuries can occur much farther away.

Launchers for 60mm mortars are a little larger in diameter than a can of baked beans and are about two feet long. They are lightweight and can be fired either with no baseplate or with a small baseplate that weighs only one pound. The rounds weigh only around four pounds each. One man can employ a 60mm mortar by himself, while 81mm mortars require a team. Those tubes are the length of a baseball bat and the diameter of a roll of paper towels. The tube weighs over forty pounds, and the system must be used with a baseplate weighing another fifteen pounds. The full system has a bipod and sight and takes one to three minutes for a trained crew of four to set and fire. The rounds weigh in excess of twelve pounds each. The 120mm mortar is a large, heavy system. It requires a crew of three to six men and takes up to five minutes to set up and fire. It is not man-portable for more than a few yards without a platoon-sized element to carry it. The rounds can weigh as much as thirty pounds.

Insurgents used several methods to avoid detection and retaliation during mortar attacks. Mortars are designed to fire at very high angles, which allows them to fire over cover and into things like bunkers and trenches. The rounds consist of a primer (usually a shotgun shell or something similar), propellant (rings of solid rocket fuel that attach like doughnuts around the shaft of the round), fins, a shaft, a warhead, and a fuse. When fired normally, at a high angle, high-speed radars can acquire and track mortar rounds, giving accurate locations in seconds and allowing forces to take action against the mortar team. However, if an insurgent took most of the propellant off the mortar, it could be fired at very low angles and sail to the target under the radar. Although the round is much less accurate at a low angle, that doesn't matter if you are an insurgent. Low-angle fire was the primary way insurgents avoided detection. Mortar rounds have long times of flight, as much as ninety seconds between launch and impact. Insurgents can fire and leave the scene before the first mortar bomb explodes, making it difficult to track or kill them. Finally, insurgents would fire mortars from within neighborhoods, thus ensuring that any U.S. lethal response (mortar or artillery counter-fire, air-delivered munitions, etc.) would result in civilian casualties. All of this made mortars a good tool for insurgents to keep in their inventory.

Although rockets were used less frequently than mortars, they provided insurgents with several advantages. Rockets are fired electrically and are very easy to set up and fire using a timer. This allowed insurgents to be miles away from the point of launch when the attack was initiated.

Counter-technology

We possess the most technologically advanced military in history, which gives us a great advantage over our enemies. However, none of it is infallible; nor can we depend on it to work all the time. After fighting us for many years, the insurgents in Ramadi had several techniques for countering our superior technology. The mortar technique above falls into that category, but there were many more ingenious ideas. For example, the speed-bump IEDs were built to be waterproof. After it rained, the insurgents would emplace the IEDs in puddles so that they could not be detected by thermal imaging sights. They also developed ways to hide behind walls and emplace IEDs. A favorite technique was to use long steel rebar poles to slide IEDs under fences and concertina wire without exposing themselves, or they would attach fishing line to an IED and simply walk across a road with one end of the line tied to a foot. Once across, they could hide in an alley and pull the IED across from a safe location.

When pursued, insurgents would sometimes hide in deep puddles and ditches, head under the water because they knew our thermal sights couldn't see into the water. At night, they would shine bright lights at our positions when they attacked because they knew it would wash out our night sights, and they used visible laser pointers to confuse our infrared laser aiming devices. They switched from metal to plastic IEDs to defeat our ground-penetrating radar. They learned how to defeat all these systems by trial and error and by reading all about the systems on the Internet. They used other techniques to defeat more secret systems that I would compromise if I discussed. Suffice to say, the enemy was savvy to many of our most lethal tricks and used his wits to defeat technology where possible.

Civilian Shields

Counterinsurgency is often more about who you didn't kill than who you did. Nothing serves to alienate a counterinsurgent force from the population more than collateral damage. Therefore, coalition forces go to great lengths to avoid killing noncombatants. Enemy fighters in Ramadi knew that very well, and they used noncombatants as shields often. The members of AQI, for example, had a favorite technique. I recall watching them surround themselves with children before moving a concrete barrier. By rights we could have killed them for moving the barrier, but they knew we would not while they had the children among them. Literally, they had children nearly touching them while they forced the barrier out of the road with pry bars. Each time we reacted, they scattered. Eventually, we were forced to overwatch the barrier from ten feet away to keep it in place.

I also watched, via unmanned aerial vehicle (UAV) video feed while an insurgent team emplaced a large buried IED deep in the al Iskan District. It would have taken hours for us to clear a route in to kill them. We had attack helicopters waiting for a clear shot to kill the insurgents for about ninety minutes, but there were always two or three boys (less than ten years old) within feet of the team while they worked. Eventually, we were able to destroy the team's car and blow the IED with a Hellfire missile, but the insurgents (and their kids) lived to fight another day.

The most insidious use of human shields occurred when insurgents forced their way into a home and attacked U.S. forces from it while the family still occupied it. These attacks truly put us on the horns of a dilemma, and often the results were horribly tragic.

Infiltration

Insurgents constantly attempted to infiltrate (and too often succeeded in infiltrating) Iraqi Security Forces. This occasionally resulted in devastating attacks against ISF from within their own ranks. More often, however, the insurgents would use their agents to bring discredit on the ISF by mistreating the locals. Coalition leaders and the ISF constantly guarded against this, but we were not always successful.

Propaganda

Local, national, regional, and international propaganda were mainstays of AQI. But propaganda includes more than pictures and CDs. The Arab street loves rumors, and AQI employed rumors relentlessly to attack both coalition and ISF. A favorite rumor, and one that always got traction, was the accusation of rape. It always took the same form: either ISF or Americans raided a house on so-and-so street and raped a young girl after beating her father. Nothing could whip a neighborhood into frenzy as quickly. Those types of rumors often led to demonstrations that came right to the gate of one of our positions. Often, insurgents would use the cover of the demonstration to attack, leaving us in a precarious position generally unable to respond without injuring the demonstrators.

Money

In a counterinsurgency, money is ammunition. That is not my concept; both Galula[15] and Kilcullen[16] wrote about it. Men, it seems, feel a deep-seated need to support their families, and many will do whatever it takes to accomplish this. They also don't like receiving charity. So, if one can find a way to get money into a man's hand, not as a gift, but for some noble action, that can provide very powerful motivation. Insurgents capitalize on this concept as much as do counterinsurgents.

For insurgents, the idea is to give a man a job attacking the evil fill-in-the-blank—in Iraq, it is apostate, Crusader, or traitor (ISF). So one man may only track the whereabouts of and watch a target for his pay, or he may be a full-fledged, IED-emplacing, murdering and kidnapping insurgent.

For the counterinsurgency force, the jobs they have available are to ensure safety and security, to build a better country, and to provide political and social leadership. That equates to ISF, contractors, and councilmen or government officials. Many Americans don't understand why we spend so much money rebuilding Iraq. Their mantra has become, "When are the Iraqis going to pay their own way?" I hope this book will make some of the issue less opaque and show why it was damn important for us to spend money, lots of money, in counterinsurgency.

Murder and Intimidation

The most effective and common insurgent action against the population of Iraq involved intense campaigns of murder and intimidation (M&I). Most Americans will have a hard time grasping the mind-numbing brutality of AQI's M&I campaign. In the city of Ramadi, on the mild end of the spectrum, a family could be kicked out of its house and the adult males publicly beaten if the insurgents assessed that the family spent too much time talking to Americans who came to search or census their home. If, however, insurgents had any indication that the family had given information to the Americans or ISF, the males would be dragged into the street and publicly killed (usually beheaded or shot, but sometimes beaten to death). ISF members and their immediate families were at great risk of being killed, and members of their extended family or their sheik could be publicly beaten or killed. For that reason, early members of the local ISF in Ramadi always wore masks.

The scale of M&I in some areas was truly appalling. In Albu Bali and Thar Thar (much more on both areas later), we found mass graves of up to thirty individuals, sometimes mutilated so thoroughly that one couldn't count exact numbers. We didn't find one grave, we found dozens. In the city in early 2007, it was not unusual to find bodies lying in the streets or floating downstream in the canals several times a week. Al Qaeda in Iraq's M&I was so effective that it became, without a doubt, the toughest insurgent action to break and had long-lasting effects even after the insurgents had been cleared from an area. One of the hallmarks of M&I was that the insurgents no longer considered their targets to be Muslim, so they did not "deserve" proper burial. As you'll read in the next section, it is M&I that ultimately led to the defeat of AQI.

Formidable Foes

Enemy fighters in al Anbar understood the value of multiple forms of contact. Therefore, over half of the attacks against coalition forces and ISF were complex, with several forms of contact being used simultaneously. These attacks showed a level of sophistication normally associated with organized and trained military forces. The bottom line was that the insurgents in al Anbar Province were the toughest, most organized, and best trained I had ever seen. They were the crème de la crème of the Iraqi insurgency and would be formidable foes for the battalion. In fact, the NTC OPFOR provided a good simulation of what we would find in Ramadi.

Good Guys

In order to understand what happened in al Anbar in 2006, one must understand the nature of Iraqi tribes and their span of influence. The tribe, in traditional Iraqi culture, is the basic social unit outside of the family. The tribe exerts more influence on a traditional Iraqi than any other institution. Although one may be a member of several other social groups (farmers' union, political party, professional community), nothing controls an Iraqi man's life as much as his tribe. The tribe serves many of the roles that we see as governmental. For example, the tribe may decide which farmers grow what crops. The tribe will have a strong say in who may marry whom and is the basic provider of social welfare for the indigent or those affected by disaster or other tragedies. The tribe is also the arbiter of most disputes. Finally, the tribe provides for the safety and security (yes, even in modern Iraq) of its members.

Arab tribes, for all their power, are fairly "democratic" organizations. Each tribe has a supreme leader known as the sheik of sheiks. He presides over the whole tribe. Some tribes, for example the Jabour or the Dulaim tribal confederation, may have well into the millions of members. (It's always hard to discern numbers when dealing with Iraqis.) These huge tribes are broken into sub-tribes, then clans (or extended families of thousands). Each level has a sheik.

A simple translation of the word *sheik* is *leader*. Sheiks have the power to make decisions for the tribes but often will convene a meeting of family and clan elders, or a "shura," to make decisions of importance. With this power comes responsibility. Sheiks receive great pressure from their tribes to solve problems. For many reasons, they will not refuse to hear a tribe member's complaints or concerns. In fact, the sheik's meeting hall, called a *muleefa*, is generally full all day with "petitioners." A big sheik may feed lunch to fifty people a day and rarely has much time to himself. For these reasons, although there are good sheiks and bad sheiks, tribes are generally very protective of their sheiks. Sheiks in rural Iraq are much like feudal lords were in Medieval Europe. In fact, good ones are more beneficent and popular than a modern-day American can imagine.

Initially, Saddam and his Ba'ath Party wanted to marginalize and perhaps even disband Iraqi tribes. However, during the Iran–Iraq War, then during the Gulf War, and finally during the period of UN sanctions, Saddam found the tribes so well entrenched in the fabric of Iraqi society that he decided to use them to control the population. During the Iran–Iraq War, Saddam merely tolerated the tribes, but after 1991, he openly supported sheiks with money and power in order to gain and maintain control of the suburban and rural populations. As a result, many of the sheiks became extraordinarily wealthy, in Iraqi terms.

Along came the Americans in 2003, and the money stopped. Some sheiks made inroads with us (such as the late Sheik Naji Jbarra al Jabouri, my good friend in Tikrit who was killed by terrorists in 2006 for his cooperation). But many, mostly for reasons of pride, refused to reach out to the Americans. They believed that we should have known enough to reach out to them. In most cases, we didn't. As Iraqi casualties began to accumulate, the sheiks came under great pressure from their tribes to make the occupiers go away. Their muleefas filled up with people asking them to redress issues with Americans who were causing harm (sometimes unknowingly, sometimes intentionally) to tribal members. So, as the chaos reigned in 2003–2004, many sheiks became supporters of the nationalist insurgents.

They saw the insurgency as a way to remedy the tribe's problems. (Actually, our tribe, the U.S. Armed Forces, had entered into a blood feud with many of those tribes, whether we knew it or not.[17]) This was the case in al Anbar. After the two Fallujah fights, it got worse. Many sheiks became very active in the nationalist insurgency. They raised recruits, they funded nationalist cells, and some even moved into leadership roles in nationalist groups. The tribes of al Anbar were our enemies.

M&I Backfires

The brutal murder and intimidation campaign perpetrated by AQI had, by mid-2006, begun to backfire. Although the campaign had a huge effect on citizens in the cities, it was becoming highly unpopular with the inhabitants of the tribal suburbs.

Much like the residents of U.S. cities, residents of Iraqi cities are literally rather urbane. They have lost some of the traditional ways of their ancestors by living in close proximity to people from other backgrounds. In the U.S., the loss of traditional ways is typically seen through the choices in cuisine, music, dress, and ceremony. People in cities have a wider range of acceptable behavior than those in rural America. The same is true for Iraqis. However, with these changes comes a loss of tribal identity. Iraqi city families, like those in America, tend to be rather self-contained. Although city folk have friends, they sometimes lose the bonds of their extended families. They become somewhat atomized and isolated in their homes. So, as AQI beat and murdered the populations of the cities into accepting the group's version of Sharia as the only acceptable law, there was little recourse for those in urban settings. They took to their houses and cowered from the brutality on the city streets, or they joined the insurgents. There was no sheik to ask for intercession. I wrote earlier about the extensive reconnaissance network that AQI had in Ramadi. It was fairly easy for leaders of the group to track what city-dwellers did. They only needed a spy or two on a block to know if someone pointed out an IED to Americans or spent too much time talking when American patrols visited. The punishment was a swift and public death. This often left the family without a breadwinner, or worse, susceptible to the unwanted advances of the terrorists (for all their talk about Sharia, the foot soldiers of al Qaeda are cutthroats, thugs, and rapists). The people of Ramadi had little choice but to join the insurgents, try to avoid all contact, or die.

It's a phrase many of us have actually heard in rural America, but whether or not anyone has actually said it to you, you all know the phrase, "You ain't from around here, are ya?" It's not much different in rural Iraq. Once again, the Arab saying, "My brother and me against my cousin, my cousin and me against my tribe, my tribe and me against the world" informs understanding. In the tribal areas, as AQI and the nationalists formed alliances, the leadership of AQI began to employ the same tactics they used in cities. However, unlike in the cities, if one kills a tribal member in the countryside, one must answer to the sheik. Granted, many sheiks were cowed by the ruthlessness of AQI, but many a proud sheik was not. Unfortunately, the result was often the same for a sheik as for a man in the city—public death. Several sheiks in the Ramadi area rejected AQI from the outset. Some were initially accepting of the alliance but soon ran into troubles with the M&I, and some fully embraced AQI. Regardless, by spring 2006, AQI began to target "uncooperative" sheiks for murder.

The Abu Ali Jassim sheik and the members of his tribe, although they were rabid nationalists, hated AQI. They aligned with a handful of other tribes to form the Anbar Salvation Counsel (ASC) and to encourage their young men to fight AQI. The ASC was a very small group of sub-tribe sheiks from four tribes in Jazeera, north of Ramadi—Abu Diyab, Abu Assaf, Abu Ali Jassim, and Abu Faraj—who were taking direct action against AQI. They began recruiting tribal militias to violently remove al Qaeda from their areas, and that is what caused al Qaeda to overplay its hand. On August 21, 2006, AQI made what turned out to be a fatal error. Members kidnapped and killed the sheik of the Abu Ali Jassim tribe in North Ramadi, and they committed the unforgivable offense of hiding the body so that the sheik could not be properly buried. (In Muslim culture, just as in Judaism, a body must be buried not later than sundown the next day.)

While I was working at the CIA, one of the most common discussions around the water cooler concerned if and how the U.S. government should engage Sunnis who were formerly associated with insurgent organizations. In the DC beltway, these discussions were somewhat esoteric. Meanwhile, the Ready First Brigade in Ramadi was wrestling with the problem in the real world. Leaders of the brigade were beginning to have limited meetings

with the ASC and were using these meetings to plan recruiting drives for
Iraqi Police. Nobody was at all sure that this would work, but then-Lt.
Col. John Tien, commander of the 2-37 Armor, and Col. Sean MacFar-
land, commander of the Ready First Brigade, took a huge chance. The
assassination of the Abu Ali Jassim sheik could have blown the whole thing,
but it didn't. The opposite happened. The assassination caused even more
sheiks to want to join in.

Among them was a young, energetic, charismatic sheik whose father
had been murdered by the terrorists. His name was Abdul Sittar Abu Risha,
but most people simply called him Sheik Sittar. Although the Abu Risha
tribe was relatively small, Sittar's family was wealthy. Sittar's brother, Sheik
Ahmed Abu Risha (the president of the Sahawa al Iraq at the time of this
writing) ran the family's import/export business mostly from Dubai, UAE.
In addition to having a good deal of wealth, Sittar also had another thing
that was vitally necessary to organize a movement against AQI: his house
was literally right across the highway from Camp Ramadi, the largest base
for coalition and Iraqi Army units in town. So, as a new, larger organization
grew out of the ASC, Sittar became its leader.

Why Sittar? The answer depends on who one asks. One of the original
members of the new organization explained to me that Sittar became the
leader as a sign of respect from the other founding members because he
allowed the meetings with U.S. forces to occur at his house, and because
he spent a lot of money feeding and caring for the organization in its infancy. I tend to think that Sittar became the leader because he was a savvy,
polished, Bedouin gentleman like those of old. He was also young, energetic, and well respected. Whatever the reason, it was Sheik Abdul Sittar
Abu Risha who announced the formation of the Sahawa al Anbar (SAA.)

Awakening

Sahawa al Anbar literally translates as "the Anbar Awakening." Edmund
Burke said, "The only thing necessary for the triumph of evil is for good
men to do nothing." The Arab equivalent is something like, "Evil prevails
when good men sleep." It is common for Arabs to refer to someone who
ignores a problem as sleeping with the problem. That is how the name
came about. It signaled that it was time for good men to wake up and do
something about al Qaeda.

The SAA started as a social and political movement with eleven points in its original manifesto:

1. Elect a new Provincial Congress.
2. Form an Anbar Province Sheiks Congress, with the condition that none was or will be a terrorist supporter or collaborator.
3. Begin an open dialogue with Ba'ath Party members, except those involved in criminal/terrorist acts, in order to quell all insurgent activities with all popular groups.
4. Review the formation of the Iraqi Security Forces and the Iraqi Army, with tribal sheiks vouching for those recruited.
5. Provide security for highway travelers in Anbar Province.
6. Stand against terrorism wherever and whenever it occurs, condemn attacks against coalition forces, and maintain presence of coalition forces as long as needed or until stability and security are established in Anbar Province.
7. No one shall bear arms except government-authorized Iraqi Security Forces and the Iraqi Army.
8. Condemn all actions taken by individuals, families, and tribes that give safe haven to terrorists and foreign fighters, and commend immediate legal and/or military remedies to rectify such acts.
9. Recommend measures to rebuild the economy, to entice industrial prosperity, and to bolster the agricultural economy. Also, find funds and resources to reopen existing manufacturing facilities. Fight for welfare and deny the insurgents any grounds for recruitment.
10. Strengthen sheikdom authority, help tribal leaders adjust to democratic changes in social behavior, and maintain sheiks financially and ideologically so they can continue this drive.
11. Respect the law and Constitution of the land, and support justice and its magistrates so no power will be above the law.

So, it had begun! Soon the SAA had raised hundreds of recruits for the new security apparatus of al Anbar. In a very short time, the SAA went from five tribes to ten, and that's where we came in.

CHAPTER 6

A Rainy Morning in Georgia

With our reconnaissance complete, Chuck and I returned to Fort Stewart and began to finalize our plans. Our initial analysis told us that we would have about three more platoons of combat power than the Bandits had. That meant, right off the bat, that we would have the forces to be considerably more aggressive and offensive than the Bandits. We planned to capitalize on our strength by expanding the force at COPs Grant and Sword to a full company each while using our scout platoon as a force under battalion control to surge into whatever area needed it the most. That unit would be our flexible and mobile reserve and could camp out with a company for days or weeks, giving us the ability to greatly increase our presence and operational tempo in a given area.

Our initial plan was to have E Company, 3rd Brigade Support Battalion (E/3BSB, Atlas), and the battalion headquarters at Camp Ramadi. Alpha Company (Rock) as the battalion's main effort would occupy COP Sword with its three mechanized infantry platoons plus a tank platoon from D Company (Knight) and project into the al Iskan District. B Company (Battle) would occupy COP Grant with two infantry platoons, and

C Company (Chaos) would occupy COP Falcon with its three platoons and the mechanized infantry platoon from B Company, 1st Battalion, 36th Infantry (B/1-36 Infantry) that was remaining in our AO. D Company (Knight) would occupy COP Iron with two of its tank platoons, the battalion mortars, and a mechanized infantry platoon from Battle. This plan would allow us to really expand our patrolling into al Iskan, forcing a fight with the Islamic State right at its capitol. We had plenty of capability in reserve, with the battalion scouts and the engineer company with its two mechanized sapper platoons (equipped with Bradley fighting vehicles) ready to surge into any area we needed. I was confident that with this force we could complete the clearance of south-central Ramadi and deal a significant blow to al Qaeda.

While we finalized our plan, brigade leaders began to adjust theirs. Unfortunately, every adjustment to their plan hurt ours. The first adjustment grew out of the fact that Task Force Manchu (1-9 Infantry) was currently organized with a tank company from 2-37 Armor (the unit in Jazeera, North Ramadi). Because the Manchus were scheduled to stay in Iraq and serve with our brigade, but 2-37 would leave with the Ready First BCT, that tank company had to be replaced. The replacement company would be my C Company (Chaos), commanded by Capt. Justin Colbert. Justin was my most senior and experienced company commander. He had commanded Chaos during the battalion's last deployment to Samarra, Iraq, and had a great deal of combat experience. Justin was smart and articulate, tactically savvy, and very competent and composed. He received a great deal of respect from his soldiers, peers, and superiors. Justin's only flaw was a well-deserved but nonetheless unsavory arrogance that manifested itself in a perceived aloofness, which caused people to steer clear of him. Once someone made it past that exterior, he or she would find Justin to be a fine human being who truly loved his soldiers and his wonderful, outgoing wife Courtney.

Justin and Courtney were the ultimate Army command team. They both worked hard at caring for and assisting the families of their soldiers and ensuring that their single soldiers felt like part of an extended family. For all those reasons, Charlton decided that the tank company that would go to 1-9 must be Chaos. In return, we received C Company (Steel) 2-7 Infantry (the other combined arms battalion in our brigade). Steel was commanded by Capt. Diogo Tavares. Diogo and his company turned out to be a great addition to the battalion, and this change really caused no friction in our plan.

That can't be said for the second change. The Ready First BCT was a legacy brigade and, therefore, still had an engineer battalion. That battalion was managing a hodge-podge engineer force at Camp Ramadi. Additionally, the Ready First had two engineer companies providing general engineering support to the BCT. In our BCT, we had no engineer battalion. We did, however, have a brigade troops battalion commanded by an engineer with several more engineers on staff. They would manage the engineer labor, but they had no engineer companies and the BCT commander decided to give them mine. However, that was not the largest blow to our plan. The biggest problem was that the brigade plan dictated that I detach an infantry company to the BCT's armed reconnaissance squadron (the cavalry name for a battalion-sized unit), 5th Squadron, 7th Cavalry.

The 5-7 was commanded by my long-time friend, Lt. Col. Cliff Wheeler, who I had known since 1988 when we met at Armor Officers' Basic Course. We had much in common back then, including our love for strong drink, and that led to our becoming fairly regular partners in mischief. We had not served together since 1989 but had remained in sporadic contact and were still very friendly. We were both pleased to serve together as commanders. Be that as it may, I was not at all happy about giving an infantry company to him. That would greatly diminish my battalion's capabilities and give us even less combat power than the Bandits. That was not the formula for offensive actions designed to challenge the ISI's hegemony in Ramadi. We would be fortunate to hold our own with only that amount of combat power.

Losing Every Argument
Although both Chuck and I tried to argue our case, he with the BCT operations officer, Maj. Rich Cleveland, and the BCT planner, Maj. Jason Garkey, and I with Colonel Charlton, we just couldn't win the argument. Cleveland and Garkey didn't even understand the argument. Neither of them had sufficient tactical experience to understand that we might actually win the fight in Ramadi. I believe they both thought our goals should be to hold on to Ramadi as much as possible and try not to lose soldiers

to attacks. Charlton certainly understood the argument, but my belief is that he thought our predecessors were not as aggressive as they could have been and that I could make up for my lack of combat power with aggressiveness. Charlton had significant combat experience as a battalion commander; however, it was in fighting against the old Iraqi Army and the Fedeyeen Saddam during the initial invasion in 2003. He had served as the 3rd Division's G-3 in Iraq in 2005 but had minimal exposure to insurgents, and he developed an idea that the units having tough fights against insurgents were just lazy, or worse. Charlton had no respect or regard for the insurgents, and could not imagine them to be a real fighting force (an opinion he would keep for quite some time).

The changes to the BCT plan caused Chuck and me to take a hard look at our options. I believed that we no longer had sufficient combat power to force a fight in the al Iskan District immediately, so we had to focus on another area with our initial main effort. Worse yet, we would be forced to use the Bandits' setup that had one company holding both COPs Grant and Sword. That would turn out to be a bad decision and one that I would agonize over.

One thing that makes leaders great is their ability to choose the hard right action over the easy wrong one. Whether or not I was a great leader is a judgment best left to others; however, in the case of deciding which infantry company I would detach and which one I would keep, I certainly chose the hard right. My two infantry companies and their commanders could not have been more different. A Company (Rock) under Capt. Mariano Wecer was aggressive and independent, so much so that the company and the commander had developed a reputation for impetuousness that bordered on carelessness. However, no commander in my battalion better understood counterinsurgency that did Wecer, and I knew that he would thrive, with the proper supervision and leadership, away from the battalion. Personally, I like Wecer quite a bit. He was built like a collegiate powerlifter, of average height but with a huge barrel chest, great big arms, and, unfortunately, a midsection to match them both. Although always fit, Mariano did not look like the archetypical infantry officer, which drew unwanted attention to him. To make matters worse, Mariano was the funniest, most animated company commander in the brigade. He also had a penchant for the flashy with regard to his uniform. In the field, you could always count on Mariano to have some unauthorized accoutrement prominently displayed for all (usually the BCT commander or command sergeant major) to see. Rock was my best infantry company.

B Company (Battle) was led by Capt. Dennis Fitzgerald, who was, in many ways, the polar opposite of Wecer. Dennis was a thinker—cautious and contemplative, often to the point of indecision. During the train-up, I had to counsel Mariano several times regarding his position on the battlefield. He led from so far forward that he could not visualize anything past the immediate fight before him. I counseled Dennis because he did the opposite. About halfway through our mission-readiness exercise, I found that he had not once left the camp with his soldiers. Dennis had capable subordinates, but they had not been pushed to achieve great results. Battle was a good company, but not great. I had grown up in an Army where a conscientious leader always detached his or her best subordinates to another command, therefore, I sent Rock to 5-7 Cavalry.

Other changes were occurring besides the changes to the plan, and one proved to be particularly significant and positive. On June 20, 2006, when I took command, I was embarrassed by one thing. The ceremony was a combined change of command for all the battalions and the brigade. On the field were soldiers from each unit with their guidons and colors (flags). The unit colors all proudly displayed the battle streamers from the organizations' history. Every unit receives a streamer for each campaign in which the unit fought, and most combined arms battalions in the Army have between fifty and eighty streamers. On the day of the change of command, all of the units displayed their streamers except for mine.

On that day, in hindsight, I should have fired Command Sgt. Maj. Pat Musckevitch. The command sergeant major (CSM) is the keeper of the unit colors and is responsible for ensuring both their serviceability and safety—Pat failed. He had a lame story about how the cleaners failed to return the streamers in time for the ceremony, but he had done nothing to get the streamers back, nor had he made any attempt to borrow or acquire some semblance of a replacement (two other battalions on post had streamers so similar to ours only an expert would have known any difference). Pat had been in the position for a couple of years and had served in the Army for over twenty-eight years. My predecessor sang his praises prior to his departure, and I took his word for the man—I lived to regret that.

I asked Pat on my first day in office if he planned to deploy to Iraq with us if we were called to duty. He assured me he would—he lied. When the time came, he skulked away with the excuse that "the Army won't let me stay in past thirty years, and if we deploy, I'll go over twenty-nine while we are away and would need to come back early to prepare for retirement." None of that was accurate. He had not explored the possibility of extending past thirty years, and I had assured him that if worst came to worst, we would send him home early. Long story short, in December, I was lucky enough to welcome Command Sgt. Maj. Randall Sumner back to the battalion. Randy had been the Chaos first sergeant for the battalion's last rotation in Iraq, and Justin Colbert and all his leaders spoke very highly of him. Randy was the perfect complement to my leadership style. Where I thrived in fluid, chaotic situations, Randy brought stability and predictability to the unit. Not only did we match professionally, but we became best friends and found great comfort in the camaraderie we had in Iraq. Don't misunderstand, we had our share of disagreements, but we handled them as two professionals who had the utmost respect for one another, and our disagreements were mostly invisible to the rest of the command.

Campaign Plan

With the reconnaissance complete, the task organization decided, and the area of operations defined, it was time to figure out how we would win this fight. We knew how the Bandits were conducting the fight, and, although they had experienced significant tactical success, I believed that their method was not likely to lead to operational or strategic victory in the long run. I thought we needed to do some things completely different. Because we would focus on the tactical defeat mechanism, after the MRE and PDSS, Chuck Krumwiede and I set out to ensure that every leader in the battalion understood it. We talked to leaders about it every chance we got, culminating in a class I gave to every platoon sergeant and above. We stressed that destroying the enemy was important and that we couldn't win without it. But, it was no more important than separating the insurgents from the population, and there was no way to win in Iraq without winning the average Iraqi over to our side.

It is impossible to defeat an enemy if one doesn't know the goal the enemy wants to attain. During my time at the CIA, I searched for a document that outlined the overall goals of al Qaeda and AQI. I could never find such a document. Because I felt that it must have been my own inadequacy that limited my search, one of the first things I did as a commander was put my staff to work finding this document. My intelligence officer was a young first lieutenant named Jay McGee—a phenomenal officer and an incredible human being. Jay's father is the chief of police at Texas Christian University, and his mom is a nurse. I have not had the pleasure to meet Jay's parents, but I am amazed at the work they did raising that young man. Although he's a graduate of the U.S. Military Academy at West Point, the story of his time there is not typical. In Jay's freshman year, he was diagnosed with Hodgkin's disease and spent the next year fighting for his life against a cancerous tumor the size of a human hand in his chest. Jay went through surgery, chemotherapy, and radiation. He gained over one hundred pounds because he could not exercise at all. While going through this horrible time, he continued his studies in Texas. Given a clean bill of health, Jay got himself back into top physical condition and returned to West Point to complete his education and commissioning.

The perspective that Jay gained during his illness made him one of the toughest, hardest-working men I have ever met, and it imbued him with a *carpe diem* love of life that makes him one of the most pleasant, funny, and fun-loving guys one could ever hope to meet. So, when Jay reported to me that he could not find an analysis of the goals of AQI, I began to believe it didn't exist. I told him to write it, and he did. This young, brand-new captain wrote an analysis that was more like something a twenty-year analyst from the Defense Intelligence Agency would write than a battalion intelligence officer with just over four years in the Army. Although the document is still classified, the gist was that AQI had two major goals. The short-term goal was to drive coalition forces out of al Anbar and destroy the ISF there. The long-term goal was to establish in al Anbar Province the capital of a greater "Sunnistan" from which al Qaeda (the larger) could retake the Holy Lands from what they viewed as Zionists, crusaders, and apostates. Jay described each method that the enemy planned to use to attain these goals as well as the enemy's lines of effort, including both lethal and non-lethal operations. The product was exactly what we needed to understand in order to win. In fact, a good deal of the information in the prior chapter of this book comes from Jay's analysis.

Commander's Intent

With that in mind, I began to write my "commander's intent." In Army parlance, this portion of the plan is designed to express the commander's vision to his soldiers. The commander's intent describes the purpose of the operation (or in this case campaign), identifies the key tasks to be accomplished, and describes the desired endstate with regard to friendly forces, enemy forces, and the terrain. While writing the intent, I relied heavily on three advisors: Command Sgt. Maj. Randy Sumner, Maj. (now Lt. Col.) Chuck Krumwiede, and Maj. (now Lt. Col.) Mike Rosamond.

Mike Rosamond was my first battalion XO, had served in 3-69 twice previously, including his company command time, and was a graduate of the U.S. Army's School of Advanced Military Studies (SAMS). SAMS was originally designed in 1983 to ensure that high-quality officers received a well-rounded, graduate-level academic experience that would help them transition from the tactical level of warfare to the operational and strategic, and to ensure that those officers understood and implemented the Army's new AirLand Battle Doctrine.[18] In its infancy, SAMS selected only the crème de le crème of Army Command and General Staff College graduates for attendance. For that reason, and for its grueling academic environment, graduates came to be dubbed Jedi Warriors in the early nineties. Although the school was designed to produce better staff officers and commanders, it soon came to be seen as a school for training planners and one that was shunned by many operators.[19] Mike had spent time as a planner on the Eighth U.S. Army staff—the Army component for the joint U.S. Forces Korea—and had a great perspective on how the tactical actions of units affected the operational and strategic levels of warfare. That perspective was very useful to me as I built my intent.

My intent as published in our initial campaign plan was as follows:

> The purpose of the campaign is to stabilize the security situation in South-Central Ramadi IOT [in order to] allow for a rapid transition of security responsibilities to local, Provincial and GOI [Government of Iraq] security forces. Support and assist the fledgling Ramadi city government in order to give Ramadi citizens a voice to the provincial and GOI levels. Isolate irreconcilable insurgents, terrorists, foreign fighters and anti-Iraqi forces from

their support in the population of South-Central Ramadi.

Key Tasks
- Treat all Iraqis politely and respect their culture.
- Dominate the terrain through persistent presence and observation.
- Kill or capture AQI, terrorists and foreign fighters (T&FF) and anti-Iraqi forces (AIF) who engage Iraqi Security Forces (ISF) or coalition forces.
- Identify and engage those citizens in Ramadi who wield economic, religious and political power. Assist those who are willing to support and participate in local and provincial governance and security.
- Develop, through interaction with people and the environment, intelligence that will drive our offensive operations—Every movement a reconnaissance—Every soldier a sensor.
- Coach, teach, mentor and lead by our example ISF in our AO. Ensure that they conduct themselves professionally and that they work to gain the confidence of Ramadi's citizens.

The endstate of the operation is ISF conducting routine, daily security operations in South-Central Ramadi with U.S. Forces as a supporting effort. No AQI, T&FF, or irreconcilable insurgent strongholds within AO Power [our area]. Provincial and GOI officials controlling all civil infrastructure in South-Central Ramadi. TF 3-69 poised to move from all COPs in order to return control to ISF.

I developed talking points for each of the tasks and spent a good deal of time ensuring that every soldier knew and understood my intent. Veterans in the battalion showed some resistance to my ideas because many of them didn't believe that we could win in Iraq by focusing on the population. They wanted to focus on the enemy and believed that only through killing could the insurgency be destroyed. But most of my leaders got it, and we kept plugging away. We all knew by then there would be plenty of killing, but there was more to winning than that.

While Chuck, the company commanders, and I focused on the fight, Mike Rosamond and nearly all of the rest of the battalion focused on moving the battalion's people and equipment to the theater of operations. As you can well imagine, there is nothing simple about moving a combat brigade from Georgia to Iraq. Although the U.S. Army has certainly become more adept over the last seven years, it is still quite a task. Mike and the battalion staff did a phenomenal job. Most of the move occurred well below my noise level, ensuring that I could continue to focus where I needed to, on the upcoming fight. I was able to float around to all the areas where the battalion worked on packing, moving, and loading in order to talk to soldiers about how I saw the terrain and the enemy, and how I thought we needed to fight in order to win.

No F-ing Monsters in Ramadi

Sensationalism sells newspapers. What was going on in al Anbar in late 2006 was sensational. Americans were being brutally attacked, and the casualties were adding up fast. It was not unusual to see thirty servicemen killed in action per month in al Anbar. The casualties there were accounting for nearly half of the total U.S. casualties, and the force was less than one fifth of the total American commitment. So as soldiers and their families watched the news, they began to feel great fear. In fact, the enemy in al Anbar began to take on a larger-than-life image among my soldiers. There was more anxiety within the unit than I had ever seen before. Unfortunately, the insurgents in Ramadi were, in reality, a very capable fighting force and could not be taken lightly, but I still had to do something to dispel the myth.

As December rolled around, we finally had the opportunity to take some well-deserved time off. While the battalion's personnel enjoyed their last bit of time with their families before we deployed, I tried to wrap my head around the myth of the Ramadi insurgents. Honestly, I was dealing with the same issues with my wife, Randi. Although this would be our third combat deployment as a couple, she was taking this one worse than usual. I feared this deployment, as well. I feared for my life (like most soldiers do) because I knew that I would put myself in harm's way, although I could surely avoid it. I knew that I would expose myself to danger in order to alleviate some of the fears of my soldiers. Moreover, I knew that, try though I may, I could not bring all of my soldiers home alive, and that fear was far worse than the fear for my safety.

The last time I would see my entire organization together before we deployed was at a physical training session on January 5, 2007, at a brigade run. Every soldier from the BCT was there unless he or she was injured or sick. It was a huge event presided over by then–Maj. Gen. Rick Lynch, who addressed the entire BCT prior to the run, as did Colonel Charlton. When we formed up at 5:45 a.m., it was warm for January. Ten minutes later, as the BCT commander and commanding general spoke, it was pouring rain. So, for the next hour and a half, we stood and then ran in the pouring rain. Finally, just before we finished running, the rain stopped. After the run, I gathered the entire battalion close around me and took the last opportunity I had to address our fears. I don't have a copy of that speech because I didn't write one. The speech came from my heart and off the top of my head. It was something like this:

> There are no fucking monsters in Ramadi—only terrorists and insurgents just like everywhere else in Iraq. Just like the ones I fought in Tikrit and Baquba and you fought in Samarra. They are very good at what they do, perhaps they are the most "professional" insurgents in the world. . . . But, we are better. I guarantee you that we can kill these terrorists. The thing that makes them different from the insurgents in the rest of Iraq is that every fucking terrorist in Ramadi belongs to al Qaeda.
>
> There are people who argue that we should not have gone to Iraq. That argument doesn't matter now. Al Qaeda is there now. They are there to kill us! Al Qaeda wants to destroy our way of life! This is the biggest threat to our way of life since World War II—communism was not as big a threat. People will look back in history and say that this is the time when America rose against her biggest threat. . . . And, you're going to be there. I can't promise that we will all come home from this fight. It's going to be tough. But I can damn sure promise you we will win!

I can't tell you what it is like to be a politician, but I think it hurts. From January 12 to January 14, 2007, I shook hands with over nine hundred young, motivated soldiers from my battalion as they deployed. I felt that I could pump up their morale just a bit if I took the time to spend fifteen to thirty seconds talking with each one as he got on a plane in Georgia or off a plane in Kuwait (obviously, I flew during this time). I asked them all personally if they felt they were ready, and I asked most of them if they were scared. In those fifteen to thirty seconds, I tailored my message to each of them. By the end of that period I was tired, and my knuckles were incredibly bruised, but I felt great about my soldiers. I also think that they felt good about themselves and their leaders.

CHAPTER 7

Changing of the Guard

We left Georgia and flew to Kuwait. We brought with us the lessons we had learned over the past six months and those our Army had learned over the past four years. We brought the weight of our previous experiences as well as our trepidations about heading to "the most dangerous city in Iraq." We also brought with us a powerful new idea, something that until now had been elusive—the possibility of victory in Iraq.

Upon deployment I found myself in Kuwait—again—for the seventh time in five years. As soon as I stepped off the plane, I got that feeling, so familiar to me now, that I wasn't "in Kansas anymore." For many first-timers, Kuwait is the first time that it dawns on them that they are really headed to war, and it can be jarring, strange, and frightening. For the rest of the U.S. Army and Air Force servicemen and women who have been down this road before, Kuwait is simply the gateway to Iraq, since the vast majority of flights to and from Iraq go through Kuwait.

New arrivals to a theater of war undergo what the Army terms "reception, staging, onward movement, and integration" (RSO&I) prior to conducting combat operations. The R, S, and O are all done in Kuwait.

Reception includes a series of briefings and mandatory training; staging is the process of finding all your people and equipment and preparing them and it for movement, which is the mundane loading of planes, trains, or automobiles. The reception training includes sessions on improvised explosive device (IED, or roadside bomb) awareness, cultural awareness, rules of engagement, how to extract yourself and others from rollover accidents in humvees, proper procedures to avoid unintended application of force (called escalation of force [EOF] training), the current rules of engagement (ROE) governing U.S. forces, and test-firing and calibration of all weapons. Additionally, company commanders and those in higher positions are required to attend a counterinsurgency academy at the U.S. Army Counterinsurgency Center of Excellence in Taji, Iraq.

Most of the training is fairly rote. However, I saw opportunity in two of the classes to address each of my soldiers one more time, so I taught the "rules of engagement" and "escalation of force" classes personally. During these classes, I stressed the importance of killing the right people and avoiding injury to civilians. Once again, I stressed that we were there to win and that we could not do so unless we could get the civilians on our side. I told all of my soldiers that it was unlikely we would go through the entire deployment without killing the wrong people, since in the heat of battle, accidents occur. The key, I explained, was to always tell the complete truth about these incidents. I told them that I had personal experience as both investigating officer and investigated party and that I would not allow a lynch mob to come after them as long as they fully cooperated with any investigation. It's a simple concept: tell the truth.

It was only two days before someone broke that rule. While in Kuwait, one of my young officers made a mistake that many young people have made. How he handled the aftermath made him a negative example for all to see. This particular lieutenant—I'll call him Lieutenant P—came to the battalion just prior to our train-up; he was transferred from my best friend's battalion as a result of some issues he had there. While in Kuwait, he was responsible for running a range and bringing soldiers there to fire their weapons. En route to the range, however, Lieutenant P got lost in the vast Kuwaiti desert. (This is not uncommon. In fact, as a young lieutenant, I got lost for twenty hours in the Saudi desert—with twenty-five soldiers in tow!) Lieutenant P was in a Mitsubishi Montero leased vehicle, and in order to find his way, he decided to stand on the roof of the vehicle in an attempt to see the road that he knew must be nearby and, consequently, caused damage to the vehicle. Had he merely told his leaders what happened, the incident would have been chalked up to experience. Instead, he lied and forced his soldiers to lie about the damage to the vehicle. I was furious! I relieved the lieutenant of his position and recommended that he receive non-judicial punishment—military punishment below court-martial, similar to pleading no contest in the civilian world. The incident was an eye-opener and did much to reinforce the standards that I prescribed. Unfortunately, he wouldn't be the last to break that rule.

The remainder of our two weeks in Kuwait passed without incident. Major Mike Rosamond handled the difficult task of accounting for all our soldiers and equipment and organizing the people and gear for movement to Iraq. Though tasks like these sound easy enough, they are drudgery—such is the life of the XO. I remember thinking as a young officer how powerful XOs were, but when I became one, I realized the truth; although you learn an awful lot about how the Army works, it is no fun to be the XO. My company commanders, Maj. Chuck Krumwiede and I, along with several of my staff officers, went on to Taji, Iraq, for our training at the Counterinsurgency Center of Excellence. While we were re-blued in U.S. Army doctrine in Taji, and Rosamond made sure everything and everybody shipped up to Iraq, Command Sgt. Maj. Randy Sumner was getting things ready in Ramadi. As the senior enlisted advisor to the commander, he advises the commander on everything from soldier welfare to tactical employment of tanks. The command sergeant major has generally spent close to twenty years in battalions. Compare that with officers who spend relatively little time in troop units—I, for example, had spent a good deal of time in battalions for an officer and had only about eight years—the rest of my career had been spent doing other jobs away from soldiers and tanks.

The "I" of "RSO&I" is integration. This occurs when the unit arrives in its battle space, and for us that meant Ramadi. Physically, Ramadi in January 2007 was the nastiest, most unpleasant place one could imagine. First, there was Camp Ramadi, a former Iraqi Army school and artillery center about the size of a large U.S. airport. Most structures at the camp looked like they were built in the late 1970s or early 1980s, probably during the Iran–Iraq War, and were fairly typical of third-world military compounds, with headquarters complexes that were single-story brick or block, U-shaped arrangements with single and multiple offices and a few conference or meeting rooms. The barracks were two-story, open-bay, brick or block buildings that were as drab and dreary as any I'd seen. The place was probably designed to house about two thousand Iraqi soldiers, but we had over four thousand soldiers, sailors, airmen, and Marines living there day in and day out. At peak times, there would be as many as seven thousand while units came and went.

Like many large installations in Iraq, Camp Ramadi grew rapidly in 2003–2004 with little thought for how it might look in three years. Therefore, there were myriad temporary structures of all sorts spread chaotically throughout the camp. Although it had several paved roads, they had been covered in dust and gravel and mud early on in American use. What a stupid move! The Euphrates River Valley has some of the most fertile land in the world, and because it is not sandy, the deep, rich soil makes mud the likes of which I had never seen before and haven't seen since. I am a tanker and have taken seventy-ton vehicles off road in all weather conditions all over the world—which makes me a mud expert. I have seen knee-deep mud in Germany, Kansas, Texas, Georgia, and Kentucky. I have seen the deserts of Saudi Arabia and Kuwait become drenched in three inches of rain in one hour, but in all my experience, I have never seen mud as sticky, heavy, and difficult as that at Camp Ramadi. Allowing it to cover the paved surfaces of the camp meant that for the residents, there was no way to escape it.

The rainy season in Iraq runs from November through April, and the 2006–2007 season was horrible. So, as we arrived at Camp Ramadi, the mud was at its worst—not merely deep and sticky but churned by vehicles into deep ruts. The Ready First BCT was undisciplined in its control of the camp, allowing unrestricted driving that left deep ruts in nearly every part of the camp. One couldn't walk from the headquarters to the barracks without going through huge ruts and adding two or three pounds of mud to the weight of one's boots. At night, there were no lights in the camp. Stupid, because the enemy knew we were there and darkness didn't hide our presence—there was no reason not to have lights. Well, add pitch dark, and you have a recipe for misery. (Most Americans rarely see pitch dark, but shut yourself in a closet with all the lights in your house out if you want to see Camp Ramadi on a moonless, rainy night.) It was not uncommon to fall down on your way back from supper or a meeting or the shower on a dark night. If you wore footgear less sturdy than boots, you risked losing them in the mud. The BCT even had a soldier who suffered a compound fracture of his femur walking from the dining facility to his room.

RIP/TOA

As we arrived in Iraq, we had a complex task. We would replace the 1st Battalion, 37th Armor Regiment—the "Bandits" commanded by Lt. Col. V.J. Tedesco. The community of armor officers is fairly small, but, oddly enough, I had never met V.J. Tedesco. We were very different men as leaders: V.J. was fairly formal with his subordinates; I was rather casual. He had seriousness about him that I found troubling. I think he mistook my casual, personable behavior for weakness. All in all, we were not compatible, but for the next ten days we would have to try to get along.

When one unit replaces another in Iraq, there is a procedure to ensure that the new unit and the old have an orderly exchange. The process is similar to the ceremonial changing of the guard that one sees at the Tomb of the Unknowns in Arlington or by the Beefeaters at Buckingham Palace. It's called relief in place, or RIP. The usual U.S. Army model is a ten-day RIP with the outgoing unit, culminating in the official transition of authority (TOA). For the first five days, all of the forces, incoming and outgoing, work under the command of the outgoing commander; for the last five days, all forces work for the incoming commander. In my previous experience, units always took advantage of the extra combat power—two units instead of one—to conduct major operations during RIP/TOA. During my tour in Diyala Province in 2004, my brigade planned and executed a major clearance of Baquba during our RIP with the incoming brigade. For about three days, we had almost twice as many soldiers on the ground, and with these we forced the enemy out of Baquba, allowing us to leave the new unit with a relatively safe environment as it started its operations. The concept is simple: take advantage of the overlapping time to put the enemy on his heels. But I arrived in Ramadi to find that no such plan existed.

The Ready First Brigade was the first U.S. Army unit to serve fifteen months in Iraq. The brigade's tour had been extended by three months in order to await our arrival while the unit that was to relieve them after one year was pushed to Baghdad. Although the formal "surge" had not been announced yet, we were actually the first surge unit to arrive in Iraq. (Three months later, all U.S. Army units would be extended to fifteen-month deployments.) The extension hit the soldiers of the Ready First Brigade hard. They had been in some of the worst fighting in Iraq non-stop since June 2006 when they arrived in Ramadi, and I believe they had run out of energy and ideas. I had come back to Ramadi after our initial recon in November hoping to find that the Bandits had made some progress, but they hadn't. Ramadi was worse than it had been during our reconnaissance in November.

Occasionally in my career I would meet soldiers, sergeants, and officers who fancied themselves larger than life. I'd call these guys "movie characters" and always warned my subordinates against behaving like them. "Be yourself," I'd say. I usually told them that being themselves had gotten them where they were and that other soldiers would always know if they were faking. The Bandit battalion was an organization full of movie characters. In most circumstances, such behavior was benign, even laughable, but in combat it was dangerous.

Command Sergeant Major Randy Sumner had arrived in Ramadi a few days prior to my arrival. When I got there he immediately bent my ear about the conditions in which the Bandit soldiers were living. Their positions were filthy, unkempt, and disorganized. Ammunition was strewn from one end of the positions to the other. Sanitation was atrocious. These are symptoms of movie characters—they want their lives to be viewed as extreme, so they make them so. Much more dangerous was that many of the soldiers and leaders of the Bandits didn't seem to want Ramadi to get better but wore their condition as a badge of honor. They liked the chest-thumping that grew from being attacked every day. One company even had a unit coin made that captured this attitude; on the back, it said, "We were in Ramadi killing. Where the fuck were you?" Randy and I had several discussions the first day with our subordinates and told them to be respectful of their hosts, "but don't you dare think you'll act that way." We had a lot of work to do.

On February 1, 2007, we sent our first group of soldiers—the headquarters contingent from Dennis Fitzgerald's B Company—to live on COP

Grant, just south of the city's al Iskan District. The soldiers arrived about 11:30 p.m. At 1:25 a.m. on February 2, V.J. Tedescu woke me to say that there had been an attack on COP Grant and two soldiers had been killed, including one from my battalion. Several others had been wounded and were being transported to the Camp Ramadi hospital. I asked Tedescu about the nature of the attack, and he told me it was a complex attack that had included mortars and small arms fire. The initial report was that the two soldiers had been killed by 82mm mortar fire. I quickly dressed, and we went down to the hospital. What I found there was a sight that would become all too familiar to me over the next two months.

Camp Ramadi's "hospital" was not a full-service hospital at all. The U.S. Army identifies three levels of combat medical treatment. Level I starts with the soldiers on the ground, including first aid rendered by non-medical personnel, called "buddy aid," up to lifesaving measures rendered by one of two professional medical providers in the battalion's area. I was fortunate to have two excellent providers. Major (Doctor) Mike Roundtree joined the battalion late in our train-up. Mike was an excellent physician and had great management skills. Our other provider was Captain Will Booker, who was an Army physician's assistant (PA) and had been with the battalion for several years. He was a phenomenal PA and had more trauma experience than most doctors. He was so good, in fact, that he had to leave us during the tour to attend an advanced trauma PhD program in San Antonio, Texas. Our battalion ran two Level I facilities, one at Camp Ramadi and the other at COP Falcon in the city. Level II treatment is the equivalent of a hospital trauma center, and Level III is a full-service hospital with all of its departments and wards. Our closest was the combat support hospital in Balad, about thirty-five minutes away by helicopter. At Camp Ramadi we had a Level II hospital, augmented by a U.S. Navy advanced trauma lifesaving team that included three surgeons and the appropriate surgical staff, but its core was provided by the brigade's medical company—Company C, 3rd Brigade Support Battalion. We called the facility, simply, Charlie Med.

Charlie Med was located in a cinder-block building left over from the original Iraqi Army base that was now Camp Ramadi. The facility included two triage rooms, the larger holding six triage stations and the smaller only three. Immediately adjacent to the smaller triage room was the surgical suite. There was also an outdoor ambulance bay and triage area that could hold up to twenty more casualties and, in an adjacent building, a holding area for the less seriously injured where they could rest and recover from their wounds.

Whenever I made these trips down to Charlie Med, Command Sgt. Maj. Sumner was at my side; this night was no different. The scene when we entered was well-managed chaos. The medics and doctors were all "gloved up," waiting in the ambulance bay, and ten stretchers were on the concrete floor in the bay. After a few minutes, three Bradley fighting vehicles came barreling in. (Because the roads were so unsafe, the Bradley fighting vehicle was the ambulance of choice in Ramadi.) Within seconds, medics and doctors were unloading casualties from two of the vehicles. The chief surgeon went into the third vehicle and pronounced dead the two casualties who were inside it. Just like that! He quickly stepped out, and the ramp went up. The Bradley crewmen who had just evacuated Pvt. Matthew Zeimer and Spc. Alan McPeek reacted violently, one soldier throwing his helmet and another going down to his knees. Trying to save these two warriors, they had just spent forty minutes driving through the mean streets of Ramadi in the pitch-black night and now, in less than a minute, a surgeon had pronounced them dead.

When I went inside Charlie Med, the small triage room was full and the larger nearly so. I honestly don't recall how many of my soldiers were there and how many Bandit soldiers were. I do recall that 1st Lt. Ryan Clinton was there with a gunshot wound to his elbow. Ryan was one of my favorite platoon leaders. When I had arrived at the battalion, he was a new, fairly timid leader, but I knew he had great potential, and I had spent a good deal of time mentoring him (along with my other lieutenants) through the summer. There really is a very strong bond that develops between a battalion commander and his lieutenants. Here was one of my boys, very much like a son to me, lying on a table with a bullet in his arm. I did the only thing I could think to do. I walked to the table and put my hands on his head, as if I were petting him. I told him he would be okay. I think I even made some lame jokes that we both laughed about. Ryan's first thoughts were not about himself—he asked me if everyone else was okay. I had to tell him no, that Private Zeimer was dead.

After half an hour, V.J. Tedesco found me and said we needed to go to "graves registration," which is the U.S. Army's equivalent of the morgue. At Charlie Med, it was across from the ambulance bay in a separate building. V.J. and I walked over and knocked on the door. This really was one of the two or three places on camp that a battalion commander or command sergeant major could not just barge into. After a few minutes, a soldier told us that we could go in. Inside, there were two stainless steel tables on which lay McPeek and Zeimer, still clothed and partially covered by body bags that had been opened to allow us to view the remains. When I saw the two, I immediately knew they had not been killed by 82mm mortars. They didn't have any fragmentation wounds, but rather their young bodies had been badly crushed and torn by blasts.

I am not a religious man. I was raised a Southern Baptist and was, as a teen, so devout I thought I might become a minister, but that thought had settled into philosophical skepticism in 1984. I am still profoundly spiritual, but the only times I've truly spoken to God since 1984 were when laying hands on soldiers killed under my charge. Iraqi or American, Muslim, Christian, Jew, or atheist, I would always lay my hands on their bodies and silently ask God to commend their everlasting souls to heaven. Mere words could not convey the sense of loss and grief I felt at those times. But my job—my sole function in life—was to bring honorable victory to my unit, my Army, and my nation. I had to look, 100 percent of the time, as if I were in control and we were winning. At times, it was the most difficult thing I would ever do.

When V.J. and I left graves registration, as soon as we stepped out, I told him those soldiers were not killed by 82mm mortars. If they had been killed by mortars at all, it would have to have been a 120mm. He scoffed. I found myself in a difficult position. I was the new guy and he was the veteran. He had been commanding his battalion for fourteen months in combat, the last six months during the toughest fighting in Iraq. But I knew I was right. I was not really a "new guy." I had seen thirty-plus soldiers killed in Operation Iraqi Freedom in 2003–2004. I had personally experienced nearly one hundred mortar attacks, and I was one of the few U.S. Army officers still around who had lived through a full-scale enemy artillery attack. During the 1991 Gulf War, as a young lieutenant, my unit had been hit with artillery fire from the Adnan Division of the Iraqi Republican Guard. We suffered nearly forty wounded in action (WIA) in the attack. I had seen scores of soldiers with fragment wounds and an unfortunate few with blast wounds. I had seen gunshots, burns, traumatic amputations, and even decapitation. I knew that what had killed McPeek and Zeimer was no 82mm mortar.

The attack on COP Grant that morning had been a brutal one, but it was actually the second such complex attack within five hours. The first had started at 8:40 p.m. on February 1, when COP Falcon was attacked from multiple positions by terrorists using small arms, RPGs, and machine guns. In response, the commander of B/1-37 Armor (the Bandit Company at COP Falcon) requested clearance to engage the enemy with tank main gunfire. Most tanks (including our M1A1 Abrams tanks) are equipped with multiple machine guns linked to various sighting systems and the main gun. The main gun packs the high-explosive wallop. Because it can cause such severe damage, there is often a unit rule that dictates battalion-level permission to fire it. The Bandits had such a rule, and we would keep it in place. In addition to granting the use of the tank main gun, Col. Sean McFarland, the Ready First Brigade commander, authorized the firing of one guided multiple-launch rocket system (GMLRS) round. The GMLRS is a one-thousand-pound high-explosive warhead mated to a GPS-guided rocket fired from the Army's rocket artillery launchers. It was a new and devastating contraption that had only been used a dozen or so times by early 2007.

As the company at COP Falcon responded, four blocks east, C/1-37 Armor reported being attacked by small arms fire from the west, but the unit's soldiers couldn't identify the enemy firing at them so didn't return fire. By 9:20 p.m., the attack had ended, and B/1-37 counted fifteen terrorists killed in the engagement, while fires from the tank and the GMLRS strike continued to burn for hours. Immediately after that attack, the convoy bringing the first 3-69 Armor soldiers left for COP Grant, arriving at 11:30 p.m. At 12:55 a.m. on February 2, the attack that claimed the lives of Matthew Zeimer and Alan McPeek began with small arms and machine gun fire from several different locations. As the soldiers on COP Grant responded to the attack, the volume of fire grew rapidly. Shortly after our soldiers began to return fire, the COP was hit with four RPGs causing no injuries. The commander on COP Grant requested and was granted clearance to fire tank main guns.

At 1:05 a.m., four blocks east, the soldiers at COP Eagle's Nest (a 1-9 Infantry position) reported that they were being engaged from the south by a large enemy force. They requested that a two-tank quick reaction force respond to assist them in their fight. Meanwhile, the fighting continued to rage at COP Grant. At 1:15 a.m., the command post at COP Grant reported that two mortar rounds had struck on its roof, causing two American deaths. The contact was done by 1:35 a.m. or so. The attack resulted in a reported seven more terrorists killed in action. And there were four more engagements that night! Welcome to Ramadi.

There are some things for which you just can't train. Try though we may to simulate them, they are too difficult to reproduce. Actions that a unit takes after a soldier has been killed in action are among those things. My battalion had developed a standard operating procedure (SOP) for how we would deal with casualties. During our MRE in Georgia, the battalion suffered about one hundred simulated WIAs and probably twenty simulated KIAs and had a battle drill associated with those actions, but it was grossly insufficient. The rest of that night (or rather, early morning) was spent on the first of those actions.

First and foremost, my organization had to begin the process that would culminate with notification of next of kin; for Matthew, this was his mother, stepfather, and father. This is one of the tasks that must be accomplished immediately—indeed, the Army's standard is that the family must be notified within twenty-four hours of the incident, and usually notification is much sooner than the standard requires. Most have seen depictions of this process on TV or in the movies, and these are generally accurate. It is a very difficult duty for the notification officer or noncommissioned officer, and obviously the most horrible day in the next of kin's life. The notification team consists of an officer or senior noncommissioned officer and a chaplain, if one is available. They must go to the house of the next of kin between 6:00 a.m. and 10:00 p.m. The team members must be in dress uniform and use a government vehicle. They knock on the door and ask to come inside. Then they speak the dreaded script: "The Secretary of the Army has asked me to express his deep regret that your son, Matthew, was killed in action in Ramadi, Iraq, on 2 February 2007. He was killed during an enemy attack against Combat Outpost Grant in the city. The Secretary extends his deepest sympathy to you and your family in your tragic loss."

While that notification is taking place back in the United States, several things must happen in theater. It is the commander's responsibility to ensure that the unit stays focused on the mission. When the sun rose the next morning, I needed to go to COP Grant to do so; however, February 2 was day one of our RIP, and the schedule said that we would be in briefings all day. Because we were still in the first half of RIP/TOA, I had no authority to deviate, so it wasn't until February 3 that I went to COP Grant. Still under the control of the Bandits, I had to tag along with V.J. Tedesco and his PSD. I brought Randy Sumner and our chaplain, Capt. J. Nathan Kline, with me. Nathan Kline is the best chaplain in the U.S. Army, and he is also an amazing human being. Nathan came into the Army after 9/11, leaving behind a successful business in Chicago that focused on interfaith relations. He also holds a master's degree in divinity from the University of Chicago, making him the first Latter-day Saint chaplain in the U.S. military to possess such a degree. He's a man's man, as well. He can carry on a meaningful discussion about nearly any topic, from existential philosophy to college football, and never comes off as a nerd or a bible-thumper. Soldiers sought Nathan whenever they had a problem. The job of an Army chaplain is to keep the unit's morale as high as possible, but he is not the "cruise director" making sure everybody has fun. Nor is he merely the cleric who serves the religious needs of the outfit. Nathan understood his role better than any chaplain I have ever seen. On this day, his role was to do something called a "post-traumatic incident debrief," which serves two major functions. First, it allows Nathan, or another professional counselor, to assess the states of mind of the soldiers who were involved. Second, it allows the soldiers to talk about the incident and begin to process and categorize something that is like nothing they've ever experienced. I know full well how "touchy-feely" all this sounds, but the fact is that every soldier who has been involved in a firefight like the one that had happened the night prior at COP Grant has post-traumatic stress. Nathan's job was to do everything he could to ensure that our soldiers didn't develop post-traumatic stress *disorder*.

While Nathan did his thing, Randy Sumner, Chuck Krumweide, and I spoke to some of our leaders, including Sgt. Clint "Mad Dog" Madron. Mad Dog and I had history. Having served together in Operation Iraqi Freedom 1 in 4ID, he and I had a good relationship. I remember seeing him at the headquarters a few days before I took command of the battalion back at Fort Stewart. It was good for both of us to see a familiar face. He had only recently arrived at the unit, and we were both happy to find that we would serve together in combat once again. I had a great deal of faith in Mad Dog, and he in me. Sergeant Madron was the fire support team chief for my B Company, and as Private Zeimer's immediate supervisor, he was taking the loss very hard. Clint had never lost a soldier in combat before. Randy, Chuck, and I did our best to reassure him that Zeimer didn't die due to anything that he did or failed to do.

One of the procedures we must perform after a mortar or artillery attack is called "crater analysis," which really is part art and part science. It involves finding the impact crater from a strike and finding all the pieces of the projectile that caused the crater. You might be surprised by how much of a bomb, artillery round, or mortar round survives the explosion. One of the first people I ever watched do crater analysis was Sergeant Madron. I had seen him do it several times while in Tikrit in 2003. Mad Dog easily found the impact crater—a large portion of the roof of COP Grant had been destroyed by the blast. He also found several pieces of the round, including some fairly intact tail fins. Mad Dog described his crater analysis to Randy, Chuck, and me. He also gave us the pieces of the round that he had found. His assessment was that the crater was consistent with a 120mm projectile and that the round had been traveling at a very low trajectory.

When Mad Dog gave me the fins, they looked strangely familiar. They were definitely from a 120mm projectile, based on the size of the fins. They also had a very unique stabilization mechanism—they were what's called fin-stabilized, which means that the fin has a T shape at its outer edge. Imagine looking at a dart's fins from the rear of the dart. What you see is the three fins forming the inner lines of a peace sign. Now imagine that each of those fins has a portion of the outer circle of the peace sign attached roughly perpendicular to the fin itself. That's what these fins looked like. I knew I had seen them before. I just couldn't place where.

When I returned to Camp Ramadi, I gave the fins and a report about the crater analysis to my intelligence sergeant, Sgt. 1st Class Brian Dotson, and instructed him to get the fragments to Camp Ramadi's senior explosive ordinance disposal (EOD) technician. Then I went to see Major Rosamond, who told me that the 15-6 investigation for Zeimer and McPeek's deaths was complete. The U.S. Army investigates every combat death. These investigations are normally performed by an officer as an additional duty and range from formal to informal; they are governed by a document called "Army Regulation 15-6: Investigations," thus the slang term 15-6 investigation. Usually, if a soldier is killed in action, these investigations are completed within twenty-four to forty-eight hours, and this one was no different. I don't recall who did the initial 15-6, but Mike gave the results of the investigation to me that evening. Commanders approve or reject findings, conclusions, and recommendations for these investigations. Since we were still serving under the Bandits, however, V.J. Tedesco approved the investigation. The investigating officer concluded that Zeimer and McPeek were killed by unknown enemy fire and that the two were killed in action. The investigator speculated that the two were killed by mortar fire. Day Two of the relief-in-place was complete.

On Day Three, I again told V.J. Tedesco that I didn't think Zeimer and McPeek were killed by mortar fire. He barely contained his disdain for my opinion, and we continued with the more mundane aspects of the RIP process. However, simultaneously, we prepared for Zeimer and McPeek's memorial ceremony. Militarily, there is only one purpose for a memorial ceremony: to allow the unit its grief and immediately refocus it on the mission. In the 3ID, we had a very rigid SOP for these ceremonies. The ceremony would start with a slide show displaying pictures of the deceased collected from his buddies; this is typically set to music according to the deceased's tastes and usually lasts no more than three minutes. After the slide show, the unit chaplain offers welcoming remarks and an invocation. He is followed by one of the soldier's immediate leaders (usually a sergeant), who reads a brief biography of the deceased. Then one of the soldier's buddies offers personal comments similar to a eulogy. After the friend's comments, the company commander makes brief remarks, followed by the battalion commander. In my remarks, I always strove to put the soldier's death in perspective with our overall mission. My remarks were crafted in such a way as to bring the unit back to our larger goals. After the battalion commander, the chaplain gives a meditation. Nathan's meditations always strove to give soldiers a way to focus their grief and not allow it to overcome them. Finally, the company first sergeant performs the "last roll call," which is an Army tradition where the first sergeant calls several names from the unit. The soldiers answer, "Here, first sergeant." After calling three or four soldiers, he calls the deceased by rank and last name . . . no answer. He then calls him by rank, first and last name . . . no answer. Finally he calls rank, first name, middle name, and last name . . . no answer. Immediately a firing detail fires three volleys and a bugler plays taps. The final roll call and taps is a sobering and heart-rending moment; it is the defining moment of the ceremony. Once it is complete, the chaplain offers a benediction and then the attendees, individually or in groups, offer honors to the soldier. At the front of the space is a photo of the soldier and the traditional display of his helmet placed on an inverted rifle with a bayonet that is either stuck in the ground or, more often, held in a stand. Around the butt of the rifle, below the helmet, is a copy of the soldier's dog tags, and in front of the rifle is a pair of boots. When rendering honors, the attendees walk up to the display and salute the soldier. Often those rendering honors will leave a memento that is then sent to the family. In the 3ID, we prided ourselves on keeping these ceremonies dignified and brief, not more thirty minutes.

The Ready First Brigade had no such standard operating procedure, and because we were still in the RIP, that unit had the lead on the ceremony. The lead for planning the ceremony for my outfit fell to Nathan Kline and my operations sergeant major, Ray Curtis. Ray was the oldest soldier in the battalion, a crusty old infantryman whose six-foot-six-inch, 255-pound frame was impressive at any age. Ray and I had developed a good relationship prior to deployment not only professionally but personally, especially since Ray and I are both crazy about American motorcycles. Ray had two Harley-Davidsons prior to deployment, and I had an Indian. He and I had developed a motorcycle safety program for the battalion that included periodic rides for all soldiers with bikes. Prior to deployment, we had over seventy bikes on our first battalion ride and received quite a bit of attention throughout the division. Ray Curtis had also written 3ID's memorial service SOP when he served in the division operations cell. As he and Chaplain Kline worked with the Bandits to plan the ceremony, he began to have serious misgivings about how it was shaping up.

Similar friction was occurring between Randy Sumner and the Bandits' command sergeant major. Mike Rosamond had issues with the unit's executive officer, and the staffs were at odds. Meanwhile, as Chuck Krumweide and I toured the combat outposts with Tedesco and his operations officer, I saw things I didn't like. For instance, most of the Bandits never met an Iraqi they didn't hate. Even when they spoke about Iraqi police or Iraqi soldiers, they had a general disdain for them and never trusted them or treated them as equals. What troubled me was that I started to see some of these attitudes spread to my soldiers. I pulled my commanders aside and warned them about this behavior. I also reiterated to them my commander's intent.

During RIP, each company commander briefed me on his area and how he saw his fight. The first company I visited was the company that had led me on the patrol back in November where the soldiers failed to speak to the women of the house or to attempt to assuage the fears of the children. I must say their attitudes were even worse than before. Ramadi was bound on the south by a set of railroad tracks that were built up about twenty feet. The berm upon which the tracks were built provides a natural barrier to north–south movement. There were a few roads that crossed the berm, but they were blocked with obstacles, so one would have to walk over the railroad tracks to cross into or out of the city. A few small villages were just south of the berm. During my briefing at COP Iron, that company commander told me that he didn't allow the villagers from the south to cross the berm into the city and said he fired warning shots to keep them from crossing. I asked if the villages had a market. He said no. I asked how those villagers could get food from the markets in Ramadi. He said they had to travel about four miles around the city to get in. I asked if he thought that was reasonable. He told me, "Sir, I don't care if they get to the market or not!" It was this hatred for common Iraqis that I had to keep my soldiers from developing.

RIP Day Five was the day of Zeimer and McPeek's memorial service. Once again, I felt surrounded by movie characters. The ceremony was designed, it seemed to me, to illicit an emotional response not of resolve but of pity. I disliked its tearful and sorrowful tone and felt that it did nothing to motivate and direct my soldiers. I tried to keep my thoughts to myself, but I think that I wore my feelings on my sleeve. Between the ceremony and my outspokenness about my disbelief in the cause of death of the two soldiers, there was finally open tension between me and V.J. Tedesco.

That night he informed me that EOD had made a final ruling about the attack on Grant: The enemy had employed a 90mm recoilless rifle. I asked if anyone had ever seen the enemy use such a weapon (a huge, truck-mounted contraption weighing hundreds of pounds). He said no. I was furious. I went into my intelligence cell and asked Sergeant Dodson if he had delivered the fins found on COP Grant to EOD. He told me no. I told him to take them there the next morning. At the end of Day Five, I was in charge. I think I only saw V.J. four or five more times over the next five days.

Investigation

During the ten-day RIP, we were attacked eighty-four times. Many of these were complex attacks, so if split into their parts there were way over one hundred attacks just in our portion of Ramadi during this brief period. The attacks resulted in eleven U.S. and three Iraqi Security Forces (ISF) personnel wounded and two U.S. deaths (McPeek and Zeimer). During these attacks, we killed nine insurgents and wounded another five or six. I enforced very strict rules about how we determined enemy killed and wounded. I would only count an enemy killed under three circumstances: First, if we touched the body, we counted him dead. Second, if a soldier watched the body being rent to pieces either through a thermal sight or some other reliable means, we counted the insurgent dead. Last, if the enemy was in a house or vehicle that was so destroyed his survival was unlikely, we counted him dead. These rules are very strict compared with the rules that many units used. In particular, the Bandits used a much different standard. In the months leading to our RIP, the Bandits counted an average of twenty enemy fighters killed in action per week. The Bandit standard was that if a U.S. soldier thought he killed an insurgent, they counted him dead. My experience in Iraq was that "body count" was not the most important measure of effectiveness. I also found that if one made body count important to soldiers, they would react by over-reporting or—much, much worse—over-killing as the first response to any action. As I wrote earlier, sometimes in counterinsurgency, who you don't kill matters more than who you do. Be that as it may, the result was that for our first ten days in Iraq, we reported considerably fewer enemy casualties than our predecessor had been reporting. To the casual observer, it made us look soft.

The one thing that troubled me about the above statistics was that Americans were dying and being injured while Iraqi policemen and soldiers were not. This didn't sit right with me. Ever since 2003, I had firmly believed that the solutions to Iraq's problems needed to be Iraqi, a conclusion I had come to based on prior experience. Indeed, Operation Iraqi Freedom was not my first exposure to the Middle East. Like many of my contemporaries, I had fought in the Gulf War of 1991. That experience, however, contributed little to my understanding of Arab culture and society. Most of the Arabs I dealt with there were Iraqi prisoners of war. We took thousands of them. I did spend some time interacting with them, but not much. My real experience came from a different time and place.

In 1999, I was finishing up a three-year tour teaching ROTC at Tarleton State University in Stephenville, Texas. It was time for me to move on. I was on the verge of being promoted from captain to major and was hopeful that I would be selected to attend the Army's Command and General Staff College that year. If so, I would begin the course in August 2000, so I needed a job that I could do for just one year—and at the time there were few places that the Army would move an officer to for one year. I was offered two choices: Korea or Saudi Arabia. For several reasons, Saudi Arabia seemed more interesting, so I accepted an assignment as an advisor for a Saudi Arabian National Guard mechanized infantry battalion. (This is their royal guard—it is a full-time military, not a reserve force like our National Guard.) I spent one year as the advisor to the 4th Mechanized Infantry Battalion in Riyadh, Saudi Arabia, and it was a great experience. I was the only American in a battalion of eight hundred soldiers and officers, and my role was to advise and assist the battalion commander, his staff, and his company commanders on all aspects of training, operations, logistics, and administration. I worked with the unit every day and had an office in its battalion headquarters. Because I didn't speak Arabic, I had a full-time linguist assigned to me. I found myself completely immersed in Arab society and soon grew to like it a great deal. I learned the customs and courtesies and began to understand the cultural differences between us.

One of the cultural traits that stood out most starkly was that Saudis, like many Arabs (I make no apology for the stereotyping), would rarely claim a problem. In fact, the phrase "success has many fathers, but failure is an orphan," though often credited to Tacitus, must have come from the

Middle East. The Saudi officers would let me fix every problem for them, mainly because I let them assign its causes to me. For a few weeks I bit, but soon I realized that if I forced their hand, they would develop and implement their own fixes for their own problems. My mantra became "make every problem a Saudi problem." It worked. Not only did the problems get solved, but the officers began to develop the foresight that is so critical to military operations.

So when I went to Tikrit, I used the same model. Now I had to apply it to Ramadi. I began to talk to my leaders and soldiers about getting the Iraqi Security Forces much more involved with our operations. It was initially a very difficult thing to do.

Thursday, February 7 was RIP Day Six. We had been running things for two days, and if we use a crawl-walk-run analogy, we were just beginning to stand on wobbly legs. When I came back to the headquarters that afternoon, Brian Dotson, my intelligence sergeant, pulled me aside. He said that he had taken the fins from the attack on COP Grant to EOD and that the senior EOD technician wanted to speak to me when I arrived. I immediately got Mike Rosamond and Randy Sumner and called for the EOD tech to come over. The senior EOD technician was a Marine Corps warrant officer with many years of experience doing post-blast analysis. In fact, he had been to COP Grant and examined the wall where Zeimer and McPeek had died. It was his opinion that V.J. had passed to me about the blast being from a recoilless rifle. He had made that assessment without the benefit of seeing the remains of the round. He told me that now that he had seen the rounds he agreed that the blast was from a 120mm projectile, but, he told us, the blast was inconsistent with a mortar. He suspected that it was from a 120mm tank round. The only 120mm tank rounds in Iraq were fired from U.S. tanks. He also told me that he was not willing to go any further without my "clearance." He said that if he proved that the incident had been fratricide, he would have to file an official report.

I was stunned. Of course he would continue his investigation. I told him to proceed and I would take full responsibility. The technician informed me that his reference books didn't have illustrations of U.S. weapons, so he asked if he could have a tank round to take apart and match to the fins. We gave him one, and he went back to work.

Holy shit! Of course! It all made sense to me then. The attack in which

Zeimer and McPeek died was an attack against multiple U.S. positions. COP Grant is three blocks southwest of the Abdul Rahman Mosque, at the corner of Baseline Road and 20th Street. At Baseline Road and Easy Street, five blocks east, was OP Eagle's Nest—five blocks straight down the road. On the night of the attack, enemy forces fired at both COP Grant and Eagle's Nest. During the hour-long firefight, a tank section (two tanks) responded to 1-9 as a quick reaction force. They had engaged "enemy forces" on a roof with their tank main gun and machine guns. They thought they were facing south when they fired, but clearly, they were facing west—right at COP Grant. The M1A1 tank is an extraordinary machine. Day or night through the worst battlefield obscuration, tankers can acquire targets with their high-powered thermal sites. If you can see the target, you can hit it with main gun fire. But while looking through a thermal site, all humans look alike. The tankers must have seen the soldiers on the roof shooting toward them and engaged. McPeek and Zeimer were killed by friendly fire.

Every Thursday evening, all the battalion commanders and their operations officers met with the brigade commander and his staff. The meeting was called the commanders' planning group and was designed to allow us to give the brigade commander an assessment of our current friendly and enemy situation, a summary of the week's operations, and a thumbnail of our future operations. The meeting also allowed the brigade commander to discuss his vision, both short- and long-term, for upcoming operations. These meetings were the only time that the entire BCT leadership was together during the week. I went to the meeting early to tell Colonel Charlton what I had just learned. Randy Sumner came with me.

John Charlton was in his new office. The BCT leaders were a few days behind us on their RIP, but Col. Sean McFarland had already vacated his office. Colonel Charlton was watching the news on TV when Randy and I knocked. I told him that we needed to talk and that we should probably have his command sergeant major, Cap Stanley, with us. Command Sergeant Major Clarence "Cap" Stanley and I had quite a bit of history. We had served together at Fort Riley from 1993 to 1996, where he had been a company first sergeant and I a company commander, then again at Fort Hood and in Iraq for OIF 1, when I was the 1st BCT operations officer and he was one of the subordinate battalions' operations sergeant major.

Known as Big Stan for his massive size—six feet five inches and every bit of 250 pounds—he was a fair, intelligent man who was focused on enforcing standards. He took pride in mentoring the battalion command sergeants major and spent each day out on the road visiting soldiers, as did Colonel Charlton.

John Charlton and I didn't always agree, but I have immense respect for him, and we have a good personal relationship. He is a genius and truly was the architect for much of what happened in Ramadi. As we all do, Colonel Charlton had his weaknesses, three of which affected me regularly. First, he was painfully introverted. Although he could break out of his introversion really well when addressing a group, he had difficulty interacting one on one. Second, he was *very* stubborn. Once he made his mind up that something was a certain way, it was nearly impossible to dissuade him with something as trivial as facts. Last, he relied upon his staff too much and didn't seek input from commanders prior to making decisions. But his staff was bad. I dislike saying that, and I'd love to apply the rule "if you can't say something nice . . . ," but the BCT staff is critical to the story. When I served as a BCT executive officer, I forced my staff to understand that although they worked for the brigade commander, they had a duty to support the battalions below. I saw it as our job to make life easier for the battalions. I also filled the role of the guy who told the brigade commander he was wrong when he was wrong. It was a difficult job. Then–Col. Dave Hogg was an awesome brigade commander, but he ripped my face off more than once. However, there was no one on Colonel Charlton's staff who dared tell him he was wrong. Furthermore, the brigade staff members were quite comfortable merely passing tasks to the battalions instead of doing things themselves or, at least, doing some analysis and providing some assistance.

All of that was in play when Randy, Cap Stanley, and I went into Colonel Charlton's office that day. He was watching the TV as I began to explain to him that I thought Zeimer and McPeek were killed by friendly fire. I described what I knew about the incident and told him I was going to assign Mike Rosamond to reopen the 15-6 investigation. He barely turned from the TV during the entire conversation. All he said was, "Okay, Mike. Thanks for the report. Keep me informed."

While we were in the commanders' planning group that evening, EOD disassembled a tank round. After the meeting, they were waiting to go in to see both BCT commanders with me. This time it was Randy Sumner, John Charlton, Chuck Ferry (the 1-9 Infantry commander), the EOD tech, and me. I started by telling Colonel McFarland what I had told Colonel Charlton earlier. Then the EOD warrant officer brought in the fins and the tank round—they matched perfectly—and told the group that he was 100 percent sure that the blast that killed the two Soldiers had been from a 120mm tank round fired from a friendly tank. After a question or two from the group, he was dismissed. I then told the group that I intended to reopen the investigation. Colonel McFarland tried, it seemed to me, to dissuade me. McFarland said that the fragments "looked old." "They had corrosion on them," he said. "They have been there awhile. I think they were left over from when we seized COP Grant." I didn't have the heart to explain to him that the fire and heat associated with firing the round caused the metal to oxidize. He was a tanker, like me, and I didn't want to make him look stupid. I think he was trying to keep me from reopening the investigation, which was bound to cause bad press for him. I simply said, "Sir, I think we need to figure it out." He couldn't disagree. Chuck Ferry took the news very hard.

Chuck Ferry taught me a lot about fighting in Ramadi. His battalion was tough and smart and understood that there was more to winning this war than killing insurgents. The Soldiers of 1-9 Infantry had arrived in Ramadi about ninety days before we did. They, therefore, left about ninety days before us, but in the year we spent together, they were excellent partners. Chuck saw almost immediately that the account I had given was probably what had happened. He was sick over it. He told me that he would cooperate in any way he could with the investigation.

I got the impression that people perceived me as an idealist. Perhaps I am—doing the right thing matters a lot to me. I did see moral reasons why we needed to figure out what really happened, but there were also pragmatic ones. Someone's next of kin deserves to know exactly how their loved one died, and we owe the dead soldiers an accounting as well. But, most important, if we know exactly what happened, we may be able to prevent it from reoccurring.

Immediately after leaving the meeting, I sat down and tried to wrap my head around what had happened that night and how I could keep it from happening again. The more I thought about it, the more concerned I became. I began, that evening, to look at the number of times multiple U.S. positions had been attacked in the Bandits' area of operations in the past and where they were attacked from. What I found was shocking. My AO in Ramadi was geographically small. Although it contained nearly one hundred thousand people, it was only about 1,800 yards across at its widest point. The range of our weapons was twice that. Indeed, I found that in many instances, a U.S. position was attacked from one direction, then, within minutes, an adjacent position was attacked from the opposite direction. Imagine you are in Florida and have a giant gun. If someone from Georgia were to attack you with his giant gun and you fired back, some of your bullets might reach South Carolina. Within minutes, South Carolina might report that they, too, were being attacked from Georgia even though it was your rounds from Florida that were hitting near them. The Bandits, it appeared, had been shooting at each other for months. It was plain as day to me when I looked at the incidents.

Mike Rosamond started the investigation the next day. Ultimately, he found conclusive evidence, including unmanned aerial vehicle (UAV) video that showed the tank round flying through the air and impacting COP Grant. There was no doubt about what had happened. As it turned out, several sergeants and officers from the Bandits had been pointing out the fact that this was occurring for some time, but they had been ignored. Shooting at each other, you see, doesn't fit in with the movie characters they played, so, I believe, they ignored it.

The next morning, my staff and I developed a plan we hoped would remedy the situation. Each U.S. position was required to fly a recognition device—which had a visual signal that could be seen day or night—from the highest point on the COP, and every soldier was required to view every adjacent friendly position both with his naked eyes and each sighting system so that he could memorize the appearance of the friendly position. Randy Sumner and the company first sergeants developed a product that was used in every one of our fixed positions; it was a panoramic photo taken from the position that aligned exactly with what a soldier saw in real life. Marked on the photo was every reference tool we used to refer to build-ings, and there was a large red-hashed area on the photo that covered every friendly position so that a soldier would immediately know that was a "no-fire area." Our plan did not immediately fix the problem—we still had a few incidents with spillover fire—but it did raise the awareness of the soldiers on the ground, and I don't think we had any more fratricide injuries.

CHAPTER 8

The Dark Days

My tour in Ramadi was my third combat tour. I had endured many stressful situations, so I thought I was ready for what was to come . . . I was not. I will forever remember my first forty-five days in Ramadi as the darkest time of my life. I hope I never experience anything worse. I am generally a very optimistic, positive person and have always tried to use that as my strongest leadership tool, but Ramadi nearly broke me. Had things not changed, I am not sure that I could have endured the situation for a year, much less fifteen months.

As I wrote earlier, Ramadi in January 2007 was the nastiest, most unpleasant place one could imagine. Camp Ramadi sucked, but over half of my soldiers didn't even have its rudimentary safety and shelter. They lived in the city on combat outposts. They were literally in harm's way every day, all day. If they were lucky, they would maybe make it to Camp Ramadi once a week for a few hours to get a hot meal and a shower. Upon leaving the camp, you entered the surreal world of the city of Ramadi. Chuck Krumwiede once called it "Jihadland" and compared it to an amusement park for terrorists. First, Ramadi is a sprawling, fairly modern, poorly planned city. It is made up of confusing, crisscrossed roads, some of which dead end with little warning. Most of the city at that time had multi-story buildings, as tall as six stories in business districts but mostly three-storied in the residential and mixed commercial areas. However, there were damn few buildings in Ramadi untouched by combat. Bullet holes and pock-marks were ubiquitous. Major blast damage was not unusual.

The roads, like those at Camp Ramadi, though mostly paved, were covered in up to ten inches of packed mud and dirt. The ever-present speed-bump IEDs left shot holes in the roads that we drove on. Often, these holes reached to the sewer and water lines, causing the streets to flood with stagnant water and sewage, in some places so deep that it came over the hood of a humvee. There was a sewage pond on the way into COP Sword that was well over four feet deep, and I feared getting stuck in it and having to get out of the truck to hook up recovery cables while stand-ing waist deep in raw sewage almost more than I feared being injured or killed. There was no trash collection, all trash was either piled up on the corner or burned. Packs of wild dogs ran loose all over the city, digging in the trash piles and strewing it all over; they rotted where they died. No major road was without a rotting carcass or two. There was no silence in Ramadi—barely five minutes passed without the sound of gunfire or an explosion. We had "unexplained" explosions every day. Imagine that! A place that has so many explosions that a couple of times a day something explodes and no one can figure out what it was. I always hoped it was some son of a bitch installing an IED who blew himself up.

The residents of Ramadi were the most unhappy and hate-filled people I've ever seen. No one would smile or wave at a passing American convoy or patrol. The best response one could hope for was that they would avert their eyes and try to move away. More likely the members of the convoy saw the usual look of hatred. They, too, were dealing with mud, stink, dogs, and explosions, but they had no hope of leaving one day. Every trip outside the camp had a measurable, statistically significant chance of bring-ing about your death or serious injury.

Deep down inside most combat soldiers exists a morbid desire to kill the enemy, and that did give one a rush of adrenaline each time he left camp. But, as many adrenalin junkies can attest, it is physically and mentally exhausting to stay hopped up on adrenaline for hours on end—

you feel nauseated, and it gives you headaches. Warfare is exhausting. My equipment consisted of helmet, earplugs (if not wearing a headset), body armor (about forty pounds' worth), elbow and knee pads, eye protection, fireproof gloves, uniform, boots, M4 carbine rifle (like a short M16), M9 pistol in a leg holster, seven rifle magazines, five pistol magazines, first aid kit, and water source. I'd say my total kit weighed over eighty-five pounds. That was the standard uniform anytime one left camp. All that kit induces fatigue even sitting in a truck; in a tank, in a Bradley, or walking, it's even worse.

My day started at about 7:00 a.m. I rarely had a full breakfast, normally just coffee and a Pop Tart or cereal. At 8:00 a.m., Jay McGee would brief me on the day's intelligence update, and then I'd spend an hour or two with the staff. Between 9:00 and 11:00 a.m., I'd roll out to visit the companies, in the early days normally with Randy Sumner and Chuck Krumwiede. We'd visit from one to three positions each day. The routine was as follows: when we arrived at the COP, Chuck and I would get a situation report from the senior officer who was awake. Because many of our operations occurred in the wee hours of the morning and we all had twenty-four-hour-a-day security requirements, there was no set "work day" for the soldiers on the COPs. Although I had a fairly straightforward schedule most of the time, my company commanders certainly didn't. In fact, during this time period, I became so concerned about their lack of sleep and how it affected their ability to think clearly, I dictated that they all come to Camp Ramadi on Friday afternoon for a meeting, then stay for supper and sleep at Camp Ramadi that night. It was my way to ensure they had at least one full night's sleep and one decent meal per week. Usually soldiers will get their food and rest; it was the leaders I had to watch out for.

While Chuck and I got our briefing, Randy would go on a tour with the first sergeant or one of the platoon sergeants who had to show him living areas and all the guard positions. During our early days in Ramadi, our positions were pigsties. The Bandits really had little care for cleanliness or orderliness. They left trash and junk all over the COPs, and ammunition was everywhere, including in sleeping areas. I don't need to tell you that ammunition is dangerous; especially in a place that the enemy attacks every day. If a mortar or rocket round hit some randomly stored ammo, things would be very ugly. In addition to being all over the place, the ammo was unmaintained, filthy, and rusted. Randy and I were not going to have our soldiers live like that—so he would take his tours with first sergeants and rip asses about getting things clean and orderly. He also emphasized guard positions having everything they needed and the soldiers manning them having great situational awareness. He embarrassed many a sergeant-of-the-guard by quizzing a soldier on the enemy situation or the rules of engagement or the location of friendly positions. Randy was the enforcer!

After our individual duties, we'd meet up and spend some time talking with soldiers and leaders, smoke a few cigarettes (it is amazing how many people still smoke cigarettes in combat—there is no mostly non-smoking population there), suit up, and roll to the next position, where we would do the same thing. More than occasionally, we would be at a COP while it was attacked. Normally, Randy, Chuck, and I would stay out of the company commander's way and let him handle his business. I used these instances as training sessions for company-grade leaders. We would conduct after-action reviews once things calmed down and use these to shape the company's procedures. On very rare occasions, if things were not going well, I would set Chuck and my PSD sergeants loose to "help out."

Early on, the battalion only had one PSD, and it was mine. If Randy and Chuck needed to get out, they had to go with me. Many other battalions fielded two or even three PSDs, but I decided we just couldn't afford to do so. The cost of a PSD was a minimum of four trucks and about sixteen to twenty-five soldiers—a platoon. I knew I barely had enough platoons as it was, and I certainly wasn't going to take another platoon's worth of assets out of the daily grind. My PSD was made up mostly of my tank crew and Chuck's Bradley crew. We augmented those crews with soldiers drawn from all across the battalion—Randy and I hand-picked most of them. The PSD soldiers were a combination of the absolute best in the battalion and some whose companies thought they could spare. Although we did toss some off the job, most were very solid and only left the PSD duty if they were promoted to a leadership position in a company. The PSD rapidly became the best small unit I've ever worked with. We started with two very young sergeants. Sgt. Darrell Woodall started as my humvee driver in the summer of 2006 and impressed me so much that I moved him to be my tank gunner, although he had never fired a tank before. D.J.

Woodall grew into one of the finest sergeants in the battalion—mature, smart, and hard-working with a natural leadership style that allowed him to get things done with little drama. His equal was Sgt. Chris Bates. Chris was the best Bradley gunner in the battalion and had impressed me from my earliest time in the unit. So, when it was time for Chuck to get a new Bradley gunner, Chris was the choice. He came into the Army with a bachelor's degree and is now an officer. These two young sergeants took a platoon that didn't exist until November 2006 and had it ready for combat when we arrived in Ramadi.

On my truck and tank crew were then–Private First Class James Beck and Specialist Michael Yaroch. James Beck was, truth be told, my good luck charm. He was the only crewman I kept for the entire tour. Beck was a California kid who had a couple of years at UC–Sacramento before his unwavering commitment to his fraternity (and the partying associated with it) landed him in the Army without a degree. With his self-deprecating humor that kept him the butt of many jokes in the truck and the tank and his generally positive attitude, Beck kept me sane. Mike Yaroch is also a stellar soldier. He was the quietest of the crew, but he would suddenly and spontaneously come out of his shell and have some pithy, meaningful observation that could either leave us in stitches or make us aware that something in our environment wasn't quite right. With his keen skill for observation, Yaroch was our hunter.

Back to the daily routine. After visiting two or three COPs, we would make our way home, usually around 4:00 p.m. This routine put the PSD on the road for several hours each day. In an American city, even with moderate traffic, one could travel the distance from Camp Ramadi to any of the COPs in only a few minutes. The farthest drive was only about four miles. In Ramadi, that could take over an hour. Speed is not your friend in these conditions. Slow, methodical movement was the best way to go. The intensity was unlike anything in civil society; I would literally forget to breathe for periods because I was so focused during some of these moves. It was utterly exhausting.

Upon our return to Camp Ramadi, I would sit down and talk with Mike Rosamond, who kept the headquarters and staff running and on track. We'd discuss whatever the catastrophe de jour might be and figure out our solution. After our chat, we would go to supper. Normally the supper bunch included Mike, Chuck, Randy, Ray Curtis, and Sgt. 1st Class Richard "Jay" Johnson. Jay was our personnel service sergeant. Usually, the personnel section has a captain and a sergeant first class, but Jay was so good at his job that I had no personnel officer. Jay also served as Randy's and my personal secretary, a crappy job that he did without complaint. After supper I would go through my email and physical inbox until midnight or later, and every day before I went to bed I called *my* Randi. Speaking to my beautiful wife of twenty-plus years was one of the highlights of the day. When the phones were down, which happened often enough, I felt as if my days were incomplete. No matter how tired or frustrated I was, the fifteen minutes I spent on the phone was my only time away from the problems of Ramadi. After our talk, I'd sleep. During the dark days, I rarely slept through the night. Each commander establishes "wake-up criteria." Because the commander and command sergeant major are the most experienced soldiers in the battalion, there are some things that require their personal attention. My wake-up criteria (which Randy shared) were as follows:

- Any death or serious injury to an American in our area of operations (AO)
- Any injury to a soldier assigned or attached to 3-69 Armor
- Any enemy contact lasting longer than five minutes
- Any major breach of discipline by a 3-69 soldier
- Any new enemy tactic, technique, or practice discovered
- Death of more than one Iraqi Security Force member in our AO
- Any incident not covered in the above list, at the battle captain/ battle sergeant's discretion

That was the daily routine, and that routine was overlaid on activity like this:

On February 11 at 8:15 a.m. it was raining, as it had been since we arrived. In the heart of Ramadi at COP Falcon, a tank was scanning Route Sunset from the northern entrance. The crew was about an hour and fifteen minutes into its three-hour shift, and crewmembers were bored. Boredom is omnipresent and dangerous as hell in combat. Some smart soldier once described combat as long periods of mind-numbing boredom followed by brief periods of intense terror, and this crew was in for a little of both.

The gunner and tank commander were taking turns scanning through the tank's thermal sight. The sight images heat in a glaring green-and-white display that is hell on the eyes, and looking through it for more than thirty minutes at a time causes a kind of temporary blind spot that tankers call "green eyes." The tank commander had just bent forward to take his turn on the sight extension near his chest when *whap, whap, whap!*—three Kalashnikov rounds impacted the turret near the area his head had just vacated. Within a few seconds, five more rounds impacted the tank. Through the sound of the whipping wind and driving rain and over the sound of the tank's humming engine, the crewmembers couldn't hear the sound of the rifles at all, just the bullets splatting against the armor. They scanned madly. A few seconds later, the soldiers in the tower on the roof behind them opened up with a heavy machine gun; two quick bursts, then silence. They never saw the enemy who fired from the third story of a building two hundred yards away, just one of the thirty-five buildings it could have been.

Staff officers asked me often, "Why did your soldiers not search the buildings?" Until you're looking down the street, lined with multi-story buildings as far as you can see (which is only about six hundred yards), it's hard to understand. By 8:17 a.m. the attack was over . . . back to boredom.

Steel's company commander was Captain Diogo "D.T." Tavares. Diogo is a great leader with a lot of energy, but he's also quite thoughtful. For our first weeks in Ramadi, Diogo's company included two of his tank platoons; a mechanized infantry platoon from B Company, 1-36 Infantry (a unit cross-attached to the BCT); and my scout platoon. Diogo also had an Iraqi Army (IA) company and our only Iraqi Police station. We had two IA companies in the task force at the time. Both of them really fielded a reinforced platoon of about thirty-five soldiers, and both were pretty sorry. They were grossly under strength due to poor retention and a high AWOL rate. The units were undisciplined and lazy. For example, at COP Falcon, the IA had a separate house. When we moved in, I went to the IA house after a few days, and what I found appalled me. The IA soldiers had been slaughtering their animals (most Arabs eat freshly slaughtered meat daily) on the front porch. It had not been cleaned in days and stunk something fierce. Inside the house there were dirty clothes and sleeping mats and dirty dishes scattered all over. The IA company commander, when he came to meet me, was completely nonplussed. He didn't even comment on the condition of his house but instead started telling me how great and brave his company was. I stopped him quickly and proceeded to tell him how lazy and ill-disciplined I thought his unit was and what a poor leader I thought him to be. He was mortified that he had lost a great deal of face to the American who was now in charge. He never recovered and was fired a few weeks later.

Continuing with that day's actions, at 9:00 a.m. Steel sent out a census patrol consisting of two Bradleys, twenty-six U.S. infantry, twelve Iraqi infantry, and six Iraqi policemen. In early 2007, our Iraqi police were all Sunnis from the Ramadi, area, and most of our Iraqi soldiers were Shia from Baghdad or the south—they were like oil and water, physical altercations were not uncommon, and it was not unheard of for them to shoot at each other. At 9:42 a.m., patrol members were engaged with one round of sniper fire but couldn't determine where the sniper had fired from, so they took cover in a house. As they were moving into the house, they were attacked from two nearby locations with machine gun and small arms fire, seriously injuring one American, one Iraqi soldier, and two Iraqi policemen. The patrol returned fire but lost visual contact as the enemy fled out the back of the houses. While the patrol treated and evacuated the casualties, Steel sent out a quick reaction force of two tanks. As the tanks moved to the area, Battle company soldiers at COP Sword, about three blocks northeast of the contact, observed two insurgents firing toward Steel's tanks. The soldiers at COP Sword engaged from their guard tower, wounding one of the insurgents. Both insurgents fled toward the al Iskan District.

I was at headquarters when the initial contact occurred, but I immediately moved to the battalion tactical operations center (TOC). The TOC is the nerve center for the entire battalion. Our battalion TOC occupied a room in the battalion headquarters that was about thirty-five by forty feet with a large horseshoe-shaped table (about nine feet per side) facing a wall that had a large projected image of the battalion's area of operation and several large, plasma-screen TVs displaying data from various computers in the TOC. On one side of the TOC table, farthest from the entrance, were workstations for the battalion's intelligence section and for our fire support (artillery) section. At the head of the table was our aviation section (which included Marines from the 1st and later the 4th Air and Naval Gunfire Liaison Company [ANGLICO] and airmen from our Air Force Liaison Team). On the side of the table closest to the entrance were the two radio/telephone operators (RTOs) who were the voice of the TOC (and the battalion headquarters) on the radio. About four feet behind the closed end of the U was a huge paper map of the battalion's area. Just beside the paper map, on a platform, were the desks of the battle sergeant and battle captain.

The battle sergeant and battle captain were the decision-makers for the vast majority of decisions on any given day, and my two full-time battle captains were Capt. Matthew McCreary and Capt. Mel Lowe. Matthew spent the train-up as my personnel officer, and when the battalion is home, the personnel officer (or S-1) spends more time with the commander than anyone. He has two functions: first is to supervise the administration and personnel section, and second is to serve as the battalion's adjutant, the commander's secretary and right-hand man. Matt and I became very close during the months leading up to deployment. A former collegiate wrestler from *the* Ohio State University, Matt would seem to be the prototypical jock, but there is much more to McCreary than that. While extremely intelligent and socially astute, he maintains a humble, down-to-earth personality. McCreary, more than any of my officers, has the wherewithal to be a general one day. After the MRE, Mike Rosamond and I decided that we needed Matt's talent in the TOC.

Mel Lowe had been the assistant operations officer through the entire train-up, and he impressed me early with his maturity and ability to plan and organize operations. Both would move on to command companies before the rotation ended. The ultimate supervisor of the TOC, however, was the XO. At our headquarters on Camp Ramadi, Mike Rosamond's office was just across the hall from the TOC, but he kept a speaker in his office that allowed him to monitor the battalion radio network while he worked—he could be in the TOC immediately, if needed.

I only spent ten minutes or so in the TOC that morning. Mel was on shift, and Mike Rosamond and Chuck Krumwiede were in the TOC to control the battalion's action. Randy Sumner and I went down to Charlie Med. The injured American was a soldier from B Company, 1-36 Infantry who was attached to Steel. As I recall, he was shot in the ankle, breaking both his tibia and fibula. One of the Iraqi policemen was shot in the chest, but, fortunately, the bullet had missed everything. He had a simple through-and-through and would spend a day at Charlie Med before being transferred to Ramadi General Hospital. The other Iraqi policeman was not so lucky. He had been shot in the neck and upper chest. He underwent emergency surgery at Charlie Med (I went into the OR and watched for about fifteen minutes). He was then evacuated to the combat support hospital in Balad for more surgeries. I don't know how it turned out for him. The Iraqi soldier had been shot in the belly and was also evacuated to Balad for surgery; he was stable when he left Ramadi.

After spending forty-five minutes at Charlie Med, Randy and I headed back to the headquarters, grabbed Chuck, suited up, and headed out to COP Falcon. When we arrived at Falcon, I spoke with Captain Tavares for about forty minutes about that day's attack. We then headed across the compound to meet with the Iraqi Police Chief at the station there on COP Falcon.

The al Forsan Police Station was the only police station in south-central Ramadi and only one of three in the city proper. COP Falcon occupied seven buildings on the corner of routes Central and Sunset. Al Forsan IP Station was in what was previously (and would be again) a school. As we walked into the police station, I was greeted by the chief, Col. Mohammed Zaidon, whom I had met, albeit briefly, during my PDSS visit. This was our first really substantive meeting. I gave Mohammed an update on the status of his two wounded policemen, which he appreciated, and then he invited me to stay for chai (tea). Mohammed and I spent the next thirty-five minutes introducing ourselves and giving a brief history of how we each came to be in that room. We enjoyed several jokes and several cups of tea, then the conversation transitioned to what he needed from us—guns, body armor, trucks, weapons. Some of his IPs had not even had the most rudimentary training, and none had any advanced training. I listened intently and took notes, then asked Mohammed to give me a tour of his station. Mohammed proudly showed me his rag-tag police station. This was a big spectacle for the IPs there—the new American colonel taking the time to walk through the station and meet a whole bunch of IPs. I sensed this hadn't happened before.

As we completed the tour, we were attacked with mortars. (This was a daily occurrence at COP Falcon.) Two 82mm mortars impacted about thirty feet from where Mohammed and I were standing. By this time, we were surrounded by a throng of Americans and IPs who scattered for cover. Mohammed and I simply stepped into the doorway of the room we were looking into and continued our chat. No one was injured, but he and I had just demonstrated our prowess to the gathered throng. As I left that afternoon, I told Mohammed that we had to have more of his IPs conducting joint operations with my soldiers. I told him that although I knew his IPs still needed training, we could not beat al Qaeda without them. I promised him I would work hard to get him the things he needed, but we could not wait to act. He hesitantly agreed.

As we mounted up to leave COP Falcon, the tank at their northern gate identified a suspected IED on the route we were going to take. We decided to head out the east gate. During our fifty-minute drive back to Camp Ramadi, D Company (Knight) reported an unexplained explosion in the vicinity of one of the company's positions. We made it back to Camp Ramadi just after dark, and I slept through that night. Our first attack didn't come until 11:38 a.m. the next day.

For the first fifteen to twenty days, the enemy tried us and worked hard to find our weaknesses. The enemy attacked all of our positions equally for our first fifteen days, and we won our fair share. On February 17 at about noon, the enemy tried to overrun one of our positions. The attack started when a sedan pulled into the intersection about three hundred meters east of COP Falcon and two insurgents in the car engaged the IPs at the gate. One IP was critically wounded; the others returned fire, driving off the attackers. Seconds later, about twenty insurgents began firing from the south side of the COP at the towers. Little did they know that in a tower was one of my snipers. The sniper, we'll call him Specialist T (because I don't know how his mother might react to all this killing), was pulling his normal guard shift in the tower. He had two weapons, his

M4 carbine and an M25 sniper rifle. The enemy fighters who attacked that day used standard military fire and maneuver tactics—moving by teams while a heavy machine gun provided suppressive fire.

COP Falcon was bisected by a feature called "Shit Creek"—just as the name implies, a wide canal full of raw sewage. Because it ran right through the COP, we had no vehicles covering the south end of the position, only guard towers. While the other towers engaged the enemy with automatic weapons, Specialist T went to work with his sniper rifle. At the end of the engagement, in the broad daylight, Steel counted fourteen dead terrorists and eleven injured. Specialist T later told me he thought he *only* killed nine of them. Due to the brave action of the IPs and the Americans in the tower, we averted a disaster and dealt AQI a blow that day, but it worried me. I was disturbed by the brazen daylight attack that clearly attempted to over-run our position . . . I was worried about COP Sword.

On February 18 at 10:00 a.m., a tank crew from my D Company that was attached to Battle had just been relieved on its observation post just north of COP Grant. Crewmembers went back to COP Grant, parked their tank, and dismounted. COP Grant was a fairly small position, not large enough to park the tanks and Bradleys inside. There was a motor pool outside the COP partially surrounded by concrete "T-walls" called the "bullpen." T-walls were everywhere in Iraq and ranged from the thirty-six-inch-tall Jersey barriers that are familiar to most Americans as the temporary vehicle blockers used for traffic control to the massive eleven-foot-tall Alaska barriers. The bullpen had Alaska barriers on two sides. We all knew that getting into and out of the tank was a dangerous and vulnerable time because all four crewmen needed to enter and exit the tank from either the top of the turret or the top of the hull. So, we did our best to move quickly and used smoke grenades to obscure the area while dismounting. On February 18, neither T-walls nor smoke helped. As the crewmembers dismounted their tank, COP Grant was attacked by machine gun fire from three different positions. As the COP reacted to the machine gun fire, a single round, much louder and closer, rang out. The round struck the tank's driver, Pvt. Kelly Youngblood, squarely in the side of his helmet. The U.S. Army's current helmet, the advanced combat helmet (ACH), is a great piece of equipment that stops almost all non-ballistic fragments one may encounter as well as pistol and low-velocity rifle rounds (like the AK-47) . . . but not a sniper's bullet. In the 3ID, we proudly wear the division's patch on both sides of our helmet. This round went right through the patch on Kelly's right side.

I was just preparing to leave Camp Ramadi when I got the call that we had a soldier wounded in action and that his status was "urgent–surgical." We use three levels of classification for casualties: routine, priority, and urgent, either surgical or non-surgical. En route to Charlie Med, I was told that the soldier had a head wound, and I knew this would end badly. I arrived about ten minutes before the Bradley that evacuated Kelly pulled into the ambulance bay and told the waiting medics and doctors what I knew of the wound. As the Bradley pulled into the ambulance bay, the surgeon climbed into the back. After only thirty seconds, he came out with the medics who were carrying the stretcher. They were "bagging" Kelly, breathing through an airway tube with a manual (bag) respirator. I was somewhat relieved to see Kelly come out on a stretcher receiving treatment. The surgeon and all the medics worked very hard to save Kelly's life for about twenty minutes, but his body core temperature eventually began to cool. The chief surgeon left Kelly's side and walked to the foot of the table where I was. He looked at me and said, "Colonel Silverman, I don't think this soldier's wound is survivable." He led me to the side of Kelly's head where the exit wound was. When I looked at Kelly's head, I knew that the doctors' actions were more for the living than they were for him. In retrospect, having seen this more than once, I believe that the surgeon in this case executed an elaborate Kabuki dance that was designed to send the message to the unit leaders present that "no matter how bad you or your soldiers are hurt, I will work my ass off to save them." I put my hands on his face and prayed.

That evening at 5:05 p.m., there was a complex attack against COPs Grant and Sword. This time the AQI terrorists allowed us to hone in on their positions. We asked for and received authorization to drop two five-hundred-pound aerial bombs on the building that the AIF fired from. It killed twelve terrorists. We had another seriously wounded soldier, and I went to Charlie Med for the second time that day. There was also a tank destroyed on COP Sword during the attack.

When I left Charlie Med, I went to the BCT headquarters to talk to Colonel Charlton. We talked about the sniper incident and the counter-measures that I would take at COP Grant. I also told him about my concerns about COP Sword. As I wrote previously, I had four major positions in Ramadi and only three companies to cover them. That is why we argued so strongly with Charlton and his staff while they developed the plan regarding allocation of forces. I reiterated to Colonel Charlton that I needed another company to put at COP Sword. He countered that our vulnerabilities had come from not being aggressive enough. He told me that clearing the al Iskan District would solve my issues. I told him that I agreed that al Iskan was the problem area, but I could barely hold what I had with my forces, and I needed my engineer company back to put a company headquarters and another platoon at COP Sword. He said I couldn't have them. The conversation was not nasty, but we certainly didn't agree. I left unpleased, pissed off, and with no solutions to my problems.

The enemy started to focus on COP Sword, where I originally wanted to position my most aggressive infantry company but wound up with a hodge-podge. I put what I believed at the time to be my best mechanized infantry platoon, my mortar platoon, and a section of tanks there. But, by February 17 I was having doubts, and between then and February 25, a chain of events occurred that absolutely convinced me I had to change things. On February 19, we had eleven attacks against our forces. Four of them were complex attacks against COP Sword. By the grace of God, we suffered no injuries in the attacks, and I went out to COP Sword the next morning. I sat down with the leaders at the COP and told them how concerned I was. During the discussion, I came to learn that the tank that was destroyed on the 18th was blown up by an IED—on the COP! I couldn't believe it. Some goddamn takfiri had crawled through a hole in the perimeter wall and put an IED under a tank, then detonated it. I was livid. I had to do something to reinforce that position, but I didn't have any good choices. When I left COP Sword, I stopped at COP Grant to have a talk with Dennis Fitzgerald about the state of things at COP Sword. I asked him when was the last time he had been to Sword and was shocked to learn it had been three days. I had been there twice in the same time period. I told him that I wanted him or his first sergeant there at least once per day.

That afternoon we had an ambush against one of Steel's joint patrols with the Forsan IPs. An IP was seriously wounded, and two terrorists were killed. I went to Charlie Med for the third time in four days and watched as an IP died. I prayed for him.

From Charlie Med I went to my tank. Chuck and I were going out with D Company (Knight) as part of an operation that we were conducting from the 18th through the 24th. Knight Company was commanded by Capt. Chris Haun, a skinny kid who grew up as an Army brat—his father was a full colonel who has commanded several medical service organizations. Small in stature, Chris is larger than life; so much so that I had, frequently, to knock him down a notch. Chris commanded from well forward in the foxhole, always finding himself in harm's way. Chris is brave and smart but unusually cocky. He smokes like a freight train and has a swagger in both his step and his voice. Chris's soldiers affectionately called him "The Duke." So it was; Chuck and his Bradley crew and my tank crew and I were going to man OPs all night as part of Knight's efforts. As we rolled out in our tracks, I was told that a Bradley had been destroyed by "possible RPG fire" at COP Sword but that no injuries occurred. It went in one ear and out the other as just another attack against what was becoming our Achilles' heel.

Chuck and I remained vigilant all night as Knight's forces performed a cordon and search of a few blocks just north of COP Iron without a hitch. The goal of the mission was to open up one of the last no-go areas in Knight's AO and search several blocks within that area for signs of insurgents, weapons caches, and IED materials. The area was called Hay al Dhubat Thania, or the officer's district number two, and bordered an area called Hay al Aramil, or the widows' quarter—both of these areas were bad. The mission concluded by about 10:00 a.m., so Chuck and I rolled back in with Knight's forces to get some sleep. Two tanks stayed behind to man the new OPs that would secure the route into the area. About an hour after we left, all hell broke loose. As Knight's first two tanks on the OP were relieved by two Bradleys, they moved back to COP Iron on the same route we had all taken an hour earlier, but they were attacked by a series of IEDs. First, one tank was attacked and then, as his wingman moved over to assist him, the second tank was attacked. Both IEDs were large speed bumps. One tank had a large hole breached in the hull, the other had damage to its suspension and turret. Knight sent two more tanks with a recovery vehicle to assist the two damaged vehicles back to COP Iron.

The operation we had just conducted was on the far side of Shit Creek, which also ran through Knight's area. To cross the creek, the Bandits had installed an armored vehicle launched bridge (AVLB). An AVLB is a steel bridge that rides folded on top of an old tank hull. Once the tank hull reaches the area to be bridged, it uses an arm to "launch" the scissors-type cantilever bridge over the gap so that other vehicles may pass. These heavy metal bridges are designed for very limited use, not to stay in place for months. You see where this is headed? Of course, the AVLB collapsed with the trail "rescue tank" on it, depositing the tank on its side, most ingloriously, in Shit Creek and leaving two Bradleys, a tank, and an M88 tank recovery vehicle stranded. What a mess! It took the rest of the day for Knight to get a new bridge in place and get the vehicles recovered. There was no rest for that company that day. They had all been up all night on the mission and had been looking forward to a little sleep. Instead, several soldiers, including the Duke, stood waist deep in Shit Creek that day.

A Bad Mosque

That evening, while Chuck and I were at the commanders' planning group, COP Sword had another complex attack. February 22 was a quiet day—one attack. Battle's nightly logistics patrol was attacked with an IED, destroying yet another Bradley. That evening, Knight had a "Pathfinder" mission. Pathfinder was the call sign of the 321 Engineers, an Army Reserve unit that deployed to al Anbar in 2006 to serve as the route-clearance element for al Anbar. Early in our tour, we had Pathfinder platoons available about four nights per week. The Pathfinder teams were equipped with a variety of strange equipment resembling farm implements. The workhorse was the Buffalo—a mine-resistant vehicle the size and shape of a small bus with a remote-controlled arm about twenty feet long capable of probing, scratching, and digging at IEDs. Before the Buffalo can dig at an IED, however, someone has to find it, and that mission went to two different types of vehicles and their crews. The RG 31 is a mine-resistant, general-purpose vehicle that looks like a giant Land Rover with a crew of four soldiers and big, bright floodlights used to search for IEDs. The craziest vehicle of the lot is the Husky, which looks like a small road grader, but instead of a blade riding under the cab, it has two flat panels that travel parallel to the ground—ground-penetrating radar that can detect metal and other dense materials buried below the surface of the ground. The operator (of the one-man crew) sits about eighteen inches off the ground that he is searching—he drives *directly over the IED*.

All of these vehicles can really take a blast. In fact, having seen the results of over a dozen IED strikes on these things, I never saw a soldier gravely or fatally injured inside one of these vehicles, though I have seen them take blasts that would have broken a tank or Bradley in half and killed the entire crew. These vehicles and the soldiers who operate them are phenomenal. Chuck Krumwiede and I had both taken the opportunity during our first couple of weeks to ride in a Buffalo on a route-clearance mission. During my time, we had a small firefight and found and removed several IEDs. I was the first battalion commander and Chuck was the first operations officer to do so, and it garnered quite a bit of respect and admiration from the crews, platoon leaders, and company commanders of the outfit.

The Pathfinder unit vehicles were escorted and secured by either a tank section or a Bradley section when they worked for us, giving them excellent security to allow them to focus on clearing the road. On this particular pathfinder mission with Knight, they were clearing the roads we had opened the night prior in the al Aramil. The al Aramil, like every other district in Ramadi, had a mosque, the Abdul Qadir Mosque. In Arabic, wherever you see the word *Abdul* or *Abd*, it means "servant of" and is always followed by one of the ninety-nine names of God. The Prophet Muhammed is reported to have said that he addresses God by all of his beautiful names. In the Quran, Allah is referred to by these ninety-nine different names, such as the Exalted, the All-Seeing, the Defender, the Bringer of Death, etc. *Al Qadir* means the All Able.

Bad things were happening in the Servant of the All Able Mosque. During the Pathfinder mission, the team found a large buried IED on one of the adjacent roads. The control wires for the bomb ran into the mosque compound. So, at about 3:00 a.m. on February 23, the battle NCO woke me and said that Chris Haun needed to talk to me. Chris explained the situation and asked that I get permission for him to enter the Abdul Qadir Mosque. Chuck Krumwiede and Mike Rosamond were already awake. The battle captain had awakened one of them before me and one immediately after. Jay McGee had not yet gone to bed. (Jay had a really bad habit of staying up all night to work, then pumping himself full of energy drinks during the day.)

We got to work building the substantial packet required to receive authorization to enter a mosque. Permission for U.S. forces to enter a mosque (except in "hot pursuit") came from the first general officer in the chain of command. For me, it was Marine Corps then–Brigadier General Charles M. "Mark" Gurganus, who had previously commanded a Marine Corps regiment during some of the most difficult fighting in al Anbar. I respected Gurganus a great deal because he didn't stay in the headquarters in Fallujah and have visions of "how it should be"; rather, he got out and spoke to soldiers and Marines and found out what the reality was. He also listened to subordinate commanders and took their advice, understanding that nobody knows an area better than the commander who is there every day. My one complaint about Gurganus is that he hardly ever came around to see my battalion. Eventually, I took this as a compliment. I think he was confident we were doing a good job and felt his time was better spent with guys who may have needed help.

By 5:00 a.m., we had enough info put together for me to have Charlton awakened. I spoke to him by phone at about 5:15. By 6:30 a.m, he had received permission from Gurganus for a mosque entry with one stipulation: U.S. forces could search the entire compound but couldn't enter the actual building of the mosque; that had to be done by Iraqis. Knight had a platoon of IPs with him, so it was no problem.

Mosques in the Middle East come in two varieties. There are small mosques that are really only prayer rooms, called *masjid*. There is a masjid on nearly every block in many Muslim countries. If you have the need to pray five times a day, you really can't drive across town to do so. Larger mosques are called Jamma or Friday mosques. Friday mosques are the large compounds that most people think of when they hear the word *mosque*. Abdul Qadir was a Jamma. Most Jammi (plural for Jamma) are not just one building but include several out buildings, what we would call a parsonage, where the imam and his family live, and often they have a madrassa. Many Americans have become familiar with the term *madrassa*. In the War on Terror context, it has come to mean those terrorist-run, anti-Western schools found all over the world that fill children's heads with ideas of hate and takfiri fascism. The truth is that the word *madrassa* is simply Arabic for school, and most of them are completely innocent. Having said that, the madrassa at Jamma Abdul Qadir was definitely a terrorist training camp. Knight found an insurgent sniper school in the madrassa complete with diagrams showing U.S. body armor and helmets that highlighted the most vulnerable spots. Outside the school, on the outer wall, were drawn target silhouettes that had been shot many times. Most damning was the U.S. helmet that the soldiers found in a shed with several bullet holes through it. Only a high-powered rifle could have done that. Not surprisingly, the compound was abandoned—Americans had, after all, moved into the neighborhood the previous day. The IPs searched the actual mosque building but found nothing significant.

Meanwhile, things at COP Sword got worse. There was a video posted on an al Qaeda website that purported to show a Bradley and its crew being blown up. It pictured a lone terrorist crawling up to a Bradley at the front of an American position. The terrorist slipped underneath the Bradley twice, dragging under a speed-bump IED and a jug of explosives, and five seconds later the Bradley exploded—horrible picture. As the camera panned out, I saw a familiar sight—something that always scared me— the sewage moat at the front of COP Sword. The Bradley that was reportedly destroyed by RPG fire two nights prior—this was it! In one week, both a tank and a Bradley on COP Sword had been destroyed by infiltrators.

Sometime that week, I got a phone call in the evening from Colonel Charlton. He told me that he had received a report from a government assistance team working in the city of Ramadi that alleged that U.S. soldiers had assaulted Iraqi civilians, including one of the deputy department heads for the city government. Apparently this man, who was a great friend of the coalition, missed work several days in a row. When he finally came in to work, it was to tell his American advisor that he quit and would be relocating his family from Ramadi, since he deemed it no longer safe. His face and back bore the marks of a serious beating. When the American asked what happened, he gave this story: About three days earlier, in the dark hours of early morning, a U.S. Army census patrol had come to his house with no interpreter and no Iraqis. The patrol entered his house by force and began, very roughly, to separate the men from the women and children. Because the department head spoke English, he approached the patrol leader, who became enraged and struck him several times. From there, things got worse. He reported that the patrol members became very rough in their treatment of the whole family, including the department head's seventy-five-year-old father. When they handled his father roughly, the department head's brother defended his father, and members of the patrol beat his brother severely before detaining him. I told Colonel Charlton that I would go to COP Sword the next morning and begin a commander's inquiry. A commander's inquiry is the step before a 15-6 investigation. It is basically designed to judge the veracity of a charge and decide whether or not the charge should be formally investigated.

Many things about the report troubled me. First, if true, it directly violated the first concept of my intent, "treat all Iraqis politely and respect their culture." This concept was my prime directive. It informed every single action that I wanted my soldiers to take. I had a saying, "Treat every Iraqi politely and with respect right up to the moment you have to kill him!" What I stressed to my soldiers was that there was no need have a huge emotional build-up or develop hate in order to kill someone. One can decide in less than a second to kill a man, like flipping a switch. One second you are the rational actor, the next, if necessary, you are a killer— cold blood. It is the passionate, emotional escalation that can lead to trouble. What I believed was that if we treated every Iraqi with respect and maintained our humanity and patience, we would kill fewer Iraqis and would disarm a major al Qaeda propaganda theme. We would no longer be seen as the hate-filled American imperialists who came to steal oil as agents of Israel. We would become human beings who treated others decently and who were fighting to free Iraq from the throes of terrorists. Second, it violated one of my direct orders: that all census patrols include interpreters and Iraqi Security Forces. How the hell can you ask questions without an interpreter? Third, the actions, if they happened as described, were criminal, war or not. Finally, and most importantly, these actions were a recipe for defeat, and I wanted to win!

The next morning I received a full copy of a compelling packet that included statements from the victims and photographs of the injuries caused by the beating. There was no doubt that two men had been severely beaten. The story in the statement rang true. In the meantime, I pulled the patrol debrief that corresponded to the reported time and place of the incident. I required a written report from every patrol leader every time a patrol left its base, whether for a ten-minute trip from one position to the other or for a ten-hour mission. These reports were critically important, and from them I gleaned a great deal of insight. Often, issues that would normally not reach my level came to light in these reports. They also contained clues about the population or about the enemy that became central to our efforts. Most of them, however, were boring and listed the acronym NSTR for nothing significant to report. This patrol debrief, written by a man who I had previously described as my best platoon leader, described a typical census patrol with no remarks about any unusual actions and specifically listed that the patrol had taken no detainees. I was more concerned than ever. The fact that I definitely had a patrol in the area at the time the alleged abuse took place further confirmed my growing suspicions. So Randy Sumner, Chuck Krumwiede, and I headed out to COP Sword.

When we arrived, I received the usual update from the platoon leader; we'll call him Lieutenant Z. Z gave me a thumbnail sketch of his activities and his assessment of the enemy situation. While Chuck and I did that, Randy met with his platoon sergeant; we'll call him Sergeant M. After Z's update, I told him that I was there to conduct an investigation into an accusation of assault and detainee abuse. I reiterated my standard spiel about how bad things happen in combat and the way we deal with them is honesty, and reminded him that as officers and soldiers nothing was more important than our honor and integrity. As soon as I finished my speech, Z assured me that he understood and agreed wholeheartedly with everything I said—then he lied to me, without flinching, for two hours. I dismissed him from the room and had him go sit in another room isolated from the members of his platoon.

Meanwhile, Chuck had all the soldiers who were on the patrol write sworn statements. They all told an identical, bullshit story about one Iraqi who had attacked members of the patrol so they detained him. Randy had gotten a similar story from the platoon sergeant, who added that the patrol brought the detainee to COP Sword, where they treated his wounds and released him. I brought Z back in the room and told him he was relieved. I said that I knew he had lied, both to my face and in the patrol debrief about taking a detainee. With a deadpan look, he said, "Well, sir, I lied to protect my squad leader. I didn't want him to get in trouble because I knew how the incident would look. I'm sure that the squad leader did nothing wrong." He then proceeded to explain to me how he had split his patrol in half that night and sent half the patrol, with no interpreter or Iraqi soldiers, to do one half of the block while he took half the patrol to the other half. The two did not link up again until Z returned to COP Sword, where he learned that his squad leader had taken a detainee and that the detainee "had resisted." Z and Sergeant M believed the half-assed story the squad leader and his squad members gave about how this man had physically attacked the patrol while they were in his house, but they knew that the incident would bear the appearance of impropriety, so they decided to cover it up.

So Z admitted he had lied to cover up his platoon's actions. M was complicit but would not admit to any crime. The squad leader, one of my smartest and most aggressive, was clearly lying. He stuck to the story that his squad had only beaten one man and only did so to subdue him after he attacked them. I knew that to be a lie because I had seen pictures of two men badly beaten: the city government official, who was not detained, and his brother, who was. Every member of the squad told the same lie in each written statement. Ultimately, when confronted with their lies, the squad leader and every member of his patrol invoked the Fifth Amendment right of silence and avoided prosecution. Even though I turned the investigation over to the Naval Criminal Investigative Service (NCIS), who pursued the case doggedly for weeks, there was nothing any of us could do to develop credible evidence that would stand up in court-martial. The testimony of two Iraqis against that of nine Americans just wouldn't be enough to convict anybody.

The issues with the investigation played out over several weeks, but that day I had larger and much more immediate concerns. I had a platoon about which I was already very concerned that now appeared to have several corrupt leaders. There was no way I could leave that element in combat—the platoon was a massacre waiting to happen. Here we were with barely enough combat power to hold the ground we had, losing soldiers to injuries and death, and I had these sons of bitches abusing locals and then lying about it. I relieved Lieutenant Z and brought every soldier who had written a false statement back to Camp Ramadi to guard the gates.

The author discusses the U.S. Army's new counterinsurgency doctrine with then–Lt. Gen. David Petraeus during the train-up for deployment. Petraeus took the time to spend two hours one-on-one with each battalion commander in the Raider Brigade prior to deployment, imparting his vision for the fight ahead during the surge. *Photo courtesy of Brian Dotson*

The skills that soldiers honed during the train-up didn't always match the task ahead but rather stressed fundamentals and principles. Tank gunnery at Udari Range, Kuwait (the last stop before Ramadi), however, served the battalion well. *Photo courtesy of Jim Irwin*

A speed bump IED and three "black jugs" of HME from large buried IEDs retrieved by PSF members in Albu Bali. The IEDs used in al Anbar were simple and highly effective. Although no 3-69 Armor soldiers were killed by IEDs, six Americans were killed while working in the battalion's area—four EOD technicians and two route-clearance crewmen. *Photo courtesy of J. Nathan Kline*

COP Sword as seen from a friendly sniper position. Although the battalion discovered several enemy sniper positions, finding them all was impossible. *Photo courtesy of J. Nathan Kline*

This house adjacent to COP Falcon shows the results of multiple firefights and gives the reader a sense of the plethora of covered positions from which insurgents could attack. There were dozens of houses like this adjacent to all of our positions and no way to prevent the enemy from using them all. *Photo from the author's collection*

A tank platoon is only sixteen men. Members of Sgt. Adrian Lewis' platoon—which lost three killed in action by the same sniper—mourn his loss. Ultimately, the sniper was reportedly killed by his neighbors; in counterinsurgency, victory can only be achieved by winning over the population. *Photo courtesy of J. Nathan Kline*

A Bradley Fighting Vehicle burns outside COP Sword. Insurgents were able to crawl under the parked vehicle in broad daylight, without being seen, and place two large IEDs under it. Because of this incident and others, the author assessed that COP Sword was days away from being overrun. *Photo courtesy of J. Nathan Kline*

Protests, like this one outside of COP Sword, were a manifestation of AQI propaganda, which often included rumors of rape and kidnapping. The signs read, in part, "We ask the coalition forces to release the women." The protests were designed to elicit a violent response and tested our discipline. *Photo courtesy of Eric Beltz*

Scouts from 3-69 Armor patrol on one of the many paved roads covered in mud, sewage, and water in Ramadi. It was only months later that we knew they were paved. Concertina wire lined the roads to prevent IED emplacement but instead collected trash and trapped animals, adding to the macabre mess. *Photo courtesy of Eric Beltz*

The attacks against COP Sword culminated with a truck-bomb attack that was repelled only by heroic actions. Below is Thunder Alley viewed from COP Sword. Eric Beltz and his scout platoon were patrolling in Thunder Alley during the attack. Two scouts and a medic were injured as the building they were in collapsed. *Photo courtesy of Eric Beltz*

"You'll never drive on 20th Street." A mere forty days after our warning from the Bandits, tanks and Bradleys from 3-69 Armor set blocking positions on 20th Street. The Raider Brigade's Operation Call to Freedom dislodged al Qaeda from Ramadi and sent the group's leaders looking for new safe havens. *Photo courtesy of Jesse Lujan*

The sheiks of the Awakening Movement put themselves at great risk to fight al Qaeda. In this meeting in Hamdiya, Iraq, over one hundred sheiks representing nine tribes and around sixty sub-tribes or clans met to discuss the improving security conditions in al Jazeera. *Photo courtesy of Jim Irwin*

Production of homemade explosives at facilities like this one in Albu Bali demonstrated AQI's sophistication and level of international support. The similarity of these facilities across Iraq showed a high degree of centralization. The chemicals bore labels from both Syria and Jordan and were, apparently, procured in and smuggled from there. *Photo courtesy of Jim Irwin*

Above and below: Fahadawi sheiks from Hamdiya survey the scene while Iraqi policemen get the Vise Grip checkpoint up and running after a truck-bomb attack killed three IPs. Most of the IPs at the checkpoint were not paid by the government of Iraq, rather sheiks paid a small stipend. Mostly, patriotism and guts spurred the IPs' volunteerism. *Photos from the author's collection*

Chaplain (Captain) J. Nathan Kline converses with Sheik Abdullah Jalal al Faraji, the director of the Sunni dowry for al Anbar Province. Nathan's religious engagement efforts were on the cutting edge of U.S. Army doctrine and made great headway with the population. *Photo courtesy of J. Nathan Kline*

The author and his linguist, Mostafa Remh, walk beside then–Lt. Col. Abbas al Balawi, the chief of the Albu Bali Police, in a September 2007 cordon and knock. These operations usually resulted in nothing significant to report (NSTR) but provided a great opportunity for both IPs and Americans to bond with locals. *Photo from the author's collection*

Pieces and parts spread in a trail of carnage after car- and truck-bomb explosions. An IP stands over the leg of the truck-bomb driver. In the scene are also car parts and a large portion of scalp (top center). *Photo from the author's collection*

Lieutenant Jim Irwin looks on as leaders from 2/1/1 IA question a local man about insurgent activity near Albu Gorton, Iraq. By the end of our tour, Americans were taking a backseat to capable and disciplined Iraqi forces. *Photo courtesy of Jim Irwin*

Albu Bali Police and Rock Company infantrymen load up for a clearance mission in Albu Bali. The exposed IPs, riding in the backs of pickup trucks, were always at great risk, and many paid the price, suffering injuries or death from attacks from which Americans, in our armored vehicles, would have walked away. *Photo from the author's collection*

"The Iron Bridge" (above) was our only means of reaching the east bank of the Haluwa Canal. When al Qaeda destroyed it, the group's leaders must have thought they could prevent our disruption of their safe havens. But installing the military bridge (below) allowed us to continue the chase. *Photos courtesy of J. Nathan Kline*

The author interacts with local children during a school supply distribution. These types of "operations" were foreign to most soldiers in the battalion, and getting them to make the mental leap was often challenging. But these types of missions are at the heart of counterinsurgency. *Photo courtesy of J. Nathan Kline*

A patrol passes under a permanent OP on an overpass along Route Mobile. These OPs were eventually manned by PSF members. Securing Route Mobile was critical to the economic livelihood of al Anbar, and the leaders of AQI knew that. Over twenty ISF died as a result of car and truck bombs during the fight to control Route Mobile. *Photo courtesy of J. Nathan Kline*

The argument ender: a Cold Steel tank engages insurgents just outside of COP Falcon. Tank cannons had devastating effects on insurgents, but the collateral damage the machines caused was one of the main reasons 3-69 Armor was moved from the city. After al Qaeda was cleared out, it was time to rebuild.
Photo from the author's collection

The author presents Sheik Muhammad al Heiss with a replica of the battalion's colors. Without firing a single shot, Heiss was the best partner the author and his battalion had in the fight against al Qaeda. During several sensitive interactions that could have gone badly, Heiss served as the author's sheik and led him through the fragile negotiations. *Photo from the author's collection*

The unit sign in front of the headquarters on Camp Blue Diamond.
Photo courtesy of Carl Wheless

A view from the entrance of COP Grant looking east-southeast. Two garbage trucks from our first mission into al Iskan wait to be returned to the city. *Photo courtesy of Carl Wheless*

An explosive ordinance disposal team safely detonates a speed bump IED ahead of a patrol leaving COP Grant. It was actions like this that turned routine travel of a few miles into hours-long combat patrols. There were no safe routes in Ramadi! *Photo courtesy of J. Nathan Kline*

The author and members of the battalion staff and PSD share a last meal at Sheik Heiss' *Muleefa*. Although they were putting the violence of Iraq behind them, leaving al Jazeera was difficult for many of the battalion's soldiers. *Photo courtesy of J. Nathan Kline*

Battle Company Soldiers share a meal with "their" sheik in Albu Aetha. Because of their total immersion, the soldiers assigned to a tribal area would often be part of the tribe's welcoming committee when American officers came to visit the area. *Photo courtesy of Jesse Lujan*

Two Battle Company infantrymen move down an alley in Ramadi. Every movement in Ramadi had a measurable, statistically significant chance of bringing about your death or serious injury. There were no safe movements. *Photo courtesy of Jesse Lujan*

Strangers to partners, partners to friends, friends to brothers. A young tanker trains the Iraqis that he lives with on close quarter battle tactics. Through these daily interactions these young men with seemingly so little in common developed nearly familial bonds with each other. *Photo courtesy of Jim Irwin*

"Nothing significant to report." Jim Irwin and his platoon conduct a patrol with members of 2nd Provincial Security Force (PSF) in Hamdiya, Iraq circa September 2007. These patrols were excellent tools for American and Iraqi security forces to meet and greet the locals, further bolstering their confidence in the security situation. *Photo Courtesy of Jim Irwin*

I was now down by half a platoon at the position that I thought could be overrun at any minute. I ordered my scout platoon, which had been attached to Steel at COP Falcon, to move to COP Sword that night. My only regret was that I didn't relieve the squad leader and Sergeant M as well. The squad leader would have two more reports of abuse (this time against U.S. soldiers) but would avoid prosecution every time. I finally relieved the platoon sergeant for lying to an investigating officer in a subsequent investigation. Charlton refused to punish him. He found that although M lied, the incident he lied about was "not as bad as it looked." Maybe I am an idealist, but I don't see how one tolerates liars, especially in a combat environment. It just isn't that much of a stretch in my mind from lying to cover your ass in a misdemeanor investigation to lying about murder.

My scout platoon was an excellent unit. The platoon leader, Capt. Eric Beltz, has a unique story of patriotism. Eric started his career as a U.S. Navy officer. He spent two years in the Navy but then decided that he wanted to make a bigger contribution to the War on Terror. He transferred to the Army under a program called Blue to Green and became an infantry officer. Eric is conscientious, brave, smart, and disciplined. His leadership played a big role in turning things around at COP Sword. (He is now a federal agent and still works to counter terrorist threats.) His platoon sergeant was Sgt. 1st Class Michael McDaniel. McDaniel was a good leader when we were at Fort Stewart but fairly young and lacking experience, which manifested itself in a tendency for him to be overprotective of his soldiers. During our time in Ramadi, he developed into one of the best platoon sergeants I've seen.

But a new platoon was only half the solution. I needed some more senior leadership at COP Sword. I needed a company but had none to use, and Charlton was not inclined to give me one. Dennis Fitzgerald had his hands full with COP Grant. Things were so bad I actually entertained the idea of moving Chuck Krumwiede out to COP Sword, which would have hurt my headquarters. There was one other option that was very unconventional and probably had about a 50 percent chance of success. Each battalion has a headquarters company that is designed to provide administrative control to the personnel who work in the headquarters. It is not manned, equipped, or organized to fight, but it has a commander, a first sergeant, and some of the administrative and support personnel that an infantry or tank company has. Specifically, it has no fire support team and no soldiers dedicated to running its command post, nor does it have combat platoons. In addition to the issues of equipment and personnel, I had the soldiers of my headquarters company doing something else. They were my "mayor's office."

As you might imagine, there is a full-time job associated with running the on-base life support for an organization of nine hundred soldiers. There are myriad issues associated with living spaces, office space and automations, utility services, laundry and bath, food, and a dozen other ankle-biters that all entail dealing with the local Kellogg, Brown, and Root (KBR) contractors. There is also the responsibility of coordinating security on the camp: guard towers and reaction force. Without the headquarters company taking care of those mundane details, the job would fall to my battalion staff or, worse yet, my forward support company.

My forward support company, E Company (Atlas), 3rd Brigade Support Battalion, was the best I have ever seen. All of my other companies had "combat" soldiers: infantry, tankers, engineers. Atlas was made up of the soldiers who would have been described in earlier times as "non-combat" soldiers, or "REMFs." REMF is the pejorative term for combat support and combat service support soldiers. The acronym stands for "rear echelon mother-fucker" and has been around as long as I have been in the Army and surely many years before that. In the old Army of linear battlefields, there was doctrine that defined the part of the battlefield closest to the enemy as the "combat zone" and the part farthest from the enemy as the "rear," or rear echelon. Of course, in the old days, the rear echelon was relatively safe and secure. Picture the fat supply type in some World War II movie sitting around the depot with his feet resting on ammo boxes drinking a hot cup of joe while some infantryman was getting stuck with a bayonet because he was out of ammo. However, any such image is less appropriate now than at any time in history. The truck drivers, supply types, fuel handlers, and mechanics of my support company were in the thick of the fight every time I turned around. They spent as much time "out of the wire" as most of my tankers and infantrymen, and put more miles on bad roads than any platoons other than my PSD.

Captain Adrian Bailey, commander of Atlas, had been in 3rd Brigade

Support Battalion since he was a second lieutenant. He had spent several years in the Army (eight or nine) and had been promoted to staff sergeant before seeking a commission, so he was far from the average brand-new captain. He also inherited a company that was a mess. The previous commander (though I never met him) was horrible—deploying with his company in 2005 and then spending around half the deployment back at Fort Stewart because he had a minor injury and "personal problems." For whatever reason, his chain of command tolerated his behavior, and one can only imagine how his terrible example impacted the overall morale and discipline of the unit. So when Adrian took command a few months before I arrived, he had a real nightmare on his hands. Luckily, he brought 1st Sgt. Nixon Camper with him, and together they started "cracking skulls." Adrian and Nixon were a tough-love team bordering on extreme; I had to rein them in occasionally to keep them from going over the edge from strict to mean, but I never had to worry about them becoming over-protective or ignoring bad discipline.

Atlas was responsible for providing supplies and services of every nature for my soldiers who were off the camp as well as for providing the vast majority of logistical transport to move anything on the battlefield and for providing every bit of maintenance for our fleet of around four hundred vehicles. Nearly every time I left the camp (and I did so about four hundred times), I passed an Atlas patrol coming or going. When I passed any one of my patrols, I scrutinized everything I saw. I never had any compunction about stopping the patrol, or more often, calling the company commander to rip his ass if I saw something wrong. Randy Sumner did the same, and he had a much better eye. We rarely had to correct Atlas patrols. I am as proud of those soldiers as I am of any combat soldier I commanded. I couldn't afford for Atlas to assume responsibility for all the actions on the camp, nor did I want to have my staff and Mike Rosamond take their focus off our combat operations, but I had no realistic alternative. My instincts were screaming that the mess at COP Sword was days away from becoming a disaster, and it was certainly critical already.

The logical choice was to assume some risk at the camp and send my headquarters company out to COP Sword. Ray Curtis stepped up and took over the mayoral duties with a couple of sergeants at his side. Head-quarters Company (Hellcat) was commanded by Capt. Mike McBride, the most senior of my company commanders. He was an infantry officer who had waited longer than most for company command. Mike was very aggressive and had a good grasp on the basics of combat actions. Although I had never seen Mike in the role of a combat leader during our training, I was confident in his abilities. The Hellcat first sergeant was Stan Balcer, and Stan was something else! Stan had spent time at the National Training Center as a trainer and had a very strong foundation in doctrine and tactics. Stan was also a really personable and caring leader whose soldiers loved him. He was comfortable interacting with officers, no matter how senior, and I always got the impression from Stan that he knew damn well he could have been an officer had he wanted to, and for that reason he related to officers in a near-peer relationship. Don't get me wrong, he was not insubordinate or disrespectful, he was just . . . comfortable. Mike McBride moved out to COP Sword that night. After a couple of days, Stan and the rest of his small headquarters joined him, and around March 5, they assumed full responsibility for COP Sword. The next several weeks were critical, and I am convinced that without those two, I would have lost that position.

Another hugely significant thing happened March 1. I was informed that an additional Marine battalion, 2/5 Marines, was coming to Ramadi and would relieve me in the south-central area. I would move my battalion to relieve Cliff Wheeler's 5th Squadron, 7th Cavalry Regiment (Warpaint) in Jazeera, the tribal suburbs north of the city.

CHAPTER 9

Expensive Garbage Trucks

I didn't quite know how to take the news that another battalion would replace mine in Ramadi and that we would head out to Jazeera, one of the safest places in al Anbar Province. Cliff Wheeler's Warpaint Squadron had suffered few attacks during its time there and had not been doing much in the way of killing. (In Jazeera, the exception to that rule would be my A Company [Rock]. Mariano Wecer and his boys were in a major fight on the eastern outskirts of Jazeera—more about that later.) Most of my soldiers looked at Jazeera as a vacation spot—strictly non-lethal. And they thought they knew how to take the news—as an insult. They saw it as a slap in the face that some *Marine* battalion was going to take over our battle space while we went to Jazeera to "pass out candy."

Chuck Krumwiede was particularly upset. By March 1, he and I felt we were starting to turn the corner on our operations in the city and that all we needed to completely clear our area, as we had argued many times, was more infantry. We had damn sure learned some tough lessons, and Chuck believed that 2/5 Marines would be forced to start from scratch and relearn all those lessons, the hard way, once we left. I discussed the issue with Charlton and he assured me that his decision was not based on any shortcomings in my unit. He explained to me his assessment that the city was a mess, both in terms of enemy activity and in terms of infrastructure damage. Not only had al Qaeda done incredible damage to the city, but six months of tanks and Bradleys driving around and fighting was wreaking havoc, and for what? We were still suffering casualties. Our tanks and Bradleys didn't make us indestructible. He thought Jazeera, with its wide-open farmland and villages, was much better terrain for a mechanized force. I counter-argued that my battalion already knew south-central Ramadi and that a better solution was for Charlton to give me an infantry company from 2/5 Marines and let me stay in the city; with the extra boots on the ground I could easily clear the al Iskan District. He was unconvinced.

The 2nd Battalion of the 5th Marine Regiment is the most decorated battalion in the Marine Corps. Headquartered at Camp Pendleton, California, the battalion had already had two tours in Iraq and was returning for its third. Marine Corps units were not doing long tours like the Army; theirs were only seven months. These mini-tours are, no doubt, better for both the service members and their families, but they are not good from a tactical or operational standpoint, and I think it no coincidence that the vast improvements in al Anbar Province came after Ramadi returned to the control of a U.S. Army brigade. Seven months is not sufficient for the Marine on the ground to become an agent for change. It takes soldiers about forty-five to ninety days to adjust to the environment each time they re-enter combat, and there is a point about thirty days before the tour ends when units tend to become over-cautious so as not to lose any more warriors. Using those horizons, that gives the average Marine battalion four months of focused time on the ground, which is an awfully short amount of time to make real changes. No battalion used its brief time better than 2/5 Marines, however.

In my fifteen months in al Anbar, I saw five Marine battalions come and go in Ramadi. Lieutenant Colonel Craig Kaczynski's battalion was the best I saw and worked more closely with my battalion than any other Americans. A Marine infantry battalion is a much different organization from my Army combined-arms battalion. Where I had forty-plus tanks and Bradleys, they had none; their strength was in numbers of infantrymen. My two mechanized infantry companies had fourteen Bradleys and three thirty-six-man platoons each. In a mechanized infantry platoon, it takes twelve soldiers to provide the three-man Bradley crews, leaving only twenty-four to fight dismounted. One mechanized infantry company detached to Warpaint left me fewer than one hundred infantrymen I could count on day in and day out. Craig's battalion had four infantry rifle companies, a weapons company, and a headquarters and services company. His rifle companies had four platoons each with forty infantrymen per platoon and no vehicles (although they would use humvees in Ramadi). His battalion could count on having about seven hundred infantrymen each day, and that is why I quickly came to realize that moving his battalion into the city was, indeed, the smart thing to do. Charlton was right. We would have to swallow our pride, and I would have to set the example to my soldiers how to do so.

In the meantime, we were still embroiled in a brutal fight. The enemy was taking a huge toll on my tanks and Bradleys. By March 1, I had lost about five tanks and seven Bradleys, mostly to IEDs, and was up to about twenty-five casualties (mostly minor injuries). So, when I said we thought we had started to turn the corner in our operations, it was really only in three ways: First, we were initiating more attacks than we had in our first twenty-five days. The total number of engagements had not dropped substantially, but my boys were surprising the enemy much more often, and as a result, we were killing more insurgents. Second, we were getting the Iraqi Security Forces (ISF) more integrated in our operations. Steel had Iraqi police from Forsan Station integrated into every patrol by the first week of March as well as having IPs with the U.S. forces at both entrances to COP Falcon. Tavares was having better luck than he had previously in getting his Iraqi Army unit integrated as well. At COP Sword, my scout platoon was also conducting joint patrols with Iraqi troops there and beginning to develop some trust and fellowship. Soldiers, Iraqi and American, were beginning to spend non-patrol time together—training, eating meals, and even just BSing during their off time.

Finally, 90 percent of my soldiers understood and followed my guidance. They began to interact with Iraqis on the street and in their homes with dignity and respect, and that had started to make a difference. My patrols were now greeted inside many of the houses by Iraqis who were not outwardly hostile or aloof. Many started to speak spontaneously with the Iraqi police and soldiers and with my soldiers, through their interpreters; sometimes about the weather, usually about the problems that the war had caused and what we owed them in terms of reparation, but on rare occasions they began to talk to us about al Qaeda. We started to glean significant intelligence from some of these reports. Often people at two or three houses on a block might tell of the same AQI terrorists who were responsible for murder and intimidation in that area, and nearly as often, once the names made it to the Iraqi police, an IP might know where to find that person or where to find a member of the AQI fighter's family who might have more info. This information started to lead to arrests by the IPs of some of the terrorists in my area, which significantly tightened the noose on the AQI members outside of al Iskan.

Up to this point, I have used imprecise terms to describe al Qaeda areas to the reader, but there are some terms that give me a better way of describing these areas, to give the reader a clearer understanding and inform much of the remaining discussion in this book. I must, once again, give credit to Capt. Jay McGee for defining these terms as tightly as he did. Once again, these are concepts that should have been codified by intelligence officers at the highest levels, and, in fact, the terms were used fairly widely, but it was young Jay who was the first to present ways to identify these areas and to describe their characteristics with some precision.

Ratline, the first of these terms, describes a terrorist or insurgent logistical route that can be used to move things or people into or out of a particular area. In order for a ratline to be useful to an insurgent, it has to possess several attributes: it must provide reasonably good transportation infrastructure—meaning road networks, waterways, footpaths, etc.—that allows relatively safe and predictable delivery of supplies or personnel to terrorists so they can maintain a certain level of activity or prepare for temporary increases in activity. A ratline must also possess the ability for these supplies and personnel to move free from interdiction by counterinsurgent forces; this attribute can be achieved either by simply avoiding areas where counterinsurgent forces operate or by possessing the ability to have these movements blend in with similar-looking innocent traffic. It is very useful if a ratline provides access to the next type of insurgent area—support zones.

Support zones are areas that, although not controlled by insurgents, allow insurgents some freedom of action. Support zones provide things like temporary holding areas for materials, or "safe houses" for personnel, communications structure, reconnaissance and surveillance structure, temporary command and control facilities, and non-terrorist-owned commercial entities that are willing to provide goods or services for money, regardless of affiliation. Support zones may also include illicit or semi-legitimate terrorist-owned commercial interests. These interests can range from kidnapping and hijacking operations all the way to perfectly innocent-looking shops, stores, or service providers. The key is that a large portion of the profit from these enterprises goes to fund terrorist operations.

Ratlines and support zones support the remaining two types of insurgent areas: attack zones and safe havens. *Attack zones*, quite simply, are the areas in which terrorists conduct their offensive operations and are really defined by the terror targets. If one wishes to attack American forces, you have to go where we are, so the attack zones are either near our positions or along routes where we move. Not all attacks, however, occur in attack zones because terrorists and insurgents also conduct defensive operations. Often these defensive actions occur on the edges of the final type of area: the *safe haven*. An insurgent safe haven is where the majority of insurgent operators and leaders reside, and these areas are controlled by the terrorists. Any Iraqi unlucky enough to reside in such an area would be subjected to the worst and most brutal intimidation and forced to live with the insurgents' rules or suffer beatings, torture, or murder as the result of resistance. Safe havens include the major command and control facilities for the insurgents, their training facilities, their manufacturing facilities, and their housing. Many times, insurgents would go so far as to move their families into these safe haven areas. Destroying these safe havens became a major focus of our operations.

When we arrived in Ramadi, we assessed that there were four safe havens in our AO. The first was, obviously, the al Iskan District, where the Islamic State claimed its capital. Literally, no American or Iraqi Security Forces member had entered the al Iskan District since October 2006. We knew it was the major command and control area for AQI because the group had announced it. There was also Hay al Dubat Thania (Officers' District Number 2) and the Aramil (Widows' Quarter) area where we had searched the Abdul Qadir Mosque. As you recall, Knight had cleared that area, and we now held it. We also assessed a smaller safe haven in the Hay al Hawz (the gated district). Al Hawz was an area just north and west of COP Falcon. We had encountered several IEDs on its periphery, and Steel had several significant engagements in the area. The last safe haven was a small area just north and east of COP Sword called the Masada Street District. After our success in gaining a foothold in the Officers' District Number 2, we began to form plans to clear the remaining safe havens. I was comfortable that we could clear al Hawz and Masada Street easily. But, as I wrote earlier, I didn't think I had enough combat power to clear al Iskan, and going in half-assed was not my intention.

Meanwhile, Knight was working to hold what we had recently cleared down south in the Officers' District Number 2 and the Widows' Quarter, but it wasn't easy. On the evening of March 1, a few hours after dark, a tank crew conducting surveillance of the Widows' Quarter saw four AQI terrorists stretching wires to what appeared to be an IED on the north side of the area. The Widows' Quarter was the poorest and most ramshackle area in the whole city and was, before the war, literally a government housing area for the widows of soldiers and junior officers who had died in service to Iraq. Only the poorest, most socially isolated widows wound up there. If a women or her husband were from even a modestly successful family, the family or the tribe would care for the widow and her children. The families who wound up in the Widows' Quarter were utterly hopeless. What better place for a young, poor, AQI extremist to find what he was really after—sex. For any devout Muslim, pre-marital sex is forbidden. Nearly all interpretations of Sharia, whether extreme or mainstream, agree on this concept. However, in the warped minds of al Qaeda, it was perfectly acceptable to force a woman to marry you (via threats of murder and torture) in order that one might get sex. We suspected there were quite a few of these insurgent instant marriages in the Widows' Quarter. These poor, unprotected women and their children were easy prey for al Qaeda because they had no one to defend them. There came a time when we could almost assume that any male over the teen years seen living in a house in al Aramil was a terrorist, and eventually, our IPs would spend a great deal of time patrolling the area (hopefully not for the same reason the terrorists did, but who knows).

At any rate, it was clear to the tank crew that they were watching takfiris install a large buried IED. The tank crew engaged with machine guns, wounding one of the insurgents, who was dragged by his three accomplices to a nearby building. Once in the building the terrorists moved to the roof and began shooting at the tank with AK-47s at a range of about five hundred yards. As I wrote earlier, there is nothing more Darwinian than an insurgency, and this was a great example. While the terrorists moved to the building, we brought an unmanned aerial vehicle (UAV— observation drone) to a position above the house. From the headquarters, we watched as the three uninjured terrorists fired at the tank. They had zero chance of hurting the crew with AK-47s, since the tank is nearly impenetrable to anything that light, but they did ensure that both the tank crew and the UAV could easily track where they were. Captain Chris Hahn requested permission for the tank crew to engage with its main gun, and I granted permission. Thirty seconds later, we all watched from the operations center as the UAV crew sent live video of the tank firing two 120mm rounds into the roof of the building—the insurgent gene pool was decreased by four idiots who probably thought they were headed to heaven to be greeted by virgins.

About thirty hours later, another tank crew at the same location observed four more insurgents on the same roof. These knuckleheads had RPGs, and I'd bet they were coming to avenge the deaths of their buddies. The crew watched the terrorists climb onto the roof and get themselves set to "ambush" the tank that was watching them. The tank crew had already reported the enemy and requested clearance to fire their main gun, which I granted. The insurgents spread out across the roof and readied themselves to fire from four different positions. The tank engaged like the well-oiled machine that it is; four rounds, four positions on the roof, four more dead takfiris, all in the span of less than thirty seconds. We had a saying in Ramadi: nothing ends a disagreement faster than a 120mm cannon. AQI hated tanks!

Later that day I went to COP Iron to visit Knight, went to COP Falcon to visit Steel, and was on the way to COP Grant to visit Battle when Chuck Krumwiede's truck suddenly erupted in a flash of flames and metal. The explosion was on the left rear side of the truck between the door and the turret. Chuck's truck was leading that day (as he normally did), followed by Randy's, then mine, and then the rear truck. When I saw the explosion, I waited for the small arms attack that might come for a full twenty to thirty seconds, but nothing happened. Then I called Chuck for a report; he came across the radio broken and scratchy because his antennae had been ripped from the truck by the explosion. He told me that he had two casualties and was going to continue to COP Grant (five hundred feet away), then his truck pulled off.

Randy and I spoke on the radio while our gunners scanned the area. Neither of us saw any signs of the enemy, and after another two minutes, we followed the lead truck into COP Grant. As we passed an alley on our right, James Beck saw a pipe sticking out from under a parked car. It was an improvised rocket launcher and had been used to fire a 20mm aerial anti-tank rocket at Chuck's truck. Luckily it failed to explode where it hit (squarely on the passenger-side rear door) and skipped into the heavily armored turret instead, doing little damage to the turret itself but ripping a huge hole in the roof of the truck right above the rear seat occupant, Spc. Kelly Blansett, our PSD medic.

Kelly is a big, strong kid and could easily have picked any one of the PSD up and extracted him. That fact, as well as his motivation and skill, was the reason Randy and I selected him to be our medic. Kelly was knocked out by the blast for about five seconds. When he came to, his first words into the headset were: "Is everybody okay?—Aw shit, I'm not." The explosion caused significant shrapnel to enter the truck right above Kelly's head, shredding his combat helmet and his body armor; his ballistic plates had several pieces of fragment in them. In any previous war, Kelly would have died, but with the advanced protective equipment he had, his injuries were serious but not life threatening. He had lacerations on his face and shoulder, and his right forearm had been badly lacerated by the blast. By the time I made it into the COP, Kelly was being treated by his fellow medics. He was conscious and alert and was busy directing their actions as they treated him.

Chuck's driver, then–Specialist Joe Picon, was knocked completely silly by the blast. He was able, however, even barely conscious, to drive the truck into COP Grant before losing consciousness completely. Picon is a Mexican-American and has dark skin, thick black hair, and brown eyes. During his time receiving treatment at the combat support hospital in Balad, Iraq, he was, based on his looks, roughly segregated into groups with Iraqi insurgent detainees twice. Both times, as he reports, he looked at the offending military policeman and said, "Dude, I'm a fucking American." He got a sheepish, "Sorry," in response. We loaded up the casualties in one of Battle's Bradleys and raced like a bat out of hell to Charlie Med.

Masada Street

In any given week, a good battalion can do no more than two major operations, and usually the right number is one. The last week of February, we focused on Knight's area and managed to open a new route and break the AQI safe haven near the Abdul Qadir Mosque. The first week of March, we turned our attention to the Masada Street District. Masada Street was on the northern boundary of our area immediately south of Route Michigan, the main thoroughfare transiting al Anbar Province south of the Euphrates River and running from the outskirts of Baghdad across the province to the Saudi border. In our area the road ran due east–west and connected Ramadi to Fallujah. Route Michigan was not like a U.S. interstate highway; it was a commercial and residential four-lane highway lined with shops, apartment buildings, and upscale residences—Route Michigan was a ratline as well as a major route for U.S. traffic.

Masada Street—a small, two-lane, residential street that had easy access onto Michigan—was one of many support zones that provided staging areas for attacks against U.S. forces on Michigan. In late 2006 or early 2007, U.S. forces stopped going into Masada regularly for several reasons: the area was right on the boundary between the zone controlled by the Bandits and the area controlled by the adjacent Marine battalion to the north (1st Battalion, 6th Marine Regiment). Also, the Bandits had seized their areas mostly from south to north, and COP Sword was their last position—they had simply not had time to make it there.

It wasn't that we couldn't get there; in fact, the route-clearance mission I rode along for in the Buffalo had taken place in Masada weeks earlier. But, the lack of regular presence, we thought, had allowed the enemy to turn a support zone into a safe haven. Things at Sword were going much better with the Hellcats in charge, and by early March, we had begun to coordinate our actions well with 1/6 Marines, so we decided to begin to focus some efforts into Masada. We started by conducting reconnaissance with both patrols and UAVs in preparation for a clearance operation by the second week of March, but things took a turn and began to indicate a quicker operation would be necessary. On the second night of UAV reconnaissance, Matt McCreary called me into the TOC just before midnight. A UAV had observed a vehicle enter the Masada Street area from the southeast. It stopped on a corner and dropped two men, who unloaded some items from the vehicle and began digging in the road. The vehicle then left by the same route and parked at the Abdul Rahman Mosque in al Iskan. Once the vehicle parked, the UAV returned to look at the two men who were now, clearly, installing a large buried IED just off of Masada Street.

The advent of UAVs and real-time video feeds into command posts has spawned a new technique I call "remote control killing," and I was a master of the art. I started using this technique extensively during the second half of my deployment in 2003–2004. As a brigade XO, my workspace then was in the brigade operations center. Most UAV pilots don't get the opportunity to see Iraq from the ground, which puts them at a disadvantage. When you team someone who has good experience on the ground with a UAV crew, you can get great effects. Because I had spent time out on the streets in Iraq, I was good at correlating what I saw on the video with what I knew happened every day in Iraq. I started to be very successful at identifying suspicious actors and directing the UAVs to watch them until it became clear what they were doing. Using this technique, I had killed scores of insurgents, and I continued this as a battalion commander. I'd estimate that I have attacked close to fifty insurgents this way in my career, and this one was a no-brainer.

Once I was sure that the two were emplacing an IED, we requested and were given air support. Two FA-18 Hornet aircraft came on station, identified the target, and dropped a pair of five-hundred-pound bombs. The first bomb struck the target but failed to explode, skipping off the road and burying itself in an adjacent home. The second struck immediately after and killed both insurgents, detonating the large IED they had emplaced. Unfortunately, the secondary explosion from the large IED caused massive damage to a nearby house. After a few minutes, a small crowd gathered at the scene of the strike and began looking through the rubble of the damaged house. I ordered Hellcat to send a patrol to the area at first light to make an assessment of the situation in the neighborhood. Then I ordered the UAV to observe the Abdul Rahman Mosque, and what the UAV showed raised major suspicion.

We had already seen the vehicle clearly associated with the IED team we had just killed park at the Abdul Rahman Mosque compound. That may have been enough to build a mosque entry packet, but that wasn't all. We had been receiving a lot of information about a truck-bomb factory in al Iskan. Truck bombs are much larger versions of the car bombs that had seen widespread use in Iraq from as early as mid-2004. Truck bombs are made using commercial truck chassis, usually either semi-tractor trailers or fifty-ton dump trucks, and contain thousands of pounds of explosives. Many of the truck bombs being employed in Baghdad were purported to have been built by the Islamic State in al Anbar Province, but no major truck-bomb factories had been located. Well, as we all looked at the video coming from the Abdul Rahman Mosque compound, we could clearly make out six large trucks parked in the courtyard of the mosque. There was no innocent reason that these trucks should be in the parking lot of a mosque, especially a mosque that AQI had claimed as the capitol of the Islamic State. Although we weren't ready to clear all of al Iskan District, we had to go search this place before those trucks were turned into giant, mobile bombs. We started processing the mosque entry request and a plan to gain entry to the al Iskan District and the heart of the Islamic State.

While Chuck and the rest of the staff began to build a plan to enter and search the Abdul Rahman Mosque, Hellcat launched its patrol to check out the area we had bombed the night before. What the soldiers found there was mostly insignificant. Some of the neighbors claimed that a family was killed in the house damaged by the explosion, but the claim was not universal, and there was no physical proof that any innocents were killed. As the patrol members returned they were engaged by a single shooter, causing them to take cover in what we would later learn to be a dentist's office. It was one strange place.

The patrol called on the radio after some time and reported that the contact was over, but they had found something very strange: rooms full of chemicals, molds, and cookers filled the building. Outside in the courtyard were a cement mixer and one hundred or so bags of cement; definitely not something we had seen before. We sent tons of questions to the patrol leaders, and they started to gather more facts: What are the chemicals? Are there any people in the building? Did you find any documents or other evidence? Slowly the answers came back. We finally had a list of the chemicals after about three hours: four gallons of methanol, one gallon of sulfuric acid, one and a half gallons of zinc oxide, one and a half gallons of magnesium hydroxide, one and a half gallons of ammonia, and one hundred fifty-pound bags of concrete. What the heck? I asked my chemical officer (Chemo) to do some research and figure out what those chemicals can be used for. I suspected that one could make explosives from them. After another ninety minutes (the patrol had now been on scene for about five hours), he told me he had no clue what they could be used for. I told Mike Rosamond to call the brigade headquarters and request some experts to analyze the site.

Mike came to me about an hour later and said that the brigade XO refused to send anyone; he wanted us to blow the place up and move on. This was one of the many times the brigade staff proved an impediment to my operations. They had absolutely no interest in supporting us and felt we were merely a nuisance to their schedule of briefings and workouts and bullshit. I called the brigade XO personally and told him we would absolutely not blow up some shit without some idea of its explosive potential. I told him I didn't think the bags were full of concrete. I thought it was explosives and, if so, it was five thousand pounds worth. He refused to help, and I eventually had to call Charlton directly and explain the situation—he was unhappy with *me*, not his staff, but eventually agreed to send his Chemo and an EOD team to look at the site.

The patrol had been there ten hours by then, and another three hours passed getting the brigade Chemo and EOD rounded up. So about fourteen hours after our first report, the patrol bringing the Chemo and EOD arrived. They reported to First Sergeant Balcer, who was running the show at the scene. Stan Balcer reported to me that it took him thirty-five minutes to get the brigade Chemo out of her truck. I don't know if this was her first time off Camp Ramadi, but I'm positive she had never been in the heart of the city. She had spent her time in the brigade headquarters reading reports about horrible attacks and injuries and deaths, and she was scared. Meanwhile, EOD told Stan that they really don't do site exploitation, and they would blow up whatever he wanted, but they had no clue if all those chemicals made explosives. They looked at the bags of cement and pronounced, "Yep, it looks like cement."

Finally, the brigade Chemo got out of her truck and spent about three minutes looking at the chemicals and the lab. She said we should load it up and bring it back to Camp Ramadi for analysis. This had been going on all day. (I never traveled to the site because we were briefing Craig Kaczynski, the commander of 2/5 Marines, and his operations officer, Maj. Jeff O'Donnell. Kaczynski arrived the night before to begin reconnaissance, which would last nearly a week. They would then leave Ramadi for about ten days and return as their Marines began to flow into Ramadi just after mid-March.) I called brigade (I think it was the XO) and reported the analysis and recommendation of their Chemo. I told them that we absolutely would not carry that shit in our vehicles through IED-infested streets and that I thought the brigade headquarters was worthless. I then told Balcer to dig a separate hole for each type of chemical and dump it out. I also told him to leave the cement and destroy the cement mixer. They happily complied and went back to COP Sword just in time to prepare for the next morning's mission to clear the Abdul Rahman Mosque.

About two weeks later, Chuck Ferry's Soldiers discovered a similar site and went through the same issues analyzing it. His leaders decided to blow up the "bags of cement" that they found—it turned out to be high-grade, homemade explosive. The blast destroyed about six buildings and damaged nearly half a block. Luckily, no Americans were killed by the blast. The site he found had contained less than half as many "bags of cement" as the one on Masada Street.

Al Iskan's Not So Bad
While Stan Balcer had been running things at the explosives lab, Mike McBride had been at the battalion headquarters receiving his mission for the next day. It was fairly straightforward. His company would set up a series of overwatching positions west of the mosque while Battle set up positions south of the mosque, then we would remove the barriers that closed off the roads into al Iskan and bring an assault force to the mosque with Iraqi Army and police and conduct a search of the compound. At 4:30 a.m., I mounted my tank with Yaroch, Woodall, and Craig Kaczynski. The mission went off without a hitch, and by 9:30 we had cleared the

entire compound. The only thing we found was some machine gun ammo in one of the outbuildings. The trucks, as it turned out, were municipal garbage trucks that had been stolen from the city's motor pool. My best guess is that they weren't going to be bombs; rather, the Islamic State was going to start providing services to the residents of al Iskan, à la Hezbollah in Palestine. They understood, as did we, that we were embroiled in a battle for the people of Ramadi. Whatever they were there for, we couldn't destroy them; instead, we needed to recover them and return them to the fledgling city government, but they wouldn't start. I tasked Hellcat to keep them secure and ordered Atlas to put together the assets to haul the trucks out of al Iskan to the Ramadi Government Center. Adrian Bailey, my support company commander, told me that he would do so ASAP, but it would take at least a couple of hours for him to gather his recovery section and get the requisite security together.

Meanwhile we met the schoolmaster for the madrassa of the Abdul Rahman Mosque, and he seemed a decent fellow. He toured us around the school, and I saw nothing that would lead me to believe this madrassa was anything more than a simple school for Iraqi children. Maybe we had over-estimated the enemy's presence in al Iskan. Being content with what we had found, I left the area so that Chuck and I could continue with our initial coordination with 2/5 Marines. I ordered Mike McBride to continue to secure the garbage trucks while Adrian prepared to come recover them. While he was there, I also wanted his soldiers to census the homes in the immediate two blocks around the mosque so that we could begin to assess the atmosphere in the neighborhood. Kaczynski, O'Donnell, Krumwiede, and I and our crews mounted up and rolled back to Camp Ramadi.

About 12:45 p.m., Adrian Bailey and his recovery patrol turned north onto 20th Street and put COP Grant at their backs. Bailey had a tank and a Bradley from Hellcat escorting him. The Bandit PSD told Sergeants Woodall and Bates during our relief-in-place that there were three things we would never do during our tour in Iraq: They said we would never stop our patrol in central Ramadi to talk to locals; never eat a meal at an Iraqi's house; and never drive on 20th Street. We did them all in the first forty days of our tour, but on this day there was a high price for driving on 20th Street. In hindsight, it is really easy to see how we made our mistake: When we entered al Iskan, we established security along its perimeter and had soldiers in tanks and Bradleys observe the routes that we needed to move into and out of the area. They scanned the area, looking for enemy shooters or IED emplacers who might move on, near, or across the roads. But, the vehicle crews could not see into the buildings adjacent to the roads, and we underestimated the enemy fighters' ability to put speed-bump IEDs on the ground without exposing themselves.

While Bailey's patrol moved north on 20th Street, a speed-bump IED was thrown from a second- or third-story window onto G Street, where they would turn east. As they made the turn, the vehicles moved in the following order: first came an escort Bradley, followed by Bailey's humvee, an M88 tank-recovery vehicle, two wreckers, and a tank trailing the patrol. The speed-bump IED hit Bailey's truck, tearing out its engine and ripping the front clip from the frame. Immediately after, the lead Bradley was attacked with another speed-bump IED that tore through the hull near the driver and broke a huge section from the engine block, disabling the vehicle. Simultaneously and almost instantaneously, the first wheeled wrecker moved up to Bailey's truck to begin recovering it and was attacked with a third speed-bump IED, flattening all ten of its tires but not disabling it. A tank from the vicinity of the Abdul Rahman Mosque (four hundred meters east on G Street) began moving to support Bailey's patrol, but it was attacked with a fourth speed-bump IED, destroying the tank's hydraulic system.

The crew continued to move toward Bailey's patrol as both the tank and the patrol came under withering enemy machine gun fire from the buildings lining G Street. The damaged tank began to return fire, as did the tank with Bailey's patrol, and all the soldiers who were now on the ground recovering Bailey's truck immediately began firing at the enemy. Meanwhile, the damaged tank was attacked with yet a fifth IED, disabling it completely. The soldiers on the ground fought so aggressively (most were mechanics, truck drivers, and supply types) that the enemy, even though fighting from buildings with a huge advantage, was driven from the area.

Once the firing stopped, the patrol identified six more speed-bump IEDs in a four-hundred-yard stretch of G Street, and there were two more found behind the patrol on 20th Street within fifty yards of the tank position that had guarded that route during the entire action. It was obvious that all the IEDs were emplaced after Chuck and I had moved through there about 10:00 a.m., and the majority were probably emplaced while Bailey's patrol came through. When EOD came out to destroy the IEDs, they found that several of them had fishing line attached. The insurgents had prepared the IEDs and tied lines to them, then used children or women to walk the lines across the street into buildings adjacent to our route. The IEDs were then pulled out, probably immediately in front of each target vehicle. EOD speculated the others had been thrown into the road with command wires attached, most likely from second-story or higher windows. The enemy had emplaced 13 speed bump IEDs in less than 2 hours, maybe within minutes, and we never saw it happen. The terrorists had used the IEDs as the cornerstone of a complex attack that resulted, thanks to the prowess of my support soldiers, in no serious injuries, but the members of AQI proved their ability to move in and through buildings and courtyards without showing anything unusual to either the UAV that had watched the whole day's actions or the tank and Bradley crews who watched the routes.

The recovery took well into the night. At 4:00 p.m., Stan Balcer was taking his turn on the Bradley OP at the west end of G Street when he observed a terrorist throw an IED into the street. As Stan watched, the man stepped into the street and attempted to adjust the IED—perhaps he didn't like the throw, perhaps the command wires came loose, we'll never know. First Sergeant Stan Balcer is a Bradley expert. He fired eight rounds from the vehicle's 25mm gun, launching eight little bombs about the size of a large cigar at the terrorist, striking him in the chest. As Stan watched, the man disappeared in a shower of spray. That day's actions had cost the U.S. government about 4.5 million dollars in armor and trucks; the enemy's bill was one takfiri. The people of Ramadi got four garbage trucks back, and Mayor Latif—the nearly powerless Ramadi mayor—was so very pleased we rescued his garbage trucks that he went out of his way to offer his personal thanks. Awfully expensive garbage trucks; there had to be a better way to win this war.

CHAPTER 10

Call to Freedom

We had made our first foray into the al Iskan District, and although it hadn't seemed so bad at first blush, it had proven in the end to be just as bad as I had expected. I considered myself lucky that I hadn't lost anyone on the garbage truck mission. It did, however, confirm in my mind that al Iskan was the major safe haven in the city. So, for the next several days, I toured Kaczynski around what would soon become his area, while at night he and I and our respective operations officers began to build a plan to clear the district. This would not be the first major clearing operation in Ramadi, but it would be the last and the biggest in the city.

In the summer of 2006, the entire city of Ramadi was an AQI safe haven. Although there were several Marine battalions in and around the city, they had been unsuccessful in dislodging the enemy. When the Ready First Brigade came in, the unit immediately embarked on an effort to systematically seize, hold, and build within the city. Starting in the suburbs, the Ready First Brigade cleared much of the city's periphery and moved on to clear some of the heart of the city. Ramadi is bound by the Euphrates River in the north, and the Habbaniyah Canal connects the Euphrates with Lake Habbanniyah and bisects the western edge of the city from north to south. In the east, an industrial canal separates the city from its suburbs, and in the south, the rail line separates central Ramadi from its southern suburbs. Lieutenant Colonel Bill Jurney's 1st Battalion, 6th Marine Regiment (1/6 Marines) cleared much of the northern edge of the city proper between the Euphrates River and Route Michigan. West of the Habbaniyah Canal Lt. Col. Miciotta "Bear" Johnson's 1st Battalion, 77th Armor Regiment (Steel Tigers) had cleared major portions of the western outskirts. And, of course, the Bandits had started the clearances in their area. All of these battalions did their part in liberating Ramadi, but the lion's share of the work had fallen to Lt. Col. Chuck Ferry's 1st Battalion, 9th Infantry Regiment (Manchu).

The Manchus were on our eastern flank and controlled east Ramadi as well as the eastern suburbs of Jalaiba and Sophia along route Michigan. Chuck had a huge task force of seven companies and the majority of an Iraqi Army brigade when we arrived. As we came into Ramadi in February, the Manchus were preparing to clear Hay al Mulab, or the Stadium District. Al Mulab was a major safe haven just east of al Iskan and was filled with evil. Ferry's Operation Murfreesborough cleared Mulab from mid-February to early March and it was a bloody battle for both insurgents and coalition, but at the end of the fight, another major portion of central Ramadi was clear of AQI presence. The clearance of al Iskan would be a much larger, more complicated operation with at least two battalions, mine and Kaczynski's, and we hoped a significant number of Iraqi forces as well. We continued to build the plan and synchronize it with the 2/5 Marines' arrival in the city.

Meanwhile, the battle for Ramadi continued to rage. The attacks continued to come at a furious rate, but we were really beginning to get in the groove with our combined operations with the Iraqi police and Army. They, in turn, were beginning to have a positive effect on the people in Ramadi. Every Friday, we conducted monitoring of the mosque messages in our area. Friday is the Muslim holy day and the day when, at the noon prayer, the imam delivers a sermon that usually lasts about an hour. Unlike the sermons we are accustomed to at churches, this sermon is played on a loudspeaker outside the mosque and can be heard for blocks. In order to monitor the sermons (because they were often inflammatory and violent), we sent patrols with an interpreter to the vicinity of the mosques to either record the sermon or write a summary and characterization on the spot. During the month of February, every sermon in our area (we had over twenty mosques) was negative. We later became aware that a good number of the imams from Ramadi had been killed or driven away by al Qaeda and replaced with their muftis.

An imam is a prayer leader and spiritual guide while a mufti is, in addition, a judge of Sharia (Islamic law) who may pronounce judgments as part of his sermons. (In fact, the concept of *mufti* is a relatively modern phenomenon and many moderate Muslims don't recognize the role as legitimate.) Many of the al Qaeda muftis used their Friday sermons as *dawa ela al jihad*, the "call to jihad." They beseeched their followers to enter the "jihad" against the crusaders and often described how Americans had come to Iraq to steal the oil and oppress the population at the behest of Zionists. In addition to hearing this vile trash during their Friday sermons, we often heard a *dawa ela al jihad* during attacks against our positions, with the speakers of the mosques closest to us coming to life while the enemy attacked. These sermons were illegal under Iraqi law, but neither we nor the Iraqi Security Forces were prepared to raid the mosques during Jamma and arrest the offending clerics, so we simply tracked the sermons and tried to counter the messages during our patrols.

On Friday, March 9, I was at COP Sword when the outpost's mosque-monitoring patrol returned very excited. The patrol leader and his interpreter, "Adam," entered the command post at Sword to make their report. None of our interpreters used their real names because doing so could bring retribution on their families. The vast majority of our interpreters were Iraqi nationals, and most hailed from areas outside al Anbar. A good number of them were Shia from Baghdad or the southern areas of Iraq. Adam was a twenty-two-year-old former college student who had majored in English literature at Baghdad University. His parents were both college professors and had urged him not to get involved with the ongoing war, but Adam was a true Iraqi patriot. I had had several discussions with him, since he was one of my favorite interpreters. On that day, Adam came into the command post and began to tell about a positive mosque message he had just heard. It was from a mosque in the recently cleared Masada Street area, and the theme of the imam's sermon was the story of Cain and Abel.

He spoke about how evil Cain slew his brother, and then he drew an analogy between Cain and Abel and the Iraqi Sunni and Shia population. He stressed to his congregation that the al Qaeda terrorists who co-opted the Sunni population were turning good, God-fearing Sunnis into Cains, and they were evilly slaying their own brothers, the Shia, who were like Abel. Adam had been in Ramadi for three years and had never heard a sermon condemning al Qaeda. He was very excited and felt, suddenly, optimistic about the future of his beloved nation. Adam and I had a brief but meaningful conversation that afternoon about the future of Ramadi and the future of Iraq. It was a truly enlightening experience for me and did much to improve my insight into the current state of affairs. I left COP Sword feeling that we had made our first significant inroad with the population and that this advance was a direct result of the increased exposure of the Iraqi police and soldiers to the population of Ramadi.

About three hours after our conversation, Adam went out with a patrol composed of a U.S. scout squad and six Iraqi policemen that ventured east down G Street toward the al Iskan District. The patrol was performing reconnaissance to find a house from which to set up an ambush to kill IED emplacers who had been using G Street to move toward COP Sword. About fifteen minutes into the movement, the patrol was ambushed by two teams of insurgents with Kalashnikovs, grenades, and medium machine guns. The initial contact left two soldiers injured. While the patrol attempted to suppress the enemy, Capt. Eric Beltz and Adam moved through the withering fire to evacuate the wounded. As Beltz, Adam, and the team's medic, Spc. Jarrod Pounds, reached the soldiers and began to pull them back to the remainder of the patrol, Adam was shot in the left shoulder, just above the ballistic plate in his vest. The bullet traveled through his chest, piercing his heart and right lung. Adam died in the arms of Eric Beltz and Jarrod Pounds. Pounds did all he could for Adam but to no avail, so he immediately focused on the other wounded. The patrol killed four insurgents during the attack. I felt Adam's loss nearly as keenly as if he were one of my soldiers. Although all of our interpreters were contractors and were very well compensated, it was clear to me that many did the job for reasons other than money. Adam's remains were to be airlifted that evening back to his parents in Baghdad.

All human remains were flown from Ramadi as quickly as possible (with the exception of the IPs whose families were in al Anbar). For U.S. remains, they were given a brief but poignant ceremony called a "hero flight," which occurred as the remains were moved from the graves registration building to the helipad about two hundred yards away. The ceremonies were simple events where soldiers, sailors, airmen, and Marines lined both sides of the trail as stretcher-bearers carried each soldier's body from the graves registration site to a waiting ambulance. Those gathered honored the procession by saluting the deceased as the body was loaded in the ambulance, then a chaplain offered a brief prayer. The attendees followed the ambulance at a walking pace while it moved to the helipad and again rendered honors as the body was moved into a helicopter. Historically, interpreters had not been given this honor but had been flown out with no pomp and circumstance as if they were cargo. Nor had they been given a memorial service. I broke that convention. Since there was to be no memorial service for Adam, I had Chaplain Kline put together a special hero flight. We combined elements of a memorial service with the hero flight ceremony. Adam was part of the unit, and though I felt his loss, so much more did the soldiers who lived and worked with him every day. They needed to say goodbye in order to refocus on their tasks, so we did.

Partners in Blue Shirts

At COP Falcon, Steel Company and the IPs of Forsan Station were building a close relationship. Diogo Tavares and Muhammed Zaidon were becoming great partners and good friends. In fact, the Forsan IPs were, unbeknownst to me, beginning to patrol on their own with Diogo's soldiers standing by as a reaction force. The response of the community to this patrolling was very positive, and the IPs were developing intelligence and making several arrests. On one of these patrols, IPs discovered and marked several IEDs, allowing us to send EOD teams to destroy them. Tavares told me about his development of IPs patrolling alone during one of my visits to COP Falcon, and I hit the roof. Although it was great initiative and was showing some success, I believed that it would lead to disaster because al Qaeda was more than capable of wiping one of these patrols out. If that happened, it would be a huge propaganda victory for AQI and would set us back months in our relationship with the Iraqi Security Forces. We developed guidelines for the support required for these patrols and continued to use IP-only patrols, but only with very close overwatch by U.S. patrols within weapons range and capable of bringing overwhelming force to bear if the IPs were attacked; and they were attacked.

The IPs worked on seven-day shifts, during which they slept at the station and worked roughly twelve hours a day. Most of the IPs who worked at Forsan lived in Jazeera, the wealthy, agricultural tribal area north of Ramadi that was the home of the Awakening movement and also housed the majority of the tribal sheiks who had begun to resist AQI in late 2006. So every seven days, like clockwork, five or six IP trucks would load up with about twenty IPs per truck and, with an escort provided by U.S. forces, travel from Jazeera into the heart of the city. We tried to get the IPs to vary their routine and maybe go randomly from five- to eight-day shifts in order to keep the enemy guessing, but they wouldn't hear of it. The result was fairly predictable: AQI attacked the patrol two times in our forty-five days in the city, and they were brutal. The attacks came at two different places along the route and involved multiple enemy positions, with the enemy firing Kalashnikovs, RPGs, and medium machine guns from second- and third-story positions directly down into the IP trucks. Both of the attacks resulted in serious IP casualties, with the total for both attacks being five WIA and two KIA. The IPs acquitted themselves very well during these attacks, returning withering fire and, in one case, overrunning one of the enemy firing positions leading to the capture of one terrorist and the death of four. The IPs in the city were becoming a force to be reckoned with and were having a big impact on all three sides of the tactical defeat mechanism: eroding enemy resources, destroying AQI capabilities, and truly beginning to isolate the population from the enemy.

As a direct result of this success, AQI launched an "information attack" from March 9 through March 12. The group spread a rumor that U.S. forces and Iraqi policemen had detained several Iraqi women during a raid and that the women were being held, incommunicado, at COP Sword. This attack first manifested itself to us on March 9 as a large demonstration that marched to the gates of COP Sword. The demonstration was peaceful. The crowd of about forty to sixty individuals descended on the front gate of COP Sword carrying signs, in English and Arabic, that said things like "coalition forces, please release the women." The crowd also chanted in Arabic for the "coalition to release the women." Simultaneously, the mosque closest to COP Sword erupted in a call to jihad. The message was, "Brave citizens: do not help the Iraqi Army or the police. They are the servants of the crusaders. Attack them and the coalition forces." The situation was quite tense and could easily have turned violent, but the leaders at COP Sword reacted well to the situation. Mike McBride put all his soldiers on alert and manned the roof fighting positions with both U.S. and Iraqi soldiers. Meanwhile, he moved to the front gate and asked a representative of the demonstrators to come inside the COP. The demonstrators refused and moved away from the COP. We watched on UAV as the group grew to about one hundred and marched through the city to the Abdul Rahman Mosque in al Iskan. Once they arrived, they loitered for about twenty minutes and then dissipated. I believe that the leaders of AQI wanted us to overreact to the situation. I also believe that they hoped for the crowd to become violent. They may have hoped for violence, but the discipline of my soldiers at COP Sword thwarted their effort. We won a small victory that day, and there was another demonstration on the 10th with a similar outcome.

Finally, on March 12, there was a third demonstration, larger and louder than the previous two. This time, a spokesman for the protesters approached COP Sword brandishing a white flag. Both Mike McBride and the new Iraqi company commander (the commander I had embarrassed about his filthy headquarters had been removed) met with the spokesman. He initially asked if there were female detainees at COP Sword. Both men assured him that we had no female detainees, nor had we detained any women since arriving in February. The spokesman then asked about a new barrier we had installed to reroute traffic onto the main roads where it could be monitored by security forces. He told Mike that the new barrier was inconvenient for the residents near COP Sword. Mike explained that we had installed the barrier to help keep AQI terrorists from having free transit across the city. Unhappy but satisfied with the answer, the spokesman rejoined the crowd, and the demonstrators moved away. Once again, we watched via UAV as they followed a march route that brought them to the Abdul Rahman Mosque, where they dispersed. Boring story? That's the point. AQI's attempt to discredit both U.S. and Iraqi forces and whip the population into a violent frenzy hadn't worked. In fact, it led to a rational and calm discussion between a U.S. Army leader, an

Iraqi Army leader, and a civilian in Ramadi.

With Mike McBride and Stan Balcer, as well as some of my very best junior leaders, at COP Sword, I could finally stop worrying about the position being overrun. I knew that there were not enough insurgents in Ramadi to do so with the team assembled there now. Diogo Tavares and his company were fully integrating their operations with the Forsan Police and seeing real results. Dennis Fitzgerald and his soldiers at COP Grant now had a smaller area to focus on and were showing more initiative than they had when they owned COPs Sword and Grant. Chris Hahn was still aggressively developing relationships in his areas, both with the Iraqi police who lived with him and with the locals who were now beginning to come out of their shells. But life was still very difficult for all of my companies, and the attacks didn't stop.

On March 14, at a little after noon, a tank pulled into the bullpen at COP Grant. It was the same tank crew that had lost Kelly Youngblood to a sniper nearly a month earlier. Kelly's replacement was new to the battalion. The flow of replacements from the United States was steady through our entire time in Iraq. Although my battalion deployed near full strength, we had already been depleted by over ten soldiers just from those wounded in action, and two who had been killed. Also, we had lost a few more to "normal" things that occur wherever you are, such as death or serious injury of an immediate family member that requires a soldier to return to the States. So, we had already received a large group of replacements. Randy Sumner and I briefed every new soldier who came to the battalion. My rule was that—in addition to a few briefings about the threat, how we conducted our operations, what the IEDs looked like in Ramadi, and the like—no new soldier could go "out in sector" until he or she had been through a newcomers' briefing with Randy and me. I spoke for about thirty minutes about my "commander's intent" for the campaign, stressing that we needed to win the support of the population. I discussed the tactical defeat mechanism with every new soldier, whether he or she was a brand-new private or a new platoon sergeant with twenty years in the Army, and that's where I first met Forrest J. Waterbury.

Forrest (John to his family) was a great addition to the unit. He was experienced, motivated, and friendly, and was fitting in with his crew and his platoon very well. He had been assigned to the unit very shortly after we deployed but had to complete a series of training courses and events at Fort Stewart before joining us in Ramadi. Forrest had had a few issues at his previous unit, but nothing serious. My sense is that he ran afoul of some junior leader there, which made his work there difficult. However, he loved 3-69 Armor. His wife told me that from the time he arrived he felt at home, as if he were part of a team. He had been impressed with the leaders and soldiers and with the state of discipline and the family feel of the unit. I had seen Forrest at the newcomers' brief and once more at COP Grant since his arrival. The third time I saw Forrest John Waterbury was at Charlie Med. He was dead when he was pulled out of the Bradley that had evacuated him, but the doctors and medics of Charlie Med tried their best to revive him. His wound was nearly identical to Kelly Youngblood's. As Forrest exited the tank on March 14, a sniper's bullet penetrated his helmet in the same place as the one that struck Kelly Youngblood's. The same sniper had now killed two of my soldiers, and we were no closer to killing him.

I threw every asset I had into the effort to kill that sniper. I ordered patrols to find his firing positions and canvass everyone living near where we believed he shot from. I pulled all of my sniper teams, who were executing missions all over Ramadi, in from the other companies and consolidated them at COP Grant with orders to spend all their effort trying to find and kill the sniper who was menacing my soldiers. I didn't know it until months later, but while I was doing everything I could, MNF-W, with its headquarters in Fallujah, had recently received a plethora of counter-sniper technologies. Although I had lost two soldiers in thirty days to a sniper, I didn't see a single piece of technology from them. In fact, it was late March before I even knew the systems existed. The first time I saw one of those systems in person, it was on General Gurganus' truck. Although I'm sure he didn't intentionally keep the technology from me, I'm quite sure that he never went to his staff to see how he could help either. Nor did the Raider staff do anything to help. Not one member of that staff contacted me to ask how they could help us find and kill that sniper or what they could do to help us fortify our positions—not once! Not one sergeant called to say that there were new counter-sniper tools in the U.S. Army arsenal. Not one officer called with a tactic or technology that might work—they were far too busy building briefings for Colonel

Charlton to be bothered with anything as trivial as that.

The next day, one of my counter-sniper patrols found several prepared sniper positions overlooking COP Sword. The positions were in two adjacent abandoned buildings three blocks over from our COP. The wall between the buildings had been breached to allow shooters to move from building to building without going outside or through any existing door or window. One could enter the building from the ground floor with no fear of being seen from any U.S. position. In the building closest to COP Sword (maybe 175 yards), there were two prepared positions. The first position was a built-up platform about three feet off the floor of a corner room. Two small holes, about eight inches in diameter, had been punched through the wall adjacent to the plywood platform. The platform was padded and had a shooter's rest built in; it was clearly designed for a sniper. On the roof of the building were several holes cut in the parapet that would allow insurgents to engage Sword from the roof but behind the cover of the knee wall. In the adjacent building on the side facing COP Sword, behind a broken-out window, hung a piece of cardboard, painted black, with a small hole cut out facing the COP—clearly this position was for a spotter who would have called out targets and passed them either by voice or by radio to the sniper in the adjacent building.

These were two buildings out of the roughly eighty to one hundred from which one would have a clear view of COP Sword. One may ask, "Why not just raze the buildings from which you can see into COP Sword?" Logical question, but doing so would have been a huge propaganda victory for AQI. Although the buildings with the prepared positions were abandoned, nearby buildings were still occupied by families, who were not complicit in the attacks. So if we razed all the buildings, we would have displaced maybe thirty or forty families; multiply that by our four positions, and it probably totals upwards of six hundred people we would have displaced. Every action in counterinsurgency must be weighed against its potential damage to the population; it would have been too costly and would have potentially caused more harm than good. The choice that I made, however right it may have been, was painful to live with.

Unfortunately, one more soldier would give his life in order to let those Iraqi families keep their homes. This time the soldier was a tanker from COP Sword. Late in the afternoon of March 21, another tank crew prepared to dismount its machine. COP Sword was big enough for tanks and Bradleys to fit inside the position, but, as described, there were buildings blocks away that could give one a view into the COP. We had set ambushes on the sniper position that the patrol on March 15 had found, but with no luck. Again, the enemy had an excellent network to know where we were and when we were there. Insurgents had simply adjusted their plans and set up a different sniper location, this time on the northeastern side of the COP. As the tank crew dismounted, a storm of small arms fire rained into COP Sword. The tower guards were engaged from at least three separate locations; they immediately began to return fire. As that shootout occurred, another well-aimed shot went through the side of a tanker's helmet. This time it was Sgt. Adrian Lewis, whose four children lost their father that day. Adrian Lewis' best friend and immediate supervisor, Staff Sgt. Demitrie Lott, struggled with the rest of his crew to evacuate Adrian, but it was too late. Once again, I waited at Charlie Med for Adrian to arrive. I had seen over thirty of my soldiers brought into Charlie Med by now, and I was nearly sure that Sergeant Lewis would be dead. This was the fourth death we suffered, three of them from the same sniper. I've only cried, in public, twice in combat. That day, while I waited in the ambulance bay, was the first time. I walked to the far side of the ambulance bay and wept. In all my life, I have never felt as helpless as I did that moment. Nor had I ever felt more culpable for the death of a soldier. I still don't know what more I could have done, but I'm sure there was something. Chaplain Nathan Kline saw me and, after a few moments, walked over to comfort me. I simply told him, "I don't know how long I can do this."

A City Sheik

Sometime between Specialist Waterbury's death and Sergeant Lewis' death, I received a call from Lt. Col. Bear Johnson, whose Steel Tiger battalion owned the west side of Ramadi. He had been at Sheik Sittar's house one day when he was approached by a young sheik named Khattab of the Abu Alwan tribe. The Alwan tribe had several areas primarily west of the city and south of the Euphrates, but the tribe also had a high concentration in the suburbs and in the city. In fact, the Alwani sheik of sheiks had lived in Ramadi before the troubles began. His compound, large and once splendid, was about three blocks north of COP Falcon. Sheik Khattab was his son.

He wanted to get back into his home (in the compound) and rebuild the damaged buildings, so he wanted to meet with me. I told Bear I'd be happy to meet with Khattab, and within a few days we pulled off the meeting.

Sheik Khattab was probably in his late twenties, was slightly overweight, smoked cigarettes like there was no tomorrow, and wore a huge "gold-tone" watch. He also carried a big-ass gun and was fairly full of shit. In other words, he was not unusual for an Iraqi sheik. We met at the city government center downtown. Sheik Khattab was accompanied by two Iraqi police officers, a captain and a first lieutenant who were genuine. (There were lots of pseudo-police—more about that later.) For a sheik, Khattab was fairly quick to get to the point—he wanted to bring about thirty Alwani policemen in from the West Ramadi IP Station and set up an IP station in his father's compound. He would clear the entire district of al Hawz (about fifteen blocks) and take responsibility for everything that happened there. Because Bear met him at Sittar's place, he had some credibility; but still, I was skeptical. I told him that I had a police station right down the road from his father's compound, so all he had to do was move in and start rebuilding. He told me, in so many words, "I met your IPs, and they are idiots; I prefer my own, thanks." I wanted to have Khattab as a partner but knew that I couldn't just build a police station on my own. I explained to him that I would need to negotiate his proposal with my boss and with the Ramadi chief of police, Brig. Gen. Khalil Abu Ali Jassim. We agreed to meet again, and I went to work trying to get approval for a new police station.

Dawa Ela al Horea

The original plan for the clearance of al Iskan included only my battalion and Craig Kaczynski's 2/5 Marines. My boys would have cleared the routes and provided blocking positions on every road that went through the district while the 2/5 Marines conducted the house-to-house searches with support from Iraqi forces. As we finished the plan for the clearance of al Iskan, however, the operation grew. Lieutenant Colonel Chuck Ferry and his Manchu battalion volunteered to perform the majority of the on-the-ground clearance; that is, they would be the ones inside the district going building to building searching for insurgents and their resources—bombs, rifles, RPGs, money, etc. Units from the 1st Iraqi Army Brigade, which were partnered with Ferry's battalion at the time, would work hand in hand with Ferry's soldiers. Roger Turner's 1/6 Marines would provide a couple of checkpoints north of al Iskan along Route Michigan to limit movement into and out of the area. My battalion would be responsible for isolating the entire area by clearing routes in and barricading all those routes with concrete obstacles and concertina wire, which would allow us to completely shut down all vehicular traffic into and out of the district and ensure that we could monitor all foot traffic in and out.

Under the adjusted plan, Kaczynski's Marines had multiple tasks as they came in to replace my battalion. First, they would take over my positions at all four COPs and then build several new positions that would secure his main routes the way the single-vehicle OPs that I manned secured ours. As I wrote before, 2/5 Marines had no tanks or Bradleys and therefore couldn't use vehicles to keep routes safe from IEDs and ambushes; but Kaczynski did have lots of infantry. The plan that Craig's staff and mine developed in conjunction was that he would strongpoint houses near my OPs and man these new OPs with infantry squads in order to provide the same level of security on the routes. The second task that we would accomplish jointly was to build those new positions. Finally, once al Iskan was secure, Kaczynski was going to build a new COP for his Marines in conjunction with a police station on 20th Street, less than five hundred yards from the Abdul Rahman Mosque, the capitol of al Qaeda's Islamic State of Iraq.

Much had changed since the planning for the operation began a month earlier, but several things remained the same. We would use the surge of incoming and outgoing forces to overwhelm the enemy, entering and clearing the last major safe haven in Ramadi and crushing the Islamic State of Iraq. The operation would be the largest the city had seen and would involve over 1,000 Iraqi security forces and about 2,500 U.S. forces (a few more if one counted supporting and minor roles). My staff had named the mission *Dawa ela al Horea*, poking fun at the al Qaeda calls to jihad so often heard from the mosque speakers. Our operation translated as "Call to Freedom," and the name stuck.

Call to Freedom was a great example of the kinetic and non-kinetic marriage used in the operations that we conducted in 2007 and 2008. Clearly, we would use obstacles and our presence to provoke the enemy and to force a fight, causing significant personnel and capability losses that would impact AQI's ability to organize and resist in Ramadi. Just as important, though, was communicating with the population of the city. First, we had extensive information products ready to distribute to the population, ranging from flyers to loudspeaker broadcasts to a message carried by every one of my leaders as well as all of the Iraqi police. The message was simple: "It's time to stand up for what is morally right and remove the murdering terrorists from your neighborhoods. Both coalition and Iraqi Security Forces are here to stay and will not allow the terrorists back into your neighborhoods." We even received help from Brigadier General Khalil, who brought his own bawdy, backroom language to the message, often questioning the sexual preference of terrorists and the sexual habits of their female family members in his loudspeaker pitches (political correctness has not yet hit Iraq). Mayor Latif, who still owed us a debt of gratitude for the garbage trucks, recorded a tamer message explaining to the population that their dark days were over and that they could expect to begin receiving city services shortly. His message also referred them to his office if they needed to file a claim for damages resulting from the clearance operation. In addition to the information message, we brought real help in the form of food, water, blankets, heaters, fuel, and various other "humanitarian assistance" that both we and the Iraqi Security Forces could distribute.

On March 18, 2007, my battalion increased the tempo of operations like raids, searches, and route clearances toward the al Iskan District. The idea was to get the enemy fighters off balance and worried while making them believe we had no intention of entering al Iskan for these operations. This increase in tempo caused a peak in enemy contacts. On the evening of March 19, Dennis Fitzgerald's Battle Company had a pitched engagement with a substantial enemy force just between COP Grant and al Iskan. The fight started while two Bradleys were conducting a relief at the OP that overwatched the intersection of Baseline and 20th Street. As the incoming Bradley crew moved into position, crewmembers spotted two speed-bump IEDs between them and the Bradley they were to relieve. This was only five hundred yards south of the area where the enemy had emplaced the plethora of IEDs during the garbage truck mission, so everyone was prepared for the worst. Both Bradleys needed to stay in place until we could get EOD on site to detonate the IEDs. In order to secure the area more completely, Dennis committed his quick reaction force (QRF) of two more Bradleys and alerted his two tank crews (Dennis only had half a tank platoon—the other half was at COP Sword with Mike McBride) to prepare to deploy, if needed. They would be.

The Bradley commander in the lead vehicle in the reaction force was then–Staff Sergeant Jose Rodriguez. Rod, as we called him, is an incredible leader. At the time, he was the Battle Company master gunner—the commander's key advisor on all technical and tactical aspects of the Bradley Fighting Vehicle. In that role, he spent a good deal of time with me both during our train-up and during our time in Ramadi. Rod is a true expert on both infantry dismounted tactics and employment of Bradleys in an infantry role. In addition to his qualification as a master gunner (no easy feat, the Bradley master gunner's course had a high failure rate), he was also a trained sniper (also one of the most difficult Army schools). Rod is a genuine genius—I would guess he sports an IQ in the mid-120s—but he wears it very well. Rod never came across as nerdy or overly contemplative. I had seen Rod a day or two earlier and was concerned about his well-being. You see, he had the dubious distinction of having been blown up more than anyone in the task force; he had lost three Bradleys to IEDs since arriving in Ramadi. Several soldiers in Battle Company affectionately referred to Rod as "Shit Magnet." When I saw him days earlier, he was limping from a minor back injury and had been knocked unconscious by one IED. He was a wreck, physically and mentally. Rod was tough, but there is only so much one can take . . . and he was about to be blown up a fourth time.

As his vehicle rolled up to secure the near side of the IEDs that had been previously spotted, he rolled right over one that had been missed. The speed bump was hidden in a mud puddle in the sewage-filled road. The blast was right under the engine compartment in the Bradley and caused a shower of sewage to cover the front half of the vehicle while it breached the hull and broke the engine. As the hot engine leaked its oil and fuel, it began to smolder, threatening to burst into flames and filling the crew compartment with caustic, acrid smoke.

Most guys in Rod's place might have hunkered down, safe in their Bradley, or, fearing the fire, evacuated using the vehicle for cover and waited to be rescued. Jose Rodriguez isn't most guys, though. What he did won him yet another distinction in the task force: He became the only soldier from my battalion to win the Silver Star. His gunner, next to him in the turret, was okay, but he could hear his driver, whose seat was right next to the engine, coughing and gasping for air. Rod exited the turret and pulled his driver out of the smoke from the burning engine. He assessed that the vehicle was still safe, at least for now. The second Bradley from the QRF returned to COP Grant to lead the recovery vehicle to Rod's position. As it turned around, it struck an IED. Then, all hell broke loose. Twenty to twenty-five insurgents moved through buildings into positions to engage the two disabled Bradleys. As the members of the second Bradley crew evacuated their vehicle, the insurgents opened fire with medium machine guns and Kalashnikovs. Both Bradley crews on the OP saw the enemy and opened fire with machine guns and 25mm cannons, but the enemy's positions in the concrete building were too tough. For the next ten to fifteen minutes, the Bradleys and insurgents exchanged fire. Rod's Bradley was still able to engage and joined in the fight. The damaged Bradleys were too close to the insurgents to use F-18 air support, so we requested helicopter support for the fight, but it wouldn't get there in time.

While the Bradleys fought, two tanks left COP Grant with the recovery vehicle. Rod's Bradley was getting worse; it lost power. Rodriguez moved outside the Bradley in order to prepare the vehicle for recovery. He could hear but not yet see the tanks and recovery vehicle. The enemy fire had, for the moment, subsided; they, too, could hear the tanks and wanted to finish this fight. As Rod surveyed the terrain behind his vehicle, an IED went off in front of his vehicle. He peered around his Bradley and saw a group of insurgents crouching and crawling toward his position. The lead two insurgents had a couple of speed-bump IEDs each and were preparing to throw them toward Rod's track. He opened fire with his M4 rifle, killing the two almost instantly. Their "support team" behind them opened fire on Rod. When the shooting stopped, eight insurgents lay dead in front of him, and several more had run back toward the building. The tank crews had seen most of this exchange, and as the insurgents entered the building, they unleashed two main-gun rounds each.

As the dust cleared, the pulverized, smoking building collapsed, and a total of eleven more insurgents were dead. Once again, nothing ends a disagreement like a tank! The engagement lasted ninety minutes and cost us two Bradleys. Fortunately, we had no one seriously injured in the fight. The enemy emplaced six IEDs during the fight, and there were four more carried by the insurgents Rodriguez killed. Nineteen insurgents died. It was a good night. The next major attack came a few days later.

On March 20, the Marines from 2/5 began moving their leaders out to the COPs. During all this increased activity and throughout the clearing of al Iskan, both my battalion and Kaczynski's had multiple procedures going on. We were moving out to Jazeera and moving my headquarters to a new operating base. Craig and his Marines were arriving in Iraq, receiving their equipment and training, and moving in to replace us. On the afternoon of March 23, we were scheduled to begin the route clearances into al Iskan, and by 6:00 a.m. on the 24th, we were to have our blocking positions in place and the area isolated for Chuck Ferry's Manchus to begin the clearance. The afternoon of the 23rd was busy for us all. Knight, Battle, and Steel Companies all made final preparations for what would be seven days of twenty-four-hour operations with little time for rest. At COP Sword, Hellcat Company made other preparations.

As the Marines moved into Sword, we planned to expand it so they could put a larger force there. Eric Beltz and his scout platoon led several of the Marine leaders on a recon of potential positions that could be integrated into the COP. The patrol left COP Sword about 11:00 a.m., and by 1:00 p.m., patrol members were in a set of abandoned buildings just across the street to the east of COP Sword along a flooded, sewage-filled section of road we called Thunder Road. The buildings had been a school and a medical clinic. They were relatively intact and would make an excellent extension to COP Sword. They would also have great value as a project to restore both the school and the clinic, once we were able to think about rebuilding. This put us on the horns of a dilemma: Should we take the property and have a great expansion for the COP, or leave it for an indeterminate time when Ramadi would be, once again, ready for schools and clinics? This was a tough choice, but AQI, in one stroke, solved the dilemma.

As patrol members looked through the buildings, the soldiers in the guard towers on the roof of COP Sword overwatched the road. Thunder Road wasn't used by anyone. The sewage lake at the front of COP Sword, as I wrote earlier, was easily four feet deep, and it dumped right into Thunder Road. I assume the road was paved, but I never saw its surface. While the soldiers in the guard towers watched, a team of insurgents moved through a labyrinth of buildings and walled compounds to get into positions. Suddenly, the towers were engaged by RPGs and machine guns from seven different buildings along Thunder Road. Apparently, the attack was aimed at COP Sword, and the terrorists were unaware of the patrol in the buildings on the south side of the street. For various reasons, COP Sword had more heavy machine guns than any other position. Instantly, three of them returned fire, quickly joined by a Bradley 25mm cannon, and the fight was on. The members of the patrol moved to the closest edge of the adjacent compound trying to find positions from which they could join the fight, and about two minutes into the firefight, a bongo truck turned onto Thunder Road.

The Kia Bongo is an Asian pickup truck with a cab that looks like it belongs on an old minivan and a wide truck bed with short, panel sides and a short tailgate. Such vehicles are ubiquitous in Iraq, but this was not your run-of-the-mill Bongo truck. It looked like a pickup truck built for "mud-bogging" near my home in Georgia. The truck had been fitted with extra suspension and big tires in order to navigate its way through the cesspool. As it turned onto the road, it accelerated directly toward the entrance to COP Sword. Instantly perceiving the threat, the machine guns on the roof began to engage the truck. One of those guns, manned by Pvt. 1st Class Sixto Garcia, scored several hits on the cab of the truck; however, unbeknownst to him, the truck had been modified there too. The cab of the truck was fitted with thick steel plate to protect the suicidal driver. Whether Garcia's fire had killed the driver or merely disabled the truck, we'll never know. In the back of the truck was an estimated six hundred to one thousand pounds of explosives, and as Garcia hit the truck repeatedly, it exploded before it could reach COP Sword.

The force of the explosion was substantial. It knocked Garcia, who was five hundred yards from the truck, out of his tower, and he landed on the roof of COP Sword about six feet below. Had that truck reached the COP, it would have completely destroyed the building, wounding or killing most of the forty soldiers and twenty Marines inside. However, we had not escaped unscathed. The blast had leveled the wall of the compound and damaged the buildings where Eric Beltz and his patrol had been moving into positions to engage. The wall collapsed onto several soldiers, causing serious injuries to two of them and knocking three others unconscious. Worse yet, with no wall left, the members of the patrol were completely exposed to the insurgents who were now well aware of their presence. As Eric rallied his forces, Garcia stood up, still dazed, with his glasses broken and face bleeding, and manned his machine gun, bringing brutal fire onto two of the insurgent positions while directing another machine-gunner onto the remaining ones. His actions allowed Belz and his patrol time to evacuate their wounded to safe locations, and ultimately, the combined fire from the patrol, the Bradley, and the towers drove the remaining terrorists off. We had suffered five wounded in action including "Doc" Jarrod Pounds, Eric's medic, who had both of his legs badly broken when the wall collapsed. Six terrorists had died in their failed attempt to destroy COP Sword. For their actions that day, both Sixto Garcia and Eric Beltz received the Bronze Star for Valor.

Less than two hours later, Operation Call to Freedom began in earnest. At 3:00 p.m., the Pathfinder teams from 321 Engineers linked up with Steel and Knight for their final briefings, and at dark, they began clearing the routes into al Iskan and the Widows' District. Our big concern was not speed-bump IEDs; we had encountered hundreds of them, and although they caused significant equipment damage, they were rarely lethal. I was worried about large buried IEDs . . . and it wasn't long before my fears materialized. Just a short distance east of where the truck bomb had exploded earlier that day, the Pathfinder team with Steel hit a large IED with a Buffalo.

The Buffalo is the most mine-resistant vehicle in the U.S. Army's inventory and one of the most mine-resistant in the world. It can drive away from all but the most serious blasts with the crew intact, but even it was no match for this four-hundred-pound monster IED. The Buffalo was thrown about thirty feet, and the entire crew was beat up by the blast. The vehicle commander, a young staff sergeant, suffered a broken femur and a concussion. Within an hour, however, the mission continued. By 4:00 a.m., Steel and Knight had occupied about half of their blocking positions, and Adrian Bailey's Atlas Company (my support company) was beginning to lay in the concrete barriers that would completely block the west side of al Iskan and the Widows' District. At first light, al Iskan was isolated, and Chuck Ferry's soldiers, along with his Iraqi partners, began to clear the last AQI safe haven in the city of Ramadi. Chuck Krumwiede in his Bradley and I in my tank trooped the line that morning. I drove down 20th Street where I had tanks and Bradleys occupying places that had been al Qaeda territory twenty-four hours earlier. I rode through the Widows' Quarter that was now locked down by Knight's tanks and Bradleys. After my first pass, the thing that was missing was Iraqi police. So I spoke to my commanders and told them to get their IPs out. We also made some adjustments to our positions and our obstacles. Ferry's force was having some enemy contact and lost a few Iraqi soldiers to small arms fire, but things were going well overall.

On my trip down 20th Street the next day, I could not believe my eyes. The place was crawling with IPs, both in their trucks and on foot. The population had responded enormously. They were out and about, including children, talking to my soldiers, talking to IPs, and just going about their business. My third trip down 20th Street was in my humvee. In sixty days, my PSD had done all three things the Bandits said we wouldn't do in a year: we had stopped many times in the city to talk to shop owners and residents, so often that some knew us by sight. We had eaten meals with Iraqis more than once. And now, we had driven our humvees down 20th Street!

Operation Call to Freedom spanned from March 23 to April 6. Although there were some attacks and casualties, and we didn't kill the hundreds of terrorists we had hoped to, it was one of the most successful operations in all of Iraqi Freedom. Prior to March 23, 2007, U.S. forces in Ramadi averaged over twenty attacks a day. In April 2007, there were fewer than sixty attacks for the month. The Marines of 2/5 replaced us and did excellent work. Within a few weeks, Sheik Khattab's IP station was open, and there were IPs on every street corner in our old area. They could now go out on patrol without being attacked at every turn. By June of that year, U.S. forces were attacked in the city at the astoundingly diminished rate of once every eight days.

Clearly, the Islamic State of Iraq, if it still existed, had moved away from Ramadi. But the question was, where had it gone?

CHAPTER 11

Out to Jazeera

Iraq is divided into eighteen provinces or states, each one is further sub-divided into municipalities, and each municipality is subdivided into districts. I've already described several of the districts in Ramadi within the city limits—al Iskan, for example. Though it is the largest (in area, not population) district within the municipality of Ramadi, Jazeera is outside the city limits. I suppose the closest American analogy would be to think of Jazeera as an unincorporated suburb of Ramadi. Literally, *al Jazeera* is Arabic for "the island," and that is a fairly apt description of the al Jazeera district of Ramadi. The district is generally bounded by the Euphrates River on the south and west, the Thar Thar Canal on the east, and Lake Thar Thar on the north. These canals are not small ditches but rather grand canals the size of small rivers. Jazeera is one of the most fertile and productive farming areas in the Middle East and has been constantly farmed since the dawn of agriculture around 8,000 BC. The population centers in Jazeera range from fairly dense, modern suburbs that house some of the wealthiest businessmen and professionals in al Anbar Province to rural farming villages that have changed little in the last couple of centuries.

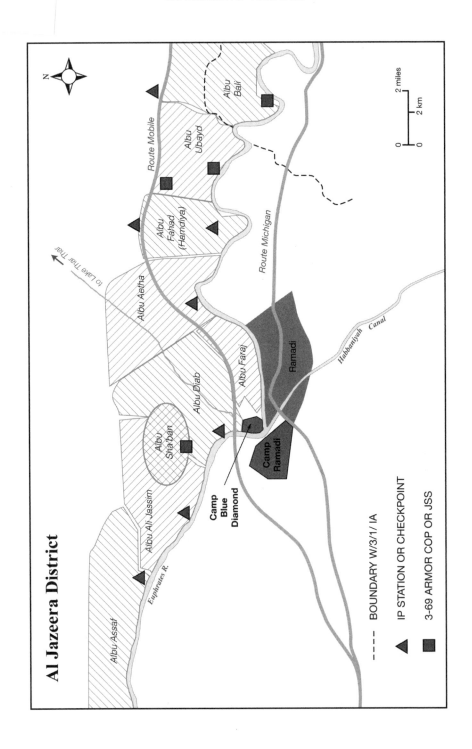

Al Jazeera District

The city of Ramadi was ugly, with its fetid streets and buildings crumbling from the nonstop combat, and it festered with the diseases of war, poverty, and hatred. The population was disconnected, fragmented into factions and downtrodden. Jazeera stood in stark contrast. Although Jazeera had been touched by war, the pockmarked buildings and cratered roads could not detract from the pastoral beauty of the place. One needn't try too hard to imagine Jazeera without war, and many of the farms and sprawling manors had actually remained above the fray. The people of Jazeera were just as different, for although they had been affected by the war as the land had been, they wore their struggles well. Many families, if not the majority (remember, they have large, extended families), had lost a loved one either to the terrorists or the Americans, or both. The people of Jazeera, however, were very well connected to their land and to their tribes, and even during the war's worst times they didn't live in constant fear (with some exceptions that I'll discuss later). When one drove through Jazeera, it was not at all unusual to see women and children attending to their chores or merely enjoying their otherwise normal lives. Smiles and waves were not rationed in Jazeera, and, indeed, we learned to judge the extent to which an area may still be susceptible to the influence of al Qaeda by the reception we received from the children.

Al Jazeera is home to eight subtribes of the Dulaime Confederation and three non-Dulaime tribes. The Dulaime Confederation is a large group of tribes that has members living in Iraq, Syria, Jordan, Saudi Arabia, Bahrain, Qatar, and the UAE. They count their tribal home, however, in Iraq, where they range from the Syrian border east along the Euphrates River into Baghdad Province and north up the Tigris River into Diyala Province, with another area of Dulaime presence in Saladin Province around Bayji. Debate exists within Iraq over whether or not the confederation is the largest tribe in Iraq, since the Jabouri tribe also claims to be Iraq's largest. Be that as it may, the confederation is huge and accounts for at least half of the Anbari population. The three non-Dulaime tribes in Jazeera are Abu Fahad, Abu Mahal, and Abu Obaid. The Abu Fahad consider themselves the largest "single" tribe in al Anbar, although they recognize that the Dulaime *Confederation* outnumbers them. The Abu Obaid tribe is one of the oldest in Iraq and lends its name to a major period in ancient Mesopotamian history.

The farms in Jazeera are mostly primitive in their techniques and equipment, and the majority of the farming is done with hand tools. Tractors are rare. The irrigation systems are much the same as they must have been a thousand years ago, except that the diesel engine has mostly replaced donkey power to run pumps. Each community has a large pumping station that pulls water either from the Euphrates or from one of the major irrigation canals. The main canals are concrete and up to fifty feet wide. When pumped to full capacity, they can be as deep as twenty feet. Each major farm uses a smaller pump to bring water into hand-made, mud-sided irrigation ditches that then bring the water to each row of crops. The smaller ditches need constant maintenance and are rebuilt every season because the harvest process destroys the ditches. Each farm also has a series of drainage ditches that keep salt from building up on the land. The irrigation system flows straight river water, unfit for any other purpose. The beautiful Euphrates River retains its deep green color because of its high level of organic matter that provides an excellent source of food for algae. Although this water is nasty, it is all that some of the poorer people in Jazeera have, so they use it for everything, which can lead to afflictions ranging from really nasty skin rashes to cholera. Half a mile from the nearest river or canal you're in barren desert, but still there are occasional houses. These houses belong to the other farmers of Jazeera, those who raise animals, mostly sheep, goats, and donkeys. Some of these modest homes in the middle of arid stretches of desert have flocks of several hundred sheep grazing in what first appears to be just sand. A closer look shows small grasses and succulent plants that thrive with nearly no water.

I have never been a big fan of cities, and Ramadi had so many reasons for me to hate it that coming out to Jazeera did much for my outlook on life. It's not that we were no longer at war because certainly we still were, but the space and light of Jazeera were good for my mind, and for most of my soldiers. As most of my soldiers finished up their last few days in the city, under the command of Craig Kaczynski, my command group moved to its new home at Camp Blue Diamond (CBD). CBD was literally just across the Euphrates River from Camp Ramadi, but it was a world away. It had been the capital compound for al Anbar Province prior to the war; therefore, it was large, state of the art (for Iraq), and in an idyllic location, sitting right on the banks of the Euphrates. The centerpiece of the camp was a huge palace that had formerly served as both the personal residence for the governor and the capitol of al Anbar. The camp also came with a series of large villas right on the water, complete with boat docks and huge waterfront verandas, and a series of solidly built buildings along the main road through the camp, which went its way through a pair of huge, ornate arches complete with guard towers on top. All the roads on CBD were paved and in very good repair. The "Angel Arch" in the center of the camp was five stories high and commanded a view of several miles of Jazeera.

After the initial invasion in 2003, the camp became headquarters to the Marine division in al Anbar, but after the second battle of Fallujah, division leaders decided to move to Fallujah. (The reasons they moved made no sense, but that is another story.) Their loss was our gain. Although the camp was a little worse for the wear and covered in junk, there was nothing we couldn't fix. I sent Sgt. Maj. Ray Curtis over several weeks before the move with a small team to work with Cliff Wheeler's 5th Squadron, 7th Cavalry (Warpaint), the unit we would replace, to ensure that we would have a smooth transition.

I had ventured into Jazeera twice before I was ordered to move there. The first trip was to attend a funeral (actually the mourning period after the funeral) for a nephew of Brigadier General Khalil (the Ramadi chief of police). The second trip was to visit my A Company, which had been detached to Cliff Wheeler's outfit. Those trips helped Chuck Krumwiede and me begin to develop our plan for how we would organize and what we would focus on for this mission. Once ordered to Jazeera, I made one more recon, which allowed us to finalize the plan. Our relief of the Warpaint Squadron was to be abbreviated; instead of the standard ten days, we would only use six. One day after I arrived in Jazeera, my company commanders would move there and begin their transition. As we moved out of the city, we made the first change to company commanders. Dennis Fitzgerald had reached one year in command, and I chose to have Matt McCreary replace him. So, in addition to the transition from the city to Jazeera, my B Company would also transition to a new commander.

Compared to my area in Ramadi, Jazeera was huge. It was about thirty-five miles wide (east–west) and fifteen miles deep (north–south). Running through most of the area was the main highway that connected Baghdad to Syria, a six-lane divided highway complete with 120-ton overpasses, steel guardrails, and eight-foot shoulders that we called Route Mobile. From a construction standpoint, Route Mobile could have been an interstate highway anywhere in the United States. It ran generally parallel to the Euphrates River, which bounded my area to the south and west. Adjacent to CBD, the Euphrates took a northerly turn and ran north and south for about five miles, making it my western boundary for that stretch. There, where the river turned, Route Mobile passed over the river on a six-lane, twin-span, modern bridge about three hundred yards long and standing two hundred feet off the water. In the east, about three miles outside my boundary, the highway passed over a smaller bridge at the Thar Thar Canal, leaving al Jazeera. Both the highway and the river played huge roles in the lives of Jazeera residents. In fact, a good deal of the population lived between the river and the highway (which were separated by less than two miles in most places). Most of the remaining residents lived within ten miles of the northern bank of the river.

Camp Blue Diamond was located right at the bend in the river, putting it less than two miles from the highway and just west of center in our area. Surrounding CBD, adjacent to the highway, was the home of the Abu[20] Diyab[21] tribe. The Albu Diyab tribal area[22] was one of the most suburban in Jazeera. It had few farms but instead was a wide belt of middle-class and upper-middle-class neighborhoods dotted by the homes of the very wealthy. There were no slums in Albu Diyab and only an occasional poorer family abode. The area had both boys' and girls' grade schools, a middle school, and a high school. Albu Diyab had several market areas, some of a general nature and some including specific categories of shops. The population of Albu Diyab was generally well educated (high school graduates and above) and relatively well employed. As did many of the tribes, the Diyabis (plural for members of the tribe Abu Diyab) experienced turbulence with their sheiks from 2003–2007. The man I came to know as the sheik of the Abu Diyab tribe (and the man I would later consider my sheik) was Sheik Muhammed Farhan al Heiss al Diyabi, or simply, to most who knew him, Sheik Heiss.

Sheik Heiss had two older brothers and one younger. The eldest brother suffered from significant mental retardation and mental illness. Although he could carry on a conversation, it was barely at the adult level and clearly not grounded in reality. Muhammed loved his brother and treated him well, caring for him as if he were a son, but he kept him out of sight most of the time. The next oldest Heiss brother was the sheik immediately preceding Muhammed, but he was slain by al Qaeda in 2006, leaving Muhammed to fill in as the sheik of the tribe.

Muhammed is a contemplative, bright, kind-hearted man who truly cares for the well being of the tribe and all the residents of Jazeera. He received some college education but no degree. Before 2003, he had served as a traffic cop in Ramadi and had always run a business of one sort or another on the side. Sheik Heiss was, most of all, a businessman who understood how to turn a buck (or a dinar, as the case may be) like few I've met before or since. I met him in his capacity as the president of the Jazeera Council, an unofficial adjunct to the city government of Ramadi. In early 2007, the Ramadi city government was a mess. The fledgling institution had a mayor and a cabinet with a few administrative branches that were functional, but not many. The city had just seated a city council, and several of the larger suburbs had formed supporting councils to address neighborhood issues and present them to the government. These councils really formed the backbone of the local government and provided the link between the official government and the people. As you'll recall, true democracy was a new thing in Iraq and, as one would expect, a real struggle. The Jazeera Council was one of the first of these advisory organizations to stand up. It was composed of about fifteen members with about half coming from the three most prominent tribes in the area: Abu Diyab, Abu Ali Jassim, and Abu Assaf. The council met regularly and focused on three areas: security, economic development, and infrastructure improvement.

My first meeting with Sheik Heiss was the day before the Jazeera Council meeting for April 2007. Cliff Wheeler brought me there as part of the transition process. Cliff had built a relationship with Heiss during his time in Jazeera, as had his predecessor. In the sixty days that Cliff had spent there, he had between a dozen and a score of meetings with Heiss, and Cliff expressed that he felt they were on the cusp of making some breakthroughs in Jazeera. They had only had two or three previous Jazeera Council meetings, and those had been somewhat contentious and disorganized; really nothing more than a chance for the sheiks on the council (who were nearly all general contractors and businessmen) to propose projects they could bid on to "make Jazeera better."

In counterinsurgency, as I have previously written, money is a very powerful weapon. Recognizing that, in 2003, the U.S. Army and DoD developed the Commander's Emergency Relief Program (CERP). CERP was designed to help commanders on the ground impact the populations of their areas directly through short-term, preferably immediate, projects designed to improve one of several categories of public infrastructure: primarily sewage, water, electricity, academics, trash, medical care, or security. (Of course, these categories of infrastructure received an Army acronym: SWEAT-MS.) Each level of command had authority to propose and approve CERP projects, and at my level I was authorized to approve projects up to $50,000, and Charlton, as a brigade commander, could approve up to $250,000. Company commanders could approve micro-projects of $2,500 or less. As I moved into the area, we assumed about $400,000 worth of approved or pending projects ranging from school renovations to new construction of facilities. All told, there had been about $1.1 million in CERP funds expended in Jazeera. I'll write more about CERP later, but suffice it to say that my primary weapons during my time in Jazeera would be CERP and personal relationships with prominent citizens, not bombs or bullets.

The Tribes of Copland

Starting in the far west is the area of Turapsha, a small corner of the larger Albu Mahal area. This remote village of about four thousand had never been touched by the insurgency—the roads were not cratered by IEDs, and the homes were intact. Turapsha had not suffered from the AQI murder and intimidation campaign, and many of the families suffered no deaths associated with the war. Turapsha had no police station.

Just east of Turapsha is the tribal home of the Abu Assaf tribe. Albu Assaf was a very safe area teeming with policemen. As original Awakening members, the Assafis had recruited hundreds of their able-bodied men to become policemen in the Ramadi municipality. Many of the police in the city proper came from the Abu Assaf tribe.

Why did the Awakening leaders and other sheiks send their sons to be policemen instead of soldiers? The answer sounds really simple—police forces were under local control while the Iraqi Army was under central control—however it hides complexity that bedeviled the Sahawa al Anbar (Anbar Awakening or SAA) for its entire existence. The SAA was a Sunni, grassroots organization that ultimately raised large numbers of local security forces in Anbar Province. Although these forces were, by March 2007, having real success against AQI, the central government in Baghdad was scared of the Awakening. The Shia-dominated government saw these security forces, no matter how effective they were, as a Sunni militia capable of sustaining a fight against central control, or worse, a coup d'état to install a new Sunni regime. Bear in mind, too, that the Shia militias, primarily Muqtada al Sadr's Jaysh al Mahdi (Mahdi Militia, Mahdi Army, or JAM), were out of control. JAM fighters were attacking U.S. forces and ISF regularly. They formed, in fact, the core of the Shia insurgency that plagued Baghdad and the southern provinces. I suspect Prime Minister Maliki and others thought, "If we can't control the Shia militias, how in the hell will we control Sunnis?"

This matter informed nearly every interaction I had with the sheiks and police chiefs in Jazeera, both formal and informal. They distrusted the Maliki government just as much as Maliki distrusted them. The result was a constant tension between Baghdad and Ramadi that was reflected in both official and unofficial matters. For example, the police in al Anbar Province were grossly underequipped, and the central government was reticent to discuss the issue, much less address it. The Iraqi Army, on the other hand, was well equipped and reflected the national demographics—i.e., it was mostly Shia. The Iraqi Army in Anbar was the de facto force to "contain" the Awakening, and the tensions were ripe for major violence. So the Assafis had two police stations, one in their tribal area, called the al Samoud Station (*samoud* translates as "steadfastness"), and one in Ramadi.

East of Albu Assaf was another original Awakening tribe, the Abu Ali Jassim. You may recall that the Awakening movement began when AQI killed and dumped the body of the Abu Ali Jassim sheik. Several of the most active leaders in the SAA and the Iraqi police in the area were from the tribe. Most prominent were Brig. Gen. Khalil Ali Jassim, the municipal chief of police for Ramadi; Col. Jubair Ali Jassim, a real Iraqi patriot who would work to spread the Awakening to Baghdad; and Col. Adnan Ali Jassim, the chief of my largest police station called the al Jazeera IP Station. The Albu Ali Jassim Police Station was called al Salaam (peace) and was commanded by Col. Walid Ali Jassim, a rotund and happy man who put on the best luncheons in all of Ramadi. Hundreds of Abu Ali Jassim tribesmen served as police in both their tribal area and in Ramadi proper.

The area between Turapsha and Albu Ali Jassim is almost completely rural. The main road running adjacent to the river had a few businesses that were either agricultural in nature or were small family stands with little more than a shack beside the road. However, east of the Abu Ali Jassim area is the heart of al Jazeera, and the river road passes through several good-sized markets. Where the river road intersects Route Mobile was the biggest police station in my area, the al Jazeera Station. Even though the station was in the Albu Diyab tribal area, the commander there was not a Diyabi. Jazeera Station was the first IP station in al Jazeera in 2006 and had the longest history of fighting AQI directly. Surrounded like a donut hole by the Albu Ali Jassim and Albu Diyab tribal areas was the small but wealthy Albu Sha'ban tribal area. The Sha'banis also had an IP station.

South of Albu Diyab was Albu Faraj. The Farajis were a unique tribe who were at the center of the nationalist insurgency in Jazeera until late 2006 and early 2007. Albu Faraj was a hotbed of discontent. Their police chief was a crotchety old former school headmaster named Col. Sa'adi al Faraji. Sa'adi became the police chief largely by default as a strange and wonderful thing happened there. In a nutshell, the Faraji sheik was so central to the insurgency that as the Awakening movement grew, he decided he could not reconcile with U.S. forces and ultimately was detained and removed to Abu Ghraib Prison. When he left, there was a dearth of leadership in Faraj. The void was filled not by a tribal sheik but rather by a sheik al jumma, an imam: Sheik Abdullah al Faraji.

When you think of an imam you may think of a slight, contemplative, scholarly man who is more a man of words than action . . . wrong! Abdullah was six feet tall and every bit of 255 pounds, and although he was very intelligent and well read, he was anything but a mere man of letters. Abdullah had, in his younger days, played semi-pro soccer in Iraq and, like many athletes of that caliber, he was tenacious and energetic. Abdullah was an original member of the Awakening and had taken part in several gun battles against AQI terrorists in Jazeera. In fact, he had lost his elder brother (also an imam) in one such fight against Abu Musab al Zarqawi's henchmen. Abdullah's brother had been the president of the Ramadi Sunni

Endowment, the official apparatus of the state religion, and upon his brother's death, Abdullah was voted into that august chair. Abdullah played a huge role in engendering trust between the U.S. forces and the population, and I owe him a good deal.

The other man in Albu Faraj who played a huge role in this story was named Col. Daoud al Faraji. Colonel Daoud was, like many of the IPs and new Iraqi soldiers with whom we worked, a former Saddam-era Army officer, but two things about him truly made him unique. The first is highly speculative: we suspected that Daoud was, until late 2006 or early 2007, a leader of the 1920s Revolutionary Brigade unit in North Ramadi and Jazeera—a major player in the anti-coalition nationalist insurgency. I am not sure to what extent Colonel Daoud conducted or planned attacks against Americans; he and I never had a frank discussion about his previous activities. However, there were plenty of intelligence reports that implicated him. The second thing that really makes him stand out is that this Iraqi officer with a truly tainted path played one of the biggest roles in my mission in Jazeera. Daoud raised, trained, and commanded a unit then known as the 2nd Battalion, Emergency Response Unit, or 2nd ERU.

The ERUs were the first units raised by the sheiks of the Awakening (in fact, even before it was called the Awakening). There were three ERUs, and the 1st and 2nd ERUs worked for me in Jazeera. The 1st ERU was commanded by Muhammed Ali Jassim and was about 50 percent Abu Ali Jassim members. The unit's headquarters was originally in Albu Diyab, right around the block from Sheik Muhammed al Heiss' house. The 2nd ERU, Daoud's unit, was stationed in Albu Faraj and contained about 70 percent Farajis. The 3rd ERU was across the river in Albu Risha—the home of Sheik Sittar, who was then the president of the Awakening. The ERUs—which would later be renamed Provincial Security Forces (PSFs)—were the Sunni militia that everyone from Baghdad to Washington feared. My soldiers and I could not have enjoyed half the success we did without the PSF.

My first exposure to the ERUs was anything but collegial. On day four of our relief of Cliff Wheeler's squadron, the first day that I was in charge, I got an early evening visit from Captain Mariano "Rocko" Wecer, my Alpha Company commander. Mariano was, by far, my most aggressive commander, and that is what often landed him in hot water. Luckily, for us both, he chose to seek my guidance that evening before acting. Mariano came to me that night with Captain Jay McGee (my intelligence officer) and asked me if he could arrest or kill Colonel Daoud. The two of them laid out a case "proving" that Colonel Daoud was a terrorist. They showed me intelligence about Daoud's checkered past (some of which may have been true, but all of which was sketchy), and they showed me what they considered to be the clincher—a report that said an Abu Mustafa, also called "al Assad" (the Lion), was going to attempt to assassinate a U.S. officer. The report had no references to areas and could have been talking about anywhere in Iraq, but the two young captains told me, "it all adds up." *Abu* means "father of," and in most Arab cultures close friends refer to each other as Abu plus their eldest son's name. For example, if your eldest son is named Ahmed, your friends would call you Abu Ahmed. Wecer told me "many locals" called Daoud "al Assad al Jazeera" (the Lion of Jazeera) and that he "had a feeling" about Daoud, that he "just wasn't right." He explained to me how he could lure Daoud to his headquarters for a meeting then "neutralize" his guards and take him prisoner. I told him he could not detain Colonel Daoud on such flimsy evidence. By the end of the hour-long discussion, things calmed down to the point that Chuck Krumwiede made several jokes about Mariano killing Daoud in a local restaurant with a gun that was taped to the commode (à la *The Godfather*). Wecer yukked it up with that idea, even demonstrating how he would have difficulty dropping the weapon on the way out of the restaurant because our pistols are connected to our gear by retaining cords. Wecer with his pistol dangling from his hand like a yo-yo is one of those images that are forever burned on my brain. Anyway, the coup de grâce for this plan finally came a few weeks later when I asked Daoud the name of his eldest son—much to the chagrin of Wecer and McGee, he told me it was Farhan. He had no child named Mustafa.

East of Albu Faraj was the most idyllic and placid of my areas, the Albu Aetha tribal area, which was mostly untouched by war. The area's southern half consisted of rolling farmland that terminated at the river, dotted by both large and small houses in the most traditional architecture. Along the river in Albu Aetha were a series of fruit groves containing date palms, orange trees, olive and fig trees, and a few others that I couldn't identify. It was a quiet, peaceful place, but the tribe was not quiet and was populated by several of the most self-centered and underhanded people I know. The Aethawis argued like children, and the tribe was in constant internal turmoil. The good news was that it never turned violent, so it became just an amusing distraction, but not to the police chief, Lt. Col. Jumma Abu Aetha.

Jumma was my favorite policeman in many ways. He was smart and well spoken, quiet and competent, and he was a former tanker in Saddam's Army who loved to talk about tanks. Jumma was the Andy Taylor[23] of Jazeera, both because of his calm and personable demeanor and the fact that he presided over the "Mayberry" of Jazeera; in fact, Jumma often didn't carry a gun! Even in the worst of days, attacks in Aetha were rare, and few insurgents lived there. Jumma's major challenge was to manage the three competing power brokers of Albu Aetha: Sheik Mohan, Sheik Sa'ad, and Haji Salah.

Mohan was (and I'm sure still is) an effete jerk. His beard was always overly trimmed and oiled, his fingernails were impeccably manicured, one could smell his cologne from four feet away, and he created more drama than a soap opera writer. Mohan was the brother of the genuine tribal sheik of the Aethawi tribe who fled to Jordan during the "troubles" and returned in late 2007. The tribe never really recognized Mohan as his brother's successor. He was supposedly the son of a former Iraqi foreign minister during the "Free Officer's Regime" of the late 1950s, and, according to Mohan, his grandfather had been a highly influential sheik during the British occupation and briefly fell out of favor during the Hashemite Kingdom period. Mohan had once told my interpreter that I should address him as Imir (Prince) Mohan. That was the last time that I called him sheik—from then on he was simply Mohan. Although he had little charismatic influence over the population, he was fairly wealthy, and that bought him some following.

His polar opposite was Sheik Sa'ad al Aethawi. Sa'ad was a fake sheik; that is, he was not a sheik until the Americans came. He was a portly man of about forty-five years who had started life in a very modest family and worked his way into the upper middle class. Sa'ad was a building contractor by trade but dabbled in several businesses. When I met Sa'ad, I quickly figured out how he had become successful: he is one of the most affable and hospitable men I know. I loved going to see Sa'ad and usually did it for no real reason other than to stay in touch. Sa'ad had an easy manner and charm, and he had a rare gift: he could tell stories and jokes in such a way that they translated into English as funny as they were in Arabic. (If you've ever tried that, you know how hard it is.) He would keep us all in stitches from the time we arrived until we left. Sa'ad knew how to handle Mohan (who was his third or fourth cousin), but he had real trouble with Haji Salah.

Haji Salah al Aethawi was not a sheik and didn't want to be one. His honorific, Haji, is a common title given to those adult males who have completed the Hajj—but don't let that fool you into thinking that Salah was a pious or religious man. Haji Salah was a glutton of the first order, weighing in at over four hundred pounds. He smoked like a muscle car in need of a ring job and drank quite openly. Rumor has it that Haji Salah was the party king of Jazeera before the war, reportedly throwing multi-day keggers with lots of food and live, mostly female, entertainment—some stories said belly dancers, but others intimated that he brought prostitutes from all over Iraq. Haji Salah was one of the wealthiest men in Jazeera and made his money in real estate, construction, and wholesaling of goods from Jordan and Syria throughout Anbar and Baghdad Provinces. As I came into Jazeera, Haji Salah had no relationship with the Americans, largely because his son had somehow found himself at the home of a major insurgent in Albu Faraj when the house was raided and wound up in Abu Ghraib. I later arranged for his son to be released, endearing our side to Haji Salah (at least for a little while).

East of the Albu Aetha tribal area was Hamdiya, the only area in Jazeera not named for its tribal affiliation. About 80 percent of the population belonged to the Abu Fahad tribe. Hamdiya had been, as late as December 2006, a major home for both nationalist and AQI insurgents. In fact, from Hamdiya east to my boundary, all along the river had been a no-go area for the coalition until late 2006, and a small section remained a no-go area as I moved into Jazeera. The local sheik in Hamdiya was a young engineer named Sheik Jabbar al Fahadawi. Jabbar was a complicated man. Although he was an engineer by education and worked as one, I always got the impression that he had done intelligence work in the Saddam-era security apparatus. Be that as it may, he was a real fighter and completely committed to building a new Iraq. When Hamdiya was still held by insurgents, he resisted them and joined the Awakening. Jabbar funded the Hamdiya

Police Station (led by Lt. Col. Khalil al Fahadawi) with his own money, buying weapons, generators, light sets, radios, and uniforms. Jabbar was a real hero and very politically astute, but was always aloof and angry.[24]

East of Hamdiya was Albu Obaid, the most recently cleared place in my AO. Obaid had been the host to Abu Musab al Zarqawi several times before his death. In fact, he was nearly killed there in early 2006. Obaid had a weak but large police station and a horrible sheik. Mariano Wecer's soldiers were attacked on the outskirts of Obaid five times a week, and one could not safely drive the roads on its eastern side. Not one of the 350 IPs in Obaid was getting paid by the Iraqi government. They received some money from the sheik (a grouchy alcoholic) and some money from the IP chief, who was a nice enough guy but really ineffective. However, the majority of their money came from selling the fuel we gave them for their vehicles and generator on the black market and splitting the proceeds among the IPs. I was complicit in this effort, and although I certainly didn't like it, I had no better solution immediately available. It took months of hard work to get any of these IPs paid, and eventually only about two hundred of them became "real IPs."

East of Obaid and south of the River Road was our last area, called Zuwei'a, a tiny enclave of Fadawis. Because they were Abu Fahad, they refused to be in the Obaid Police and had their own sub-station, led by Sheik (Lt. Col.) Bassim al Fahadawi, who was not a *sheik al shire* (tribal sheik) but rather a *sheik al jumma* (imam or religious sheik). Bassim was my youngest IP chief and a genuinely kind and good man—he was only marginal as a police chief, however.

Eighty percent of what my soldiers did in Jazeera centered on the Iraqi police. In the city, for the last three months, our mission and our lives had been focused on finding and killing AQI insurgents. Although I had wanted to focus more on partnering with Iraqi Security Forces and separating the population from the insurgents, the reality was that my soldiers had been focused on killing the enemy. Because of our hard work and the hard work of many others, Craig Kaczynski's Marines would now be able to focus on the population in central Ramadi.

Killing the enemy is the traditional role of a soldier and what one thinks about when invoking the word *combat*. For my young soldiers, the constant cat-and-mouse game with insurgents in Ramadi was exciting, and it made them think they were in "real" combat (never mind the fact we had lost four heroes killed in action and another thirty or so wounded—that doesn't really figure in the imagination of the twenty-year-old infantryman or tanker). What most of my young warriors didn't understand was that killing insurgents was not the formula for victory. Victory was getting the Iraqi population to reject the insurgents and therefore to starve the insurgency to death through lack of support, lack of safe havens, and violent attrition. Key to that victory were the Iraqi police and the tribes they represented.

As we moved into Jazeera we partnered with eight IP stations, composed of about 1,400 IPs, and the two ERUs, which numbered another 1,500 pseudo-IPs. Of these stations, only one, al Jazeera IP Station, had a U.S. transition team. Transition teams are groups of American military advisors who live and work with indigenous forces. Those who work with police are called PTTs, for "police transition team" (There are also MiTTs, or military transition teams, and BTTs, or border transition teams. In Afghanistan, there is a whole new lexicon of TTs.) The PTT at Jazeera Station included fifteen soldiers from 1-41 Field Artillery (Glory's Guns) commanded by then–Lt. Col. Noel Nicole. Noel was tasked with managing police transition for the entire brigade area of operations and was the primary interlocutor and advisor to Brig. Gen. Khalil Abu Ali Jassim. I liked Noel, but he was a constant thorn in my side. He went native and embraced the Iraqi bureaucracy wholeheartedly, making it very tough for me to get my IPs onto the payroll. He also meddled in my area quite frequently by bringing fuel and guns and other baubles to the Albu Ali Jassim area behind my back, thereby causing consternation among my eight other tribes. Noel was also famous for making promises (most of which he couldn't keep) to my police chiefs without my knowledge, thus undermining my efforts to keep those guys working while we all waited on the Ministry of Interior in Baghdad to add the stations to the payroll and equip them accordingly.

Guns and Cars

Occasionally I see rap videos, usually by accident as I am channel surfing. When I do, they always seem to be about the allure of guns, cars, and half-naked women—all of which I can appreciate, but none of which validate my worth as a man. If someone were to mistakenly equate those videos with American culture writ large, they may result in some wrong generalizations. Well, perhaps I spent my time with the Iraqi equivalent of the hip-hop culture, but if you take away the half-naked women, then you understand how many Iraqi men derive their worth: guns and cars. So, many of the conversations I had with police chiefs and sheiks, especially early in my time in Jazeera, centered around guns and cars—actually guns and trucks. Why? Because, Iraq is not America. At most police departments in America, every policeman has some type of conveyance: car, motorcycle, truck, Segway, horse, or bicycle. Granted, there are big-city departments where cops still walk the beat, but mostly they ride. I have never seen a police department in the United States in which there was less than one gun per cop. In fact, here many policemen have two or three guns—shotgun, pistol, and rifle is not rare. In Jazeera, and throughout Anbar Province, that was not the case. Most of my stations were lucky to have one truck per 70 policemen, and a station of 150 would be lucky to have half a dozen pistols and forty rifles issued by the Iraqi government. These were not London bobbies keeping the order in an already orderly place; these policemen were counterinsurgent paramilitaries who were fighting against AQI terrorists.

The problem of equipment was multifaceted. First, remember that from mid-2006 to April 2007, the Ramadi municipality went from about two hundred policemen to over eight thousand, and the force was still growing. Fallujah, though several months behind Ramadi in the Awakening, was by April 2007 growing its own police force, and Hit and Qaim were just coming online. So even if the officials at the Ministry of Interior in Baghdad had wanted to supply all the police in al Anbar, they would not be able to do so quickly.

Secondly, there was the issue of transportation. The two main storage depots were in Baghdad and Taji, separated from Ramadi by fifty miles of very dangerous road. Third was the issue of the bureaucratic nature of the regime. In fact, there were some trucks and weapons stockpiled at Camp Ramadi, but cutting through Iraqi red tape took time—months. One really can't fault them; the centralization imposed under Saddam will take years to overcome. Under Saddam, initiative was discouraged, and an error of commission, no matter how well intentioned, could get one fired . . . or worse.

Finally, it is hard to ignore the fact that the leaders in Baghdad were scared senseless of arming what they still considered the Sunni militia, so Baghdad took a wait-and-see posture regarding the security apparatus of the Awakening. And it wasn't just guns and cars; they also withheld more mundane things like generators for the police stations (most areas in the Ramadi municipality had fewer than six hours of municipal electric power per day in early 2007), uniforms, radios, boots, equipment belts, helmets, and body armor. As a result of all that, the police were grossly under-equipped and really only had two sources to get what they needed quickly—the Americans or their sheik. There was huge pressure on the sheiks—who, after all, had convinced their tribesmen to join the police—to produce these items, and they all did produce, to varying degrees; some to the equivalent of a hundred thousand U.S. dollars. We did what we could, greasing the skids of the district and provincial police headquarters, providing confiscated weapons and vehicles, and delivering fuel in huge lots. Diesel fuel was as good as money, and we had lots of it, so we delivered fuel to the stations. If a station had two trucks and two generators, it may have gotten as much as five hundred gallons per week (easily five times what it took to run the station's fleets). Policemen sold the excess to equip, man, and run their stations.

Pay was another huge issue. When I moved into Jazeera only about 600 of the 1,400 policemen got paid every month. The ERU battalions had a higher percentage: about 1,000 of the 1,500 ERU members (they hated it when I called them police, but they weren't soldiers either) were on the payroll. Again, there were several ways that individual sheiks and IP chiefs dealt with the issue. Some took all the pay and put it in a kitty, then parsed it out to cover their entire force. Some of the sheiks kicked in for a small stipend. There was the fuel black-marketing, and we delivered food, blankets, and other necessities to police families. The average IP made about three hundred dollars per month on the payroll. In Jazeera, because of the pay issues, most of our IPs saw less than one hundred dollars a month on average. What did they do for that pay? They manned checkpoints where in any given week they had about a 50 percent chance that some terrorist would try to kill them. I have heard many ill-informed Americans belittle the contributions of these Iraqi patriots, but I doubt I could get many of those Americans to borrow a rifle and stand an eight-hour shift with little or no protective equipment on a badly fortified, over-exposed checkpoint, knowing that al Qaeda wanted to kill them in order to reinfest their neighborhood.

Strangers to Partners, Partners to Friends, Friends to Brothers

In many cases, perception is reality. What follows is my perception of how Cliff Wheeler's outfit conducted their military operations in Jazeera. I believe they spent the lion's share of their time and effort keeping themselves safe. When we moved into Jazeera, there were three combat outposts (COPs): Anvil, Aggressor, and Warrior. Anvil was the farthest west, and the area for the company (called "troops" for Wheeler's cavalry unit) there included Turapsha, Albu Assaf, Albu Ali Jassim, Albu Sha'ban, and Albu Diyab. COP Anvil was located on the northern outskirts of Albu Sha'ban near an oxbow lake we called C Lake, which had separated from the Euphrates some centuries ago. The first time I visited COP Anvil was during my RIP/TOA. I visited all the COPs without Wheeler. C Lake had a two-lane dirt track that ran around its shores and was the primary route to get to COP Anvil, although one could take a more circuitous route through Albu Sha'ban proper. I chose to take C Lake Road for this visit. As I turned off the paved two-lane road that ran through a market in Albu Diyab, I was immediately greeted by a checkpoint manned by the Albu Sha'ban IPs. The checkpoint was atrocious—no shelter from rain or sun, no fortifications or blast shields, no proper barriers—and was manned by four IPs with Kalashnikovs and decent uniforms. After being waved through by the IPs, I continued on the road for the remaining two or so miles to COP Anvil. A couple of small, one-lane tracks intersected with C Lake Road from the east, and one of these had a two-man IP checkpoint no better equipped than the first. Just north of that checkpoint, I spotted two Bradley Fighting Vehicles in the palm grove adjacent to C Lake Road. The crewmen were milling about, and the turrets were stationary (normally indicating no active searching or scanning). Finally, I arrived at the entry point for COP Anvil.

COP Anvil was located in a three-story house of about five thousand square feet of typical Iraqi construction—concrete walls, tile floors, and an open and accessible roof with a parapet around its edge. COP Anvil was home to about 110 of Wheeler's soldiers, so every room had sleeping quarters for someone. Just off the entryway on the bottom floor was the troop operations center with the commander's and first sergeant's quarters in a connecting room. That's where I went for my operations briefing from the outgoing troop commander. For about the next two hours, he explained to me how he saw the enemy and friendly situations in his area and what operations his unit was conducting. I probably don't recall all the positive things that he told me. What I do recall is that he was using about half of his combat power to man the Bradley OP that was in the palm grove adjacent to C Lake Road merely because C Lake Road had been a hotbed of insurgent violence in 2005 and 2006. The last attack there was in August 2006 as the Awakening was gaining ground; that was, in fact, the last attack in this troop's AO, and it had occurred six months prior to them moving in. These soldiers had never experienced an insurgent attack. Still, another third of their combat power was manning guard towers on the roof of the COP. That left enough manpower for about three patrols per day outside the gates. The young troop commander knew the names of his IP commanders and only a little more. He visited each of them once a week. He saw Col. Abdul Ghafor almost daily, since the Sha'ban IP Station was four hundred yards outside his front gate—the guard towers on the roof had a great view of it.

The next position I visited was COP Aggressor, located at the northern edge of the intersection of Albu Diyab and Albu Aetha just north of the populated areas of Jazeera in the desert. COP Aggressor was in a gravel factory. The main road to the COP was a two-lane dirt road that ran next to a large irrigation canal. Like COP Anvil, COP Aggressor was very well protected. The soldiers from COP Aggressor manned three OPs, the first a single-vehicle OP located not one thousand yards south of the COP. There, where the canal road had a twenty-foot dip, a large buried IED completely destroyed a Bradley sometime in mid-2006. Pieces of the armored vehicle were still on the road. For that reason, a Bradley Fighting Vehicle with a three-man crew stood watch over that spot 24/7. The canal road ran south until it intersected with Route Mobile, where a Bradley section (two BFVs with full crews) manned an OP overwatching the highway and the road to the COP. Another Bradley section manned an OP about three miles east on another overpass on Route Mobile. For the troop assigned to COP Aggressor, well over half of its combat power was stuck on static positions watching places that had seen no enemy activity for months. The unit at Aggressor had responsibility for Albu Aetha and Albu Faraj but rarely went to the IP stations there.

Farthest east, in Albu Obaid, were Mariano Wecer and my A Company. They were partnered with the Obaid and Hamdiya IPs and had a "sub-station" in the tiny village of Zuwei'a. Mariano and his boys were knee deep in hand-grenade pins—I'll write about that in the next chapter. Mariano stayed in his area and was returned to my control.

Wheeler's last cavalry troop was assigned the mission to secure Route Mobile. Those soldiers conducted day and night patrols and manned some random OPs. They were responsible for one full-time OP at the far east of our area overwatching Route Mobile.

Matt McCreary, my newest commander, and his Battle Company moved into COP Aggressor and held down the center of our area. I assigned Chris Hahn and his Knight Company to COP Anvil and my westernmost area, and Diogo Tavares and Steel Company were responsible for Route Mobile. I ordered Chris Hahn to remove the Bradley OP from C Lake Road and cut his number of soldiers on the rooftop by half. After much irritating debate, I ordered Matt McCreary to get rid of the Bradley OP just south of COP Aggressor and cut his rooftop security as well. I ordered Diogo to prepare to take over all the permanent OPs on Route Mobile and to continue his security patrols on the road. In most of Jazeera, we were in the hold and build phases of the clear-hold-build model, but these positions were manned as if we were in a bare-knuckles brawl.

My soldiers were coming out of an area where they, literally, fought for their lives every day. We had made some inroads into working jointly with Iraqi forces but not as much as I would have liked. We handed Craig Kaczynski and his Marines an opportunity to greatly expand that cooperation, and they ran with it. Now my soldiers were going to have to come to a new and different place and figure out how to turn these odd Arabs living around them from strangers to partners, partners to friends, and friends to brothers.

CHAPTER 12

On the Eastern Front

"Don't worry—the IPs do all the hard work."
—Graffiti from a Porta Potti on Camp Blue Diamond

My Soldiers settled into their new roles reluctantly, mostly. It is very difficult to convince a twenty-year-old infantryman or tanker that winning a war is not, necessarily, about killing the most people. Gradually, they began to come around. The transition was difficult for me too, but I was happy that I could sleep through many nights without either being awakened by potentially catastrophic events or lying awake wondering what the next catastrophe might be and how I could prevent it. My daily routine in Jazeera was similar to that in the city. I woke up shortly before 7 a.m. and took about forty-five minutes for personal time. By 7:30 I was in my office (in the same building as my sleeping quarters) reading the latest news and checking my official email. At 8:30 every day but Sunday, I walked across the hall to our conference room for my daily battle update brief (BUB) from my staff, where Jay McGee or one of his intelligence analysts gave me the latest enemy situation both for our area and broadly for all of Iraq, then my other staff officers or sergeants would fill me in on their activities for the past twenty-four hours and the plans for the next three days. The briefing, if delivered pro forma, was designed to take about half an hour, but I rarely adjourned this meeting before 9:30. I used this meeting as a brainstorming session, conducting it much more as an informal discussion than a formal briefing. Although that technique is not the most efficient way to run a military operation, it certainly is an effective way. It was in these sessions that, as a group, my headquarters came up with some of the most unorthodox and unusual aspects of our operations. I loved this chance to interact with the leaders on my staff and used this opportunity to ensure that the leaders in my headquarters understood my vision for the fight. Without this daily meeting, we would not have had the innovation that ultimately shaped our victory.

After the BUB I took a few minutes to talk about administrative issues with my executive officer, Mike Rosamond, then suited up and left the wire. Whereas in the city, my daily outings (militarily, they were patrols) revolved almost exclusively around visits to my soldiers, and any visit to an Iraqi leader was ancillary, in Jazeera, the roles were reversed. There, within just a few weeks, my calendar filled up with Iraqi events: tribal meetings where I would sit with sheiks from the highest level all the way down to the lowest; grand openings of CERP projects like water pumping stations, schools, clinics, or market renovations; routine visits to IP stations or the ERU battalion headquarters; and, several times a week, a couple of hours with Sheik Muhammed Farhan al Heiss. It didn't take long before I ceased to be an observer of this culture and became part of it. Not in the "oh, he's gone native" way, but in a way that allowed me to have great access and influence with the population.

These meetings were, in keeping with Iraqi tradition, combinations of highly social gatherings and business meetings. Whether adversarial or completely cooperative, they mostly followed the same routine. I would arrive at the site with a good deal of hubbub and pomp like some grand potentate, representing to the gathered folk the entire might of the United States. (Truly, it amazed me—and still does—how much I, as a military leader of middle-management ranks, represented the entire might of the United States government.) Once my procession of security entered the compound, I would emerge from the truck and make my way to a receiving line including the who's who of whatever area I was visiting. After a brief greeting outdoors, we would move inside where I would greet, individually, every member of the group, sharing handshakes with those who were new or less familiar acquaintances and kisses for those with whom I was most familiar—a custom that my prior experiences in Saudi Arabia had prepared me for but one that is quite jarring to the uninitiated Western man. The man-kiss process is very well codified: right cheek, left cheek, then another right cheek double for good friends. This little dance can lead to some funny outtakes for those just learning; the biggest blunder occurs when the new initiate goes for the wrong cheek first and winds up, not with the cheek-touch air-kiss, but with a full-on kiss on the lips. Normally, one's Iraqi counterpart would be adept enough to play it off, but don't think for a minute that the other Americans present would let a soldier live down such a faux pas.

Once seated, the group will greet the new arrival by placing hands over hearts and saying, "Allah buhair," roughly translated as "may you be welcome with God's goodwill." The next four or five minutes bring a chaotic, repetitive, and somewhat strange routine of asking each other "how are you?" (in Iraqi Arabic, "schlonek" or, literally translated, "what's your color?"), then expressing how one hopes everyone is good ("enshallah mobsut," or "if God is willing, you're happy"). By now you are a good fifteen minutes into the "meeting," and to the average type-A, ex-jock, military man, nothing has happened! In the most formal of settings, those rituals would be followed by a flowery and poetic (it's these times that I really wished I was fluent in Arabic) welcome speech from the host, to which the senior guest would reply as eloquently as possible (always just hoping that your translator would get it right) with his own remarks. Then came chai— the syrup-sweet Iraqi tea.

Now, easily thirty minutes into the "meeting," the business discussion could begin and, if you were lucky, would stay on topic and under control for an hour. You knew when the business was nearly done because the lunch ritual would begin. The lunch ritual was quite a production and began with the tables. Depending on the venue, from four to twenty men would start setting up metal folding tables, sometimes in the same room in which your meeting was held, sometimes, if you were lucky, in a separate room or outside in the courtyard, but you would always know that it had begun. No matter how small the crew doing the setup, there was always one guy who was in charge. He would, while the others began to put plastic tablecloths over the tables, make the most minor and trivial adjustments to the table's positions, often accompanied by head shaking and clucking of the tongue, *tsk-tsk-tsk*.

Once the plastic was in place, next came the veggies—plates full of fresh, salted tomato wedges, cucumbers, pickled vegetables, olives, and onion, all locally grown. (I still miss the tomatoes from Iraq—the best I've ever eaten.) The man in charge would, again, make the most minor, merely ceremonial adjustments to the plates while the rest of the crew brought the main course of lamb, fish, or chicken served on a bed of seasoned rice on a large, communal platter, always more than the collected group could eat. The next trip of the preparation crew was for bowls of soup, usually a thin, tomato-based soup with okra that could either be eaten with a spoon or poured over the rice, which was always eaten with the right hand, as was the rest of the meal. Then, either the gathered crowd was asked to go outside to wash their hands, or the host's sons would bring in pitchers, soap, and large basins and would go around the room to each person. One son would hold the basin while the other poured the water as each man washed his hand; the ritual and symbolism were every bit as important as having clean hands with which to eat.

During the meal, the host would pull the best selections of meat from the lamb and place them in front of the honored guest(s) on the communal tray. (Unfortunately, for many Americans, the best cuts are often the fat of a "fatted lamb," so one must try his hardest to eat some of it to make his host feel good.) After the meal there was a less symbolic washing of the hands, then a brief chat, some more chai, and it was time to go—a group goodbye was an acceptable adieu, as opposed to the long individual greetings. These meetings, whether with sheiks, policemen, local businessmen, Iraqi government officials, or Iraqi soldiers, were where the vast majority of my crucial business was done. More importantly, I developed personal relationships during these meetings, and those relationships became as essential as money in my counterinsurgency in Jazeera.

As I made my rounds, however, these meetings were not all goodness and light. These men all wanted things from me, and I wanted things from them. The IP chiefs wanted equipment, pay for their IPs, and training—most of all, they wanted official recognition for their stations from the MOI. The sheiks wanted contracts for projects and the money that they brought. I cannot stress enough how important money is to counterinsurgency. By 2007, Iraq's economy, which had already been weakened by twelve years of United Nations sanctions before the 2003 invasion, was a wreck. Long-term unemployment was high, median incomes were low, and even if you had a job, you had poor electricity services, water that was largely unfit for drinking, and major league fuel shortages. Men were still required to put food on the family's table, and this is where CERP was the most effective tool available for fighting the insurgency.

As I moved into Jazeera, the majority of the CERP money was going for large projects designed to build or renovate community facilities. There were water pumping stations, a couple of clinics, school renovations, and lots of canal work—repairs, cleaning, and a few new canals—all being completed by a handful of contractors (all of whom were local). Some of these projects had been initiated by the Jazeera Council, and several of the sheiks on the Jazeera Council had benefitted, personally and greatly, from these contracts because they owned the companies doing the work—clearly a conflict of interest. At an early Jazeera Council meeting, one of the members even had the moxie to make an official motion that the Jazeera Council members should get 15 percent of the total cost for projects they recommended to the coalition; one of the few times when I exercised my absolute veto.

Why did I tolerate this seemingly corrupt behavior from the Jazeera Counsel? Why did the United States government tolerate this behavior? First, because these were the men who recruited, equipped, housed, and even paid the ERU and IP recruits who were in the process of kicking al Qaeda out of Iraq. We needed their cooperation and participation. Second, because Iraqi tribal culture operates based on a patronage system that has been in place for hundreds of years. The tribal sheik is at the center of the system. It is he who paves the way for Iraqi government officials to receive their appointments, and in return, he demands access to the governmental position of his tribal members. In Iraqi culture, it is completely appropriate and expected that government officials would grant contracts to their sheiks or other tribal cousins in return for the political and social support of the tribe. This was not a system that was invented after the U.S. invasion, but rather, we eventually learned to embrace this system. Hell, there are city councils in the United States that are just as corrupt, and they don't provide the kinds of services that these men did. The bigger and more powerful the tribe, the more political sway and access they demanded. The resulting power that the sheik develops is known as *wasta*—and my friends were developing major *wasta* in al Anbar.

Within a couple months, my most junior leaders' days looked very much like mine, but I have to give some credit for that to Col. John Charlton, who really started to "neglect" my battalion once we moved to Jazeera, or, at least, that's how I perceived it. I wrote earlier about the strange relationship between Charlton and me and about my belief that if one is tasked to send away a subordinate unit, one should send the most capable one, keeping the less capable. Well, I'm not sure if Charlton agreed with that technique or not, but I was now the last remaining "maneuver" battalion from our Fort Stewart unit that remained under his command, giving me the perception that he thought my unit was the weakest. On several occasions, he told me that he didn't feel that way, but I never really believed him. So, there I was, the sole remaining Raider Brigade unit with a tank battalion from 1st Infantry Division, a light infantry battalion from 2nd Infantry Division, and two Marine infantry battalions all serving under a 3rd Infantry Division brigade combat team. (The convoluted mess that put the U.S. military in this predicament is another story.) When it came to resources—support teams, equipment, small unit attachments—Charlton definitely favored the "guest" units. So, although I had more police stations in my area than any other battalion, I had only one Police Transition Team (PTT) from outside my organization.

Be that as it may, Charlton ordered me to man transition teams for all my IP stations and the ERU battalions because he understood, maybe even earlier than I, that helping the Iraqi Security Forces to become as capable as possible as soon as possible would be the key to sustaining the progress we had seen thus far in Ramadi. Charlton originally proposed that I man teams at each station and that they would work for Noel Nicole's "Glory's Guns" battalion. I fought back and ultimately won the fight. The result was that, after only having been in Jazeera a few weeks, I ordered each of my companies to assign a platoon as a full-time partner unit to each IP station, and but for two exceptions, we wound up with one platoon assigned to each Iraqi unit, whether it was an IP station or one of the ERU headquarters. This meant that every day, my platoon leaders, platoon sergeants, and even squad leaders met with their Iraqi counterparts, going through the same routines and developing personal relationships just like me. My company commanders each had responsibility for several tribal areas, and they met with IPs, sheiks, and other leaders on a regular basis. I don't mean to imply that, like me, the bulk of their duties involved sitting around, chatting, and sipping chai. They were responsible for assisting their counterparts with all aspects of training, administration, and operations, and they conducted patrols, checkpoints, raids, and searches with their partnered units.

As my soldiers came into Jazeera, few had any real experience working with Iraqis every day, much less going to work and seeing the *same* Iraqis every day. Many of my soldiers (probably a majority of them) distrusted all Iraqis and bore significant prejudice based on their time in Ramadi. However, over the course of the next several months, their distrust and prejudices faded. I told my leaders that if they wanted to know how to behave with their Iraqi counterparts—sheiks, policemen, and civilians—they could just watch me. They began to emulate my behavior, and so did their soldiers. Once platoons were partnered with IP stations, they quickly became partners with an entire tribe, so much so that when I went to visit that tribe, I would be greeted as a guest, but often the lieutenant and sergeants who worked there every day would be with the tribe as I arrived and, for all intents and purposes, be part of the tribe's "welcoming committee."

I was the senior advisor to all of the IPs and ERUs in Jazeera, and I took that role very seriously. I spent a good deal of my time coaching the IP chiefs on leadership, training, and administration as well as explaining my requirements, intent, and orders. These men all worked for me, at least technically, since al Anbar was still under U.S. control. Although they showed occasional consternation about the arrangement, especially the few who had been successful officers in the Iraqi Army, they mostly accepted my orders graciously and followed them diligently. But these were not American policemen, and this was not America. Often there would be tensions and issues internal to the police station or tribe, or between tribes, that I just wouldn't understand. At those times, I turned to Sheik Heiss. As I wrote earlier, I saw Sheik Heiss several times a week. Sometimes it would be just his entourage (Heiss had a PSD of his own as well as a chief of staff—Saddam Hussein al Diyabi—who was in charge of his small household and business staff) and my PSD, but just as often, he would invite guests for our discussions. When no "outsiders" were present, Sheik Heiss taught me about the recent history of Jazeera, Iraqi tribal traditions and values, and generally the who's who of the area. I soon came to realize that Sheik Heiss, perhaps more than anyone I knew, wanted the United States to succeed, and, first merely by extension but later because of friendship, he wanted to see me succeed. I quickly came to trust Sheik Heiss completely, and there were few ideas I didn't pass by him before we executed them operationally. Muhammed Farhan al Heiss had become my senior advisor, my partner, and my friend. In return, Sheik Heiss became wealthy.

AQI and Albu Bali

While most of my leaders and I got our legs under us in Jazeera, Capt. Mariano Wecer and his Rock Company (A Company), who were now returned to my command, continued their fight on the eastern edge of Jazeera. Where the rest of Jazeera was in the build phase, eastern Jazeera was still in the clear phase, and just over our boundary was the Albu Bali tribal area, which was a bona fide al Qaeda safe haven. Mariano's soldiers made contact with the enemy nearly every day in several forms. Rock Company's infantrymen and tankers had done a hell of a job taking the initiative against their enemy. They had a series of "small kill team" (or SKT) positions and one OP, occupied 24/7, which they used to keep the enemy at bay.

Rock Company's headquarters, with its two infantry platoons and one tank platoon, operated from Joint Security Station (JSS) Warrior. A JSS differs from a combat outpost in one critical way: it includes, within its perimeter, both Iraqi and American forces, and we were working to make all our positions JSSs. JSS Warrior was a three-house compound that had belonged to a sheik named Abdul Sittar Abu Obaid, who was a businessman and was absent from Jazeera when I arrived. I heard various stories about him—some accusing him of cowardice and some accusing him of complicity with al Qaeda. When I asked Sheik Heiss about Sittar Obaid, he laughed; he and Sittar were best friends and business partners. Heiss told me that Sittar fled to Jordan when Abu Musab al Zarqawi moved into Albu Obaid. That settled the matter for me—Sittar was okay.

JSS Warrior was a well-protected compound that was generally in good order. Randy Sumner still found substantial fault with it, however, and he and 1st Sgt. Freddy Gonzales set about to make several changes to both the quality of life and force protection aspects at the JSS. Warrior was located next door to the Albu Obaid IP Station, and the company had a great working relationship with the IPs.

The second compound that Rock Company used was an unfinished gas station, also owned by Sittar Obaid, on Route Mobile called Firebase Dragon. Firebase Dragon housed a small medical aid station and my mortar platoon. Wheeler had occupied Firebase Dragon with his mortar platoon at Mariano Wecer's insistence so that he could have the range to provide mortar fires into Albu Bali. When I visited Firebase Dragon, I was appalled by the conditions. Soldiers were living like pigs; there was no shade from the sun and no stand-off from the highway—a truck bomb could have driven right past the wall without raising any suspicion. I knew that I would close Firebase Dragon soon.

But Firebase Dragon was not my biggest concern in Rock's area. More troublesome still was the eastern frontier. As stated before, Albu Obaid was formerly the home to Abu Musab al Zarqawi, the founder and leader of al Qaeda in Iraq. Obaid was cleared in late 2006, but all that did was drive the enemy across our boundary into Albu Bali. Indeed, for the first several weeks of my time in Jazeera, nearly every meeting I had with either sheiks or Iraqi police eventually turned into a discussion of the security issues in Albu Bali. All of the Iraqis urged me to "go into Bali," and all of the police told me they would come with me. I got tired of explaining that Albu Bali was not in my area and that I needed to get permission to go there, but I also made it clear that I would work as hard as I could to make it into Albu Bali.

This boundary, between Obaid and Bali was not merely my battalion boundary, nor just the BCT's boundary; this was a boundary between U.S. forces and the Iraqi Army. Back in 2005, most American strategists thought that victory in Iraq was merely getting out, and the way out was to get Iraqi forces stood up as quickly as possible. So it came to pass that some genius decided to give a wedge-shaped area north of the town of Habbaniyah to an Iraqi Army brigade and one of its battalions—1st Battalion, 3rd Brigade, 1st Division, or 1/3/1 IA—owned Albu Bali. The soldiers from the unit rarely entered the place, however, and when they did, it cost them in blood.

Albu Bali sat in a bend in the Euphrates River that made a peninsula about two miles wide just north of Habbaniyah. It was a relatively isolated tribal area and had only two roads in and out: the first was the River Road, a paved road in poor repair that ran along the elevated dyke between three hundred yards and one mile north of the river. About two miles east of Albu Bali was the Habbaniyah Bridge that connected the north and south banks of the Euphrates. It was the only bridge over the river between Ramadi and Fallujah. The second road was a north–south two-lane dirt track that ran from Route Mobile directly into Bali. While the battle for Ramadi was ongoing, Albu Bali was a major safe haven and support zone for AQI and the Islamic State of Iraq. Bali housed many of their senior planners and leaders, and it was a major area for homemade explosive (HME) and IED construction. Many intelligence analysts theorized that Albu Bali was the home of a major truck-bomb factory that sent death into Baghdad on a regular basis.

In fact, everyone knew how bad Bali was, but nobody really did much about it. The Marine regiment that owned the Fallujah and Habbaniyah areas had conducted a few operations into Bali with 1/3/1 IA, including one in late March 2007, but the unit never went in with any intention of staying, and the operations rarely yielded much. Before moving to Jazeera, I had told Charlton that I wanted to extend my boundary to include Bali, and he agreed. He and his headquarters had run into major resistance attempting to do so, however. The obstacles to extending our boundary were complicated. First, there was a bit of inter-service rivalry. As stated previously, my BCT, the Raider Brigade, worked for a Marine Corps head-quarters, Multi-National Force West or MNF-W. MNF-W owned all of al Anbar and had owned it for years. It was a U.S. Marine general who made the decision to cede Bali to the Iraqi Army in 2006. The U.S. Marines still believed that putting Iraqis in charge was the way home—regardless of their ability to actually fight al Qaeda. Asking the Iraqi government to give the area back would require them to admit their previous decision was wrong. The second major impediment was that the Iraqi government could ill afford the loss of face that would come with admitting they couldn't handle fighting the takfiris in Bali. Finally, by March 2007, it was clear that "The Surge" was not going to be permanent because the Army and Marine Corps could not sustain the deployment load as it was indefinitely; therefore, senior leaders in Iraq were not looking to acquire more area but rather to give some away to Iraqis. These three things conspired to make it difficult to get my boundary extended, but I made it my single-minded goal to get it done. Every time I met with Charlton or spoke to one of the Marine Corps generals, I spoke about Albu Bali and the need for me to own it. Charlton was in complete agreement and worked just as hard as I did to convince MNF-W leaders, mostly Brig. Gen. Mark Gurganus, that we needed to own Bali.

My first personal exposure to the insurgents that roamed Albu Bali came during my transition with Wheeler. On the day that I visited Mariano Wecer's company, after he gave me an ops briefing, I went on a dismounted patrol with him and one of his infantry platoons. The plan was for us to walk to a house near his boundary and establish a small kill team for several hours overwatching an area where the enemy had conducted several attacks against his forces. Once set, a mounted patrol of Bradleys and tanks would move to an adjacent position and man an OP in an attempt to draw enemy forces into an ambush. It was a good plan, even though it was a daylight patrol, but, as we say in the Army, the enemy had a vote that day. As we walked toward the house, we were covered from observation by an over-grown irrigation canal with reeds twenty feet tall between us and Albu Bali; however, we could be seen by insurgents south of the river. About an hour into our walk, we were engaged by insurgents south of the river and forced to take cover in the canal (that was twelve feet deep and had about three feet of water at the bottom). We could not see the insurgents who engaged us, and after about twenty minutes, we left the canal and completed our movement to the SKT position.

I believe that the insurgents south of the canal called those in Albu Bali (at the time they were using both walkie talkies and cell phones) and alerted them to our movement. Once we were set, we called for the mounted forces to move to their OP, but while en route, the lead Bradley was attacked and disabled by an IED—no injuries, but the Bradley was immobilized and would have to be extracted by a recovery vehicle. Twenty minutes later, the huge, ungainly Hercules recovery vehicle arrived on scene, and as it moved into position to hook up the Bradley, it hit a pressure-plate IED, destroying the vehicle. At that point, the enemy clearly had the upper hand. We had yet to see a single insurgent, but we had lost about $4 million in equipment. Wecer and I consulted and decided to extract the vehicles and the dismounted element and live to fight another day. Once again, much like in the city, I found myself in a position where the enemy could use an effective safe haven and support zone, only transiting to his attack zones when he saw fit. Because we couldn't drive him out and couldn't cover our boundary 24/7, he had a huge advantage. The difference was that this time, with my ERUs, IPs, and soldiers, I knew I had enough combat power to crush him.

Shortly after that patrol, within days I think, I ordered Chuck Krumwiede and my planners, in cooperation with the BCT staff and Mariano Wecer, to develop an operation to clear-hold-build in Albu Bali. When we moved to Jazeera, we changed our naming convention for our operations, adopting the names of Savannah, Georgia landmarks for all of our operations. This one became our first and most famous operation in Jazeera—Operation Forsyth Park. Operation Forsyth Park was an ambitious plan to envelop Albu Bali by attacking along both the River Road and the northern route while simultaneously clearing the IEDs from the routes. (We knew there would be some—we didn't have a clue how many.) We coordinated to have two route-clearance platoons from 321st Engineers (Pathfinders) 24/7 for the duration of the operation (which we thought would be about ninety-six hours). The plan was for Wecer's forces to be the main effort while my scout platoon isolated the northern routes into and out of Albu Bali. At the same time, 1/3/1 IA would set up a checkpoint east of Bali on the River Road to cut off all insurgent escape routes. As Wecer's forces attacked, we planned to establish a series of checkpoints on the roads into Bali using the 2nd ERU (Colonel Daoud) on the River Road and the Obaid Police on the northern route. Once in Bali, we planned to establish a new JSS on the River Road from which Wecer's platoons, ERU, and Iraqi Police would systematically clear the entire area. We were hopeful that we could recruit locals into a "neighborhood watch" to augment and guide our forces, since local scouts knew the area and the enemy better than we did.

In April 2007, the neighborhood watch concept was relatively new. I believe that Lt. Col. Roger Turner, one of the Marine battalion commanders in Ramadi, was the first to employ the neighborhood watch. The concept was that one would recruit and *rapidly* vet local men who would immediately begin to augment both U.S. and Iraqi forces in a newly cleared area. It was a dangerous proposition because it gave relatively unknown men close access to coalition forces, posing a major risk for suicide attacks. Lieutenant Colonel Chuck Ferry made extensive use of neighborhood watch both in the city of Ramadi and in his rural areas south of the river.

Around April 15, I briefed General Gurganus about our intelligence assessment of Albu Bali and the plan for Operation Forsyth Park. He was convinced of the need to clear Bali and comfortable with the plan, so he agreed to fight hard to get us a temporary operating area (TOA)—a temporary extension of our battlespace for a specific time and reason—in Bali. The fight he had was invisible to me, but I'm certain it was difficult. About a week later, Gurganus' staff informed Krumwiede that the TOA was approved.

Hindsight and a captured insurgent after-action report allows me to describe, with only a little speculation, what was going on in Bali from the enemy's perspective. March had been a disastrous month for the leaders of AQI as they lost their headquarters and capitol in the al Iskan District. They had a well-entrenched safe haven and support zone in Bali and knew that Bali belonged to the Iraqi Army, meaning they could operate there fairly unmolested. So, as Ramadi fell, they moved the leadership of the Islamic State of Iraq and most of their Ramadi-based cadres into their already established refuge in Bali. Because Bali was an area of significance to them even before the fall of Ramadi, AQI had established a robust defensive belt there. The area's isolation made it simple to close off from the outside; the Bali-based insurgents simply emplaced nearly eighty IEDs on the two major roads into the area. The IEDs on the outer edges were armed and ready to go—if insurgents needed to use the road, they simply unhooked the victim initiators, drove over the IED, and reconnected the initiator—while the IEDs on the inner ring were emplaced but had no power source or initiator installed. When insurgents wanted to arm these devices, they had to bring a battery pack and initiator to the device and take five to ten minutes to hook it up. Just as important as setting the IEDs on the roads was controlling the population of Albu Bali, and AQI was more ruthless in Bali than in any area I saw. The Bilawis had been a tribe in turmoil even before 2003. They had several factions that regularly competed for power within the tribe, resulting in the tribe having no real leadership of which to speak. AQI leaders took advantage of that as easily as they capitalized on Albu Bali's remoteness with a horrifying murder and intimidation campaign that included, at least, five mass assassinations over a several-year period. AQI ruled Bali with the most evil techniques and inhuman cruelty of any area in Iraq, leaving long-lasting scars on the Bilawis. With the population completely controlled and the roads fortified with bombs, the leaders of AQI thought they could withstand the might of the coalition; so, even though they suspected a major assault was coming, they chose to stand and fight.

They knew a major assault was coming, in part, because I told everyone who would listen. As I wrote earlier, I discussed Bali at many of my meetings with sheiks and IPs, and although the vast majority of IP chiefs did an excellent job keeping secrets, sheiks didn't, and I didn't expect they would. I wanted both the AQI operatives in Bali and the civilians to know that the fight was coming. I knew that we would ultimately win the military engagement and hoped that AQI would stand and fight instead of running to new safe havens. I also knew that we needed a sheik and neighborhood watch recruits to help us manage the place, and the only way we would get them quickly was to broadcast our intentions. I also wanted to ensure that we had minimal collateral damage and avoided accidental killing and injuring of civilians. It's possible that, by broadcasting the attack, I may have made it more difficult for us, and perhaps I gave the enemy an advantage. The most extreme argument, although no one made it to my face, is that by violating routine secrecy, I cost four Americans their lives. (Later you may decide for yourself.) At the time, it was a controversial decision and could have landed me in trouble, but, it has since become a widely accepted best practice in counterinsurgency, and, I believe, it has saved countless civilian lives, thereby winning the population's support. Whether or not you agree, it worked. Although I don't recall the exact sequence—I think we got a call from an American outfit in Fallujah, but the initial contact could have come from IPs—we were soon in contact with a sheik from Bali, Sheik Sirhan al Balawi, who assured us we would have recruits for the neighborhood watch the day we entered Bali. I was happy to speak to him—we met twice before the operation commenced—but thought he was full of shit.

The A Shau Valley of Iraq

Once we had approval for the operation, we began our considerable preparations. Operationally, we had to brief the orders to all the participants, including Iraqi police and ERUs, which meant that the whole kit and caboodle had to be translated to Arabic. That task, and many others, fell to Capt. Bryan Dennison, who was technically my fire support officer, but as we moved up to Jazeera, I made him and his section our Iraqi Security Forces coordination and liaison cell. For that mission, we assigned one of my brightest infantry platoon sergeants, Sgt. 1st Class Derek Kitts to be his sergeant-in-charge. Dennison and Kitts were both extraordinarily bright and very hardworking—Kitts was also the biggest smartass in the battalion—and made a great team. We also gave them a very capable but quite cantankerous interpreter whose pseudonym was Jack—a grouchy, naturalized U.S. citizen who had been living in the States for about thirty years when the war broke out.

Jack was Cliff Wheeler's personal interpreter while he was in Jazeera, but my interpreter, Mahar (also a U.S. citizen), came from the city with us. As we moved to Jazeera, Mahar took vacation to return to the States, and I used Jack for about two weeks—it was disastrous. Jack and I got along fairly well personally, but professionally I found him unacceptable. Jack was a Shia and had deep-seated resentment for the Sunnis in al Anbar, and he wore his emotions on his sleeve. Although I'm by no means fluent in Arabic, I speak enough to know that Jack was editorializing my words quite a bit. He did a great job for Bryan, though. After the translation was done, we had to brief the orders to all involved, receive back briefs from the units, and finally conduct rehearsals of the entire operation. Back briefs are a critical part of our preparations. Simply, the subordinate units and staff members tell me, as the commander, how they plan to do the things that I ordered them to do. It is during these briefs and the subsequent rehearsals that the commander and his staff ensure that everyone is "on the same sheet of music" and that there are no glaring omissions or issues. If there are issues (and there almost always are if you're really thinking through the operation), then they are either fixed on the spot or the staff corrects them later in a written order.

We did find a few issues with this operation: first, I was concerned about how quickly we could build some type of fortification for the IP and ERU checkpoints along the roads. Second, we were all concerned about identifying markings for the new neighborhood watch recruits. Finally, I was concerned that we didn't have communications with the ERU members and that they didn't have sufficient radios to communicate among themselves. To correct the first issue, I ordered that Wecer leave U.S. OPs at several spots along the road to provide covering fire should an IP or ERU checkpoint come under attack. For the second issue, I had my logistics officer acquire as many marking panels as he could. "VS 17" marking panels are six-by-three-foot colored panels, pink on one side and orange on the other, that are used for visual marking. We cut them into strips and made armbands for the new recruits until we could get something better. The last problem was the hardest—we needed the ERUs to carry their load but couldn't have them running around unless we knew their location. To solve the problem, I ordered that either Colonel Daoud or his second-in-command needed to be with Mariano Wecer at all times, and no ERU element would move more than one thousand yards without U.S. forces accompanying.

With preparations complete and approvals given, Operation Forsyth Park kicked off at 6 a.m. on April 26, 2007, after I had been in charge of Jazeera for twenty days. Things went exactly as planned—but only for the first three minutes. The pathfinder unit on the northern route found the first IED at 6:03 a.m. when it detonated against the lead RG-31 personnel carrier, destroying the vehicle and injuring all four crewmembers (one was evacuated to Baghdad with a severe concussion). The IED was in a culvert that crossed a major irrigation canal that ran east–west about halfway between Route Mobile and River Road. The entire culvert was destroyed, making the forty-foot-wide by thirty-five-foot-deep canal impassable for vehicle traffic.

There were two other culverts within three miles that crossed that canal into Bali, and we needed to check them out, but there was a stretch of uncleared dirt road we had to clear first. At about 9:30 a.m., a large buried IED detonated against a Buffalo mine-clearing vehicle on the River Road, destroying the Buffalo's remote arm, without which it was just a big armored bus. Within an hour, an IED detonated on a Buffalo on the northern route, destroying the vehicle but injuring no one. The two Pathfinder platoons had one extra Buffalo between them, and it had already moved to meet the route-clearance patrol on the River Road. So we were at a standstill in the north. There were other backup Buffalos at Camp Ramadi, so, after coordinating with 321st Engineers, I sent my PSD to go bring two more of them forward. The clearance proceeded on River Road, where we had our first contact (other than IEDs that were unmanned) around 11:00 a.m. when a pair of insurgents fired an RPG at the lead RG-31, knocking one of its antennae off but exploding harmlessly on the road adjacent to the vehicle. No one saw the insurgents, and they escaped back toward Bali. Over the next several hours, we discovered two large buried IEDs on River Road; both were ten-gallon plastic gasoline jugs full of HME (probably fifty pounds) buried in or beside the road with multiple pressure strips and booby traps so that if they were moved, they would explode.

My PSD returned with the backup Buffalo and crew at about 3 p.m. and got back to work on the northern route. The operations officer for the 321st Engineers came back with them, and he, Krumwiede, and I had a brainstorming session about how we should proceed. Obviously, we were all concerned about how the operation had gone so far. We were now nine hours into the route clearance and had cleared only about a mile, and that mile had been quite costly in both human and equipment terms. Although we only had one serious injury, and that one was not life threatening, we also had a couple of minor concussions and some cuts and bruises. Furthermore, we all knew we had been lucky so far; it was only a matter of time before we had some very serious injuries or deaths. While we were having that discussion, we heard another explosion in the distance, followed by a second explosion and machine gun and Bradley cannon fire. Another RPG attack on River Road, ineffective again.

With the replacement Buffalo, Wecer's infantrymen and the explosive ordinance disposal (EOD) team supporting them had made it to the next closest culvert over the huge east–west canal, but, like its twin a mile and a half away, it was rigged with a large buried IED. The EOD technicians went down to check out the bomb and found that it had been ingeniously placed by cutting a section from the top of the culvert pipe with a torch, hollowing out a large spot for the bomb between the pipe and the road above, then welding the pipe back into place. The massive IED had been hooked to a pressure switch, but there was no way to know if the device had other initiators or not, and it was too risky to attempt removing it without such knowledge. The only acceptable choice was to blow it in place, leaving a second of the three culverts impassable. We had cleared less than a mile on River Road and had already lost two Buffalos there, and the northern route was apt to be even more difficult. It was time, already, to adjust the plan. After huddling with Chuck Krumwiede and the Pathfinder company commander and talking to Wecer on the radio, I decided to establish blocking positions with IPs and my scout platoon along Route Mobile north of Albu Bali, isolating the area. We would have to focus on clearing River Road to gain access to Albu Bali.

But River Road wasn't easy. At 6:00 p.m. another RG-31 was destroyed by an IED, and this time there were four injured, two serious enough to require evacuation to the level III hospital in Baghdad. At 7 p.m. another RPG attack, but this time the failing daylight caused the insurgents to come too close, and one of Wecer's Bradley crews killed them. As that engagement occurred, a replacement Pathfinder company came to relieve the B Company, 321st Engineers, who had done a phenomenal job. All told, they had suffered twelve WIAs and had four vehicles either destroyed or damaged, but even with all their hard work, we had only cleared about two miles on River Road. C Company, 321st came in as their relief. That night the going was very slow. The Pathfinder platoons that came in for the night shift were tentative and frightened (for good reason). From about 7 p.m. until about 4:30 a.m., the unit only cleared about six hundred yards of the River Road, finding two IEDs and losing one Husky mine-detecting vehicle to an unseen one. No one was injured that night.

As daylight came, C Company, 321st Engineers picked up the pace. They had covered about another four hundred yards when they found their first IED that day—another large buried one. As they worked to clear that IED, one of Wecer's Bradley crews jockeyed for position on the road to provide better overwatch. About two minutes after the Bradley had set in position, a large buried IED exploded beside the vehicle, blowing the track off and causing some suspension damage but no injuries. It was this IED that started a buzz among 321st Engineers that eventually grew to a roar, nearly bringing Operation Forsyth Park to a screeching halt. Every IED that had been discovered thus far on the roads to Albu Bali had been set up with pressure-detonating devices of one sort or another. A few IEDs also had command wires run to them—command wires allow an insurgent to trigger the IED remotely—but none of the command wires terminated near a power source. Basically, one needs a car battery to set off an IED from a distance, and insurgents don't typically run off carrying a car battery after an attack, but we had not found any batteries thus far.

Regardless of the facts, the 321st Engineers had been attacked with more IEDs in the thirty-six hours up to that point than they had in the three weeks prior to it. They were the experts at finding these IEDs but had still been attacked nearly as often as they had found and diffused the bombs on these roads. I believe they were beginning to feel like my soldiers were questioning their abilities. I certainly wasn't, and I'm unaware of any of my soldiers who did. I thought that the insurgents in Bali were excellent IED emplacers and the roads leading into Bali were the most difficult type on which to identify IEDs. Regardless of reality, the Pathfinders were beginning to look for a scapegoat, and my soldiers were it. C Company, 321st Engineers began to talk among themselves, telling each other that most of the IEDs they had found thus far had been command detonated and that the reason insurgents were able to attack them was that 3-69 Armor soldiers were providing poor security for them. This misconception would continue to build to the point of crisis.

Meanwhile, real progress was occurring behind the route-clearance teams. As soon as the roads were cleared, my soldiers began to emplace OPs that could provide security while IPs and ERUs emplaced their new checkpoints. In the north, the Obaid IPs had two new checkpoints working in conjunction with my scout platoon. Farther east, at the eastern edge of my AO, Diogo Tavares' Steel Company was overwatching a new checkpoint the Hamdiya Police had put in due north of Bali. The Hamdiya Police were neither part of the plan nor operating in their area—they were, by far, my most aggressive police station—but the checkpoint they put in was a great idea, and I had soldiers in a permanent position nearby who could respond if needed. On River Road, the Zuwei'a IPs had emplaced a checkpoint, and Colonel Daoud's 2nd ERU had emplaced two checkpoints and two OPs that were hidden in fields watching the road. The ERUs were also conducting mounted patrols behind the route-clearance teams to keep the routes open. One of those patrols had attempted to enter a side road from River Road and had found an IED, eventually getting a report to Wecer, who passed the info to a Pathfinder who destroyed the IED hours later.

The enemy immediately reacted to the success of the Iraqi Security Forces. Three times on April 27, insurgents attacked IP or ERU checkpoints with gunfire, RPG fire, mortar fire, or some combination. The IPs and ERUs acquitted themselves well, suffering no casualties and claiming to have killed seven insurgents. Also fighting like champs were the soldiers of B Company, 321st Engineers and their EOD detachment, who had come back on duty at about 6 p.m. on the 27th. A little more than an hour after they returned, the enemy launched a complex attack with three groups of insurgents wielding RPGs and machine guns against their element. B Company, 321st Engineers killed three insurgents in the engagement and wounded several others, sustaining no casualties themselves. While that firefight raged, all hell broke loose along the line: Wecer's soldiers had two more complex attacks nearly simultaneously, and the ERUs were engaged with RPGs. We killed five more insurgents and wounded an unknown number; one ERU member received minor shrapnel wounds. What was most significant was that, by all accounts, the enemy had attacked with at least a dozen insurgents simultaneously, perhaps as many as twenty-five. It had become clear that the leaders of AQI had decided to stand and fight for Albu Bali. However, during those complex attacks, we had broken al Qaeda's defense. There were five IEDs discovered and destroyed in a row before and after the complex attacks, and no IED attacks or injuries; the route clearance progressed very quickly. By 11:30 p.m. we were checking out the first of three possible locations for the new JSS, but the enemy wasn't done yet.

As B Company, 321st Engineers began checking the route toward the driveway of the large compound in which we might have set up our JSS, they discovered another large buried IED. Insurgents emplaced this one by cutting a square out of the asphalt road and then repairing the asphalt in an attempt to hide the bomb. After checking around it with the Buffalo, they found they could not expose the IED through the asphalt patch and called for the EOD team to come forward and disable the device. Marine

Sergeants Peter Woodall and William Callahan dismounted from their huge Cougar mine-resistant, ambush-protected (MRAP) vehicle and proceeded to the spot of the IED.

I had worked with U.S. Army EOD during my previous tour in Iraq and could remember a time in Baquba when insurgents had targeted EOD technicians, killing five or six over the course of a month. In my previous experience, I had never known EOD techs to pick up IEDs or approach them without bomb suits on, but here in Ramadi, I had not seen a bomb suit employed yet. I am not an EOD expert and certainly don't know much about what they call "render safe procedures," and I don't want to second guess these two sergeants, who had a good deal of experience with IEDs. Furthermore, I'm not sure that any safeguards would have prevented what occurred next. As the two Marine sergeants placed a disruption charge on the IED, it exploded, instantly killing them both. What occurred for the next hour was sheer chaos—Wecer's soldiers and the Pathfinder soldiers went on a manhunt for the triggerman who, I believe, didn't exist. They combed through the dense palm grove surrounding the area and searched nearly to the river about four hundred yards away.

Meanwhile, back at Camp Blue Diamond, my battle staff had been monitoring the operation via reconnaissance drone, or UAV. There are some things that UAVs don't do well and some they excel at—UAVs can't distinguish good guys from bad guys and can't track individuals that move through a group, but they certainly can find human beings hiding in the bushes very well. Unless there is a solid canopy in an area, a person can't really hide from an overhead thermal image sensor. These things detect temperature changes as subtle as one degree and can easily distinguish the shape of a man from above five thousand feet. From my location at JSS Warrior, I could speak with my staff, and both Maj. Mike Rosamond and Capt. Jay McGee (who had extensive experience using UAV images) said that there was no one, other than our forces, within five hundred yards of the site at the time of the explosion, nor had they seen anyone move from the area since the explosion. I was given a report that night that said the post-blast investigation identified a command wire buried three feet deep and running two hundred yards toward a palm grove, but in subsequent reports (and there were several), there was no mention of such a wire, and I doubt that in the confusion that occurred that night anyone was able to pull a wire buried three feet deep to its terminus two hundred yards away. I believe that this IED, like so many of the others we saw in Bali, was rigged with a booby trap that went off when it was molested. Regardless of how it happened, two brave young Marines had lost their lives to liberate Albu Bali from al Qaeda, and I wasn't about to stop now. Nothing else happened that night as we spent the rest of the darkness recovering from that gruesome attack.

The next morning dawned bright and clear, but things were anything but for me. That morning I had a visit from the commander of the 321st Engineer Battalion, an Army Reserve full colonel who looked about fifty-five years old. I don't remember his name, and that's probably good. What I do remember is that he was whiney and passive-aggressive in his dealings with other battalion commanders. In fact, a couple of my Regular Army and Marine counterparts had some really heated exchanges with him. He often said that, although he outranked us all, he always wanted other battalion commanders to treat him as a peer, but his actions rarely showed that to be the case. National Guard and Army Reserve units often are cobbled together at the last minute before deploying into combat. The truth is that they are usually not fully manned and certainly not trained for the missions at hand. This was the case with the 321st Engineers. I'm not sure if this guy commanded them before they were activated or merely came in to command them for deployment, but either way, he didn't have my respect.

As stated earlier, Chuck Krumwiede and I rode with the Pathfinders early on in our time in Ramadi while they conducted route clearance, and we were the first field-grade officers to do so—neither the battalion commander nor his executive officer or operations officer had done so, according to one of their company commanders. In fact, I never saw this guy off of Camp Ramadi until that morning. My personal feelings aside, this commander came out to JSS Warrior because he was genuinely concerned for the safety of his soldiers and mine. After a very brief exchange of small talk, he told me about the theory his soldiers had developed that all the IEDs we had encountered were command detonated, and he expressed concern that my infantrymen and tankers were not doing everything we could to secure his unit. We had a long discussion about what my soldiers were and were not doing and what we could do to improve security. During the meeting, he threatened to take his soldiers out of Albu Bali if I couldn't provide them security. I finally lost my temper and asked him to leave—I said I was too busy to have this conversation right then but that I would have my staff look at solutions to the problem. As soon as he left I called Charlton—something I didn't do much—to ensure I would have his support. We had nearly reached the location of our new JSS, and I couldn't afford to give up this ground we had fought so hard to take. Events would not allow me to dwell on this issue too long, though.

By noon on April 28, my soldiers had reached what would become our new JSS, and we had begun the multi-day process of fortifying the position. About an hour after they had begun setting up at the JSS, they were approached by a man named Abbas al Balawi, who declared himself to be the commander of the Albu Bali Police and called himself a captain. Abbas was a character and caused me much consternation over the next five months. He was a twenty-six-year-old jeweler who once owned a shop in Baghdad. He was pompous, loud, and uncouth and had little in the way of leadership skills, but I supported him publicly (while often flaying his hide privately) because he was brave and took charge of a place that was as dangerous as any in Iraq. We had hoped to find 50 or so recruits for the Bali neighborhood watch; Abbas brought us 140 that day. Though they were ragtag, untrained, and ill equipped, the Albu Bali neighborhood watch was a critical asset without which we couldn't possibly have succeeded. We immediately set them to work with my soldiers, the ERU, and the Obaid police to man checkpoints and establish security.

Three other occurrences that day were highly significant. That afternoon at about 3 p.m., Captain Abbas came to Mariano Wecer very worked up. He said he had reliable information that a group of twenty to thirty insurgents was planning to attack the JSS. At that point, the JSS was far from secure. Although we had emplaced some barriers, the perimeter was still wide open in several spots; Soldiers were just beginning to build proper fortifications in the building and on the roof, and we had forces spread out over five miles of bad road trying to keep our routes open. There were only about ten soldiers at the JSS at the time. Wecer called in a report to me about the intelligence Abbas had brought, and I quickly coordinated to get helicopter gunship coverage.

As they arrived on station they reported, through my Marine Supporting Arms Liaison Team (SALT) that they had identified about eleven men moving in a military formation toward the JSS. I asked, through the SALT, for them to approach the men close enough to see if they were in uniforms or marked with orange armbands. (I later found out that my questions and the answers were miscommunicated.) I was concerned that these could be Abbas' neighborhood watch (who were in civilian attire with armbands) or ERUs (who wore green camouflaged Iraqi Army uniforms). After about ten minutes of questions to Wecer and to the helicopters, I was convinced that these men were not in uniform, they were armed, they were moving directly toward the JSS, and they matched, albeit roughly, the description of the attack that Abbas had foretold. I ordered the helicopters to kill them. They made two gun runs on the target, killing two and wounding two. The rest dispersed.

About ten minutes later I received word that Colonel Daoud's ERU had had a squad attacked by helicopters and that casualties were on their way to JSS Warrior. Sure enough, ten minutes after that, two dead ERUs and two wounded—all wearing green camouflaged uniforms—were brought to Warrior. I immediately went out to talk to Colonel Daoud. I explained to Daoud what had happened and fully expected him to take his unit and leave, or at least to display his formidable temper. He didn't, rather he grabbed me by the shoulders and said something like, "Shit happens, we'll sort it out later, let's move on." Up to that point, I honestly thought of my Iraqi security partners as less professional than me—less like real soldiers. I changed my opinion that day. I have replayed and second-guessed my decision to engage those men a thousand times, but I can't take it back.

About an hour later an event took place that did more for us in Albu Bali than any other single event. Insurgents on its northern edge fired two 120mm mortar rounds at the JSS . . . and missed. The rounds landed short and hit a family compound north of the JSS, wounding six civilians, two urgently (both little girls, one seriously). Their mother and two men received minor wounds. Not knowing how we would react, the father (who some later claimed was an insurgent) brought his injured family to the JSS, where we treated them exactly as we would treat my soldiers. They were evacuated, and one of the little girls was saved after hours in the operating room. The story spread like wildfire through Albu Bali.

At about the same time, a lone al Qaeda foreign fighter (the locals all said he was a Saudi national) drove a car bomb toward Albu Bali. It was a Chevy Caprice station wagon loaded with about one thousand pounds of HME. I believe he intended to attack the new JSS. His route took him near the Hamdiya Police's temporary checkpoint on Route Mobile. When he saw the checkpoint, he attempted to evade the police, and they shot and killed the driver, capturing the car bomb intact. That was another huge victory for my Iraqi Security Forces. Also that night, without my approval and much to my chagrin, my soldiers named the new JSS in Bali "JSS Pathfinder," in honor of the soldiers who did the real work getting us in there. In the three-day fight to seize JSS Pathfinder, the 321st Engineers had discovered and neutralized fifteen IEDs, and either they or my soldiers had been attacked by another thirteen IEDs—all to clear a stretch of road about six miles long.

The battle for Albu Bali didn't end on April 28, 2007; it was just beginning. Over the next twenty days, IPs, neighborhood watch, ERUs, and American soldiers, sailors, airmen, and Marines fought to clear every house, farm, field, and storefront in Bali. The 321st Engineers continued clearing IEDs through the first week of May, and they lost two of their own soldiers on May 3 to an IED on the district's outskirts. Staff Sergeant Coby Schwab and Corporal Kelly Grothe were killed when they stepped on a pressure-strip IED as they dismounted from their Buffalo. About a dozen Iraqis from the ERU and the Obaid IPs lost their lives in that fight as well.

During the period from May 3 to May 17, my forces, both Iraqi and American, developed a new technique for finding IEDs. ERU members, who had previously been nationalist insurgents, walked the roads criss-crossing Bali and identified, based on their experience, IEDs. One was particularly proficient, so much so that Mariano Wecer asked him, "How are you so good at finding and dismantling IEDs?" After some thought, he told Wecer, "I used to be a TV repairman." From that day forward, we called him Captain Spicoli, referring to the memorable quote in *Fast Times at Ridgemont High* when Curtis Spicoli says, "I can fix it. My dad's got an awesome set of tools. He's a TV repairman." On a daily basis, the coalition forces in Bali seized weapons caches, removed IEDs, and established a safe and secure environment. All told, over seventy IEDs were destroyed, and tens of thousands of pounds of munitions and explosives, including a major truck-bomb factory, were seized. Additionally, we uncovered the gruesome signs of AQI's brutality there, finding five mass graves that held more than eighty individuals who had been killed by AQI death squads.

On May 17 we declared Operation Forsyth Park over. To this day, it remains one of the more famous small unit actions in the Iraq campaign. John Charlton, who rarely paid compliments to me or my outfit, paid us the highest compliment when he dubbed Operation Forsyth Park the A Shau Valley of Iraq. But it wasn't over yet. Six days later, al Qaeda launched its final attack from Albu Bali. On the night of May 23, an insurgent group that formerly operated in Albu Bali launched a complex attack against a police checkpoint in northeast Obaid. As my soldiers responded to the attack, a man signaled to the lead element to come over to him. By then we were accustomed to interacting with locals as we responded to attacks. The lead fire-team leader, Pvt. 1st Class Daniel Cagle (a California kid who played a mean guitar), and his squad leader, Staff Sgt. Steve Butcher (a guy who was a legend in my battalion and who had once auditioned to be a TV Power Ranger), moved over to speak to the civilian . . . who exploded the suicide vest he wore, killing both men. I never saw Cagle again; he was flown to Baghdad still barely alive but declared dead on arrival. I did see Steve Butcher—I put my hand on his broken body and prayed that God would take his soul.

Two months later, a U.S. unit conducting a raid at an AQI safe house captured a document that purported to be the al Qaeda after-action review for what they called the "Battle of Jazeera." They claimed that fighting the U.S. and Iraqi forces in Albu Bali was the biggest error they had made to date. Although we only confirmed about twenty enemy killed and sixty captured, they put the number at eighty AQI members killed and one hundred captured and swore they would never stand and fight again. Later that summer, they published what they called Zarqawi's First Rule: Always go where the Americans are not.

CHAPTER 13

Everlasting Bomb Stoppers

After Operation Forsyth Park, there was never again an insurgent safe haven in the Ramadi municipality—the entire city and the surrounding suburbs were clear of al Qaeda. With Iraqi Police (IPs) on nearly every corner in the city and about a hundred checkpoints in Jazeera, as well as a similar numbers of checkpoints in the areas south of the river, there was little chance for insurgents to plant IEDs in the area or to attack with small arms, RPGs, mortars, or rockets. Insurgents had no safe area from which to launch those attacks because the population no longer supported their efforts and would not hide them, feed them, supply them, or even tolerate their presence. Previously, the average citizen couldn't resist al Qaeda because he had no way to stand on his own, nor did he have a reliable way to reach anyone who could help. Now, all the average citizen had to do was go out on the street, and within ten minutes he could either walk to a police checkpoint or a police truck would come by on patrol. I'm sure that al Qaeda's leaders were frightened by these events and furious at the population and the Iraqi Security Forces, but I think they saw this, initially, as only a temporary setback. They needed to get their safe havens back, and that meant coercing the population one way or the other. So they went back to their "bread and butter"—murder and intimidation.

As I said, we didn't see mortar attacks, IEDs, or RPGs, but there were still attacks, and they were occasionally spectacular. Since very early in the insurgency, AQI had employed car- and truck-bomb attacks, largely, but not exclusively, against Shia targets. Now, the AQI fighters turned on the Sunni population and Iraqi Security Forces in al Anbar, and we saw a major uptick in suicide car- and truck-bomb attacks. My experience is exclusively with suicide car and truck bombs in which the driver "delivers" the ordinance to a location and the device is detonated while the driver is still in it. For our purposes here, I'm only going to make two distinctions. I'll call a car bomb any motor-vehicle-based IED on a chassis smaller than two tons; this includes everything from three-wheeled, motorcycle-engine-powered carts to the Bongo truck. A car-bomb might have as little as one hundred pounds of explosives but can have, like the Chevy station wagon that the Hamdiya Police captured, as much as one thousand pounds of HME, military munitions, or commercial explosives. These "small" bombs can still have huge effects, like destroying a building, killing a dozen people in a marketplace, or killing every IP at a checkpoint. These were multipurpose bombs, and I'm sure that AQI kept a stockpile of them pre-built.

What I'll call a truck bomb is built on a commercial truck chassis—normally either an eighteen-wheeler or a ten-ton or larger dump truck loaded with up to six thousand pounds of explosives. These massive bombs have the potential to level multiple buildings, killing scores of people, and were often set up to throw huge amounts of shrapnel. They could also be built to destroy a span on a major bridge or breach the entrance to a fortified compound, but these were always single-purpose, "custom-built" bombs and were made in special factories—probably only a few such factories existed in all of Iraq.

I wrote earlier about the highly modified, Bongo car bomb that had been used to attack my soldiers at COP Sword just prior to Operation Call to Freedom, and I'm aware of a half-dozen or so other car- or truck-bomb attacks that occurred in or near Ramadi prior to that time, but these attacks were relatively rare in the city. The attacks were less rare in Jazeera. There was one such attack against the Jazeera IP Station just prior to our arrival, and two more against the Albu Faraj IP Station and an ERU checkpoint prior to clearing Albu Bali, but from about May 1 until mid-July 2007, there were a dozen or so such attacks in Jazeera alone and probably another eight to ten in other parts of the Ramadi municipality.

Most Americans have seen images of the aftermath of these despicable suicide car-bomb attacks in the media—the blood-stained streets, the broken glass, the remnants of a vehicle or two, charred roads, police and paramedics scampering around—you can see it in your mind. Let me tell you some of what you don't know or didn't see on TV. The first thing that you can't get on TV is the smell of a car-bomb attack: the acrid smell of burned rubber and plastic, the distinctive smell of homemade explosive—a combination of cordite (gun smoke) and the odor of burned match heads. Then there is the strong smell of all the vehicle fluids—engine and transmission oil, coolant, and battery acid. Finally, there is the smell of blood; not decay, but rather the smell of large amounts of fresh blood—metallic and very distinct.

After the smell hits you, next you notice the pieces scattered around the area, sometimes as far as two hundred yards. As you approach, you recognize some pieces: a door handle, springs from the suspension, a windshield wiper, a twisted section of guardrail, a human torso, an arm, a foot, or a matted and bloody scalp. The next thing you see is that the blood, fat, and body parts often leave a separate trail for each victim, a three- or four-foot-wide swath that makes a perfect line from the blast site to the point where one may recover a large enough set of remains to bury. Just as often the trail of gore simply fades away, and there's nothing left. There's one person who rarely leaves a trail; the bomber is usually so close to the blast that his remains go up instead of out, but by some strange combination of physics and biology, his head normally survives. Believe me, there is nothing more surreal than watching a soldier do a retinal scan on a disembodied head, especially one that often has a full beard that has been singed by the explosion. In most cases, the head would be found by the Iraqis on site, and they would point it out to me by putting a foot on top of it—of course, touching the remains with the sole of a boot represented the highest disrespect they could show to the takfiri scum—then proclaiming, "He definitely isn't Iraqi." Sometimes, I could tell that the bomber had African features, but just as often he had Arab features and skin tone. Whether they could really tell that he wasn't from Iraq or they simply wanted to distance themselves from the thug whose head they were kicking like a soccer ball, I'll never know.

Inside the remains of the bomber's vehicle, if there was enough left, we would often find one of the driver's legs, normally attached either with chain, cable, or wire to some portion of the vehicle because once he made the decision to become a "martyr," there was no going back. Car and truck bombs normally had multiple initiators; they all had a switch, plunger, or button in the cab from which the driver could initiate the bomb, but they often had one or more "chicken switches" as well, rigged in a number of different ways so that if the driver changed his mind, the bomb could be initiated remotely, by time, or by some inadvertent action by the driver.

Our experts could normally glean a good deal of information from the scenes of these incidents. EOD technicians gathered the data, and it went to several different agencies for analysis. Initially, it was difficult to do these investigations, or "post-blast analyses," though later it would become better. The difficulty arose from the cultural differences between Americans and Iraqis. In America, if a car bomb went off and killed six or eight people, we would cordon off the area until the "authorities" arrived, then they would investigate for days, "releasing" the scene only once all the evidence was collected, cataloged, and stored for the inevitable trial of the suspect or suspects. Then, having finished that process, we would immediately begin plans for a monument to the heroes who had died there. In Iraq, when these events occurred, the single most compelling motive for action was to get things back to "normal" as quickly as possible—road swept off and washed down, bodies removed, vehicle towed or pushed off the road, barriers re-erected, and checkpoint operating as usual. To see just how driven the Iraqis were in these attempts, one must examine "normal" Iraqi (or, more generally, Arab) reactions and norms for roads and highways.

For example, I can recall several occasions in Kuwait, Iraq, and Saudi Arabia when a vehicle destroyed in a motor vehicle accident would sit on the side of the road for weeks without being moved; or the contents of an overturned semi-tractor trailer (be they gravel, scrap metal, garbage, or anything else of little value) would be swept to the edges of the motorway and left piled on the shoulder until time, wind, and traffic finally moved them from the road; or the glass, bumpers, fenders, wheels, and other parts remaining from an accident would lay on the shoulder until the desert eventually reclaimed them. Therefore, this zeal to sanitize the area must have been motivated by something other than mere orderliness. I believe they did this as a matter of pride and determination, in order to show AQI that they would not be intimidated, nor even taken out of their routine. So, initially, we were always in a race to get to the scene before all the evidence was gone, but eventually, through my actions and the actions of my subordinate leaders and soldiers, we got the IP and ERU leaders to understand the need to preserve these scenes.

My unit could not stop these attacks. To truly stop them, one had to attack the network that built and transported these devices, and that was out of bounds for my unit, both figuratively and literally. Literally because my outfit and my colleagues throughout the municipality destroyed all the bomb factories in our area, and figuratively because these networks were among the most difficult to penetrate (with spies or informants), track, or target because they were run, exclusively, by hard-core al Qaeda and rarely had ties to locals or mere criminals who could be "bought." Because we couldn't stop the attacks, the best we could do was to stop the bombs from making it to their intended targets, thereby limiting the damage done. That task was accomplished by setting up checkpoints to keep car bombs outside of the city and away from markets, police stations, and government facilities. That sounds very clinical and neat . . . unless you are the IP or ERU who is at the pointy end of the spear, sticking your face in the driver's window of a car or truck bomb.

As previously detailed, there were hundreds of checkpoints in and around Ramadi, but they were not necessarily designed to keep car bombs out of the entire municipality; rather, these checkpoints provided protection to small areas. In January 2007, that made perfect sense because one didn't exactly know where the insurgents were, so a checkpoint was a means to provide localized protection. It took an engineer to figure out a larger plan, and that engineer was Sheik Jabbar al Fahadawi from Hamdiya.

Sheik Jabbar, as was mentioned earlier, was hugely instrumental in setting up, recruiting, and equipping (with his own money) the Hamdiya IPs. The Hamdiya police chief, Col. Khalil al Fahadawi (I think they were distant cousins—not closely related by Iraqi standards), was a very close friend of Sheik Jabbar and, being five to seven years his elder, was also a man who had great influence on the sheik. (Both of these guys were really the salt of the earth, and I count them as true friends.) When Cliff Wheeler was still in charge in Jazeera, Jabbar decided that he wanted to build a major checkpoint right on Route Mobile designed to keep car and truck bombs, as well as insurgents and their other wares, out of Jazeera. (Really, he just hoped to keep them from repopulating Hamdiya or attacking "his" IP station.) Cliff was completely supportive of the idea and brought it to Charlton, who hated it. He ranted to Cliff that such a setup would be a truck-bomb magnet. "Just look at Baghdad," he would say, referring to the constant suicide car- and truck-bomb attacks on the IP and U.S. Army checkpoints surrounding the capital city. But Jabbar wasn't about to wait for American approval; he always thought it silly that Americans made decisions about what was best for Iraq. (In fact, he used to scourge me with his logic for any boneheaded decision that the United States made in Iraq—that's when it was no fun to represent the entire U.S. government.)

So, without Charlton's approval and with Cliff's tacit agreement, Jabbar started running a checkpoint on Route Mobile just north of Hamdiya. That week, Cliff convinced Charlton that we needed to support the effort, and Wheeler's forces began what they named Operation Vise Grip. Wheeler was only about a week into Vise Grip when we took over. To the Iraqis of Jazeera, the checkpoint on Route Mobile was always called the Hamdiya checkpoint, but to us it was Vise Grip. Vise Grip, like any other good position, was never completed; rather, we were always doing something to upgrade the level of protection, comfort, and safety of the IPs who worked there and continually working to increase the effectiveness of the operation.

On my first few visits to Vise Grip, I was harangued about the lack of generators, portable light sets, air conditioners (for the guard shack/sleeping quarters), barricades, signs, and on and on. They were all valid arguments. Because Charlton had been, more or less, forced into approving Operation Vise Grip, he had not really committed a hell of a lot of resources to it. In fact, 80 percent of the BCT's resources were going into the city. It's understandable for several reasons: first, Ramadi was the crown jewel of the counterinsurgency. AQI had designated it as the capital of the group's Islamic State of Iraq, but now it belonged to the Iraqi Security Forces, and the population was coming to our side, rapidly. Second, Charlton had begun to build quite a reputation as a result of our operations in Ramadi, but it was fragile. If the reliance on Iraqi Security Forces failed, he would be seen as a guy who had tried something new but made no lasting improvements. Charlton couldn't afford not to show rapid improvements in the city, across the spectrum. So, every light set, barrier, air conditioner, and generator was going somewhere in the city. For a month, there was little I could do for the IPs at Vise Grip. But, that all began to change during Operation Forsyth Park.

You'll recall that the Hamdiya IPs had, of their own accord, established a checkpoint on Route Mobile due north of Albu Bali and about four miles east of Vise Grip and had, while they were there, interdicted a car bomb. That did a couple of things: it gave the Hamdiya IPs a great deal of confidence in their ability to stop these bombs from entering their area, and it gave them instant credibility with both the BCT and the MEF (the Marine HQ). We were able to leverage that credibility to get commitments for some supplies for Vise Grip. Unfortunately, it would be a week or two before we really got buy-in.

On this particular day, I was required to attend the Ramadi City Council meeting, a task I always dreaded because the city council was feckless. The meetings were rambling, had no agenda, and rarely set anything real into motion. It was the neighborhood councils (like the Jazeera Council) that actually got things done. But it was a good time to see my fellow commanders and to press city officials for things that we needed in Jazeera. It was during the pre-meeting schmoozing that we all heard a huge explosion, clearly many miles away. Someone from my PSD approached within a few minutes and told me there had been a truck bomb at Vise Grip. After a brief conversation with Colonel Charlton, I headed out there as quickly as I could, arriving within twenty-five minutes of the explosion. The scene was horrific, as always (though this was my first close exposure to one of these attacks). Two IPs were killed and one very seriously injured (he had already been evacuated to Camp Ramadi), but what truly amazed me was that, although there was a traffic backup several miles long, IPs had already resumed searching vehicles on Route Mobile.

The general procedure at Vise Grip didn't change much over time. About a quarter of a mile out from the checkpoint there was a screening station manned by three IPs, two in a small machine gun bunker (to ensure compliance) and one who served as the initial screener. Among other functions, it was the screener's job to talk to the driver of every vehicle that approached the checkpoint. It was during this discussion that the screener decided whether or not that vehicle would get a cursory search or a full search. The screening discussion consisted of a few simple questions: who are you, where are you going, and what's in your car/truck? Although many Americans will shudder at the thought, the screener was conducting the basest form of social and racial profiling. If you weren't Iraqi (by admission, accent, or appearance), or you seemed nervous or ill at ease, or the soldier just didn't like the cut of your jib, you went to the thorough search lane.

The IPs and PSF put a great deal of faith in the screening process. They always told me, "Colonel Silver"—they always called me Silver; I think they assumed that my first name was Silver and my last was Man and so, in the Arab custom, Colonel Silver—"We know a takfiri just by looking. You will never be able to tell a takfiri from the man in the moon, but we know just by looking." I'll not disagree because the screening process normally worked. In fact, it worked so well that the vast majority of car and truck bombs exploded in the screening area rather than waiting to get into the search area where they would have killed twice as many, or worse, reach a crowded market where they would have killed a dozen innocents. That's the good news; the bad news is that the screener (in every incident I can recall) died in the blast.

I can remember being new in the Army and listening to the wise, old, Vietnam vets tell me that, "The life expectancy of the average point man [the first guy in an infantry formation] in Vietnam was about thirty seconds." I always thought, "Bullshit, what the hell are these old guys talking about?" I now know (not that I yet believe) that what they meant was, upon contact with the enemy, the average point man lasted about thirty seconds. Well, now that I'm the old vet, I can report that on enemy contact, the average screener lived less than two seconds. He had no chance to take cover behind a tree, or duck out of the way of bullets, or even return fire at his assailant—in the blink of an eye, his enemy hit a switch, and the screener turned into a gruesome trail of human remains that stretched across the road he guarded. But, as the result of his actions, some teeming marketplace, government building, U.S. position, or police station was protected.

If the vehicle didn't blow up while the screener made his decisions, then it went into one of two lanes: the fast search or the detailed search. In the fast search lane, the occupants would get out of the vehicle and open all the doors, the trunk, and the hood; then two IPs would do a quick walk around the vehicle, the occupants would get back in, and off they'd go. In fact, if the vehicle was local, if it contained family, or if it in some other way was familiar to the IPs, the occupants might be able to wave as they passed through the fast search lane. The detailed search lane involved a more rigorous process where drivers and passengers would show IDs or papers while three to five IPs looked in, under, on top of, and through the vehicle and its cargo. This detailed search could take as few as five minutes or as long as an hour, and (just like anywhere else in the world) if you displayed "attitude," the search got longer, and you could even wind up in jail.

The only exceptions for entering one of these lanes were for military traffic, local IPs, and "special people" who could pass directly through the checkpoint via the "coalition lane." The coalition lane bypassed all of the obstacles and barriers and didn't stop at all, but woe be on the Iraqi who thought he was special and really wasn't. Unauthorized driving in the coalition lane was occasionally punishable by death. Although I tried (as did everyone else) to force the IPs to adopt the same escalation of force procedures the U.S. forces used, I was not successful, nor was I able to equip them with the same warning devices we used. The results were predictable and unfortunate, especially at night. Confused drivers would get in the coalition lane; fail to understand what IPs were trying to communicate with lights, shouts, or flares; and wind up getting shot or shot at before they stopped. Although I only remember a couple of deaths as the result of this, I can remember dealing with plenty of angry sheiks, citizens, and even U.S. contractors who had been fired at in the coalition lane.

On this particular day in May, as the evacuation and clean up were still going on at Vise Grip, a new IP manned up as the screener, and two more were on the PKC machine gun within fifty yards of where their comrades—hell no, not comrades, but probably their cousins—had just been killed. During this time, all I heard from the United States was, "When are the Iraqis going to stand up in this fight? We're tired of Americans dying in Iraq," or "No blood for oil!" Well, these brave men, more than half of whom weren't even getting their measly three hundred dollars a month, were standing in the middle of a four-lane highway, poorly equipped and largely unprotected, knowing that the next bomb was coming, and if they did their job well, it would kill them instead of their neighbors, families, or some complete strangers in the market down the road. I tell you, these men weren't doing this for some American handout, for a contract to build a school, or because they thought they would eventually become rich. They did it because they were patriots, the likes of which haven't been seen often anywhere in the world. They wanted a place where their children could grow up in peace and have better lives than they had experienced since 2003—or, for that matter, since the rise of the Arab Ba'ath Party. When you watched these men, the Awakening was no longer an abstract principle but rather flesh and blood.

I'm not going to say that I had an epiphany; I don't think it was that dramatic, but I did know that I had to do better by these men. Luckily, when I went to see Colonel Charlton, he had swung to my side in supporting Vise Grip with assets and engineers. So far had he swung that he chewed my ass for not getting the equipment the Hamdiya IPs needed. I suppose I could have fought him and reminded him that I had asked for just such support—Lord knows that he and I were both hard-headed and loved to say "I told you so" to each other—but I think this time I humbled myself and said, "Sir, you are exactly right." Or, at least, that's how I remember it.

With new resolve to build a bigger and better checkpoint, we began to establish a much more substantial position at Vise Grip, adding concrete T-walls (Texas and Alaska barriers), Hesco baskets, sandbagged machine gun bunkers, signs, and flashing lights. But, even as we did all this, AQI increased the level of car- and truck-bomb attacks to a furious pace. The city was getting hit—markets, government center, police stations—and the suburbs north and south of the river east and west of the city were being hit as well. By mid-May, there was a car- or truck-bomb attack somewhere in the Ramadi municipality about every four days. It was obvious that this was a big problem, and the BCT was going to fix it for us all. Charlton issued a plan called Operation Squeeze Play, initially intended to cordon the city in the event of insurgent kidnapping of U.S. persons.

Basically, Squeeze Play was designed to put a U.S. checkpoint on every road into and out of the entire municipality on a temporary basis so that insurgents would be unable to transport any captured persons out of the immediate area. It was unsustainable on a semipermanent basis because it gave each battalion five or six more positions to man, supply, and fortify. If these positions were temporary, one could assume some risk on fortification. Simply, the enemy would not have the time to develop a serious attack on the position in a couple of hours, but if the positions stayed in place for days or weeks, one needed serious force protection measures like T-walls, Hescos, bunkers, etc. We could barely build the positions we had already, much less add five more per battalion. The plan was also bad counterinsurgency because these checkpoints were extraordinarily burdensome on the population; the lines backed up, causing traffic snarls that could take hours to get through. It's one thing to have IPs inconvenience the population but another thing all together for Americans to do so. As a result, we executed Squeeze Play haphazardly, and the plan was largely ineffective. The bombs kept coming.

The intelligence picture regarding these bombs was dicey. As I wrote earlier, these car- and truck-bomb cells were difficult to infiltrate, and most of the intel was strictly anecdotal. However, for whatever reason, Charlton and his staff had decided that all these car and truck bombs were transiting Route Mobile from the east and that they were getting through Vise Grip because the IPs were not searching correctly. It was complete nonsense! Vise Grip was the most thorough and professional checkpoint in the entire province, and the evidence was simple to see. There were a total of five car or truck bombs that detonated there, killing about ten IPs in May; clearly, they weren't getting through. Once again, logic was not going to sway John Charlton; he tenaciously ordered me to "get those IPs to do their job."

Operation Copland

Meanwhile, the Hamdiya IPs were taking a beating. Like all my other police, they had an area they had to secure and patrol and in which they had to maintain routine law and order, and they also had this massive checkpoint on Route Mobile. In Albu Bali, Captain Abbas and his neighborhood watch were making the slow transition to becoming full-fledged IPs. Daoud and his 2nd ERU Battalion were winding down their operations in Bali and needed some other work. They had also, of late, strayed way out of their area. Colonel Daoud, who had, by this time, developed a reputation throughout al Anbar as a formidable commander with a great unit—much of this reputation was well deserved and came from his unit's actions in Albu Bali—had, unbeknownst to me, been summoned to Baghdad to meet with several high-ranking Ministry of Interior officials who gave him some authority and latitude to conduct operations independent of Americans. Daoud had good intelligence that many of the bombs used to attack Vise Grip had come from Fallujah and one of its suburbs called Albu Ghorton. So, with his newfound charter, he coordinated with the chief of police for the Fallujah district and conducted two raids, one in Fallujah that seized a truck-bomb factory and one in Albu Ghorton that ended badly, with several civilian deaths.

I got called on the carpet for his actions, since he worked for me, and began to feel a good deal of pressure from the MEF leadership (who certainly were getting pressure from Baghdad) to get a handle on my ERU battalions. (A good deal more about that appears in the next chapter.) The 1st ERU with Colonel Muhammed was partnered with Matt McCreary's Battle Company, and the unit was beginning to do some very good work on the northern edges of Jazeera. The 1st ERU had also assumed two of the OPs formerly manned by U.S. forces on Route Mobile west of Vise Grip. I had three problems, however: first, I had to find full-time work for my two ERU battalions before they got themselves and me into a bind. Second, I had to get some relief to the Hamdiya IPs. And finally, I had to figure out how to stop the constant car- and truck-bomb attacks.

It was during this time (late May or early June), that we had the worst car-bomb attack in Jazeera. Two Bongo trucks loaded with one thousand pounds of explosives each detonated in one of the busy markets in Albu Diyab, killing thirteen and injuring another dozen Iraqi civilians. Most of my Iraqi partners thought the bombs had entered Jazeera from the north, since there were a couple of good roads through the less inhabited areas on which a terrorist could wend his way into Albu Diyab without hitting a major checkpoint. We also had more and more frequent reports coming in about insurgents operating north and east of Jazeera on the shores of Lake Thar Thar and in Saddamiya, a former Ba'ath Party resort area built on the shores of the lake. We had just suffered the attack that had killed Butcher and Cagle, and I was convinced that the suicide bombers and their vests had been able to gain entry to Obaid by coming off of Route Mobile east of Vise Grip. I sensed we were vulnerable from the north, west, and east. The solution was an idea that Krumwiede and his planners called Operation Copland.

Copland would do four things. First, we would push Vise Grip east on Route Mobile to very near our eastern boundary. Second, Colonel Daoud and his 2nd ERU would take over Vise Grip and secure Route Mobile east of Albu Diyab. They would be responsible for patrolling and checkpoints and would partner with Diogo Tavares' C Company, 2-7 Infantry (Steel). Third, Colonel Mohammed and his 1st ERU would build a new checkpoint on the northern edge of the populated areas of Jazeera and become responsible for securing our northern flank. Finally, we needed a new checkpoint on Route Mobile just east of the Euphrates River Bridge that could secure that road west of Albu Diyab (only about four miles of road). That task went to my biggest police station, the al Jazeera IPs. In effect, we would close off Jazeera from the rest of the municipality and fully engage the ERUs. The idea had really come from the BCT's Operation Squeeze Play, so the BCT's leaders were fairly happy to support the plan. The hard part was selling it to the Iraqis.

To "sell" the plan, I brought all the IP chiefs and both ERU commanders together for the first of several "Jazeera security conferences." This was a big deal. I previously mentioned the kind of pomp and circumstance that went into my meetings at the Iraqi muleefas (tribal meeting halls) or police stations. Well, this was the first time I would have all the security leaders come to Camp Blue Diamond at the same time, and I was adamant that we show them the same level of hospitality they always showed us. Holy shit, was that easier said than done! I couldn't believe the amount of bureaucracy and push-back I got from my own staff, the contractors who ran our facilities, and some of the colonels who lived and worked at *my* camp. You see, there were over seven hundred Iraqis who lived and worked on Camp Blue Diamond—the headquarters for the 7th IA Division was there—but they really were treated like second-class citizens. They had to be searched and disarmed in order to enter the camp and were restricted to "Iraqi areas" unless they were escorted. They were forbidden to use any of the U.S. facilities, including our dining hall, and only 7th IA vehicles could come onto the camp; all other Iraqis had to park about half a mile away and walk in.

Well, there was no way I was going to have that crap. When I went to their house, they didn't restrict my movement, make me park a mile away, or take my guns, and there was no way I was going to treat them differently. This conference brought to a head all these restrictions. I was the camp commander on Blue Diamond, and I was going to have it my way, but it was going to be a fight. Three of the full colonels who lived on the camp called me over my proposed changes. One of them even told me I had to make my recommendations to a security committee for the camp and they would vote on them—wrong. My own force protection officer fought me, asking, "What if one of the IP chiefs wears a suicide vest?" And Kellogg, Brown, and Root, the contractor that ran all the support activities in Iraq at that time, fought me hardest of all. The contractors refused (as if they could) to allow Iraqis to have access to the dining hall, pointing out that in 2004, a man posing as an Iraqi National Guard soldier blew himself up in a dining hall in Mosul, killing twenty-two and wounding sixty-four. But I was not persuaded by these arguments, and, ultimately, I was in charge at Camp Blue Diamond, so I made the rules.

Although this conflict may seem mundane, it illustrates a significant issue in counterinsurgency. These IP chiefs were central to any victory we would enjoy in Ramadi, and I treated them, to the extent possible, as dignified partners in our efforts and ensured that my leaders and soldiers who worked with them everyday treated them the same way; but, had I not fought to give them special privileges on Camp Blue Diamond, they would have come there and been treated as though they were likely takfiri insurgents. ("Colonel Silver, you will never be able to tell a takfiri from the man in the moon, but we know just by looking.") They would have parked half a mile away and then walked to a gate where, one at a time, they would have been thoroughly searched, disarmed, and escorted (on foot in 120-degree weather) by some private who spoke no Arabic—and probably hated all Iraqis—to my headquarters another half a mile down the road. How much of an equal partner does that make?

Here is the conundrum, and it's one that counterinsurgents deal with constantly: the actions of one soldier or U.S. contractor who doesn't get it can have a huge impact on key targets in the fight to win the support of the population. It wasn't as if these IP chiefs were going to turn into insurgents because some guy at the gate treated them disrespectfully, but it was going to impact their overall perception of Americans. And if, heaven forbid, some sheik, potential Army or police recruit, or influential farmer or contractor runs into an American who hates all Iraqis (really all Arabs), and the guy is that person's first contact with us, then we may have made an insurgent. Bottom line was that I ensured these policemen would be treated like the VIPs they were when they came to my camp, and by doing so, I pissed off a bunch of Americans.

While I was making the Americans angry, I wasn't necessarily making all of the Iraqis happy either. I knew that the leaders of both ERUs would hate the new plan. They wanted to be super-sexy strike forces that could move around anywhere they wanted and crack insurgent skulls. None of the eastern police thought that Albu Bali's force was ready for prime time, and the Hamdiya, Albu Obaid, and Zuwei'a police chiefs made it clear that they didn't yet trust Captain Abbas and his boys. The Jazeera IPs would carp that they didn't have the manpower to run a major checkpoint on Route Mobile. Only the Hamdiya IPs would be happy because they would be relieved from the deadly duty on Vise Grip that drained their resources and manpower. When the day came, my predictions were spot on—I had a bunch of pissed-off IP chiefs and ERU commanders. Colonel Adnan from the Jazeera IP Station, in an overt sign of disrespect, failed to show up, sending instead his operations officer and third in command, Major Marwan—who really was a bright and capable young officer, but that's not the point. After complaining about the plan and grumbling over the general lack of guns and trucks and the fact that they still had hundreds of IPs not getting paid, we adjourned to my dining hall (they called it our restaurant) where they ate food they really didn't like while we laughed and joked as if we were best friends . . . because we were.

Because I knew that the new plan wouldn't be popular with the IPs and ERUs, before I even unveiled it to them, I got buy-in from a couple of key sheiks. First, of course, was Sheik Heiss. Muhammed Farhan Heiss was distraught over the attack in the market in Albu Diyab, and he knew that the tribe couldn't take a whole lot more of that. So, he was more than willing to put pressure on Colonel Adnan to force the Jazeera IPs to man the new checkpoint if we built it so that it checked all traffic from both the east and west that came off Route Mobile into Albu Diyab. I agreed that we would build it that way, so Sheik Heiss began to pressure Adnan about the checkpoint. He also enlisted Colonel Tariq Yousef al Diyabi in the effort.

Colonel Tariq became one of my best friends in Jazeera over my first few months there. Tariq had been an officer in the Iraqi Army but, as a first lieutenant, went AWOL in 1991 (after the Gulf War hostilities) and never went back. He later served as a border and customs service officer during the Saddam regime (I don't know if he was really a colonel). Tariq had been one of the original members of the Awakening and had, since its inception, served as the chief of public safety and security operations for the movement. I'm not sure that I know what that means, but I think Tariq was instrumental in developing the recruiting strategy for the Awakening, and I think he did much of the macro-level planning for employing the initial forces. Tariq was well educated and spoke English with near fluency. He was always dressed impeccably, coiffed, and manicured, and one could get the impression that Tariq was effete, but I think he was a fairly dangerous man when the chips were down, and I know he had a great military mind (not just because he occasionally agreed with me). He was also brutally honest at times and really funny—we just got along. Tariq's opinions carried a great deal of weight with most of the IPs and both ERU commanders. Having him on our side regarding the changes in Operation Copland was useful. The other sheik who made a big difference was Sheik Jabbar al Fahadawi from Hamdiya. Vise Grip was Jabbar's idea to begin with, so having a Vise Grip–like checkpoint at every entry point to Jazeera struck him as a good idea. More important, the plan got "his IPs" off Route Mobile and back into Hamdiya where they belonged. Jabbar was another sheik who was widely respected, and his help pushed the idea along. Finally, by June 1, we started executing the plan.

Just a few days after the 2nd ERU assumed operations at Vise Grip, there was a terrible incident that was nearly disastrous. During a midmorning shift at Vise Grip, a truck came into the screener's area carrying the day's supply of ice for the checkpoint. Although the ERU leaders and members had been warned several times by the Hamdiya IPs about the danger associated with the screener's area, the ERU soldiers went out to the screener's area to unload the ice rather than having the truck come into the search area. What happened next was, I think, a blind stroke of luck for AQI. The truck immediately behind the ice truck, a Mercedes ten-ton dump truck loaded with about 3,500 pounds of explosives, exploded while the ERU soldiers were clustered around the ice truck, killing five of them and the ice truck driver while injuring another five ERUs, two of them critically. The truck also destroyed the two cars behind it, killing three and wounding another four, including a three- or four-year-old girl who lost a good part of her face and an eye—so nine dead (I never count the takfiri piece of work who blew himself up), nine wounded, three vehicles destroyed plus the truck bomb. It was a huge mess.

When I arrived about twenty minutes after the blast, there was chaos. The checkpoint was still closed, and the line of vehicles was now backed up about two miles. Mariano Wecer, who no longer had responsibility for the checkpoint, was already there, and Diogo Tavares was en route. Mariano was trying to get the ERU company commander on duty to get his men reorganized and get them back to work but to no avail. The company commander was a hysterical mess, wailing, crying, and yelling incoherently. Wecer's medics were working on the wounded, but the dead were still sprayed all over. The truck bomb's frame and engine were all that was still there; the rest of the huge dump truck was scattered over a wide area, and the burning hulks of the other vehicles had not yet been extinguished. Civilians were scurrying about trying to help. Chaos! I ordered Wecer and Tavares to get their soldiers to secure the area and sent my PSD soldiers out to begin the initial search of the scene so we could point the EOD technicians to the highlights quickly, allowing them to complete their post-blast analysis. While that happened, I found an ERU leader who was not hysterical and told him to get his men back to work. He told me that Colonel Daoud was on his way and that they wouldn't go back to work until he got there.

When Daoud arrived, he was furious. He got out of his truck yelling at his soldiers and leaders and then came storming over to me, where he proclaimed that this was entirely "the Americans' fault" because he had told us this place was not fortified enough and that his soldiers would not go back to work until all the discrepancies were fixed. I listened for a few minutes, then grabbed him and pulled him to the side. I told him, pretty callously, that this happened because his men completely disregarded the training that the Hamdiya IPs had given him when they bunched up at the screening area and allowed vehicles to bunch up there as well. Had they used the procedure they had been taught, there would probably be one dead now instead of nine, and there would have been no civilians killed. I also told him that I had seen the Hamdiya IPs hit by many of these bombs, and I never saw them go into a panicky mess or quit doing their jobs. While we were engaged in our less than friendly discussion, one of my PSD members came over to tell me they thought they had found the bomber's torso and head in the desert about eighty yards away. Daoud and I walked over, and when he saw the partial torso and head in the desert, he said, "No, that's not the bomber, that's one of my platoon leaders." I said I was sorry, and we spent the next thirty minutes discussing how we could improve Vise Grip when we moved it. Chuck Krumwiede and Diogo Tavares were there taking notes. It was that day that JSS Arcala was conceived.

Sergeant Kurtis D.K. Arcala was a C Company, 2-7 Infantry soldier who was killed during the unit's 2005–2006 rotation to Iraq. So, when Steel Company was ordered to build a new position for a company of the 2nd ERU and a U.S. platoon, company leaders chose to name it Joint Security Station Arcala. Arcala was Vise Grip on steroids. It had more force-protection fortifications: multiple blast-wall-protected search lanes, several elevated and bunkered machine gun positions, and a fairly decent life-support area (even though it was a tent). By late June, we were building Arcala about five miles east of where Vise Grip was. Charlton and the BCT had so embraced our plan that they issued a similar one called the Ramadi Security Plan that ringed the city proper with Vise Grip–like checkpoints. While we built, every new checkpoint in Jazeera was hit with at least one car or truck bomb, and each time, the ISF there, whether IPs or ERUs, physically and emotionally dusted themselves off and went back to work.

On July 4, we had our last fatal attack against IPs at JSS Arcala. A couple of days later was our last truck-bomb attack: a pair of eighteen-wheelers, each loaded with about five thousand pounds of explosives, came to the Route Mobile bridge at the western edge of Jazeera, the Euphrates River Bridge. The plan was for one suicide operative to attack the westbound span and another the eastbound, but only the westbound span was destroyed. At the last minute, the would-be suicide attacker who was to blow up the eastbound side of the bridge changed his mind and surrendered to IPs. Upon questioning him, they found that he had been a student at King Abdul Aziz University in Jeddah, Saudi Arabia, about two weeks earlier when he was talked into joining "the jihad." Once he made his decision, he was told to bring $1,500 and fly to Syria, where he would be met at the airport. On landing, his facilitators led him through Syria, where he was eventually handed off to AQI operatives at the border who promptly took his money, put him in the trunk of a car, and drove for two days, only letting him out to eat and sleep. Finally, he was hidden in a pump house on a farm for two days where he met his accomplice driver, a man from North Africa. They were briefed that their target was the bridge, and he objected; he had come to kill American infidels, not blow up Iraqi infrastructure. Ultimately, he played along. The cell leader briefed them on the route and told them they had to always enter Ramadi from the west because there was a huge IP checkpoint in the east they had tried but just couldn't seem to get through. They were talking, of course, about Vise Grip.

From July 2007 until May 2010, there were no car or truck bombs in Jazeera that killed civilians. On May 17, 2010, a car bomb at the checkpoint south of Albu Diyab claimed the lives of four IPs and four civilians. The IPs, the everlasting bomb stoppers who were willing to trade their lives to protect their civilian neighbors, immediately went back to work—and they are still working today.

CHAPTER 14

Dancing the Chobi

"War is a mere continuation of politics by another means."
—Carl von Clausewitz

No respectable book about war can exist without a quote from Clausewitz. Above is the most popular Clausewitz quote, but it is almost always taken out of context. Clausewitz used it in a dialectic for which its opposite was the idea that war is merely a street fight or wrestling match where the opponents use force of violence to gain some desired end. His point was that war is something between pure politics and sheer brutish violence and always ends up a combination of the two. My experience in al Anbar demonstrated to me just how right Clausewitz was.

John Charlton told me once, heading out of a sheik's house in Albu Faraj where we had been discussing council seats, contracts, and who was supporting whom, "I hate all that political shit. I'll leave all that up to you." But he didn't leave it all up to me. Charlton's deputy commander, Lt. Col. Thaddeus McWhorter, was the Brigade Combat Team HQ's political operator. Thad's job was to improve relations with the sheiks, and he was good at it. Thad is a sharp guy who fancies himself a genteel Southern gentleman and whose family was from Georgia and may have been, for all I know, the real kind of old South aristocracy whose manner he affected.

Thad and I got along well, even though we were often on opposite sides of the myriad micro-political issues with which we dealt.

First and foremost among these issues involved the health and direction of the Sahawa al Anbar (SAA), or the Anbar Awakening Movement. As stated before, the SAA was formed after the assassination of the sheik of the Abu Ali Jassim tribe and was preceded by an organization called the Anbar Salvation Council (ASC). Focused almost exclusively on the violent removal of al Qaeda from Iraq, the ASC was founded in early 2006 by the Heiss brothers: Sheik Muhammed, his elder brother, who I never met (he was killed by an al Qaeda terrorist named Khataba Dhari, the same takfiri who killed the Abu Ali Jassim sheik) and his younger brother, Sheik Hamid Farhan al Heiss. The organization was initially an alliance of only the Abu Diyab and Abu Ali Jassim tribes. These two tribes recruited small militias to hunt down and kill AQI members in their tribal areas. The leaders of the organization were not interested in the law, and the ASC wasn't chartered to fill the ranks of Iraqi Security Forces but rather to go to war with al Qaeda using tribal militia. Nor did the ASC have a great deal of direct contact with Americans. In U.S. military parlance, the early fights between the Anbar Salvation Council and AQI were called "red-on-red" violence (on a military map, enemy forces are depicted in red, friendly in blue, and neutral in green), meaning two enemy factions were fighting. Eventually, two more tribes, Abu Assaf and Abu Faraj, entered the council, and AQI stepped up the violence, assassinating the eldest Heiss brother and then the Abu Ali Jassim sheik.

After these significant assassinations, the movement began to expand and have regular contact with Americans. Although the contact was welcomed, many Americans feared the rise of Sunni militias. The U.S. military was already fighting against a powerful Shia militia, the Jaysh al Mahdi (Mahdi Army), and was not going to stand by and allow new Sunni militias to add to the sectarian violence already rampant in Iraq. So one of the caveats the Americans immediately placed on the ASC became point seven of the Awakening charter: "No one shall bear arms except government-authorized Iraqi Security Forces and the Iraqi Army." The original ASC members may have cut ties at that point, but their new leader, Sheik Abdul Sittar Abu Risha, was smart enough to see that he needed the Americans. He pushed to dissolve the ASC, and the Sahawa al Anbar was born with its eleven-point manifesto—the rest is history. But there was always tension between the Anbar Salvation Council members and the later members of the Awakening, and one could even argue that there were two camps in the Awakening: one led by Sheik Hamid al Heiss, Mohammed's younger brother, and the other led by Sheik Sittar. Both camps distrusted the government of Iraq (GOI).

Distrust of the GOI was widespread, in fact nearly universal, in al Anbar to the extent that the uninitiated observer might have seen Anbaris as paranoid. Paranoia is generally defined as an unreasonable suspicion of the motives of others; therefore, the Anbaris' suspicion of the GOI was probably not paranoid and might have been prudent. Al Anbar Province is the only province in Iraq that is over 95 percent Sunni. Even the other provinces of the so-called Sunni Triangle, Diyala and Saladin, are not nearly as religiously homogeneous as al Anbar. For that reason alone, the GOI was openly hesitant to commit scarce resources to al Anbar. Add to that the fact that al Anbar was widely recognized as the home of the Sunni insurgency and that insurgent factions in al Anbar had declared themselves no longer subject to the rule of the GOI but rather had sworn they would overthrow it, and what you have is every reason for the GOI to drag its feet in establishing strong and viable governmental entities in al Anbar.

Further complicating the matter was the unavoidable fact that the governor and his cabinet, all members of the Iraqi Islamic Party, were openly hostile to the GOI and had, several times, acknowledged support for "the resistance," though he bemoaned the fact that he had "invited the foreigners [AQI] into my city."[25] So, there was distrust between the GOI and the al Anbar provincial government, and an even stronger distrust between the GOI and the Awakening, which, to Prime Minister Maliki, looked like armed Sunni militia. The Sheik Hamid faction of the SAA took the attitude that they would just continue to do what they had been doing and to hell with the GOI. This faction had some issues with living by the rule of law and often caused major problems for the IPs and ERUs in al Anbar. The other faction, led by Sheik Sittar, was much more politically astute and sought to put the GOI at ease by displaying both the good intentions of the Awakening and the subordination of the newly recruited ISF forces in al Anbar to the GOI. Representatives from the SAA began holding regular meetings with GOI officials in Baghdad as early as May 2007, even though they still hadn't received the kind of recognition from Prime Minister Maliki that they wanted.

Several times in summer 2007, tensions between these two factions threatened to break the SAA, but none so much as the scandal arising from the extrajudicial killing[26] (EJK) of Khataba Dhari in late June. As was mentioned earlier, Khataba Dhari was the assassin who killed the eldest Heiss brother and the Ali Jassim sheik in late 2006. Khataba was the mufti responsible for "law enforcement" for the Islamic State of Iraq in the Ramadi area. That means he was the man who ran the murder and intimidation program, and he did much of the "wet work" personally . . . which ultimately led to his demise. Revenge, they say, is a dish best served cold, and so it was for Khataba. I'm not sure when that evil takfiri bastard was killed, and I may not have stopped it were I there to do so, but I do know that in late June 2007, a cell phone video of his EJK hit the airwaves on Iraqi TV and the internet. The video showed a group of IPs leading a bound and beaten Khataba Dhari into a spot in the desert in front of three IP trucks. The markings on the trucks were somewhat obscured, but enough was showing for me to know that they were from the Jazeera IP Station. Next, in the video, a chubby, balding man in Western attire comes into the frame holding a big nickel-chrome revolver and begins to curse Khataba, calling him a coward and using plenty of salty expletives. He tells Khataba Dhari that he will atone for his sins today and that he is headed to hell, then he turns toward the camera, and his face is clearly shown in the video. He takes several steps out of the frame, and then the camera watches as shots ring out. After the first one, Khataba Dhari falls over. Three more shots ring out, and one can see his body twitch with each— end of video.

Jay McGee, my brilliant intelligence officer, was the first to show me the video. He said that one of Charlton's intelligence officers, Capt. Elliot Press, had found it. Press was Charlton's tribal expert and still knows more about the tribes in al Anbar than any non-Iraqi I know. Press told McGee that he thought the man in the video who killed Khataba was Hamid al Heiss, Mohammed's younger brother. When Jay asked me about it, I lied to him—I think it's the only time I lied to any member of my staff and one of damn few professional lies I ever told in a twenty-five-year career— and told him that it didn't look like Hamid to me. Later that day, al Iraqia

TV identified the man in the video as Sheik Hamid Farhan al Heiss, the former head of the Anbar Salvation Council. My charade was over.

The next day, Colonel Charlton called me, and we spoke about the incident. He told me that he had spoken with General Gurganus and that we may have to detain Hamid. He explained to me that EJKs were a big problem in Baghdad because the Shia militias had so infiltrated the police that many of the death squads in Baghdad wore IP uniforms. Allowing a Sunni EJK to go unpunished would be a real blow to the Iraqi Rule of Law Movement. Baghdad was putting pressure on Gurganus to do something about Hamid. I told him that I thought detaining Hamid would cause big problems in Jazeera and that it could rupture relations between the SAA and us. I urged him to leave it alone and allow the GOI to take action. He told me he could do that now, but if he received orders to detain Hamid, I would have to do so. I went to Mohammed's muleefa that evening and told him I needed to see his brother. About an hour later, Hamid came swaggering in, laughing and joking about his famous appearance on TV—that cleared up any doubt in my mind. (Hamid was not new to TV, since he was one of the main spokesmen for the SAA and before that had received notoriety as a leader in the ASC.) Hamid Heiss is one of the few sheiks I have been associated with who made me nervous. I never felt threatened, but I was uncomfortable around him. Although I have never met a mafia don, I'll bet it would feel like meeting Hamid. After some very brief small talk, I told Hamid that I thought he made a huge mistake—not killing Khataba, since I'm not sure that I can morally condemn that action, but filming it and allowing the film to be released. He laughed and told me, in so many words, not to be such a worrywart. He basically told me there wasn't a policeman in al Anbar who would arrest him for such a crime. Be that as it may, I told him, there was the possibility that I would be forced to detain him even though I didn't want to. I explained that he had put me between a rock and a hard place.

Within a few days, I began to hear talk from the IPs that an arrest warrant for Hamid was forthcoming, but I never saw such a warrant and don't think it was issued. Shortly after our discussion, Hamid left for Dubai, where he stayed as the guest of Sheik Ahmed Abu Risha, the brother of Sheik Sittar who ran their import/export business in the UAE. Ultimately, Hamid was right; no one arrested him for killing a takfiri mufti who was responsible for hundreds of deaths in and around Ramadi. Charlton became a huge Hamid fan, often calling him "the Rambo of Jazeera," and even presented him with a stylized poster of Rambo with Hamid's face superimposed on Sylvester Stallone's body. Later, Hamid and I joked about his "exile" to Dubai, and he told me stories of his many exploits while he was there. Although the incident put a strain on both the GOI and the SAA, ultimately it brought the two "sides" closer, largely through the actions of then–Col. Tariq Yousef al Diyabi.

Colonel (later Major General) Tariq is, as I wrote earlier, one of my best friends in Iraq. He was the chief of police for al Anbar Province from early 2008 to early 2010 and could be found in U.S. newspapers more often than any state police chief from the United States. In summer 2007, Tariq was still the chief of security for the SAA and had the lead for SAA interactions with the Ministry of Interior (MOI) in Baghdad. Tariq is a true believer in the rule of law and did much to eventually bring full recognition and support to the IPs and ERUs in al Anbar. But that summer the IPs and ERUs were having a tough go of it. The issue is complicated, perhaps too much so to capture in a paragraph, but at its core the problem was twofold. First, there was the tension between the GOI and the Awakening. All of the new Iraqi Security Forces (ISF) in al Anbar were nearly 100 percent Sunni and had been recruited by sheiks who were, in many cases, associated with the nationalist insurgents. I'll reiterate that Baghdad was nervous about arming and paying them. Second, The GOI, like many former military dictatorships, was (and continues to be) a very centralized regime. Nothing really gets done from the bottom up but rather from the top down. In Iraq, all security forces work for the central government, and the provincial and local governments are not independent entities but rather subordinate to Baghdad. Well, the GOI sets the end strength for all ISF, and they never authorized the IPs to grow the way they did, nor did they authorize the formation of the ERUs. As a result, although I had nearly 2,500 IPs and ERU soldiers, less than half had been "authorized"— that means no pay, equipment, or operating funds for "unauthorized" stations. My staff and I burned thousands of hours trying to cut through the red tape associated with this mess and had only limited success. In the meantime, every trip I made to an IP station or to the ERUs led to discussions of these issues. I was on the side of the Iraqi Security Forces even when that meant I was against some Americans. This was often the case between then–Lt. Col. Noel Nicole and me.

Noel was the police coordinator for the BCT, and that meant that he was part of the red tape machine. Noel and I would go around and around over several issues, but none as often as his patronage of the Ali Jassim IPs of the al Salaam IP Station. Noel's main Iraqi partner was Brig. Gen. Khalil Abu Ali Jassim, the municipal chief of police for Ramadi. Khalil was only the chief because he was bold enough to step up when few others would. AQI had attempted to assassinate Khalil countless times, but he had survived with only minor injuries. Khalil was ill-educated, loud, coarse, and as corrupt as the day is long. He was a buffoon, but he was Noel's buffoon. What Khalil wanted was to funnel projects, money, guns, trucks, and anything else he could get his hands on to his tribe, the Abu Ali Jassim. Noel was forever making trips, usually unannounced, to the Salaam IP Station to hand out pistols, bring them fuel (which they promptly sold), or promise them projects. Every time Noel did this shit, my other IPs and tribes heard about it and were pissed. Everyone wanted pistols, fuel, trucks, and projects, and I explained to Noel that I had nine tribes to consider, not one, and I didn't need him giving baubles to the tribe that was, really, one of my least productive. The Abu Ali Jassim was one of my more difficult tribes—the IPs were lazy, they had ghosts on the payroll (when others couldn't even get real IPs paid), and they had constant drama. I remember having to send Capt. Chris Hahn out there one night because they had a shooting at a wedding—guess who the suspect was . . . sure, it was Khalil, who in a drunken snit shot one of his cousins. I didn't want to see that kind of behavior rewarded. Although I asked Noel not to do this, he continued. Apparently, Noel did similar things in other battalions' areas because Charlton eventually ordered him not to go to an IP station without preapproval from the local battalion commander—although that didn't really work.

But Noel was merely a thorn in my side compared with Brigadier General Gurganus (whom I like and respect a great deal). He was a real threat to the ERUs. Gurganus found himself stuck between the powers that be and the reality on the ground. If Sunni IPs made officials in Baghdad nervous, the Emergency Response Units scared them to death. The Iraqi Police had barely enough mobility and firepower to defend themselves in their small tribal areas, but the ERUs were constituted to be mobile and lethal fighting forces. ERU battalions had about twenty trucks each, and every truck was outfitted with a crew-served machine gun, from the lightweight PKC up to the more powerful and menacing DShK 12.7mm and 14.5mm machine guns.

The DShK (pronounced *dushka*) was the heaviest machine gun in Saddam's Army. The 12.7mm is the equivalent of the venerable M2 .50-caliber machine gun in the U.S. Army. It is a large weapon (weighing in at over fifty pounds and stretching over four feet in length) that can only be employed from either a fixed mount or a heavy tripod. The 14.5mm is a monster the likes of which we don't have in the modern U.S. Army. It is easily six feet long and weighs more than a hundred pounds. It fires .57-caliber rounds that are about seven inches long and can tear huge holes in a moderately armored vehicle (like a Bradley) or masonry walls. The weapon can only be fired from an elaborate mount that has a gunner's seat and hand cranks to control azimuth and deflection on the piece (like the antiaircraft weapon in the famous Jane Fonda photos from Hanoi). Thad McWhorter and I nearly came to blows over the DShKs. He called me fuming mad one day because an aviator had seen a truck from the 2nd ERU with a 14.5 DShK mounted in it. (That is very frightening to aviators and broke the rules for what ISF were allowed to have—they had no need to defend against aerial threats.) McWhorter said I needed to take all those weapons away from the ERUs. I said no, explaining that the DShK was an excellent weapon for engaging terrorists in masonry structures and that the ERUs needed them for their quick-reaction forces and strike platoons. I also reminded him that I didn't work for him and damn sure wasn't going to take such action without a written order. Eventually, I got a written order and complied, asking Colonel Daoud to deliver the DShK 14.5s to McWhorter's office, which he did, leaving the massive guns and their mounts right on the sidewalk outside the BCT HQ. I told him to keep his 12.7s.

Anyway, with all those trucks and all that firepower, the ERUs were particularly troublesome to Baghdad. The problem was that for political reasons—to please the Awakening sheiks—the ERUs were the first units fully integrated on the MOI payroll. When I got to Jazeera, over half of the ERU members were paid, and in late June or early July, the rest were added to the roles. So I had 1,500 paid ERU guys (I still don't know what to call them—policemen, soldiers, or paramilitaries) organized into two battalions that were transitioning to provide security for Route Mobile while they provided an offensive capability to support the largely defensive IPs. I knew how the ERUs were being used, and I was glad I had them.

In addition to being scary because of their capabilities, however, they were really scary because Baghdad saw them as overly responsive to the sheiks. Here, Baghdad was just plain wrong. ERU members were recruited by the sheiks, true enough, but the units were not tribal, nor were they particularly beholden or responsive to the sheiks. Let me lay it out for you so that you will understand better than most of the GOI and the senior Americans in Iraq at the time. The ERUs were not tied to one tribal area, nor were they recruited from one area. The 2nd ERU, Colonel Daoud's battalion, had members from seventeen tribes and had 10 (okay, out of 750) Shia in its ranks. The unit received its pay and almost all of its equipment from the GOI, and the battalion's leaders were, exclusively, former Iraqi Army officers whose loyalty was to Iraq, not some tribe. No sheik told them what to do. Contrast that with my IPs who worked in tribal stations where every member of the force was from one tribe (with only one exception—Jazeera IP Station had IPs from three tribes). They were responsive to one sheik, and, because not all of the policemen were yet paid by the MOI, the sheiks supplemented their salaries and in many cases bought their equipment. Knowing that, who do you think had more potential to be tribal militia?

But, the facts didn't matter much; in July 2007, Multi-National Security Transition Command Iraq (MNSTC-I, or "minsticky") pronounced that the ERUs were to be disbanded. This was classic Operation Iraqi Freedom bullshit. Here's how it worked: the officials in the MOI, who had already recognized the ERUs (remember Tariq's negotiations), given the ERUs authority to operate across U.S. boundaries (remember Daoud's operations in Albu Ghorton and Fallujah), accepted them on the MOI payroll, and made several promises to Sheik Sittar about them, now wanted to be rid of this force that scared the bejesus out of them. So, they convinced the Americans who were their advisors to do their dirty work. MNSTC-I was the headquarters, commanded by Lt. Gen. James Dubik, responsible for all the advising and training of ISF. The MNSTC-I senior leaders served as advisors to both the minister of defense and minister of interior, who, I was sure, were pulling the strings to get their American counterparts to do what they had promised not to do—disband the "Sunni militia."

Dubik pressured Major General Gaskins (the MNF-W commanding general, who I thought was a poor leader), who pressured Gurganus, who pressured Charlton, who pressured me to disband the ERUs—I basically thumbed my nose at them. I told them that the ERUs worked for the MOI, that they were all on the payroll, so I had no power to disband them; nor did I think it a good idea. For two months they told me to disband them, and for two months I said, "I can't." (Lieutenant Colonel Bear Johnson, commander of 1-77 Armor on the west side of Ramadi, had an ERU battalion too, but he had convinced them to wear police uniforms and man a police station, which got him off the hook. He used to laugh at my ranting about the pressure to disband the ERUs.)

During this time period, General Gurganus made one of his rare trips to visit me. He wanted to meet with me and the "senior ERU commander." Well, as luck would have it, the MOI had just promoted Col. Muhammed Abu Ali Jassim, the commander of the 1st ERU Battalion, to the office of brigadier and made him the titular commander of the ERUs. (Daoud really hated that.) So, Gurganus met me at Muhammed's headquarters, which was at an old, stripped-out building just adjacent to COP Aggressor. (The 1st ERU was partnered with Matt McCreary's Battle Company.) Gurganus came to tell Muhammed that the ERUs were going to disband and that half of them could become highway patrolmen. Muhammed didn't laugh in Gurganus' face, but only out of respect. He told Gurganus that that wasn't going to happen and then proceeded to explain to Gurganus that he didn't have enough trucks, guns, and equipment and that his headquarters was embarrassing and he wanted money to fix it. Gurganus, who was experienced with Iraqis, committed to nothing. One month later, I received twenty thousand dollars each for the two ERU headquarters. At some point during this time, the ERUs became PSFs (provincial security force battalions). Although I still got pressure to get rid of the PSFs, it became more and more clear to me that the minister of interior would have to be the one to do something if he didn't want them around. By 2009, there were eleven PSF battalions spread throughout Iraq, even one in Diwaniya (they must be "Shia tribal militia"). As far as I know, they are still operating today.

American Politics

By late summer 2007, Anbar was becoming more and more stable, and I perceived that there was a great deal of political pressure coming from the administration onto Generals Petraeus and Odierno, both to ensure that Anbar didn't revert and to begin spreading whatever was happening there to the rest of Iraq. "The Surge" was a huge political gamble as well as a military one. I entertained four or five print journalists that summer, although the vast majority of the media and official visitors went into the city to get the stark visuals associated with the change. Thanks in large part to the ring of "Vise Grip" checkpoints around it, Ramadi was beginning to look like a regular Middle Eastern city again, with thriving markets and renovation and repair going on everywhere. That's where one could find the TV-worthy images. My area was, by then, much more mundane, but it was interesting to print reporters who didn't need shocking images but wanted real stories. When I received media, they mostly had the same two questions: "How did you do this?" and "Will it last?" My short answers were cryptic—"We didn't do this" and "I don't know." I then explained to them that the Iraqis were responsible for the changes we saw in al Anbar. For over four years we had killed our way through this war with little regard for anything else, and it got us less than nothing. If the surge had only been about more Americans, the result would have just been more dead Iraqis. What we were doing was about the Iraqi people and their forces— we merely empowered and protected them while they got rid of the insurgency. Then I would explain to them the importance of the sheiks and the Awakening to the whole process and tell them that I wasn't sure if it could work in other places because I wasn't sure how much power sheiks wielded there.

At some point, either before or after this conversation, the reporters would go out with one of my units to meetings with sheiks and IPs, where they would eat with their hands and hear Iraqis tell them the same things I did. They never saw a shot fired in anger, and the print media ate the story up. One such encounter, though—I think it was with Greg Jaffe of the *Wall Street Journal*, who wrote a great piece[27] that has been quoted all over the place—got me in some hot water for a couple of days. Jaffe's finished piece made all the Americans in al Anbar look like geniuses, but while he was writing he had a conversation with the public affairs officer for Major General Gaskins and told him words to the effect that I said I didn't think it was "exactly" legal for us to pay Sheik Heiss to build himself a muleefa (which we did). I said I was sure it violated some beancounter's rules but that it cost about one twentieth as much as one Bradley or tank, and I could drive around freely because of what he and sheiks like him had done for us. Gaskins blew a gasket. He had some colonel call to rip my ass, while Gaskins called Charlton to rip his ass. Much ado about nothing in the end, since Jaffe's article was a big hit with all the brass.

By late summer, the sheiks of the Awakening were also working to spread what they had done elsewhere. Sheik Jabbar al Fahadawi from Hamdiya, Sheik Tahir Abu Ali Jassim, and Sheik Mezhir al Assaffi, along with another of my good friends, Colonel Jabair Ali Jassim (a former Saddam-era Army officer turned great citizen and one of several security advisors to the SAA), were working in Sunni neighborhoods in Baghdad to do what we had done in Ramadi and Jazeera—raise recruits who could assist ISF to secure the area and root out AQI and nationalist insurgents. They started slowly and without a great deal of support from either ISF or U.S. forces, who were both nervous about Anbari Sunnis coming to town, but I spoke to several of the U.S. commanders (a couple of whom I knew), and the MOI spoke to the ISF, and soon (within months) they were making big progress in the outskirts of Baghdad. One couldn't watch Arab-language TV—al Jazeera, al Arabia, al Iraqia—without seeing a sheik from the Awakening talking about the evils of al Qaeda and how they were taking back their country. As a result, an amazing thing happened: these media outlets stopped referring to us as occupiers and oppressors and started to call us coalition forces, and they started calling al Qaeda takfiris and infidels. Americans had been talking for years about the evils of al Qaeda, but we didn't speak Arabic, nor did we wear the dishdasha and shmaug (white robe and red headscarf) of Arab tribesmen—one Sunni sheik denouncing al Qaeda was worth thousands of Americans. This thing was really taking off!

The SAA was beginning a transformation that would carry it to new heights; it was becoming a national movement. Sheik Sittar wanted this to happen. He saw a chance for the Awakening movement to become a legitimate political power in Iraq, but he had some convincing to do, mostly with the former ASC members. He began to use his influence to spread Awakening councils (as they were called) throughout the Sunni Triangle. Soon there were councils in Saladin and Diyala Provinces and more than one in Baghdad. Then fortune really smiled on the Awakening.

About mid-summer—when Joint Security Station Arcala was new— a group of Shia refugees returning from Syria to Baghdad stopped at the checkpoint. Realizing they wouldn't make it to Baghdad before nightfall, and knowing that the road was treacherous, they asked Colonel Daoud if he could provide them refuge overnight. Among the sixty or so refugees were dozens of women and children who were hot, hungry, and tired. Daoud called Sheik Muhammed Heiss, who invited them to his muleefa, fed them, and allowed them to spend the night. It was truly a sign that sectarianism didn't override the Iraqi customs of hospitality and courtesy. (I cannot stress how important hospitality is in Arab culture. There is an old Bedouin saying, "An invitation that doesn't damage your clothes is not an invitation from the heart.") The story spread like wildfire, and the SAA made hay with it. Later that summer, the Shia sheiks representing those people sent word that they wanted to meet Heiss and thank him for his hospitality. It was a big deal the day they came to the muleefa, and I was there. The event included lots of pomp and circumstance, the exchanging of gifts, and, of course, an invitation to their homes in Karbala. Heiss asked me to go with him, but I couldn't because I was heading home for my fifteen-day leave in mid-August. Well, after Heiss' visit to them, they decided to open an Awakening council in Karbala—the SAA had crossed sectarian lines. August saw the SAA begin its transformation from the Sahawa al Anbar to the Sahawa al Iraq—the SAI was born, the Iraqi Awakening.

Through all this political wrangling, my "Arabic voice" was my linguist, Mostafa Remh, whose codename was Moose. Moose had been the interpreter and translator for my civil affairs detachment when I first came to Jazeera, and he and I had become friendly as we saw each other quite a bit. Moose was an excellent linguist and a patriotic American. A Moroccan-born, naturalized U.S. citizen, Mostafa had a great grasp of the intricacies of Iraqi Arabic. He was also bright, well educated, and mature. In June, Mahar, my previous linguist, decided to leave the employ of the U.S.

government and open a business in Iraq, and I jumped at the opportunity to have Moose come work for me. In every interaction I had with Iraqis, it was Moose who communicated my words, intent, and emotion. Without Moose, I would have been a caveman trying to communicate by grunts and gestures.

Reckless and Cavalier

Just before I left for my much-needed R&R, I had a bomb dropped on me. Of course, after the accidental killing of the ERU/PSF members during Operation Forsyth Park in Albu Bali, there was an investigation. The investigating officer (IO) was a Marine who worked on the MNF-W staff named Lt. Col. Peter Lynch. Pete seemed like a good guy to me and did an exhaustive investigation in which he found that although a combination of factors led to the death of the ERU members, "[The] battalion commander [me] was reasonably certain by a process of elimination that armed individuals tactically approaching the JSS when all friendly forces were twice accounted for and a reliable PSF officer advising 5 to 8 AIF [insurgents] were armed with small arms and RPGs and heading to attack the JSS were legitimate hostile targets based on hostile intent." The prose isn't great, but the gist was that, based on the information I'd had, I made a reasonable and prudent decision.

Major General Gaskins, in a move rarely done, rejected the IO's conclusion and substituted his own with no further investigation. His conclusion was that I was reckless and cavalier because I didn't ensure that the PSF had radios! This from the same son-of-a-bitch who read my reports every month about how ill-equipped those brave men were and did absolutely nothing about it. The memo (with his signature—bigger than life) gave several substitute findings of fact and made the following recommendation: "In addition, the battalion and company commanders in this incident will report to Commander, Ground Combat Element [Brigadier General Gurganus] that he may assess whether to continue allowing them to command forces under him. . . . Finally, I am forwarding this investigation to [General Odierno], as a matter under his cognizance, for administrative and/or disciplinary action."

It was clear in his tone that he wanted to see me tried by court-martial over this action. I was furious! Charlton came to my side immediately and ran the thing up to Major General Lynch (who had legal jurisdiction over me), and he spoke to Odierno about it. I called Gurganus and asked him when I should "report" to him that he "may assess whether to continue to allow me to command forces under him." He said, "Mike, what the heck are you talking about?" Gaskins never called, spoke to me about the report, or spit at me. Finally, Charlton asked Gaskins what the hell was going on, and reportedly Gaskins said, "I never signed such a memo." At the time, I was in the throes of deciding whether or not to retire after twenty-five years of military service. My lovely wife had had enough and asked me to retire, but she left the choice to me. I dropped off my retirement papers the second day I was home and haven't looked back.

There was plenty of work to be done that summer and some changes too. Majors Rosamond and Krumwiede were taken from me and moved to the division headquarters in Baghdad, and I got two new majors to replace them. Major G.A. Pivik came to us from a tour at U.S. Central Command (CENTCOM), where he worked directly for General Abizaid as a strategist. G.A. is a phenomenally bright officer and had served as a White House intern prior to his tour at CENTCOM, and studied at Havard prior to his internship. He immediately saw the strategic ramifications of what we were doing and integrated rapidly, serving as my executive officer from July 2007 until we redeployed to Fort Stewart. Krumwiede's replacement as my operations officer was Maj. Jason Garkey. Jason came to us from the BCT, where he had served as the chief of plans and was instrumental in the decisions made prior to our deployment—and many of the decisions, you may recall, I thought were asinine. I had previously told Charlton that I didn't want Jason as my operations officer, but that fell on deaf ears. I honestly tried to accept him and did so personally, but professionally, he struggled in the shadow of Krumwiede. I'm not an easy bastard to work for, and I admit it. It's possible that I couldn't overcome the grudge I had against Charlton's staff, who I felt never supported the battalions but rather merely made demands of us. In fact, Jason did a good job and is a fine officer. To make matters worse, the new BCT operations officer was a guy I truly disliked, and he bullied Garkey fiercely.

Be that as it may, we kept firing on all cylinders. As we headed toward the fall and the much-needed break in the stiflingly hot weather, my staff was doing phenomenal work. While my company commanders and I managed the political wrangling of sheiks, police, and PSFs, and my junior leaders and soldiers did the hard work of training and mentoring their ISF counterparts, my staff did all the coordination, planning, and forecasting necessary to bring my vision to reality. Each and every member of my staff was working hard and smart, and they presented me with options from which to choose that were complete, feasible, and appreciated. We were at a place I never dreamed we'd reach: attacks in Jazeera were down to zero, police were reaching new levels of professionalism, my soldiers were living with their Iraqi counterparts and fully integrated into the community, and the MOI was finally coming through with equipment, training, and, most importantly, pay for most of my ISF.

Charlton was as close to happy with my unit as I had ever seen him, but he still had it in his mind that we needed to search out and clear insurgents. So, we began to do a series of combined searches with the police. These searches were really walks through their tribal areas where IPs, PSF, and American soldiers interacted with the population. Many times we handed out relief supplies during these events—foodstuffs, blankets, infant formula, heaters (winter was coming), and various other sundries. (Heiss was my contractor for all this stuff and provided it like clockwork—and he was getting wealthier as a result.) At the end of the day, most of these searches ended with nothing significant to report (or NSTR—oh, how the U.S. Army loves acronyms). In the dark days in the city, NSTR was a bad thing. It meant we hadn't found the enemy. Now, there was no real enemy to find in Jazeera. It was Capt. Greg Ralls (who had replaced Mariano Wecer that summer in A Company) who first told me the beauty of NSTR, and he was right. Life was good, for now. But Ramadan was approaching, and we all expected al Qaeda to make noise during the holy month.

One of my staff members was going way beyond what I could have expected to ensure that Ramadan went well for us. Chaplain then–Capt. Nathan Kline was going out on a limb. The U.S. Army writ large was struggling with the new counterinsurgency doctrine, but one group struggled more than most—the Army Chaplains' Corps. Legally, U.S. Army chaplains are noncombatants and, as such, are forbidden from engaging the enemy. In the black-and-white world of big wars, that is easy to understand. Although chaplains were allowed to render religious and spiritual support to enemy prisoners of war, all the rest of their efforts were directed toward soldiers. Chaplains are more than mere ministers, although they certainly are that—rendering religious services, rites, and rituals—they are, in a larger sense, there to provide spiritual and moral support to all soldiers, be they religious or atheists. But in the grey world of counterinsurgency, there was room for a new role: they could be the interlocutors with the local religious leaders, and several had done that in Bosnia back in the 1990s. The members of the Chaplains' Corps were struggling with how to acquit themselves in Iraq and Afghanistan, where many thought that the mere appearance of a Christian (or worse, Jewish) holy man could cause major consternation. (In fact, I have reminded many Army officers that Muslims are not vampires and will not cringe at the mere sight of a cross.)

Over the summer, Nathan had approached me about going to Sheik Heiss' muleefa with me, and I had jumped to bring him. Nathan was smart, well educated, and had been very active in interfaith work prior to his time in the Army. I introduced him as my religious mentor for my soldiers, and he was immediately a big hit with the sheiks; so much so that they wanted him to meet Sheik Abdullah al Faraji, the president of the Sunni Dowry in al Anbar. Nathan and Abdullah became strong colleagues, and Nathan wound up meeting regularly with a group of imams. We didn't hide his actions; in fact, he shared them with the office of the U.S. Army's chief of chaplains, who gave the action a tentative nod. (Now doctrine reflects this new role for chaplains, due in part to Nathan's success.) Abdullah and Nathan found a way to truly bring my soldiers and the community so close during Ramadan that there would be no room for insurgents to come between us. The ingenious plan centered on the Muslim tradition of providing food for the poor during Ramadan, and had imams, IPs, sheiks, and Americans providing humanitarian relief supplies to poor areas in Jazeera during the holy month—sheer genius. By the end of the month, we had gained support from thousands of Anbaris who were still, up to then, sitting on the fence.

There is a Bedouin dance called the Chobi, a martial line dance that traditional Iraqis do at festive occasions. Holding swords or guns, the male dancers move linked together, arm-in-arm. It symbolizes the unity of the tribe and can be used to show unity between tribes as well. That summer, although I didn't physically dance the Chobi, I was symbolically dancing the Chobi the whole way. I was now a part of the tribes, as were my soldiers, and we danced the Chobi every day while we met with sheiks, patroled with IPs, and fought for the respect our ISF deserved. We were united, dancing the Chobi in the face of our enemies.

But al Qaeda wasn't done. In nine months, AQI had gone from having its own state in al Anbar to being almost totally purged from the province. Now AQI leaders saw the SAA turning into a national movement, and they were not about to let that happen. By a web of treachery, the takfiris were able to infiltrate Sheik Sittar Abu Risha's personal security, and on the eve of Ramadan, September 13, 2007, they assassinated the great Sheik Sittar with a large buried IED in his backyard. They hoped, I assume, that by killing Sittar they would kill the Awakening—another takfiri blunder. Sittar's funeral was the largest I have seen in any country and was attended by over one thousand mourners, including the who's who of Iraq. Within a week, his picture on a poster printed by the GOI appeared on every street corner in Iraq, from the Shia stronghold of Sadr City to the home of Saddam Hussein in Tikrit. The poster showed Sittar's face with a white stallion in the background and read, "The Hero Sheik Sittar Abu Risha— 'We must unite Iraq and build it based on equality without sectarianism.'" I don't think it's overly dramatic to say the Iraqi civil war that had raged, largely unacknowledged, since 2005 ended that month.

CHAPTER 15

Thar Thar Is Hot

After the car- and truck-bomb campaign ended in July, peace fell on Jazeera. Markets were safe, CERP projects and GOI projects were employing a couple thousand people, policemen were getting paid, traffic was flowing back and forth to Syria on Route Mobile, the tribes settled into their normal routines of cooperating and then bickering—life seemed very normal in Jazeera. As for my soldiers, we were pretty happy. Mid-tour R&R was in full swing, soldiers had settled into their new living arrangements with their IP or PSF counterparts, and, largely, no one was shooting at us. I can't remember a single attack against my soldiers, civilians, IPs, or PSF in Jazeera between mid-July and October 1.

Things were settling down throughout al Anbar as well. Fallujah was largely attack-free and had a PSF battalion of its own. A battalion from the 2nd Brigade, 1st Iraqi Army Division had moved into Albu Ghorton and Saqlawiya north of Fallujah, and had pushed the clearance of Albu Bali all the way to the edges of Anbar Province. Cliff Wheeler and his squadron were working the western suburbs of Baghdad where Baghdad and al Anbar Provinces met, and although they had a bloody fight for several months, things there were fairly calm. Major General Rick Lynch and the remainder of the 3rd Infantry Division (my Fort Stewart cohort) were bringing the same techniques that we had used in Ramadi and Jazeera to Baghdad and having great success, as were the sheiks of the Awakening, who were continuing to recruit Sons of Iraq (the new name for neighborhood watch) in and around the capital. Not only had AQI lost its hold on al Anbar by then, but the group was losing everything else too. For the first time since 2005, AQI was losing popularity, losing power, and could see its vision of a new homeland (à la Afghanistan) disappearing. AQI leaders knew they needed to do something, and that something was to consolidate in the rural areas northeast of Ramadi and Jazeera while attempting to mount a surge of their own.

I began to hear about it from the sheiks and IPs in July. Al Qaeda's new effort centered around an area called Thar Thar, a large reservoir lake about twenty miles northeast of Ramadi—between Ramadi in the south, Samarra in the east, and Bayji to the north—the biggest lake in Iraq and an important source of water to much of central Iraq. Like many places in Iraq, there is no real definition for the Thar Thar region. Most Iraqis called the entire vast desert area within twenty to thirty miles around the lake the Thar Thar area. Worse, some called the entire area Saddamiya.

During the Saddam era, there was a resort area for the Ba'ath Party's rich and influential called Saddamiya at the lake's southeast corner, near the main dam on the reservoir. Saddamiya was the Disneyland of the Ba'ath Party; both in amenities and scale, it was like an amusement park. The buildings and palaces were built in the style of the ancient Sumerian city-states that once dominated the area, and at its height, Saddamiya probably housed a permanent staff of about 500 and, at capacity, as many as 2,500 VIPs and their guests. Only those in Saddam's closest personal circle had permanent residences there. Although Saddamiya was, no doubt, beautiful in its day, save for the main palace and the main mosque (and those two buildings were little more than rubble), there was not much left of the main area of Saddamiya. I'm not sure if Saddam never finished Saddamiya or if it was just completely looted, but it was barren the first time I saw it in late May 2003. At any rate, I'll limit my discussion of Thar Thar to the area from the lake east to about three to five miles west of Highway 1, the Baghdad-to-Mosul highway. Outside of Saddamiya, the Thar Thar region was mostly bereft of population. One could drive for miles without finding a house in most places.

The Thar Thar region had been an important economic region for al Qaeda in Iraq nearly since the group's inception, and the reason for that had much to do with the "Iraqi Civil War" and the commerce of smuggling. Smuggling in the Middle East is not the high crime that it is in America, and most of the smuggling in the region is more about avoiding taxation than trafficking in illicit materials. In Iraq there was (and still is) a large grey market for commercial goods that were either restricted or highly taxed. During the Saddam era, many of the Iraqi tribes, both Sunni and Shia, made a good deal of money by smuggling. Sheik Sittar's family, for example, made their wealth through both legitimate and grey market import and export. (I once heard Major General Gaskins, during a briefing in which Charlton was talking about the importance of the SAA, say that Sheik Sittar was nothing but a criminal and a smuggler and that we should avoid him.) Iraqi tribes smuggled everything from cigarettes to whiskey to washing machines, and by selling them at a fair price, they kept the huge grey market flourishing in Iraq.

You may have noticed that several of the Iraqi tribal figures with whom I worked had ties to the border and customs organizations of the old regime. One way the tribes kept things running was by developing a connection at the border. Then it was a simple matter of paying a bribe or two to keep the goods flowing. Before 2003, there were few checkpoints on the major highways in Iraq. So once a smuggling truck crossed the border, it was free to move to a distribution center or straight to market. After the coalition invasion in 2003, however, that began to change in multiple ways: first, checkpoints went up all over Iraq, albeit their intent was to limit the movement of arms and munitions rather than hinder grey market trade, but they still had an impact on smugglers. They began to push smugglers off the main highways and onto secondary roads where U.S. checkpoints were much less likely to exist. Initially, the traffic didn't leave the main roads completely, but as the sectarian tensions became violent, a second thing happened that greatly affected the smugglers, especially the Sunnis.

As ISF soldiers began to take over the checkpoints from Americans, they reflected the reality of the new Iraq in that they were mostly Shia. These new Shia ISF had little love for Sunni smugglers, and if they allowed

Sunni goods to pass, it was only after hefty bribes were collected. The result was that most Sunni smuggling traffic left the main roads to avoid checkpoints. As a final change, after 2003, the number-one smuggled commodity in all of Iraq became fuel, and most of the illicit fuel came from the refinery in Bayji. Because of this, the two once-sleepy, two-lane farm roads through Thar Thar became the most important smuggling routes in northern Iraq. Thar Thar had no full-time U.S. forces or ISF presence. It was an area that units in Bayji, Tikrit, Samarra, or Fallujah would drive into to raid the omnipresent insurgent training and toughening areas, but no units stayed long. So the leaders of AQI ran their own lucrative checkpoints in Thar Thar, and by keeping their "tolls" reasonable, they made hundreds of thousands of dollars in tolls, taxes, and occasional ransoms, and there were no ISF or U.S. forces to do much about it.

Once things became normalized in Anbar, the stable markets and jobs created a huge need for fuel and goods, and the route those goods took (still needing to avoid the Shia areas around Balad and Baghdad) was through Thar Thar. But after being kicked out of Ramadi, Jazeera, and Albu Ghorton, AQI now had an ax to grind against the Anbaris. AQI's leaders began to forgo their easy taxes and tolls and pull Anbari drivers out of their trucks loaded with goods, either to kill them and hijack their rigs or to ransom them back to the sheiks, whom they now despised. The sheiks of Jazeera, Fallujah, and Ramadi, who had their hands in this traffic up to their elbows, were raising hell about the insurgents there, and their complaints didn't fall on deaf ears. The Marine Corps leadership in al Anbar decided to send an infantry battalion, the 15th Marine Expeditionary Unit (or 15th MEU) to set up a new combat outpost on the southern edge of the Thar Thar region called COP Golden. They stayed for about sixty days and didn't venture into the heart of Thar Thar often, but they did establish a base that later held a battalion from the 1st Iraqi Army, 1/2/1 IA, whose parent brigade was working out of Albu Ghorton.

Meanwhile, al Qaeda was busy setting up a new headquarters for its now paltry Islamic State of Iraq. The new area was deep in the heart of the Thar Thar region near the only place with more than two hundred people living in the same square mile—the "Tri-City Apartments." I don't know how the Tri-City Apartments got their name, but perhaps it was because they were about twenty miles west of Samarra, twenty miles north of

Fallujah, and thirty-five miles northeast of Ramadi. The Tri-City Apartments owed their existence to a former regime military base called Muthanna, or the Muthanna Chemical Complex. The complex was originally built around 1978 as part of Iraq's then-secret Project 1/75— Saddam's project to manufacture chemical weapons. It was greatly expanded and changed to Project 922 in 1980 when German contractors were brought to the remote location to build a facility for the safe and efficient production and storage of chemical agents. The Project 922 site was renamed the State Establishment for Pesticide Production once the plant became too large to hide. In U.S. intelligence parlance, however, the site was called the Muthanna Chemical Complex, and between 1981 and 1991, the facility produced and stored nearly four thousand tons of chemical agents, including mustard agent, sarin, cyclosarin, and v-series nerve agents. After 1991, Muthanna was demilitarized and used as a WMD (weapons of mass destruction) destruction facility until 1998.[28]

"Two wars, sanctions and UNSCOM [United Nations Special Commission] oversight reduced Iraqi's premier production facility to a stockpile of old damaged and contaminated chemical munitions (sealed in bunkers), a wasteland full of destroyed chemical munitions, razed structures, and unusable war-ravaged facilities. In 1998 Al Tariq State Establishment took over all remaining remnants at Al Muthanna."[29] Al Tariq State Establishment owned the Tri-City Apartments that had formerly been the military and civilian employee housing facilities for Muthanna. But, in late summer 2007, the Tri-City Apartments became the desolate, wasted home of the Islamic State of Iraq.

There were actually two different apartment complexes about one mile apart that made up the Tri-City Apartments. Intelligence reports said that the larger one had played host to several meetings attended by top AQI leaders including Abu Ayub al Masri, who had replaced Abu Musab al Zarquawi as the head of AQI after Zarqawi's death in June 2006. The meetings were also said to have included Abu Omar al Baghdadi, the president of the Islamic State of Iraq.

Reports varied about the existence of Abu Omar al Baghdadi. Some intelligence officials claimed that he was pure fantasy, while others thought he was real. The truth seems to be in between. As AQI became larger and larger from 2004–2007, the group had one big liability: all of its leaders were foreigners. Abu Musab al Zarqawi was Jordanian, Abu Ayub al Masri was Egyptian, and most of the senior AQI leaders were also likely foreign fighters. This caused recruiting issues in Iraq, especially when dealing with the tribes who had strong nationalist leanings. The solution was to invent a character to "put an Iraqi face on" al Qaeda and declare him the president of the farcical state. A quick Internet search will show that Abu Omar al Baghdadi has been killed or captured at least half a dozen times. The reason is simple: there were multiple actors who played al Baghdadi—on audio tapes and on video tapes as well as a couple who presented themselves in person to sheiks (as AQI worked to recruit the sheiks), and maybe, just maybe, one who really held some position of leadership in AQI.

The 15th MEU found some really bad things in the southern Thar Thar region—truck-bomb factories, large buried IEDs, huge caches of munitions, and homemade explosives by the ton—but once the unit's time was up there was no one to replace it in Thar Thar, and in the vacuum of U.S. forces, 1/2/1 IA began to be brutally attacked at COP Golden. As much as nature abhors a vacuum, so much more does the U.S. military—thus, a plan was hatched.

Fall 2007 was to be full of transitions for the BCT. In October, the soldiers of Bear Johnson's 1-77 Armor were heading back to Germany after their fifteen months in Iraq were up. In November, Chuck Ferry's 1-9 Infantry was also rotating back to the States. These two battalions would be replaced by one Marine Corps infantry battalion: 1/8 Marines, led by Lt. Col. Mike Saleh. With al Anbar largely under control, there would be fewer forces to go around. The plan was that Saleh's Marines would take over Bear's old area west of Ramadi, and Bear's forces would conduct one last offensive maneuver to seize a new outpost right next to the Tri-City Apartments. About five days later, my B Company (Battle) would move from Jazeera to Thar Thar, and I would inherit about three hundred square miles of new, bad territory.

The good news was that I would get more forces, the entire Iraqi Army 3rd Battalion, 1st Brigade, 1st Iraqi Division (or 3/1/1 IA) as a "partnered unit." Unit partnerships were new and evolving at the time. From 2005–2007, IA units had been under the tutelage of military transition teams (or MiTTs). These MiTTs (almost exclusively U.S. teams, although there were a few from the "coalition") were responsible for both training and employing the IA, who usually worked for an American commander. In 2007, Chuck Ferry's battalion had partnered with the 1st Brigade, 1st IA Division for much of his tour, but the partnership was limited to training the unit and then "borrowing" squads and platoons from the Iraqis to augment his forces, although he had, occasionally, used full companies. The new concept was to be a much more egalitarian arrangement. My Battle Company would conduct every operation with its new partnered battalion. Sometimes the Iraqis would lead the mission planning, and sometimes my headquarters would do so. As far as I know, no unit had ever really operated in this manner.

I had a few concerns about this new plan. First and foremost was the fact that the new outpost was about forty road miles from Camp Blue Diamond and at least thirty as the crow flies. On a good day that meant it took seventy-five minutes or so to drive there. But it wasn't just the time that concerned me but rather the conditions. There was only one usable road to get from Jazeera to the new outpost, and it looked very much like the River Road that went to Albu Bali—poorly paved, elevated on a dyke, and highly susceptible to IEDs. The tyranny of that road would leave Battle all but cut off from the rest of my outfit. There was also the problem of communications. My line-of-sight communications would not reach that far, therefore I needed another satellite node, not just to pass voice traffic, but for the substantial data that modern forces need. Finally, I was concerned about what would happen if the enemy interdicted that route (which they easily could have). I had to have an intermediate position that could serve as a logistics hub, waypoint, and communications node, but I didn't have the forces to open a new position.

After only a little wrangling, I was able to convince Charlton (who was very reasonable about this) to give me another company and allow me to build a joint security station for that company and the 1st PSF Battalion. He gave me my C Company (Chaos), which had been attached first to Ferry's 1-9 Infantry and then to Kaczynski's 2/5 for the new position, but he told me, "There's no way you can move the PSF—remember, they are going to disband!" There it was again, the American plan to get rid of a unit the Iraqi MOI had already endorsed. I told Charlton that I was going to move them anyway, that we'd call it temporary and deal with Gurganus' wrath when it came. He finally agreed. So the concept for JSS Zeimer was

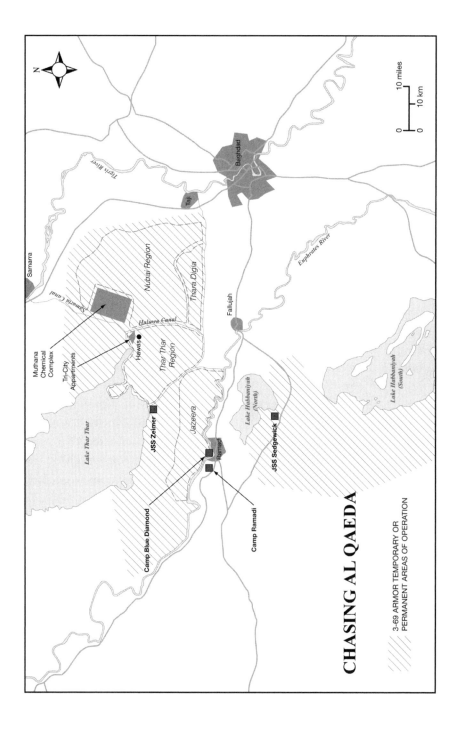

CHASING AL QAEDA

3-69 ARMOR TEMPORARY OR
PERMANENT AREAS OF OPERATION

born. As stated previously, there was not much left of the main part of Saddamiya, but there was an annex to Saddamiya immediately adjacent to the
dam that contained the shells of a dozen buildings above the dam, on both
the Jazeera side and the Thar Thar side, and the remnants of three beautiful
villas right below the dam. These villas had access to a spillway and the
main canal coming out of the lake. The buildings on the west side (the
Jazeera side) of the dam became JSS Zeimer (named after Matthew
Zeimer). The joint security station housed Chaos Company, 1st PSF
(Brigadier General Muhammed), and a small forward logistics element
(FLE) from Adrian Bailey's Atlas Company.

So, while Bear Johnson's boys did the clearance up to the Tri-City
Apartments and Battle prepared to move to its new home, Chaos set up
JSS Zeimer. But there was quite a bit of argument over where the outpost
near the Tri-City Apartments should go. I argued that we should take one
corner of the apartments, relocate anyone who may be living there, and
live right among the insurgents; there was no better way to control the area
than to live right on it. Charlton, very much out of character, argued that
we shouldn't displace any families from the apartments because that would
anger the population we were trying to sway. He said we should build "out
of the dirt" near, but not right next to, the apartments. Only one problem
with that idea, I argued: there was no legitimate population in the apartments to alienate, since nearly everyone there was an insurgent or was a
family member of insurgents. I speculated that less than 20 percent of the
inhabitants had "deeds" (really like a rental agreement from al Tariq State
Establishment) and that we needed to clean out the al Qaeda families who
were living there while "daddy got his Jihad on."

Bear Johnson, who really had no dog in the fight, agreed with Charlton
but thought we should build from the remnants of a former military facility
in an area between the two main roads running beside the formidable
Samarra Canal. The foundation of all the old buildings remained and
would make high-and-dry pads for whatever we built as the rainy season
approached. However, the old Army base was right between the two apartment complexes but resided on low ground literally twenty feet below the
roadbeds. That would be a disastrous area to defend. Bear was the guy-on-
the-ground who made the decision, and he chose the worst of both
worlds—the military base ruins would house the IA battalion and the U.S.

forces would go to a big, barren, flat piece of desert.

On the maps, we used the area that had the word *hawas* on it, and the name stuck—JSS Hawas. I went to Hawas for a reconnaissance the day after Bear's battalion "seized" it—1-77 Armor had little enemy contact on the way to Hawas, as I recall four or five IEDs and maybe one brief firefight—and I couldn't believe that Charlton and Johnson wanted to build a base on such a godforsaken spot. There was nothing there, no buildings—never had been, thus no foundations, no concrete, no water, nothing—or paved road, no fence or barrier of any kind, no shade or wind blocks. Two days later, when Battle moved there, little had changed from the dust, heat (summer had not yet broken in early October), and barren desert, except that there was now a tent for the IA on Hawas and a tent with about thirty IA soldiers located at the old Army base where the engineers were working to build another berm. All told, there were about fifty IA soldiers in the area out of a battalion of around four hundred, not a great sign that the 3/1/1 Battalion was committed to this crazy new plan.

Bear's outfit hadn't really poked around much and had made no contacts with any of the civilian population, so that became the first thing on Battle's agenda. Matthew McCreary had been in command for over six months by then and, as I thought he would, had become an excellent company commander. Although I was really fortunate with all of my company commanders, Matt was the one I thought most likely to be a general one day. He had the right combination of aggressive and analytical behaviors and had great intuition. He planned to leverage Brig. Gen. Muhammed Abu Ali Jassim, commander of the 1st PSF and a man with whom he had developed a real friendship, to help him cultivate his relationship with the battalion commander from 3/1/1. However, as he moved into Hawas, neither ISF leader was there. Muhammed was on leave (the ISF had bizarre leave cycles—sometimes half the unit would be on leave at a time), and 3/1/1 had only sent two company commanders forward to Hawas. They were really trying to slow-roll the whole process, hoping that the order to move from Ramadi to Hawas would be rescinded. So, for the first few days, it was just McCreary's soldiers and a few Iraqi Army soldiers working the area around Hawas and the apartments. The 1st Provincial Security Force was now partnered with Chaos Company and moving its headquarters to JSS Zeimer, and the unit's job was to keep the road open out to Hawas.

For the first few days, the going was rough. We had no sheiks, no Iraqi police, and no neighborhood watch; the soldiers of 3/1/1 IA were reluctant to leave the comfort of their Ramadi headquarters for the poverty of JSS Hawas, but McCreary's boys were motivated. They had begun to feel stagnant in Jazeera and were now itching for the challenge that Thar Thar brought. So for the first four days, they patrolled the area with route-clearance teams (finding a dozen or so large buried IEDs and being attacked by a few) and conducted dismounted patrols in the apartments. The patrols, always joint with 3/1/1 soldiers, were what we called "cordon-and-knock" patrols. The term comes from the doctrinal "cordon-and-search" in which an area is rapidly isolated, cordoned, and and efficiently searched, usually in the wee hours of the morning when our night-vision devices give us the greatest advantage. What the doctrine doesn't tell you, but our time in Iraq had, is that the classic cordon-and-search is a terrifying and wholly demoralizing process for the searched (and stressful for the searchers), so, where possible, most units would conduct a cordon-and-knock instead—same principle but normally done in daylight, and instead of rounding people up and segregating them while searching their homes, you simply knock on the door and ask to look around. This less kinetic action, although still not the most pleasant for the searched, was much more palatable and allowed civil interaction with the "target persons." Additionally, we came bearing gifts of staple items—sugar, flour, rice, tea—that further lessened the sting.

What we found was largely what we expected. There were a few full families in the apartments, but many of the families were obviously lacking military-aged males, and they had a plethora of lame excuses—my husband is a truck driver and he's away, my father works in Baghdad and only comes home once a month, my son was killed by the insurgents—none of which rang true. The truth was staring us in the face; this was where insurgents moved their families who were no longer welcome in their tribal areas . . . these families were the face of al Qaeda that we rarely saw.

On the fifth day, 3/1/1 IA finally moved a large portion of its headquarters to Hawas and invited my leaders and the 1st PSF leaders to dinner. We all had a nice time; the IA leaders and PSF leaders exchanged stories of their time in Saddam's Army and did the inevitable butt-sniffing that soldiers do to establish one another's bona fides. My officers and NCOs were included, and there was a sense of equality and camaraderie that made me feel as if we were making progress. The IA company commanders who had been working with Battle Company had given their boss favorable reports about the "new Ameriki partners." I left the meal that evening feeling good about where we were heading.

In fact, I felt so good about where we were heading that I took some time to goof off that evening, which was a rarity. Part of it had to do with the circumstances of the situation. Because I was so concerned about the isolation of JSS Hawas, I had decided to place a forward headquarters there with representatives from each of my staff sections and a forward command post that was to be managed by one of my senior leaders, either myself, Jason Garkey, or G.A. Pivik. Jason had the first tour as the forward commander at Hawas, but I wanted to stay until we got things running smoothly. As mentioned earlier, the communication structure there was less than adequate, so for about seven days I was freed from my email and normal administrative functions. As the operations wound down each evening, I had a few free hours before I went to sleep—a rare luxury. On this evening, the sergeants and soldiers of my PSD challenged Command Sgt. Maj. Randy Sumner and me to a spades tournament. While we played, we heard several explosions in the distance, but I knew Jason would handle it, and explosions, even at that late date, were not unusual in Iraq. We were in the process of losing at spades when a runner came out to find me (no buildings there yet, we were all sleeping under the stars). He told me I needed to come to the command post; there was a situation that Major Garkey was dealing with, and he needed me.

The Smell of Onions

In both Iraq and Afghanistan, most units that conduct operations are tied to a piece of terrain, an area that they "own." But other units have specific tasks that are not tied to terrain; rather, they are singly focused on doing some military action. The route-clearance battalions are a good example; they move throughout all unit areas to clear IEDs from roads. There are other units not tied to an area whose job it is to kill or capture key insurgent leaders. These units operate very differently from units like mine. Although they often coordinate with units that own the terrain, they are not required to do so.

As I entered the command post, Jason told me he had just spoken to the BCT operations officer, who told him that a unit had just conducted a raid to kill or capture a major AQI figure about three miles south of Hawas and that, while they had killed and captured several AQI leaders, they caused "significant collateral damage." Brigade ordered us to deal with the "consequence management" from the mission, i.e., our job was to clean up the mess. After a brief planning period with Matt McCreary, we set out for a house south of Hawas that had been codenamed Objective Monk. We didn't know if the unit was still fighting at the house or not, so we moved cautiously. About one hour after the call, we were setting a cordon at the house. I used that time to give an update to my command post and to allow McCreary to conduct coordination with the unit that was preparing to leave the site. After about ten minutes of radio discussions with Jason, I got out of my truck and walked up to the house. It was typical of the farm homes in the area, this one clearly belonging to a well-to-do farming family. As I approached the house, I was overpowered by the smell of onions. In the yard was a truck loaded to go to market, full of fresh onions—a major crop in the area. I found my company commander conversing with the commander from the other unit and allowed them to finish their conversation while I watched from a few feet away. Once Matt had received a briefing on the situation, he came to me and said, "Sir, you've got to see this. This is a fucking mess!"

I had spent twenty-four years in the military and had seen my fair share of horrors in combat, but none of that prepared me for what I saw next. As we went in the house, the marble-floored entryway, stark and white, was covered with a blood trail three feet wide. Not all blood looks the same; it ranges from nearly black to bright red, depending on where the wounded person is bleeding. This blood trail had the bright red, almost hot pink, thin and frothy appearance of punctured lungs. The trail was about twenty feet long and led to the first room on the right. This guy was still alive, frothing blood from punctured lungs when he was dragged from the house. That man, whom I never saw, had already been evacuated to a waiting helicopter. In the room from which he was dragged lay three more men of various ages, all stone dead and all shot in the face or head (not unusual for skilled close-quarters marksmen). We walked back into the hallway and followed it to the main room of the house where three more men lay dead, two with headshots and one with fragmentation and blast wounds. The walls of this room showed the telltale pockmarks of a hand grenade explosion. In the back of the house, there were two seemingly unharmed women in one room and a young man of about fifteen being treated by one of my medics for some minor fragmentation wounds. So far, I was largely unaffected; this scene was about what I had expected. McCreary then took me out the side door of the house near the kitchen, and what I saw there changed my life forever.

As I walked out the door, my flashlight played across a large dark mound twenty feet from the building. The side of the building had the flower-shaped pockmark of a large munitions impact. Closest to the impacted wall lay a woman, or what was left of one. The mind plays funny tricks at times like these, and I will forever remember thinking how she looked like the Wicked Witch of the West as she was melted by Dorothy's water bucket. (I am ashamed of that thought still.) She was clothed all in black, as is customary in Arab lands. Her arms and legs had been burned and blasted from her body, and her face was pale and crushed beyond recognition into a macabre mask. As I fought to process that, my light fell upon a tiny baby, wrapped in swaddling clothes and lying, seemingly discarded like trash, dead on the ground. The full scene was only then becoming apparent. My light played on the mound that lay another ten feet distant, revealing a mass of broken humanity: three women of various ages and nine more children, all dead and beginning to show the signs of rigor mortis, their limbs stiffly poking up at perplexing angles.

I still had hold of my faculties, and I pulled McCreary aside and ordered him to perform a full sensitive site exploitation, or SSE. SSE is the military equivalent of crime scene investigation including detailed searches, sketches, photography, and gathering any germane data associated with a military site, and the platoon leader on site began the methodical process. Meanwhile, Matt told me that two "squirters" (a *squirter* is the U.S. Army slang term for someone who attempts to exit a cordon) had been killed in the farm field adjacent to the house but that he had only found one who was lying dead about thirty yards from the main entrance. I told him to focus on the house for now, and with Randy Sumner and two of our sergeants we began to look for the squirters. We found the one closest to the house almost immediately, and since he wasn't going anywhere, we searched in vain for the other. After twenty minutes, we decided we would have to wait for daylight to find the second squirter. On our way back, we stopped by the body of the squirter nearest the house. He lay in the same position we had found him in initially, lifeless, but something wasn't right. "Sergeant Major," I asked. "What did this guy die from, fright?"

There wasn't a mark on his fat body. He watched the lifeless body for a minute and said, "That son-of-a-bitch is still alive!" Randy immediately began to check for a pulse but couldn't find one, but the body was warm and wasn't stiff like the others. "Medic, get me a goddamn medic!" Randy shouted. Out of the darkness came one of my medics, in fact my very worst one. We'll call him Specialist X. Specialist X was a bona fide dirtbag, one of my very worst soldiers. Prior to deploying, he had tried every trick in the book to shirk his duties and get out of the Army. The first ploy was to have his foreign-national father call Colonel Charlton to tell him that he had to have his twenty-six-year-old, high-school-educated son around to run the U.S. branch of his multinational corporation. Seriously, the father later told me that there was no other person who could do that. My answer was that the Wharton School produced some excellent candidates, and he should look for one there. The next ploy was for Specialist X to go AWOL. While on the lam, he went to Massachusetts with another of my less-than-stellar soldiers, a mortar infantryman, and got married. In the don't-ask-don't-tell U.S. Army, there were three conditions upon which a homosexual must be discharged. Of course, there was an acronym—SAM: statement, action, or marriage. If a soldier said (convincingly) that he was an "active" homosexual, or if he was caught in an act, or if he entered a homosexual marriage, he must be discharged. Unfortunately for Specialist X, his "husband" was already married . . . to a woman. His illegal Massachusetts marriage didn't work either, and at that point I would have gouged out an eyeball before I'd let that malingerer avoid his duty. The next twenty minutes caused me to reassess the intelligence of my decision.

Specialist X came over to the "body" and administered two clinical tests for responsiveness, an eyeball thump and a sternum rub. The eyeball thump or, more properly, the eyeball compression is simple: just push on an eyeball, and if the patient is alive and responsive, it is nearly impossible not to react. The fat guy on the ground had no reaction; his eyes, which had remained open for the last ten minutes without a blink, stood up to several hard thumps with no reaction. The sternum rub, a vigorous and painful knuckle drag across the sternum for ten seconds, also produced nothing. "This fucker's dead," pronounced Specialist X, but Randy wasn't hearing it.

"Check his vitals," he said. After about three more minutes of triage, Specialist X said, "He's got a pulse, but I think he's dying." I said, "What the hell is he dying from? Does he have any wounds?" While all this was going on, Abu Omar al Baghdadi, the fat bastard on the ground, sat bolt upright and began yelling for his daddy. Randy Sumner had captured Abu Omar. Now flailing on the ground was the man who, for al Qaeda, presented himself to sheiks as the president of the Islamic State of Iraq! He was fine and clearly had excellent, Zen master–like training at playing dead. He was flex-cuffed and extracted to a nearby Bradley.

I went back to my truck to call the command post and give them an update. I also told Garkey to get a platoon of Iraqi soldiers and the battalion commander to come up to our location. Although I was concerned about the secrecy implications of what happened that night, I also knew that I needed ISF to see our reaction. After making the call, I sat nearly catatonic for a number of minutes while my crewmembers became concerned. I now realize that I had an acute stress reaction that night, but I snapped out of it. I told my crew to give me the body bags that we carried in our trucks; we only had two. I called McCreary on the radio and told him to round up all the body bags he had with his Bradleys and meet me at the side of the house. Between the six Bradleys on site and my five trucks, we only had six body bags. I was angry. Our standard procedure was for every vehicle to have two body bags, but ninety days of peace in Jazeera had weakened our discipline. I grabbed Randy, and we walked over to the bodies on the side of the house.

The Iraqi Army soldiers had arrived, and there was a brief period of hysterical yelling as they figured out what had happened there. For about two minutes, I thought there might be a firefight, but one of the IA company commanders took charge and explained to his soldiers that "our" unit (he actually said "our" unit) had not done this, and we needed to get focused on doing what we could, now. I told my soldiers it was time to get out of there. I picked up the burned and broken woman by the house and the baby and put them in a body bag. Then, as respectfully as we could,

Randy, McCreary, and I with about five other soldiers, all of whom wore the same zombie expression that I must have been wearing, put all fourteen bodies on the side of the house into three body bags while the shocked and dazed Iraqi soldiers, some clearly seething with anger, watched. We then moved back to Hawas, where I called Charlton, waking him from sleep, and told him what I had seen and that I suspected the actions there may have been a war crime.

The next morning didn't get any easier. We now had all the bodies loaded in a truck with no refrigeration that the IA soldiers had driven back from the farm, and the time was ticking on a proper Muslim funeral. I needed ISF to go contact the family members so that they could come pick up the bodies. I appreciated everything that 3/1/1 had done the night before, but there was still significant tension on Hawas, perhaps more tension than at Objective Monk, and I needed Iraqis who knew me for this mission. I called back to Chaos Company at JSS Zeimer and told them that I needed Brigadier General Muhammed from the 1st PSF to come to Hawas, that I had urgent business and needed his help. I think the "urgent" part of the message was omitted because several hours later his "deputy commander" (really his admin. officer), Lt. Col. Thamer Abu Ali Jassim, appeared.

Thamer was a dull, dimwitted, piece of work! I was pissed off that he was the one who showed up. But I gathered Thamer, the 3/1/1 IA commander, Jason, and Matt McCreary so that we could figure out our next steps. We started the meeting by giving Thamer a synopsis of the events of the last twelve hours. He went on a three-minute rant about how Americans only understand killing; if we had just called, he could have brought twenty PSF to the house and captured the terrorists without killing anyone . . . blah, blah, blah. (Thamer was a coward. I had never seen him leave the PSF headquarters, and the reason it took him so long to come to Hawas was that he refused to go until Chaos escorted him all the way there—no great warrior was this dude.) Finally, I stopped him and asked him if he had ever known my soldiers to behave badly? No. Had he ever known us to act unilaterally, without IPs or PSF? No. Then, I politely said, shut the fuck up or I will have General Muhammed fire your sorry ass when he returns—I'm sure it was much more eloquent in translation. Needless to say, Thamer wasn't happy, but the PSF company commanders he brought with him, although they contained their laughter, were greatly amused (I'm sure he was a jerk to them too), and the commander of 3/1/1 IA was too. It seems that in the strangest ways, one often develops credibility. They began to speak in Arabic, and before I even had to mention it, they announced that they were heading out to find the aggrieved family members and their sheik and bring them back to pick up their loved ones. Thamer pouted a bit on the way out, but he never mouthed off again. He knew that in the tribal hierarchy of Jazeera, I had much more *wasta* than he.

I then turned my attention to my soldiers. When I had spoken to Charlton earlier that day, I had told him that I needed some assistance, since Chaplain Nathan Kline was on an extended R&R leave in conjunction with the Latter-day Saint General Conference, where he had been invited to speak. I was without a chaplain, and I was positive that I needed both spiritual and psychological help for the soldiers who had gone to Objective Monk. As I came out of the meeting with my leaders and the ISF, I saw the soldiers from my PSD and the platoon from Battle Company who had gone to Objective Monk huddled in one corner with the combat stress team and a chaplain from the BCT. I went over and spoke to them after the chaplain and doctors had finished. I told them that, in fact, a really bad guy, a major AQI figure, had been captured at Objective Monk. I also told them that only the unit that conducted the action knew the full story but that I would ensure that an investigation would be conducted to get to the bottom of what had happened there.

Shortly after that, the IA and PSF trucks appeared at the front gate with a group of about fifteen Iraqi men dressed in traditional attire. I grabbed Moose, and we headed out to meet them. There were no men left from the immediate family of those killed at Objective Monk. Two heads of households had died there, and one had been captured by the other unit (although I didn't know that he was alive). Therefore, the most senior representative from the family was the paternal uncle to the owner of the house. As we approached the gate, he walked toward us with another man in traditional dress escorted by Lieutenant Colonel Thamer and the 3/1/1 battalion commander. The head of the family was introduced to me as Haji Kamal al Mahali, and the man with him was a sheik of the Abu Mahal tribe whom I had not seen before and never saw again. After they were introduced, I immediately expressed my deepest sympathy for their loss and told them I was personally sorry that it had happened. I told them we had done the best we could do to treat the remains with respect and that my first thought was to get the bodies back to the family so they could be properly buried. I warned them that what they would find in the truck was shocking and would be very disturbing. The Sheik asked if a particular man was dead, and after he gave us a description, I told him that I believed that man was dead.

This news seemed to hit Haji Kamal particularly hard. At that point, the sheik began to yell and scream. I don't blame him, but neither do I remember a word he said. The events of the last twelve hours were having a huge impact on me. I had already removed my eye protection as I greeted these men, and at that point, though I tried to control myself, tears began to stream down my dirty face, leaving lines as clear as those on a map. I told the two men that I had been a soldier my entire adult life and had seen some truly terrible things, but nothing compared to what I had seen in that house. I vowed that I would see to it that a full investigation occurred into what had happened and why it had happened. When I finished speaking, Haji Kamal grabbed my hand and, turning to the sheik, he said, "This is a good man, this man is not our enemy. It's time to go." Haji Kamal kissed my cheek, turned, and left.

We drove down near the house that afternoon and saw the funeral party. It was huge and included several vehicles that I suspected belonged to international media. In the distance, I saw several of the men looking toward our trucks. We left without approaching.

That afternoon, I had the platoon leader complete his report from the SSE. I had him put the report, with photos, on a CD and erase the originals from his camera and hard drive. The last thing I wanted was to see those photos on the Internet à la Abu Ghraib. With that in hand, I headed back down to Jazeera where my first stop was at Sheik Muhammed al Heiss' muleefa. I explained to Sheik Heiss what had happened and asked him what I should do. He told me to do what an Iraqi Army officer would do, let my sheik handle it. We spent the next hour or two in a mostly pleasant conversation about what was going on in Jazeera and had a wonderful meal.

Over the course of the next ten days, Sheik Heiss, working through Brigadier General Muhammed from 1st PSF, brokered three meetings between him, me, and Haji Kamal. The meetings followed tribal custom. The first meeting at Heiss' muleefa was a quick meeting to acknowledge that there had been a wrong done. Heiss stressed to me that it was important not to say at the first meeting how I thought such a thing happened but just to acknowledge I was sorry that it did happen. The second meeting was also at Heiss' muleefa, and it included, in addition to my sheik, Haji Kamal, and me, an additional entourage from the Abu Mahal tribe and several IP chiefs from Jazeera, Sheik Abdullah al Faraji and Col. Tariq Yousef. This meeting was like a strange sort of trial where the Abu Mahalis presented their understanding of the events of that night and the Jazeera contingent extolled my virtues and defended my character. (Here I was representing the entire U.S. government, again. My soldiers and I hadn't killed a single person on Objective Monk.)

During the course of the first two meetings, I heard enough information to be able to piece together what had happened that night. Abu Omar al Baghdadi was traveling through the area with other AQI figures. As darkness fell, they decided to break their Ramadan fast (October 11 was the last night of Ramadan, the eve of Eid al Fitr, like a combination of Christmas Eve and Thanksgiving) and stopped at the home at Objective Monk. The Bedouin culture says that one must offer hospitality to anyone who attends your camp, whether invited or not. In fact, their culture says that a stranger may stay three days before you can politely ask why he's there—maybe this is where Benjamin Franklin got his "House guests are like fish, both start to stink after three days." Anyway, Abu Omar and his two men imposed themselves for supper on this unwitting family's biggest feast of the year. What happened next is the part that I don't know—although an investigation was conducted, I was neither consulted nor privy to its results. Somehow, the unit that conducted the raid at Objective Monk perceived a threat there—although we didn't find a single weapon, and the only spent casings on the property were from U.S. rifles—and went in hard, probably initiating the raid with a Hellfire missile strike into the house that just happened to impact where the women and children were cleaning up from the meal.

Most of the people who died there were innocent bystanders, and the entire event could have been avoided. With one call, I could have gone to the house with a hundred Americans and a hundred Iraqis, and we could have pulled Abu Omar and his two thugs from the house, tousled the hair of the kids, and left the families with a wish of *Eid Mubarak* (Happy Eid). I still believe that the killings there were uncalled for. I have no way of knowing if anyone was ever held accountable. I believe the units that hunt down "high-value targets" frequently kill the wrong people, and I believe that each time they do we strengthen the hand of the takfiris. Every time I hear about a "drone strike" that killed an al Qaeda leader but, unfortunately, killed civilians as well, I think about Objective Monk. And not a day goes by that the images of Objective Monk don't invade my thoughts.

The final meeting was at Haji Kamal's house. I traveled there with Sheiks Muhammed and Hamid al Heiss, Sheik Abdullah al Faraji, Sheik Mizir al Assaffi, Col. Tariq Yousef, and several others who urged the Abu Mahalis to join the Awakening Movement so that AQI terrorists would stay away and not bring war into their houses. They then chastised the tribe for allowing the Tri-City Apartments to become full of takfiris and foreigners who seek to destroy Iraq. Haji Kamal agreed that the tribe should have been more diligent and that they would work to rid the area of AQI. I then went into a back room, just Haji Kamal, myself, Moose, the eldest remaining man from the Objective Monk family, and a finance Marine from Fallujah. We counted out the equivalent of $125,000, or about 150 million Iraqi dinar—I believe that was the largest condolence payment ever made by U.S. forces in Iraq.

Haji Kamal remained one of our best friends in the area. Not only did he support our initiatives, but he told the story of how al Qaeda caused the death of his family and how hard the Americans tried to remedy the tragic loss. I think of Haji Kamal often.

CHAPTER 16

Chasing al Qaeda

The rest of October went by in a blur. Our new area was not as bad as Albu Bali or Ramadi at their worst, but it was certainly worse than Jazeera. Matt McCreary and his soldiers worked to develop a close relationship with their new Iraqi Army partners, and though we had ups and downs; the Iraqi and American Army units were beginning to feel like one unified team. The leaders of al Qaeda didn't stand and fight in Thar Thar as they had in Albu Bali. They now used Zarqawi's first rule, always go where the Americans are not. Although we suffered several major IED attacks—including lethal attacks against both the 1st PSF, which killed a company commander, and 3/1/1 IA, which killed its operations officer—we had no firefights or complex attacks. Rather, we were playing elaborate cat-and-mouse games attempting to kill IED emplacers using ambushes—both mounted (tank and Bradley) and dismounted—as well as conducting helicopter and UAV drone reconnaissance and attacks. We had some success killing the active members of the IED cells operating in our area and captured some low-level insurgents as well, but as usual, the real success came from getting the Iraqi Security Forces out on the road and into the population.

The PSF were manning two checkpoints along the route that ran from COP Zeimer to JSS Hawas, and the 3/1/1 IA soldiers were manning three checkpoints on the paved roads near Hawas. This curtailed AQI's freedom of movement in the area, and we started to see insurgent families fleeing from the apartments because their men could no longer come and go as they pleased. The control of movement into the area made Thar Thar ineffective as a safe haven or support zone, and our ability to kill IED teams made the area an increasingly less desirable attack zone, so now it was time to have real influence on the population.

About ten days after the incident at Objective Monk, we finally had a sheik who came forward to represent the population at the Tri-City Apartments, a fake sheik named Musa al Mahali. Sheik Musa was a childhood friend of Col. Abdul Ghafor al Sha'banni, the chief of the Albu Sha'ban IPs. Ghafor had introduced me to Musa before we moved up to Thar Thar and told me that when we went there, Musa would be the best guy to have with us. My impression was that Musa had been an employee at the Muthanna Chemical Complex and had lived in the Tri-City Apartments for years. I also believe that Musa was a former AQI operative—in fact, maybe a low-level leader in the Thar Thar region—but I knew he had turned against al Qaeda months earlier because he had provided intelligence, through Col. Abdul Ghafor, that had led to the destruction of a major truck-bomb and suicide-vest factory and cell in the Thar Thar region. The access that allowed him to know about the operation was what led me to believe he was al Qaeda, but the fact that he gave the cell up showed me he had turned. Either way, both McCreary and I knew about Musa's prior history and treated him cautiously at first.

Cautious or not, it was good to have someone willing to be the representative of the atomized, non-tribal population of the Tri-City Apartments, and we relied heavily on Musa. Among other things, Musa recruited Sons of Iraq (SOI) to augment the 3/1/1 IA security in the area. Although they started slowly, eventually we developed a force of over one hundred SOIs who, predictably, all wanted to be Iraqi policemen. Musa formed a council for the Tri-City Apartments and began to work with us to develop CERP projects to make life better for the families that stayed in the area. He also courted the approval of the SAA/SAI and was eventually granted a "charter" for a Thar Thar branch of the Awakening. Things gradually became safe inside our area of operations, but right along the boundary there was still violence.

East of JSS Hawas there was a major canal running through a wadi that was thirty-five yards across and twenty yards deep, and at the bottom ran a wide but shallow creek. The Haluwa Canal ran the length of our area of operations and formed our eastern boundary. The canal had narrow dirt roads that ran along either side between a sheer bluff and the drop-off of the wadi and provided an excellent place for the enemy to employ IEDs. It was on the canal road where the 3/1/1 IA operations officer was killed with an IED. Although the canal was our boundary, we were occasionally allowed to cross it to conduct operations and could pursue the enemy across if needed. One old, rickety iron bridge led across the canal in our area, and about nine miles north of Hawas, across our northern boundary, was a huge concrete bridge built during Muthanna's heyday to support the heavy traffic of the secret facility. Al Qaeda was good at observation and, shortly after we moved up to Hawas, figured out the extent of our boundaries. The group ceded those areas to us and worked to keep us out of the adjacent areas. Within a month of our arrival, al Qaeda blew up the iron bridge across the canal twice (ineffectively the first time). We responded by having our boundaries temporarily extended to the north and east and conducting a multi-day clearance, along with Chuck Ferry's Manchu Battalion, of both the Muthanna Complex and the area between Thar Thar and Highway 1. Although we found little of import on that trip, we made it clear to the leaders of AQI that we would chase them when and where we could. Five days after the boundary extension expired, al Qaeda blew the concrete bridge at Muthanna, cutting us off completely at the Haluwa Canal.

Leaving Jazeera

Meanwhile, the changes kept coming at the Brigade Combat Team's headquarters. The second phase of the BCT's plan to adjust its battlespace came out in late October. The plan called for my battalion to leave Jazeera and hand it over to a Marine Corps company from Mike Saleh's 1/8 Marines. I would keep Battle Company at Hawas and Chaos Company at JSS Zeimer, and A Company (Rock) would leave Albu Obaid and Albu Bali and move down to the shore of Lake Habbaniyah—about twenty-five miles as the crow flies south of Camp Blue Diamond but about thirty-five miles road distance—to a base called JSS Sedgwick (named after the fort in *Dances With Wolves*).

JSS Sedgwick was built during the truck-bomb campaign of the summer after AQI blew up one of the two usable bridges over the Habbaniyah Canal south of the lake. The roads that crossed the canal were major supply routes for the U.S. forces in western al Anbar. Chuck Ferry had a company at Sedgwick that Rock would relieve; on the same base was the 1/1/1 IA—the 1st Battalion, 1st Brigade. I would lose C Company, 2-7 Infantry (Cold Steel), since they would be heading to western Anbar in mid-November to provide security, with their Iraqi partners from 2nd PSF, to the Iraqi ground route for Hajj 2007. For that mission, Steel would be over one hundred miles away near the Saudi border, detached from my command and working directly for the BCT. Chris Hahn's Knights would head back into Ramadi and work for a Marine Corps battalion to provide security for the Anbar Government Center and to serve as a PSD for Governor Mahmoon.

So, with two companies co-located with two battalions of the 1st Brigade, 1st IA Division, I was to become the partner unit for the brigade. Although the partnership was working for McCreary and the 3/1/1 Battalion, I was unsure how it would work with the brigade. But after seeing how well it was working at Hawas, Charlton was sure that we could make it work for the entire 1/1 Brigade, and I must admit that this is one of the times when his vision for the way ahead was clearer than mine.

The 1/1 Brigade was, logically, the first brigade stood up in the new Iraqi Army and had been in existence since 2004. The brigade commander, Brig. Gen. Abdullah al Jabouri, was a smart, experienced Army officer and, just as importantly in al Anbar, was a Sunni Arab with ties to a strong tribe. General Abdullah had a capable staff and a particularly strong executive officer named Col. Adil Abbas al Hamdawi, who was Shia from the south of Iraq but lived with his metropolitan (read: not particularly tribal) family in Baghdad. The two made good counterpoints for each other: Abdullah was boisterous and intuitive and made decisions quickly, while Adil was smart and analytical and could usually get Abdullah to wait until all the facts were in before acting.

The brigade's headquarters was in the eastern outskirts of Ramadi, south across the river from Jazeera in the Ramadi University complex. The brigade had a full-time military transition team (MiTT) composed of about twenty Marines and soldiers and ably led by Marine Corps Lt. Col. Charles A. "Chuck" Western. Chuck was an intelligent and hard-working officer, and the cooperation and hospitality he showed to me and my officers made the partnership work well. Chuck's career and mine had several similarities. We both joined the Marine Reserves straight out of high school and served with the 4th Marine Air Wing as we went through college (although we didn't know each other—Chuck served in California, and I in Florida). Upon commissioning, our paths diverged. Chuck stayed in the U.S.M.C. as an infantry officer, and I went to the U.S. Army as a tanker, but we both served in line units and saw combat during Operations Desert Shield and Storm.

Again, in the late 1990s and early 2000s, we had similar experiences as I served as an advisor to a Saudi Arabian National Guard infantry battalion and Chuck served as an advisor to the Yemeni Armed Forces as they stood up a demining program in Yemen. These shared experiences and the fact that we both viewed counterinsurgency in the same way allowed us to have a unique and highly functional power-sharing relationship, as I commanded my battalion and took the operational lead and he took the lead regarding training and interaction with the 1/1 Brigade. It also helped that his operations officer was Capt. Mariano Wecer, who had only recently relinquished command of my A Company. Mariano, who was always one of my favorites (although he did step in shit often), really did an excellent job of working the staff interactions from the MiTT team to the battalion as well as "talking up" the battalion to the MiTT members.

As the transition plan was announced, the sheiks of Jazeera had high anxiety. They had grown accustomed to me and my staff and grew nervous about how the new unit would interact with them. They felt a little better when they learned that the new unit commander was named Lt. Col. Mike Saleh. *Saleh* is an Arabic name, and although they knew that he was American-born, they hoped that his Middle Eastern roots would mean he would have understanding for their culture and bear some level of empathy. But, as he met them, the good feelings rapidly faded.

I'm not sure what Mike Saleh's story is because we never hit it off and didn't have any conversations about family, personal, or professional background. My perception was that Mike Saleh was a racist who disliked Arabs in general and, it seemed, Iraqis in particular. I suspect that he is from a Lebanese Christian family, which means that such prejudice could be deep-rooted, but it could be simply that Saleh didn't care for the way I'd done things and wanted to see big changes. My first real clue about his feelings was when I brought him to a Jazeera Council meeting—he was awkward and uncomfortable, and he was fairly rude and aloof to the participants. It started when I introduced him as Colonel *Saleh* (with the Arabic pronunciation *sa-la*). He immediately corrected me—it's pronounced *sally* (or he may have said *sā-lè*)—signaling, in what I felt was strong language, to the sheiks that he wasn't one of them. It went downhill from there.

During transition, Saleh refused to come around with me to meet the sheiks, instead leaving the task to his company commander. In fairness, Jazeera would be the company's area, but I explained to him that I thought it sent a strong message for him to attend such meetings. In western Jazeera, I had not had a single attack against one of my positions in six months—not one attack. At those positions, Iraqis had the lead on security, not Americans. I had soldiers living in IP stations, and the only places we guarded were the entrances to U.S.-only sections of our JSSs. Saleh's subordinates reported to me that as soon as we handed over the area, that practice would change. Apparently Saleh didn't think it wise to leave security in the hands of the Iraqis. In fact, he made those changes with disastrous effects. At JSS Anvil, collocated with the Albu Sha'ban IP Station, sometime a few weeks after we handed over the position, a U.S. Marine and an Iraqi policeman had a disagreement, purportedly over the IP's use of a cell phone while on duty. The disagreement ended with the Marine stabbing the IP to death with a bayonet. I wasn't involved with the investigation in any way and can't speak to its results or the circumstances of the incident, but the sheiks and police of Jazeera certainly talked my ear off about it. They were furious that the incident happened to begin with and even more incensed by the way they were ignored and marginalized by Saleh in its aftermath. They claimed that it took him days to even discuss the matter with any sheiks, and that he treated the IPs, including the IP investigators, with contempt. Colonel Abdul Ghafor reportedly threatened to quit over the incident. What I know for sure is that even after I left Jazeera, I fielded complaints from sheiks and ISF alike over the way the population was treated by Saleh's Marines, and I saw with my own eyes an indication of their contempt.

In mid-December, Sheik Jabbar al Fahadawi set up a huge celebration to commemorate the one-year anniversary of the "liberation of Hamdiya" from al Qaeda, spending thousands, if not over ten thousand dollars of his own money to put on a huge event. I received an invitation and planned to attend, and went out of my way to ensure that Saleh and his Marines knew about this event. I told him he should attend, and I mentioned to Charlton that he really ought to and should probably get one of the Marine Corps generals there. When the big day came, the who's who of the SAA/SAI were all in attendance as well as every police chief from Jazeera. Gen. Tariq Josef, who was by then the provincial chief of police for al Anbar, was there, as well as sheiks and leaders from all over the province. My PSD soldiers and I were the only Americans, however, and the absence of others spoke volumes. The close relationship between Americans and Iraqis in Jazeera was fading, but all I could do was watch and wait—I had other fish to fry.

Through our work in Thar Thar, Jay McGee and his counterparts at the BCT HQ were beginning to build an intelligence picture of what was going on in the desert area between Thar Thar, Samarra, ad Dujayl, and the northern edges of Baghdad Province. Out in these sparsely populated areas, on the edges of both military and provincial boundaries, members of al Qaeda were enjoying their last safe havens . . . and we weren't about to let them do so. With Chuck Ferry's battalion on its last month in Iraq, Colonel Charlton put together a couple of BCT-level operations to clear some of the areas adjacent to us—the Muthanna area, again, as well as an old military compound in an area generally called Thara Dijla (literally, the "arm of the Tigris"), named after a major canal that ran west from the Tigris River into al Anbar Province. These operations netted a few large weapons and explosives caches and, unfortunately cost the Manchus one more soldier killed in action.

I had long since come to the realization that any operation that merely called for forces to enter and clear an area and then leave was of little use. Worthwhile operations emphasized that victory meant leaving behind a new group of sheiks and Sons of Iraq who could run checkpoints, control access, and root out insurgents; otherwise an area was only clear for the fleeting time that we occupied it. I began to devise a plan, with Maj. Jason Garkey, to establish a permanent presence north of our boundary on the northeast shores of Lake Thar Thar and east of the Haluwa Canal. Both of these areas were in Saladin Province and therefore outside of the MNF-W military boundaries, belonging to Multi-National Division North, headquartered in Tikrit.

We pitched the new plan to Charlton, who liked it, then to General Gurganus. Although Gurganus liked the concept, he had multiple concerns: his first concern was with the feasibility of logistically supporting a force that I moved farther out. The only secure route was the road that we were holding between Jazeera and Thar Thar. The quicker route, logistically, was to come due north from Fallujah up through the Thara Dijla area, but that was bound to subject my logistics patrols to attack. In retrospect, I think Gurganus was right on that account. (Imagine that, he had only been in the Marine Corps for thirty years.) His second concern was a more bureaucratic one but no less a problem—he was not about to ask the Multi-National Corps-Iraq (General Odierno's command) for an increase in battlespace when he knew that his replacement would have far fewer troops to deal with an already expansive area. I couldn't argue with the logic, but I did argue that, in my remaining months, we could do a good deal to free the area of AQI presence and establish a few pockets of SOIs or ISF. While my counterargument was not convincing for Gurganus, it did give me another idea—perhaps the Iraqi Army would be willing to do what the Americans were not. Maybe the answer was to put an Iraqi battalion east of the Haluwa Canal. I began, over the course of several meetings, to "socialize" the idea with Gen. Abdullah Jabouri, who was fairly reluctant to embrace the plan, but Colonel Adil loved it. Adil received permission from his boss to discuss the plan with the Iraqi 1st Division staff, and the plan began to gain some traction on the Iraqi side.

As Thanksgiving approached, our exploits in Thar Thar were bearing fruit, and Greg Ralls and his Rock Company were settling in down in JSS Sedgwick. The southern half of my area was very different from the north. Ralls' company was partnered with 1/1/1 IA and three IP stations. The IPs were fairly well along when we arrived there, and the tribal situation was very different from that of Jazeera or Thar Thar. Ralls' area stretched south of Lake Habbaniyah for twenty miles, ending at the political boundary between al Anbar and Karbala Provinces, and therefore was on a major Sunni–Shia fault line. The Sunni tribes in Greg's area were the most suspicious and anxious tribes I dealt with and, for that reason, had been the most deeply infiltrated by AQI. Although we rarely had outward signs of aggression or attacks there, the tension was thick. Greg and his leaders, along with the 1/1/1 IA, did a great job keeping the lid on a potentially explosive situation.

The other crucial aspect of Greg's area was that it was the major logistics route to support all the forces in western al Anbar, and the move was afoot to make it the major logistics route for Ramadi as well. With the improved security situation in Ramadi, Habbaniyah, and Fallujah, the civilian traffic using the routes through the populated areas had grown tenfold, leaving little room for large American convoys. Also, these logistics convoys were known for a shoot-first-ask-questions-later posture, and we could ill afford to have civilian casualties as these convoys made their daily runs; so, the route south of the lake was becoming more and more busy. What Greg and his soldiers were doing in the south may not have been as sexy as fighting al Qaeda in Thar Thar, but it was important.

On Thanksgiving Day, I drove from Blue Diamond to JSS Zeimer and then on to JSS Hawas and down to JSS Sedgwick—about a one-hundred-mile loop. That was the first time the breadth of my battlespace became concrete for me. I started at 7:00 a.m. and didn't get back to Blue Diamond until 8:00 p.m., only spending about an hour at each location. The rest of the time was spent driving through good and bad roads in Iraq. At Sedgwick, I met Charlton (he offered me a ride home, but I refused), who had flown down to meet then–Lt. Gen. Ray Odierno, who was coming to Sedgwick to have supper with my soldiers and the MiTT team there. It was good to see my old boss from 4th ID, and in the brief time that we had to speak (his visit was primarily a morale visit with the soldiers for the holiday), he asked several questions about what was going on up in the Thar Thar area. It seems that the events there had captured considerable interest in his headquarters, and he had been keeping close tabs on my battalion's actions since Operation Forsyth Park. I gave him a thirty-second thumbnail of the spiel I had given Gurganus, and he was very interested. He told me he wanted to pay a visit up to Hawas, and he wanted my assessment on the AQI situation there where Saladin and Anbar Provinces met. He asked me to ensure that his staff put that on his calendar soon. I, of course, complied.

Intelligence reports, meanwhile, were beginning to stack up about an area called Nubai, another area of nebulous size and boundaries but generally accepted to be located between Thar Thar, Karma, Taji, and ad Dujayl—this area included the large desert region east of the Haluwa Canal. The reports talked about AQI activities throughout the huge region but centered on a series of commercial quarries in the southern third of the area near the Thara Dijla Canal. Reports had these quarries as major weapons caches and bomb-making factories, and further indicated that insurgent murder and intimidation was commonplace and that the insurgents were running illegal checkpoints throughout the region. Not only was this area out of my battlespace, it was way out of MNF-W battlespace and fell within Multi-National Division Baghdad's area. But why let that stop us? The 1/1 Brigade was itching to go to the Nubai Gravel Quarries, and so were we. By now, it was pretty easy to convince Charlton to go along with these operations—he was all for chasing after al Qaeda anyplace we could.

Planning the operation took about two weeks as my staff, the MiTT team, and 1/1 Brigade planned in unison, but the lead agent was the IA unit, and it was great to see those leaders stretch their legs on this operation. They built the intelligence picture with help from Jay McGee and his shop, they developed several potential courses of action for the "attack" (doctrinally, it was a cordon-and-search), they built the intelligence and surveillance plan for putting scouts and sensors in early, they prepared the movement plan and did much of the coordination for movement through other units' areas, they built the logistics plan, and, most importantly, they built the plan for information operations (to include press releases) and civil military affairs. They briefed General Gurganus and their division commander and led the rehearsals and inspections; in a nutshell, they planned a major offensive operation and included all the things a U.S. unit would. I exercised one veto: there was some discussion early on about flying scouts in on Iraqi Air Force helicopters, but this would have been the first live assault mission for the fledgling pilots, so I said no helicopters. We planned to use a petroleum storage and distribution facility that, according to all accounts, was abandoned as our temporary headquarters. When we arrived, we found that it most certainly wasn't abandoned but rather was guarded by Ministry of Oil guards and fully functional, but hadn't made distributions of benzene or diesel in years—just one of those bizarre Iraq things.

The area at the southern end of Nubai belonged to 2-8 Cavalry from the 1st Cavalry Division, whose commander was an acquaintance of mine named Lt. Col. Scott Efflandt. Scott is a smart, very accomplished, and very savvy armor officer with whom I first became familiar during our time in Command and General Staff College. We were then stationed at Fort Hood together, Scott in the 1st Cavalry Division and I in 4th Infantry. Scott was responsible for a large area of operations around Taji, Iraq, including some areas with long histories of insurgent activities. Nubai was for him as Albu Bali had been for me: a hot spot on the fringes of his AO but one he had not yet had the opportunity to address. When my staff called and asked him if we could take an Iraqi Army brigade and two-plus companies of Americans into Nubai to conduct a clearance, link up with the Sons of Iraq who had purportedly started to conduct checkpoints in the area, and find local sheiks who might be willing to establish an SAI chapter, he was not about to say no. Scott and his soldiers had been working to build checkpoints for the SOIs in Nubai, but he had not been able to focus route-clearance teams or other engineer assets on that project, largely because he didn't have the soldiers available to secure the sites. With us there, he would be able to focus on building the checkpoints as we cleared. Efflandt also hadn't had time to fully develop relationships with the local tribes that he knew he would eventually need in his corner—a win–win situation.

The movement plan was pretty complex, since it entailed moving the better part of the Iraqi brigade and the better part of my unit through eastern al Anbar into the suburbs of Baghdad, then north into Nubai. Jason Garkey did an excellent job of moving that huge force into position, since I was at the Hamdiya one-year anniversary shindig on the day of the movement. By the time I closed on the unit, we were just moving into the petroleum storage station. We quickly and efficiently established a robust forward headquarters with most of my battle staff and the entire 1/1 IA staff. This was a truly combined area with no partitions or off-limits areas for either U.S. or Iraqi forces—we shared the same maps, same phones, and same workspaces. Our only limitations arose from our dissimilar communications architecture and, of course, the language barrier.

The operation was straightforward: we would clear the routes into the area using route-clearance patrols and then systematically "clear," in cordon-and-knock style, every dwelling and business in Nubai. We also wanted to make contact with the SOIs who were already beginning to secure their areas and link them in with the IAs and, ultimately, with 2-8 Cavalry. Finally, we wanted to meet with the sheiks to get a conversation started about the Awakening movement and what improved security could do for the economics and development of the area. Once done with the more populous area in southern Nubai, we would clear all the way to the Haluwa Canal adjacent to JSS Hawas, hopefully trapping several of the IED cells between us and the canal and developing intelligence as we went.

The operation lasted five days, one day longer than we planned. We made a few detentions, encountered several IEDs—one of which was lethal, killing one Iraqi soldier and severely injuring two others—set up five or six fortified checkpoints for the local Sons of Iraq, cleared the roads that ran through the area, seized a few weapons caches, and met with and befriended three groups of tribal sheiks, community leaders, and prominent businessmen who were willing to step forward, recruit SOIs, and work with ISF and American forces in the future. All of that would have been just another day's work save for the fact that the Iraqi Army took the lead for the entire operation. They only asked us for a little support after the operation ran longer than expected. Mostly they provided fuel, water, food, intelligence support, ammunition, maintenance, and recovery support for their own forces—and really treated us as if we were helping and coaching. They didn't wait for us to prod them into action. It was on this operation that I watched 1/1 IA become a self-sufficient unit capable of owning and managing its own battlespace.

My role in this whole "backseat driver" approach was challenging (as I'm sure it was for all my leaders) and, frankly, bizarre. General Abdullah had served as a senior officer in the Saddam regime but was asked to leave the service at the same time that his distant cousin, Hussein Jbara Jabouri (my old buddy, the former governor of Saladin Province), was imprisoned. In fact, nearly all the Sunni Jabouris who were serving in the Army were executed, imprisoned, or simply cashiered over a wide-ranging plot in the mid-1990s to assassinate Saddam. Having served in the old regime, General Abdullah had very specific and traditional views regarding the concept that rank has its privilege—he was treated like some minor nobleman—and those views transferred to me as well. Because he saw us, more or less, as equals, he decided that I would live in his command quarters for the duration of the operation. So, I shared a room in the headquarters building with General Abdullah and lived a very different existence for a couple of days.

I have given you the impression that I was a fairly low-maintenance commander because I think I was. I'm not sure if Command Sgt. Maj. Randy Sumner or Spc. (now Staff Sgt.) James Beck would agree, but I certainly never lived like Abdullah. Abdullah spent the vast majority of his days in repose in his quarters/office—not to say that he wasn't situationally aware of his brigade's activities because he was briefed constantly on any significant action. While in his quarters, Abdullah smoked cigarettes non-stop and drank chai tea by the pot. He ate the same fare as his soldiers (which wasn't bad) but ate it whenever he wanted, prepared on demand by his unit's cooks. Abdullah didn't carry his own bags, nor did he pack them. When he needed something, he just shouted for his steward (who remained outside the door all day) and told him to bring it.

Perhaps one of the funniest requests I ever heard was "jeeb tracksuit"—*jeeb* means "bring me" and *tracksuit* is, apparently, a universal phrase. Abdullah's steward went out to the general's bags (whereever that may have been—perhaps residing in their own large truck) and came back in with two new, still in the package tracksuits on hangers to display to the General. Abdullah grunted something and shook his head, and the steward left to repeat the process again—the second pair of suits was acceptable. "Colonel Silver, do you want a tracksuit?" he asked. "No, thank you, sir"—what more could I say?

So, for two days we sat in the general's quarters and accepted visitors from the area: sheiks, contractors, informants with an ax to grind. Finally, on the third day we emerged from the general's lair to actually go see what our soldiers were doing with our own eyes. When we visited, Iraqi officers scurried over to brief the general while Moose translated for me. Later, McCreary or Phil Messer would pull me off to the side and give me their own updates. When we visited houses, the general was the star. It was quite odd for me because I had been used to being the potentate in my time in Jazeera. It sent me a strong signal: The War in Iraq is finally about Iraqis, and why shouldn't they be the stars?

Christmas was, once again, a grueling but very fulfilling time for me.

Between Christmas Eve and Christmas Day, Chaplain Kline, Sergeant Major Sumner, and I (and our hard-working PSD) visited every position at which we had soldiers—Camp Blue Diamond, Ramadi Government Center, Hurricane Point (a tiny outpost in Ramadi that we inherited for closure), JSS Zeimer, JSS Hawas, and JSS Sedgwick. Spirits were good, and the soldiers were doing very well. Our Iraqi partners mostly watched respectfully as we celebrated Christmas, but at some of the positions they took a more active role with their American brothers, joining in the tree-trimming or gift-giving and sharing the generally excellent meals that our cooks provided.

Cooking has become a dying art in the Army as contractors take over the job in far too many places and provide frozen meal pabulum to replace the generally excellent meals produced by soldiers who really care about their trade. One of the real boons of moving my companies so far away from Camp Blue Diamond was that they got my cooks, who had been driving trucks or supervising civilian contractors, to prepare meals the old-fashioned Army way, in a mess trailer at their camp. Each set of cooks and "mess sergeant" put their own spin on the usual Army menu, but they all did an excellent job.

After Christmas, it was back to the fight. General Odierno came to visit JSS Hawas to hear about our operations and to get my perspective on the enemy situation. In my previous time with Odierno in 2003–2004, he had come to trust my judgment regarding insurgents and insurgency. Protocol dictated that Colonel Charlton come up to Hawas for the visit, but he also decided that he was going to give the briefing, even though I told him that Odierno had asked for me to do it. The result was fairly comical. Charlton put up a slide and talked about a subject for a few minutes, then Odierno would look at me and ask, "Mike, what do you think about that?" I would spend several minutes tag-teaming my analysis with Jay McGee's while Odierno asked questions, then Charlton would move to the next slide.

The theme of the briefing was that AQI was taking advantage of the fact that my forces and the IA couldn't cross the Haluwa Canal from the area around Hawas. This was allowing the enemy fighters to use the northern Nubai area as a safe haven and support zone. I also lobbied for a force, either an American or IA battalion, to assume battlespace in northern

Nubai and the Muthanna area, and told Odierno that I believed if we crushed the AQI fighters in there, they would have little chance to recover. He told me there were already indications that AQI was moving all of its leadership to Ninevah Province in and around Mosul, but he also believed the group needed to maintain at least a support zone in the desert areas around Hawas because they contained important routes for AQI to move around the Sunni Triangle. Because he thought it was so important, he committed to providing a military bridge across the Haluwa Canal and increasing my battlespace to include a sizable chunk of northern Nubai. He also agreed to take my thoughts on positioning a force near Muthanna to both his staff and the Ministry of Defense. All in all, it was a very successful meeting.

While we waited for the engineer unit to arrive and install our new bridge, we conducted one more huge clearance operation, this time north of Saddamiya. Saddimiya lay on the banks of Lake Thar Thar, but it was also immediately south of the Samarra Canal that came off of the lake and ran a twisting but mostly northeast–southwest route, where it connected into the Tigris River just south of Samarra. The Samarra Canal was difficult to cross in a vehicle because of its steep sides but, in places, fairly easy to walk or swim across because it was shallow and had a nice, sandy bottom. The Samarra Canal was my northern boundary, and AQI had taken advantage of that fact as well. The group used the desolate area north of the canal to stage IED cells, then walked the IEDs into Saddamiya and planted them on the roads that we patrolled. Using this technique, AQI fighters had destroyed three PSF trucks, killed three PSF members, and wounded nearly a dozen. This was a troubling and fruitless skirmish. Had there been no IEDs, there was no reason to go to Saddamiya, since the only people there lived in a few nomadic fishing camps. However, members of AQI continued to emplace IEDs, and if we didn't go there, civilian fishermen would hit them with disastrous effect, so we couldn't cede the area to AQI. Chaos Company hit several IEDs in the company's tanks, but although the tanks were damaged, nobody was seriously injured. The PSF pickup trucks were a different story.

There was also another incident about twenty-five miles northeast of Saddamiya, just northwest of Muthanna. Our adjacent unit to the north, from 3rd BCT, 101st Infantry Division, had been out on a routine cordon-and-search through the areas next to the Samarra Canal. While working their way through the ten-foot reeds surrounding the canal, soldiers from the unit stumbled into an AQI camp (probably foreign fighters— certainly suicidal) of about ten to twenty armed insurgents. The firefight that commenced must have been much like the blind firefights in the densest jungles of Vietnam, where you could only see about twenty feet through the impenetrable vegetation and, therefore, your adversary popped into visual range at the same time that he came into hand-grenade range. I don't recall the casualty count from the engagement, since our only part in the fight was to send McCreary's Bradleys there to provide support as the infantrymen evacuated the area, but I do recall a couple of American KIAs and several WIAs and about twelve AQI KIAs, including a suicide-vest bomber.

So, we had to do something to deal with this threat. The answer was a huge clearance that involved McCreary's Battle Company with 3/1/1 IA, Phil Messer's Chaos Company with 1st PSF, a U.S. Navy boat company from Riverine Squadron 2, and the 2nd Marine Reconnaissance Battalion. The operation was huge but fruitless, since the AQI fighters had hundreds of miles of open desert and occasional oases that allowed them to move freely through the area. There was a tiny permanent population in that vast area and hundreds of Bedouin shepherds and fishermen who had temporary camps along the lake and in the desert. Any insurgent who was worth his salt could fit right in with that population, forcing their compliance by the old techniques of murder and intimidation. We had chased al Qaeda as far as we could in that area; it just wasn't possible to patrol such a vast, open desert.

But while we did that, Odierno came through on his promise to send an engineer bridge company to Hawas to begin constructing a military bridge that would give us access to northern Nubai across the Haluwa Canal. Guarding the bridge site was a huge task, and both Gurganus and Charlton had made it clear to me in no uncertain terms: don't let that bridge get blown up! I found the lack of subtlety somewhat boorish, but, as we say in the South, a wink's as good as a nod to a blind horse—they wanted to make sure that even I understood. The result was that for the last sixty days or so of McCreary's time at Hawas, we had a full IA infantry platoon and half an American mechanized infantry platoon guarding first the construction site and then the actual bridge. The bridge was a real threat to AQI and, as such, there were a couple of firefights across the canal during construction, which we won handily.

Once the bridge was finished, we were able to patrol into the populated areas adjacent to the Haluwa Canal daily and began to drive AQI from the area. We conducted our last multi-day clearance operation in northern Nubai shortly after the bridge was built and had great success. During the operation, 3/1/1 IA and Battle Company discovered several large caches containing tons of munitions and explosives, including one cache in a small barn that had over two tons of homemade explosives and tens of thousands of rounds of small arms ammunition. About five hundred yards from the large cache was a slightly smaller one in a modest, unfinished house that had clearly been used to house livestock (it was full of sheep shit). On the wall of that unpretentious abode, in the middle of nowhere, with no paved roads or real population to speak of was a single, neatly painted line of Arabic script. When the IA soldiers read it they burst into laughter, then Moose read it to me. It said, "The Capitol of the Islamic State of Iraq's Saqlawiya Province."

In military parlance, we use two terms to describe victory: one can destroy an enemy, which means that a majority of his force is rendered unusable—dead, captured, retreated, routed, they can no longer resist— or one can defeat an enemy, meaning that the enemy can no longer attain his goal, though he may still have the means to fight. As I stood in the middle of an area that most Americans would never hear of, staring at a seemingly insignificant little building, I realized that al Qaeda in Iraq had been defeated. The group would never attain its goal of establishing a new nation from which to launch the global al Qaeda's final assault on the Arabian Peninsula. I also knew that most Americans would never know just how close al Qaeda had come to accomplishing not merely its goals in Iraq but its larger goals to overthrow the regimes in Saudi Arabia and Jordan. And al Qaeda might have won, save for an Awakening led by a handful of brave Iraqi sheiks and the IPs, ERUs, and SOIs who stood against all odds and died in droves to defend their homeland. I was honored to have been a part of that decisive effort, the Awakening victory.

Muddy Bookends

Camp Blue Diamond was to become an Iraqi Army base, so Charlton ordered me to move my headquarters back to Camp Ramadi. I think the order came in about September, and, like an immature child, I kicked and screamed and drug my feet and postponed what I knew to be inevitable. But finally, on January 11, 2008, my command group and headquarters moved back to Camp Ramadi. I remember the day because it was the day that it snowed throughout central Iraq. In Baghdad, according to some news reports, many of the locals proclaimed it a sign from God that the end of the war had come and a new era was beginning. All I knew was that it made Camp Ramadi once again the muddy, ugly shithole that I remembered all too well. The good news was that Sheik Heiss won a contract to demilitarize Camp Blue Diamond that was worth a good deal of money. So, for the next forty-five days, we planned and packed, all the while still conducting operations, and beginning the last week in February, all of my soldiers moved back to Camp Ramadi and ceased combat operations.

Although Camp Ramadi still sucked, having my soldiers mostly out of harm's way was the most relieving feeling I've ever experienced. But, leaving

Iraq was like leaving a piece of my soul behind. Those men—sheiks, IPs, PSF, and IA soldiers—had become like brothers to me. I will never forget my last time at Heiss' muleefa; as I departed, we embraced, both of us with tears welling in our eyes like schoolgirls. I felt heartsick as I drove away.

By mid-April, my soldiers were all back in the United States. We went through some post-deployment reintegration training and then had an extended leave of absence. I was thrilled to be home and much relieved, but things went slightly awry. I began to be plagued by nightmares, usually nightmares in which zombies with Arab faces—some men, but mostly women and children—pursued me. I didn't know what they wanted, but I knew they wanted something. The dreams were accompanied by distinct mood changes. I became grouchy (or grouchier) and impatient, and had an overwhelming, obsessive feeling of guilt and shame like none I'd ever felt—an irrational feeling of guilt, since my soldiers and I had done right by the families at Objective Monk. Fortunately, the U.S. Army had done a good job of training both myself and my wonderful wife to recognize the signs of post-traumatic stress disorder (or PTSD) and, in what was one of the smartest moves the Army's made in years, had taken the stigma away from seeking help for such disorders. I had gone my entire career not really "believing" in PTSD until I had it. Believe me, it's real. I have now learned (through intensive therapy) to deal with my PTSD, but not a day goes by that my mind doesn't, in some idle moment, settle on the horrendous memories I have of the house at Objective Monk, and I imagine that should I live to be a hundred, that will never change.

Iraq has made it through the country's second national-level election, and this time Sunnis all over Iraq participated. My good friend and former interpreter, Mostafa Remh, described it in an email excerpted here:

The election went well over here and all over Iraq; a few unfortunate incidents, but it went well. I am sure you were watching it closely . . . but Mike . . . it was a very important historical moment politically, socially and believe it or not even culturally. Believe me my dear friend, this coming from me, an Arab, who knows well his history, understands, feels and senses deeply his culture and knows his people very well . . . I definitely wish you were here for just that one week, especially you my dear friend Mike, to witness and see how much and how deep people of your caliber had touched people over here. I did not go out there, but people, "the Iraqis" came into Camp Ramadi and you know me, I am a go getter. I am curious, I talk to people, I want to know what they are thinking and how are they feeling . . . you know Mike the voting day over here specifically (Ramadi/Al-Anbar) and in Iraq in general . . . it was nothing short of an "Eid"—a religious holiday. An Iraqi contractor who knows me and I remember him from a couple or three years ago told me that kids (girls and boys) were dressed in their brand new outfits (just like Al-Eid) and they went with their mothers and relatives to the voting booths, and some kids were even seriously trying to vote, he told me, and when they were told no . . . those kids went back that evening to their neighborhoods and played kids games . . . the guy asked me: "Mostafa, do you know what were their games?" He said their games were that these kids made up a make believe voting booth and got in line and acted like they were voting. He also told me that he heard of an 85-years-old grandfather from Al-Malaab neighborhood (which you know well) who asked his grandson to find a way to get him to the voting booth since he cannot walk long distance—there was a curfew against cars, up until 12 noon, for security reasons no car was allowed inside Ramadi . . . the grandfather told his grandson: "You want to tell me that I lived to see a day where I, as a regular person can choose and say who do I want to be the next ruler of Iraq? . . . then, if you wanted my blessings then getting me there will get you all of my blessings." Mike you know well how we feel about parents' blessings culturally as well as religiously, so the person took his grandfather on his back; he carried him on his back to the voting booths since neither cars nor motorcycles were allowed. There were many other great stories like these, and they are just the very tip of the iceberg of how happy and proud people are feeling. The people here experienced something unheard of in our history, "the Arab people's history" something new they never thought could be possible, and it seems to me that people here are not ready nor will they ever be ready to let go of that right and freedom!

Will Iraq become the shining example of liberal democracy in the Arab heartland? I don't know. AQI still exists, and although the group's attacks are infrequent, its leaders still want to kill democracy in Iraq and throughout the Muslim world. But for now, the democracy in Iraq, with all its warts and flaws, thrives. In the run up to the election, many of the sheiks of the Awakening played major roles in developing, with Shia politicians, lists (the equivalent of parties) that included Sunni, Shia, and Kurd members. If not for the Awakening movement, I don't think that could have happened.

Last and most important, I learned a valuable lesson during my time in al Anbar Province: America cannot win the Long War on Terror; rather, all we can do is help our Muslim allies win. The war is not about keeping America safe from the likes of al Qaeda, but rather it is about the future of political Islam and whether the takfiris' movement—who would like to destroy individual rights and replace the law of democratic peoples with the twisted and cruel version of Sharia law to which they ascribe—or modern Muslim leaders who recognize the enlightenment values of individual rights to life, liberty, and property will rule one-fifth of the world's population. I hope that the lessons of my experience might influence America's road ahead . . . but that is for another book.

Source Notes

[1] Mundy, Carl E. III, *Save the Rod, Spare the Nation, New York Times*, December 30, 2003.

[2] GlobalSecurity.org, "Saddam's Martyrs" ["Men of Sacrifice"], *Fedayeen* Saddam.

[3] GlobalSecurity.org, "Jamaat al-Tawhid wa'l-Jihad/Unity and Jihad Group," Tanzim Qa'idat Al-Jihad in Bilad al-Rafidayn(Organization of Jihad's Base in the Country of the Two Rivers), www.globalsecurity.org/military/world/para/zarqawi.htm.

[4] Ware, Michael, "The Most Dangerous Place," *Time*, May 21, 2006.

[5] Ibid.

[6] "Situation Called Dire in West Iraq, Anbar Is Lost Politically, Marine Analyst Says," *Washington Post*, September 11, 2006, A01.

[7] Hescos are ubiquitous in Iraq. They are metal cube cages lined with lightweight fabric that can be set up and filled with dirt to create excellent fortified positions.

[8] "The al Iskan District" is a mixed translation. In Arabic, *Hay al Iskan* literally translates as "the housing district."

[9] Letter from Abu Mohammed (believed to be Ayman al Zawahiri) to Abu Musab al Zarqawi dated July 9, 2005. A translation of the letter can be found on GlobalSecurity.org, www.globalsecurity.org/security/library/report/2005/zawahiri-zarqawi-letter_9jul2005.htm.

[10] Al Qaeda's reference to the "Greater Israel" refers to Genesis 15:18: "In that day the Lord made a covenant with Abraham, saying: 'Unto thy seed I have given this land, from the river of Egypt unto the great river, the river Euphrates.'"

[11] Letter from Abu Musab al Zarqawi to Osama bin Laden and Ayman al Zawahiri, undated but purportedly seized by U.S. government officials in February 2004. A U.S. government translation can be found at www.state.gov/p/nea/rls/31694.htm.

[12] Ibid.

[13] Letter from Ayman Zawahiri to Zarqawi intercepted by intelligence officials and released

by the director of national security on October 11, 2005. A full test can be found at
www.globalsecurity.org/security/library/report/2005/zawahiri-zarqawi-letter_9jul2005.htm.
[14] Ibid.
[15] Galula, David, 1919–1967. French military officer and scholar who authored
Counterinsurgency Theory and Practice in 1964. The book was re-released by Praeger in 2006
and became wildly popular with the U.S. military.
[16] Kilcullen, David, born 1967. Former Australian Army officer, consultant, and author of
"Twenty-eight Articles: A How-to Guide for Junior Officers Engaged in Counterinsurgency"
and *The Accidental Guerrilla: Fighting Small Wars in the Midst of a Big One* (Oxford Press,
2009).
[17] This is one of the central tenets of Bing West's book, *The Strongest Tribe: War, Politics, and
the Endgame in Iraq* (Random House, New York, 2008).
[18] The AirLand Battle Doctrine was designed by the founder of SAMS, BG, Huba Wass de
Czege. It replaced a doctrine of attrition with one of maneuver and was the very doctrine
that allowed U.S. forces to win a decisive victory in the 1991 Gulf War.
[19] In the U.S. Army, there was a de facto dual track among combat arms officers, and both
tracks led, ultimately, to command positions. One could become either a planner or an
operations offier. Planners served at the division level and above and were tied to those
positions anytime they were not in troop units. Operators were the executors and often
viewed planners as effete officers who spent their entire careers dealing with the esoteric.
[20] The difference between *Abu* and *Albu*: *Abu* means "son of," so a tribe is called Abu—like
Abu Diyab. *Albu* means "land of," so the tribal area is Albu Diyab. An individual is usually
called by his name(s), then called the "al," which indicates he is a member of a tribe: for example, Saddam Hussein al Tikriti.
[21] A note about tribal names: Like all Arabic, tribal names are translated phonetically into
English. *Abu Diyab*, for example, can be spelled *Abu Thiyab, Abu Dhiyab, Abu Di-ab*, etc.
The general rule of thumb is that if it sounds the same, it's probably the same Arabic word,
name, or phrase.
[22] One can think of the tribal areas of Jazeera as neighborhoods in the suburbs. They were all
named for the prevalent tribe, and, indeed, the vast majorities of their residents belonged to
that tribe, but there was no restriction, per se, on residency. A non–tribe member could buy a
house and live there and would have the exact same legal status as his neighbors, but he
would not have the extralegal protection, mediation, and care of the tribe.
[23] *The Andy Griffith Show*
[24] Jabbar was quoted in *Time* in October 2010 saying, about Americans: "They are dirty
killers," he says, "and whether 40 years from now or 100, what they did here will not be for-
gotten."
[25] West, Bing, *The Strongest Tribe: War, Politics, and the Endgame in Iraq* (Random House,
New York, 2008), 133.
[26] *Extrajudicial killing* is defined as a deliberate killing not authorized by a previous judgment
pronounced by a regularly constituted court affording all the judicial guarantees that are
recognized as indispensable by civilized peoples. Sinaltrainal v. Coca-Cola Co., 578 F.3d
1252 (11th Cir. Fla. 2009), USLegal.com.
[27] Jaffe, Greg, "Tribal Connections: How Courting Sheiks Slowed Violence In Iraq," *Wall
Street Journal*, August 8, 2007, 1.
[28] "Al Muthanna Chemical Weapons Complex, Iraq's Chemical Weapons Program, Annex B,
Iraq WMD 2004," CIA, Washington D.C., declassified April 2007.
[29] Ibid.

Glossary of Terms and Acronyms

1AD: 1st Armored Division

1CD: 1st Cavalry Division

3ID: 3rd Infantry Division

4ID: 4th Infantry Division

APC: Armored personnel carrier

AO: Area of operations. The geographic area in which a given unit is authorized to conduct military operations.

AQI: Al Qaeda in Iraq. The Iraqi affiliate of al Qaeda started by the Jordanian ex-pat and former al Qaeda trainer Abu Musab al Zarqawi, circa January 2003. (See also JTJ.)

AWG: Asymmetric Warfare Group: A special-mission U.S. Army unit developed to assist non-special forces units as they trained for and executed counterinsurgency.

BCT: Brigade Combat Team. An Army unit typically composed of 2 to 6 combat arms battalions, a support battalion, a fires battalion (artillery), and various attachments. BCTs are usually commanded by Colonels and can have from 2,000 to 6,500 soldiers.

COP: Combat Outpost. The smallest of U.S. expeditionary positions, combat outposts normally have less than 200 Americans and are generally temporary positions.

CMOC: Civil-Military Operations Center. A military facility used to interact with local populations for actions such as filing claims and grievances, applying for work with coalition forces, or bidding on contracts that are pending award.

EJK: Extra-Judicial Killing. A deliberate killing not authorized by a previous judgment pronounced by a regularly constituted court affording all the judicial guarantees that are recognized as indispensable by civilized peoples.

ERU: Emergency Response Unit. The pseudo-police or paramilitary battalions recruited by the sheiks of the Awakening. These units were ultimately renamed Provincial Security Forces (PSF).

FIF: Free Iraqi Forces. A militia recruited by the U.S. government to work with U.S. forces during and immediately after the 2003 invasion. The FIF was largely composed of Iraqi ex-patriots who lived in Western nations and included some rather unsavory individuals.

Hesco Baskets: Large (up to 7-foot tall) wire framed, fabric lined cubes designed for use as soil-filled containers used to build bunkers, protective walls, and as reinforcement to existing structures to protect against enemy fire.

HME: Home-made explosive.

IA: Iraqi Army.

IED: Improvised explosive device or "roadside bomb."

Imam: A Sunni Muslim religious leader or scholar.

IO: Investigating Officer.

ISF: Iraqi Security Forces.

ISI: Islamic State of Iraq. The farcical state declared by al Qaeda in Iraq in October 2006, the capital of which was the al Iskan District of Ramadi.

IP: Iraqi Police.

JSS: Joint Security Station. Similar to a combat outpost, this is typically a small expeditionary position occupied by both U.S. and Iraqi forces.

JTJ: *Jamaat al-Tawhid wa'al Jihad* (followers of unity and struggle.) The precursor organization to al Qaeda in Iraq.

KIA: Killed in Action.

Legacy Unit: An old-fashion U.S. Army unit. A unit that is not organized in the most current way.

MiTT: Military transition team. A team of coalition (usually U.S.) military personnel assigned to assist and advise an Iraqi Army unit.

MNC-I: Multi-National Corps- Iraq. The headquarters responsible for all tactical units in Iraq, during 2007–2008 it was commanded by then–Lt. Gen. Ray Odierno.

MNF-I: Multi-National Forces-Iraq. The headquarters responsible for all actions in Iraq, but focused mainly on aiding and assisting the central government of Iraq. During 2007–2008 it was commanded by General David Petraeus.

MNF-W: Multi-National Force-West. The division-sized headquarters responsible for al Anbar Province; during 2007–2008 it was commanded by then–Major General Walter E. Gaskins, USMC. The ground component commander was then–Brigadier General Mark Gurganus.

MND-North: Multi-National Division-North. The division responsible for Saladin and Diyala Provinces.

MND-Bagdad: Multi-National Division Bagdad. The division responsible for Bagdad (city and province).

MRAP: Mine Resistant Ambush Protective vehicle. Any one of a family of vehicles designed to survive mine strikes ether through greatly increasing the ground clearance thereby providing stand-off from a mine or IED strike; or by shaping the vehicle hull in a way to channel the blast away from the crew compartment, or both.

Mufti: A special religious leader accepted by some Sunni Muslims. A Mufti is not just a religious scholar, but a scholar qualified to pass legal judgments based on Sharia law. The concept of Mufti was not a part of original Islamic dogma, but was developed by the Umayyad Caliphs circa the 8th century as a method to merge secular and religious political power.

NSTR: Nothing Significant To Report. This acronym is used in military jargon to denote a patrol or other operation that was absolutely routine.

OP: Observation Post. A manned position the sole purpose of which is to observe an assigned area.

PDSS:Pre-Deployment Site Survey. This is the leaders' reconnaissance conducted into Iraq (or Afghanistan) prior to a unit's deployment.

PTT or PiTT: Police Training Team. A team of coalition (usually U.S.) military personnel assigned to assist and advise an Iraqi police unit.

PSD: Personal Security Detachment. A team of bodyguards assigned to protect a key individual.

PSF: Provincial security forces. (See ERU.)

RPG: Rocket-Propelled Grenade. The ubiquitous Soviet-designed shoulder-fired rocket used by insurgents all over the world and by many developing nations' militaries.

Sahawa al Anbar (SAA): Anbar Awakening Council.

Sahawa al Iraq (SAI): National Awakening Movement.

Sharia: Islamic law based on both the Koran (Islamic holy book) and the Hadith (literally the example—the stories of the Prophet Muhammad's life).

Supporting Arms Liaison Team (SALT): Marine Corps team assigned to a maneuver unit in order to provide coordination with artillery, naval gunfire, and aviation assets.

SSE: Sensitive Site Exploitation. The forensic investigation of an enemy location such as a safe house, bomb factory, or weapons cache.

RIP/TOA: Relief in Place, Transition of Authority.

T-Walls: Concrete barriers ranging in size from the Jersey barrier, the 3-foot-tall barrier used to control traffic on US highways, to the 11-foot-tall Alaska barrier. These barriers are used both to channelize traffic and protect from explosions and other weapon effects.

Takfiri: The act of excommunication in Islam. Declaring takfiri is generally frowned upon by mainstream Muslims because it supersedes God's judgment. However, groups like al Qaeda readily excommunicate other Muslims or declare takfiri, therefore they are called takfiris by many mainstream Muslims.

UAV: Unmanned Aerial Vehicles. Remote-controlled drones used to conduct reconnaissance or attack.

WIA: Wounded in Action.